Reinventing Thailand

Silkworm Books is a general publisher specializing in select markets and quality English-language books, primarily on topics related to mainland Southeast Asia. It is the foremost publisher of serious books on Thailand in English. To date, it has published more than 250 titles by commissioning writers, licensing English-language rights, and purchasing translation rights. Based in Chiang Mai, Thailand, its books are distributed in Asia through local distributors, and in North America, the United Kingdom, and Australia through the University of Washington Press.

The **Institute of Southeast Asian Studies (ISEAS)** was established as an autonomous organization in 1968. It is a regional centre dedicated to the study of socio-political, security and economic trends and developments in Southeast Asia and its wider geostrategic and economic environment. The Institute's research programmes are the Regional Economic Studies (RES, including ASEAN and APEC), Regional Strategic and Political Studies (RSPS), and Regional Social and Cultural Studies (RSCS).

ISEAS Publishing, an established academic press, has issued more than 2,000 books and journals. It is the largest scholarly publisher of research about Southeast Asia from within the region. ISEAS Publishing works with many other academic and trade publishers and distributors to disseminate important research and analyses from and about Southeast Asia to the rest of the world.

Reinventing Thailand
Thaksin and His Foreign Policy

Pavin Chachavalpongpun

ISEAS

INSTITUTE OF SOUTHEAST ASIAN STUDIES
Singapore

SILKWORM BOOKS
Thailand

First published in Singapore in 2010 by
ISEAS Publishing
Institute of Southeast Asian Studies
30 Heng Mui Keng Terrace
Pasir Panjang
Singapore 119614
E-mail: publish@iseas.edu.sg
Website: http://bookshop.iseas.edu.sg

Co-published for distribution only in Thailand by
Silkworm Books
6 Sukkasem Road, Suthep, Chiang Mai 50200, Thailand
Tel   :   053 22 6161-3
Fax   :   053 22 6643
E-mail :   info@silkwormbooks.com
Website :   www.silkwormbooks.com

Silkworm Books ISBN : 978-616-215-000-5

*The responsibility for facts and opinions in this publication rests exclusively with the
authors and their interpretations do not necessarily reflect the views or the policy of the
Institute or its supporters.*

ISEAS Library Cataloguing-in-Publication Data

Pavin Chachavalpongpun.
    Reinventing Thailand : Thaksin and his foreign policy.
    1.   Thaksin Chinnawat, 1949–
    2.   Thailand — Foreign relations — 1988–
    I.   Title.
DS578.32 T32P33   2010

ISBN 978-981-4279-19-2 (soft cover)
ISBN 978-981-4279-20-8 (E-book PDF)

Cover photo: Reproduced with kind permission of Pornsak Saelim

Typeset by Superskill Graphics Pte Ltd
Printed in Thailand by O.S. Printing House, Bangkok

CONTENTS

List of Tables	vi
Foreword	vii
Preface	xi
List of Key Characters	xv
Abbreviations	xvii
Map of Thailand and Southeast Asia	xx
1. Introduction: Reinventing Thailand	1
2. Bamboo in the Wind: A Traditional Thai Diplomacy	63
3. Major Foreign Policy Initiatives: The Making of a Hegemonic Power?	92
4. Bilateral Relations: Tailoring of a Thaksinized Diplomacy	162
5. A Moot Foreign Policy: Shortcomings and Oversights	232
6. Conclusion: A Rickety Reinvention	266
7. Epilogue: The Post-Thaksin Foreign Policy	278
Bibliography	315
Index	333
About the Author	353

LIST OF TABLES

3.1   Areas of Cooperation and Prime Movers of the ACD   103
3.2   ACMECS's Existing Projects   114
3.3   Thailand's FTAs with Its Partners   129

FOREWORD

Thailand's foreign policy has been little studied. This is perhaps because, just as Britain is sometimes said to have no climate, only weather, a consistent Thai foreign policy stance cannot always be readily discerned. Inconsistency, or perhaps simply an overarching pragmatism, has been a recurrent feature of Siam/Thailand's dealings with the wider world. Such pragmatism was perhaps most explicitly seen during World War II, when the Phibun Songkhram government formed an alliance with Japan and declared war on the United States. However, Seni Pramoj, then ambassador to Washington, failed to deliver the declaration. When the Allies emerged as victors, Thailand was quick to claim that the pro-Allied "Free Thai" resistance movement had represented the real stance of the war-time nation, an argument which was broadly accepted by the Americans. In other words, Thailand succeeded in being on both sides during World War II, a rare feat of foreign policy flexibility. Not for nothing has the Thai Foreign Ministry traditionally prided itself on a mastery of "bamboo diplomacy".

By the 1980s, however, such diplomacy was coming under strain. Whereas both the pre-1932 absolute monarchy and the military-dominated post-1932 regimes were characterized by the concentration of power in the hands of a tiny elite, with elite diversification came a new form of inconsistency: the pursuit of different policies by different ruling groups. This was most clearly seen during the ill-fated Chatichai Choonhavan government of 1988–91, which saw a struggle for control of foreign policy towards Indochina. An elected prime minister with a group of well-educated and iconoclastic advisers — the so-called *Ban Phitsanulok* team — sought to engage with Vietnam and end the isolation of Cambodia, turning the former battlefield of Indochina into a marketplace. Meanwhile the Foreign Ministry remained wedded to the American-influenced ASEAN orthodoxy of punishing Vietnam for the "crime" of invading Cambodia in 1979, while the Thai military took matters a stage further by actively supporting residual elements of the Khmer Rouge. Three Thai government agencies, three Cambodia policies. As the first elected head of a Thai government for over a decade, Chatichai sought to wrest policy decisions out of the hands of the Foreign Ministry bureaucrats; meanwhile, the military continued to assert the right to pursue its own regional agenda, invoking the trump card of "national security".

The Chatichai government was ousted by a military coup in February 1991, but the army won only a pyrrhic victory. Within a couple of years, a UN intervention had restored Cambodia to a tentative normalcy, the ASEAN blockade was lifted, and soon afterwards President Bill Clinton restored America's diplomatic relations with Vietnam. Chatichai's team had demonstrated that Thailand's diplomats and soldiers were behind the times, failing to think creatively and to rise to the challenges of a post-Cold War environment. New ideas came from elected politicians and a team of smart advisors who were willing to think "outside the box". In the event, attempts by the leaders of the 1991 coup to assume power through civilian means ended in failure following the bloody Bangkok street clashes of May 1992. The extended 1991–92 political crisis led to the crafting of the 1997 "reformist" constitution, opening up liberal space for elected politicians to play the lead role in Thailand's governance.

Into this space stepped a new style of Thai politician: Police Lieutenant-Colonel Dr Thaksin Shinawatra. A former police officer with an American doctorate, Thaksin had become fabulously rich through winning a series of government concessions in the telecommunications sphere. While his competitors were badly hit during the Asian financial crisis of 1997, Thaksin had walked through the storm unscathed, emerging as the dominant player in Thailand's booming mobile phone business. His Thai Rak Thai Party won electoral victories on an unprecedented scale in 2001 and 2005. Like Chatichai, Thaksin sought to shake up the sluggish Thai bureaucracy and approached key areas of domestic and foreign policy with a private sector mentality. Unlike Chatichai, Thaksin quickly achieved unparalleled dominance of Thailand's key institutions and resources, presenting himself as a "CEO prime minister" who was on a mission to make Thailand more productive, competitive and goal-oriented. But again like Chatichai, Thaksin was ousted in a military coup. His shake-up of the existing order ruffled feathers and antagonized much of the traditional elite.

Thaksin's political career has been widely documented and discussed, but this book by Pavin Chachavalpongpun is the first extended study of the controversial premier's foreign policy. Based on considerable research, including interviews with many key players, and drawing upon the author's own inside knowledge of Thailand's foreign policy apparatus, this remarkable book allows us to see Thaksin Shinawatra in a new light, laying out both the boldness and often the hollowness of his numerous international initiatives. Since 2001, Thai politics has been characterized by an intense contestation between the old bureaucratic elite — including what I term "network monarchy" — and "Team Thaksin", a set of alliances centred on the ex-prime minister and his family. Most crudely, these clashes have recently been acted out between yellow-shirted and red-shirted protesters on the streets of Bangkok. Pavin demonstrates how these conflicts penetrate and polarize institutions such as the Foreign Ministry, undermining traditional sites of "aristocratic" privilege and prerogative.

More than any previous civilian prime minister, Thaksin sought to impose his own personal agenda — often difficult to separate from his family's business interests — upon the core agencies of the Thai state. Foreign policy was deployed both domestically and internationally to market the Thaksin message, through a range of policies including the ACD, the ACMECS, a range of new FTAs, and most colourfully through doomed attempts to engineer the appointment of his ministerial side-kick Surakiart Sathirathai to the post of U.N. Secretary-General. In the process, Thaksin downplayed such standard Foreign Ministry preoccupations as its snobby fixation with Europe, and stopped paying endless lip-service to the lacklustre regional body ASEAN. Deploying an Asian nationalist rhetoric, Thaksin diverted foreign policy resources into supporting economic initiatives aimed at preserving and boosting Thailand's role as a dominant player in the golden peninsula of mainland Southeast Asia. He was also probably the first Thai leader to take the sub-continent seriously, recognizing India as an emerging power, and positioning Thailand as a broker between East and South Asia.

In retrospect, it seems all too predictable that Thaksin's manic iconoclasm and his headstrong slaughter of sacred cows — both at home and abroad — would end badly. Following the 19 September 2006 military coup, Thaksin found himself charged with corruption-related offences, and was sentenced to a jail term in 2008. Yet by the time the verdict was announced, Thaksin had already fled Thailand and become a professional fugitive, flitting between London, Hong Kong, Dubai and other locations, rapidly wearing out his welcomes. This was an ironic fate for the most internationally-oriented of Thailand's prime ministers; the man who had made so many foreign policy initiatives had nowhere left to go. Pavin's excellent book goes a long way towards explaining this startling state of affairs.

Duncan McCargo
Professor of Southeast Asian Politics
School of Politics and International Studies
University of Leeds, U.K.

PREFACE

Thai politics has sunk into deep turmoil since Prime Minister Thaksin Shinawatra was toppled in a military coup in September 2006. The domestic situation has gone from bad to worse as profound polarization has continued to dictate Thailand's political well-being. Three years on, Thailand has witnessed four governments, including one military rule, two pro-Thaksin regimes, and one royalist political entity. All this time, Thaksin, now a fugitive from Thai law and charged *in absentia* with corruption and abuse of power, has incessantly manipulated politics from his base overseas. The political tug-of-war between Thaksin and his opponents is far from over. "Reconciliation" between different political factions seems to have become an alien word. The impact of internal political crisis has been devastating. It has certainly caused a huge consequence to Thailand's foreign relations. The Ministry of Foreign Affairs has been intensely preoccupied with reconstructing the country's good image, in the wake of an ongoing political war. The incident in which the pro-Thaksin red-shirt protesters stormed into the meeting venue of the Association of Southeast Asian Nations (ASEAN)+3 Summit in Pattaya in April 2009 marked one of the lowest points in Thai diplomacy. Thailand has lost its international reputation as well as its leadership in ASEAN. From July 2008 to December 2009, Thailand held the chairmanship of this regional organization. But political fragility at home prevented Thailand from playing a proactive part in ASEAN. The country's diplomatic role in the region diminished. The latest flare-up in the Thai-Cambodian conflict as a result of the bilateral dispute over the Preah Vihear temple, and the war of words between the Abhisit Vejjajiva government and Cambodian Prime Minister Hun Sen, dangerously put Thai diplomacy to the test. Has Thai diplomacy's glorious past already been forgotten?

While in power from 2001 to 2006, Thaksin began the process of rejuvenating Thailand's diplomacy. This period saw the most colourful and exciting, yet controversial, period of Thailand's foreign relations. Thaksin claimed to have elevated the Thai international standing, from obscurity to hegemonization, through a myriad of grandiose foreign policy initiatives. Thaksin, with the assistance of his foreign ministers Surakiart Sathirathai (2001–05) and Kantathi Suphamongkhon (2005–06), aspired to transform Thailand from a mid-ranged power into a leading nation in the region. Thailand was reinvented as a donor country. It also initiated Asia-wide cooperative frameworks, such as the Asia Cooperation Dialogue (ACD) and the Ayeyawady-Chao Phraya-Mekong Economic Cooperation Strategy (ACMECS). At a bilateral level, Thaksin promoted a business-oriented foreign policy that aimed at searching for more markets for Thai products. Accordingly, he supported the conclusion of free trade agreements with Thailand's trading partners. Thaksin also expressed, albeit somewhat superficially, his affinity with democracy through his idea of the "Bangkok Process", designed to bring about change in Myanmar. At the global level, he nominated Foreign Minister Surakiart for the position of the United Nations Secretary-General, deemed his most ambitious attempt to place Thailand at the forefront of international politics. Not only were changes seen in the content of Thai foreign policy, Thaksin also revamped the Foreign Ministry and reprogrammed the way this state agency had been operating since the colonial period. CEO ambassadors were put in place as part of the organizational revamp. Thaksin thus began to "colonize" the Foreign Ministry and compelled its members to produce policies that would serve his domestic needs, legitimate or otherwise.

Beautifully repackaged for the taste of domestic and international audiences, Thai foreign policy under the regime of Thaksin hid its unattractive side. Thaksin's diplomacy, occasionally referred to as "Thaksiplomacy", was a populist device. In the meantime, the line between national and private interests in the conduct of Thaksin's diplomacy remained blurry. At many points, Thaksin was paramount about protecting his business interests while interacting with countries, near or afar. His foreign policy initiatives highly reflected his ambition. But his ambition, at times, was unrealistic and disregarded the limits of the national capacity. Thaksin's attempt to rewrite the history of Thai diplomacy, from bending with the wind like a bamboo to bending the prevailing wind in favour of Thai interests, was called into doubt. Was Thailand, under his administration, ready to conquer the world? In his own mind, Thaksin might have reinvented Thailand. But whether Thailand's new look would be long-lasting and sustainable is the significant subject of this book. More importantly, I would like to emphasize that the theme of this work, "Reinventing Thailand", strictly connotes Thaksin's own aspirations and vision to use foreign policy to fulfil his diplomatic ambition for ultimately the remaking of a new Thailand. It, therefore, does not necessarily reflect my endorsement of his handling of foreign affairs. I hope that this study would provoke further critical thinking about how Thailand's foreign policy has been, and will be, managed by various political actors.

This project on Thailand's foreign policy under the guidance of Prime Minister Thaksin Shinawatra, from 2001 to 2006, was the joint initiative between myself and Ambassador K. Kesavapany, Director of the Institute of Southeast Asian Studies (ISEAS), Singapore. The *raison d'être* is straightforward. The subject of Thai foreign policy has been understudied. Although Thaksin's period was the most exhilarating moment of Thai diplomacy, Thai foreign policy has largely remained an underdeveloped area of study. I am grateful for Ambassador Kesavapany's generous fellowship extended to me from 2008 to 2009 to conduct the research on this special topic. My profound gratitude also goes to Dr Tej Bunnag, former Thai Foreign Minister and former Permanent Secretary of the Thai Foreign Ministry, for his unfailing encouragement and valuable advice. Without his help, my stint at ISEAS would not have been possible. I would like to thank Ambassador Pradap Pibulsonggram for his support in this project.

I owe a big debt to a number of people who have assisted in this study. First and foremost, my heartfelt gratitude is for Acharn John Funston at the Australian National University. He must have spent hundreds of hours scanning through the final draft of this manuscript. Acharn John unfailingly gave me valuable comments, and also suggested better ways to tackle critical issues. I would like to thank all my interviewees, namely, former Foreign Minister and

ASEAN Secretary-General Dr Surin Pitsuwan; former Deputy Prime Minister and former Foreign Minister Dr Surakiart Sathirathai; former Foreign Minister Dr Tej Bunnag; former Minister of the Prime Minister's Office Jakrapob Penkair; former Deputy Foreign Minister Sawanit Kongsiri; former Ambassador Surapong Jayanama; former ASEAN Secretary-General Rodolfo C. Severino, and all anonymous sources at the Thai Foreign Ministry. I am grateful to those who lent me their helpful suggestions and research ideas, as well as provided me with useful materials, including Duncan McCargo, Thitinan Pongsudhirak, Panitan Wattanayagorn, Arne Kislenko, Busakorn Chantasasawat, Michael J. Montesano, Marc Askew, Lee Poh Onn, Pinsuda Jayanama, and David Fullbrook. My special thanks go to Nantikan Swatdipakdi, Director of Strategy and Planning, Thai Spokesman Bureau, Government House of Thailand, for granting the permission to reproduce most of the photos contained in this book. I also would like to thank Nick Nostitz, Nirmal Ghosh, Simon Roughneen, Marinee Kittiwangchai, Atiya Achakulwisut, Kesanee Cherngvanich, Kateprapa Vaisok, Ittipong Ngamdan, Nopporn Wong-Anan, and Prachathai Editor for giving me advice on the photo selection and for offering some of their own collections to be used in this project. Special thanks go to three anonymous referees for their constructive comments made on an earlier draft of this manuscript, as well as Triena Ong, Head of ISEAS Publishing for making this book project an enjoyable mission. To Anusorn Visitsilpa, I express my thanks for his brilliant design of the book cover. Finally, I would like to thank Nick Potts for reading through the original manuscript and offering his honest comments. None of those thanked here are by any means responsible for the content of the book. Any errors that might remain are all mine.

The Thai transliteration into English is based on the RI system. I also use certain Thai names commonly found in Thailand's English-language newspapers. In some places, the use of old name of countries and cities was introduced to avoid "historical confusion", such as the use of Siam instead of Thailand, and Burma instead of Myanmar, when the old kingdoms were mentioned or discussed.

LIST OF KEY CHARACTERS

Abhisit Vejjajiva, Prime Minister (2008–present)

Bhumibol Adulyadej (King), The Ninth Reign of the Chakri Dynasty (1946–present)

Chatichai Choonhavan (General), Prime Minister (1988–1991)

Chavalit Yongchaiyudh (General), Prime Minister (1996–1997)

Jakrapob Penkair, Former Minister of Prime Minister's Office and a leader of the National United Front for Democracy against Dictatorship (UDD)

Kantathi Suphamongkhon, Foreign Minister (2005–2006)

Kasit Piromya, Foreign Minister (2008–present)

Prem Tinsulanonda (General), Prime Minister (1980–1988)

Samak Sundaravej, Prime Minister (January–September 2008)

Somchai Wongsawat, Prime Minister (September–December 2008)

Sondhi Limthongkul, Leader of the People's Alliance for Democracy (PAD)

Sonthi Boonyaratglin (General), Former Commander-in-Chief of the Royal Thai Army and former Head of the Council for National Security

Surakiart Sathirathai, Foreign Minister (2001–2005)

Surayud Chulanont (General), Prime Minister (2006–2008)

Surin Pitsuwan, ASEAN Secretary-General (2008–present), former Foreign Minister (1997–2001)

Thaksin Shinawatra, Prime Minister (2001–2006)

ABBREVIATIONS

ACD	Asia Cooperation Dialogue
ACMECS	Ayeyawady–Chao Phraya–Mekong Economic Cooperation Strategy
ADB	Asian Development Bank
AEC	Assets Examination Committee
AFTA	ASEAN Free Trade Area
APEC	Asia-Pacific Economic Cooperation
ARF	ASEAN Regional Forum
ASC	Assets Scrutiny Committee
ASEAN	Association of Southeast Asian Nations
ASEM	Asia–Europe Meeting
BIMSTEC	Bay of Bengal Initiative for Multi-Sectoral Technical and Economic Cooperation
BOI	Board of Investment
CCP	Cambodian People's Party
CEO	Chief Executive Officer
CIA	Central Intelligence Agency
CIS	Commonwealth of Independent States
CLMV	Cambodia, Laos, Myanmar, Vietnam
CNS	Council of National Security
CSEP	Civil Service Exchange Programme
EAS	East Asia Summit
ECS	Economic Cooperation Strategy
EFTA	European Free Trade Association
EGAT	Electricity Generating Authority of Thailand
EHS	Early Harvest Scheme
EMEAP	Executives' Meeting of East Asia Pacific Central Banks
ETCF	Emerald Triangular Cooperative Framework

EXIM	Export-Import Bank
FBA	Foreign Business Act
FCCT	Foreign Correspondents' Club of Thailand
FTA	Free Trade Agreement
GCC	Gulf Cooperation Council
GSP	Generalised System of Preference
ICJ	International Court of Justice
IMF	International Monetary Fund
JTEPA	Japan-Thailand Economic Partnership Agreement
KMT	Kuomintang
KNU	Karen National Union
LDCs	Less Developed Countries
LPRP	Lao People's Revolutionary Party
LST	Lao Shinawatra Telecom
MGC	Mekong-Ganga Cooperation
MNNA	Major Non-NATO Ally
NACC	National Anti-Corruption Commission
NCCC	National Counter-Corruption Commission
NGOs	Non-Government Organizations
NLD	National League for Democracy
NRC	National Reconciliation Commission
OAG	Office of the Auditor-General
ODA	Official Development Assistance
OIC	Organization of the Islamic Conference
OTOP	One *Tambon*, One Product
PAD	People's Alliance for Democracy
PAS	Parti Islam se-Malaysia
PPP	People's Power Party
SAARC	South Asian Association for Regional Cooperation
SARS	Severe Acute Respiratory Syndrome
SEATO	Southeast Asia Treaty Organization
SME	Small and Medium Enterprise
SPDC	State Peace and Development Council
SSA	Shan State Army
STEER	Singapore-Thailand Enhanced Economic Relationship
TIFTA	Thailand-India Free Trade Agreement
TNZCEP	Thailand-New Zealand Closer Economic Partnership
TRT	Thai Rak Thai Party
TTR	Thailand Trade Representatives
UDD	National United Front for Democracy against Dictatorship
UMNO	United Malays National Organization

UNCTAD	United Nations Conference of Trade and Development
UNDP	United Nations Development Programme
UNESCO	United Nations Educational, Scientific and Cultural Organization
UNHCR	United Nations High Commissioner for Refugees
UNSC	United Nations Security Council
UNSG	United Nations Secretary-General
VCP	Vietnamese Communist Party
WTO	World Trade Organization

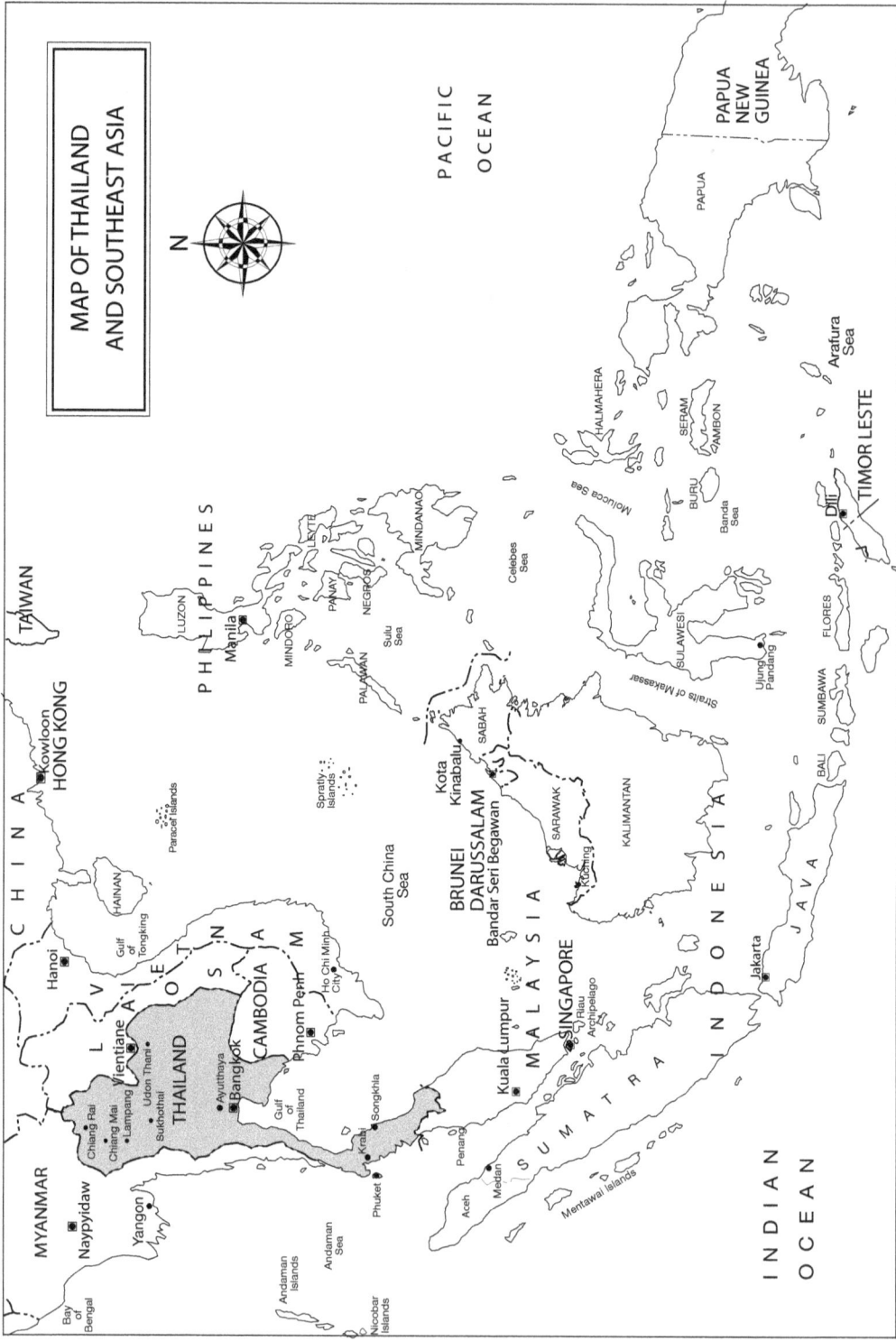

MAP OF THAILAND AND SOUTHEAST ASIA

1

INTRODUCTION
Reinventing Thailand

I decided that the primary mission of my premiership is to bring changes for a better Thailand and for the benefit of the Thai people. These changes include both domestic and foreign dimensions. My mission is to see the Thai people prosperous and Thailand peaceful and secure. The realisation of that mission depends on a result of successful domestic policy as much as a consequence of appropriate and properly implemented foreign policy.... As long as I am in charge, nothing will deter me from making changes if those changes are for the benefit of the Thai people and this country.

Thaksin Shinawatra[1]

Fortunately or unfortunately, Thaksin Shinawatra, Thailand's prime minister from 2001 to 2006, is no longer in charge of his country's domestic and foreign affairs. What he has left behind is a big question, whether the changes he made in foreign affairs during his five years in office were for the benefit of Thailand and its people as he had claimed in his speech. Thaksin Shinawatra rose to the premiership in 2001 after winning a landslide election. He claimed to represent a breath of fresh air in Thai politics, someone who, in his own words, dared to "think out of the box".[2] His party, Thai Rak Thai (TRT), meaning "Thais love Thais", formed a solid government that effectively dominated political power and challenged certain traditional institutions. Thaksin was also the first Thai prime minister to have served a full four-year term as head of a Thai government. While consolidating his power, Thaksin's inclination toward authoritarianism and his confrontation with the old establishment propelled him from the most popular elected prime minister to a wanted fugitive after being sentenced to two years imprisonment for a conflict of interest.

Thaksin might have gone, at least for now, but his foreign policy legacy can still be seen. His ambition was reflected in his myriad of grandiose foreign policy initiatives. This period in Thai foreign affairs was coloured with excitement and controversy. Thaksin was enthusiastic to shape his country's international standing, and was once tipped to become the next regional leader, like Singapore's Lee Kuan Yew and Malaysia's Mahathir Mohamad, and therefore the voice of the Association of Southeast Asian Nations (ASEAN).[3] Dubbed "Thaksiplomacy" by his political opponents, Thaksin-styled diplomacy, which was essentially commerce-driven, appeared to be the core element of Thai foreign policy — a reminiscence of Thailand's business-led policy under the government of Chatichai Choonhavan (1988–91).[4] Thaksin, in effect, reshaped the country's foreign policy with an Asia-first focus as his priority in international relations. He accordingly embarked upon restoring Thai relations with neighbouring countries, seemingly to bring about Thai economic dominance and to proclaim Thailand as the leader in the Mekong region. Rising to this aspiration, Thaksin declared that Thailand would no longer play a role of a recipient country, but would offer financial and technical assistance to its less developed neighbours. In fact, this policy was not new. Providing financial and technical assistance to Thailand's less developed neighbours first begun under the leadership of Prime Minister Anand Panyarachun in 1992.

Also during this period, Thaksin strengthened relationships with certain allies. Ostensibly, Thaksin attached great importance to solidifying economic linkages with China to the point where Bangkok often bent over backwards to avoid offending Beijing on a range of political issues.[5] As a result, the Sino-Thai relationship, already one of the closest between China and a Southeast Asian country, became even more intimate. A series of bilateral activities, ranging from the conclusion of the Sino-Thai Free Trade Agreement

(FTA), the first between China and an ASEAN country, and the first Sino-Thai joint naval exercises in the Gulf of Thailand in 2005, took place. In the meantime, Thai-U.S. relations seemed to remain solid, with the kingdom being awarded the status of a major non-North Atlantic Treaty Organization (NATO) ally, mainly due to Thailand's continued support for the American war on terrorism. This new status made Thailand eligible for priority delivery of defence materials and military cooperation. Could this be considered as Thaksin's strategy to play one power against the other — a revisit of a traditional diplomatic strategy employed by past Thai monarchs who claimed to preserve the kingdom's independence from European colonialists by adopting a balance-of-power policy?

Closer to home, Thaksin regarded Myanmar as one of Thailand's closest friends. Ties between the two countries were once again described as amicable following long years of frigid relations left over from the previous Democrat government. Thaksin often spoke on behalf of Myanmar, particularly in defence of its snail-paced democratization process. Yet, this bilateral relationship, allegedly cultivated on Thaksin's economic interests in Myanmar, drew heavy criticism from within Thai society and the international community alike. Meanwhile, as Thaksin deepened his personal ties with Cambodian leaders, the Royal Thai Embassy in Phnom Penh was burned to the ground in 2003, apparently as a result of a new surge in Cambodian nationalism against Thailand. It was the first case in ASEAN in which a member state resorted to a violent means against a diplomatic mission of another member. This incident raised the crucial question of whether Thaksin's foreign policy, built on Thailand's aspiration for political and economic dominance, was sustainable, and actually served to guarantee the continuation of Thai sovereignty, prosperity and dignity, or indeed simply served the personal ends of power-holders.

Many aspects subsumed within Thailand's foreign policy during the Thaksin administration deserve a serious and systematic study. Not only did the substance of Thai foreign policy undergo a major facelift in this particular era, but the policy decision-making process was also radically reconstructed to fit the political agendas of the leaders. The Thai Foreign Ministry seemed to have lost its grip on foreign affairs to Government House where new initiatives were manufactured and executed.[6] The diminishing role of the Foreign Ministry, in many ways, opened up a space for the Thai power-holders to pay greater attention to other non-traditional aspects of diplomacy. At the same time, it also allowed them to manoeuvre foreign affairs in a way to fulfil their own objectives. The uniqueness of this period of Thai foreign affairs with Thaksin at the helm represents a valid reason for deeper analysis. This study, however, departs from previous examinations of Thailand's foreign relations with their heavy reliance on grand Western theories of international relations, which, as the author perceives, remain useful but may not be best to explicate the Thai case. Throughout much of the twentieth century, the field of international relations (IR) was dominated by rationalist theory, a term normally used to describe the "scientific" analysis of IR practised predominantly by realists, neo-realists and neo-liberal institutionalists.[7] Thaksin's foreign policy defies the rationalist theory and its scientific way of IR analysis. Thailand's domestic and foreign affairs have increasingly been intertwined, and local political culture has emerged as an overriding factor in the formulation of foreign relations, which may not necessarily reflect the influence of rationalist thinking. This represents one of the challenging threads of recent research in international relations that involves the specification of domestic preferences in models of foreign policy and international relations. Unlike earlier work on "linkage politics" by James N. Rosenau, which asked simply if domestic factors exerted any impact on external behaviour, this study attempts to specifically model the impact of domestic preferences on types of leaders' behaviour in the area of foreign relations.[8] It is the only attempt so far to explain Thailand's foreign policy in the modern period which has been rather "understudied". Then and now, Thai foreign policy has always been an "underdeveloped study", resonating the general state of the study on foreign policy in developing countries.

The core argument of this research is that Thai foreign policy under the Thaksin administration was an extension of domestic policy, a tool for the leader to garner power, be it in the domestic or international realm, and not necessarily always serving national interests. This argument gives birth to a catalogue of critical questions and reinterpretations to be discussed in subsequent chapters. They include:

1. Since foreign policy is a continuation of the power needs in the domestic arena, a new focus should be placed on the notion of

"national interests versus private interests" of the Thai power-holders, as well as the question of whether Thailand's foreign policy was strictly regarded as purely an instrument for national interests.

2. Thaksin's reinvention of Thailand was crafted upon two elements in the country's foreign relations — first, the nature and content of, and the motives behind the foreign policy, and second, the process of foreign policy-making, with a special emphasis on the competing hegemony between the prime minister and certain powerful conservative factions inside the Foreign Ministry. These two elements are to be consistently taken into account in the investigation of Thailand's foreign relations throughout this book.

3. The book highlights an often-neglected but rather significant aspect of Thai diplomacy, christened by Thaksin as "the people-centric diplomacy", which makes this work visibly different from previous analyses of Thailand's foreign affairs. The people-centric diplomacy focused mainly on how to respond to the Thais' needs in the realm of foreign affairs and how to involve them in the foreign policy formulation process. This type of diplomacy also serves to buttress the argument of Thaksin's handling of foreign relations as an apparatus to boost his domestic popularity.

4. The myth of the success of Thai foreign policy due to its flexibility to "bend with the prevailing wind" needs a serious reinterpretation. The Thaksin period seemed to suggest that Thailand did not conform to the specific patterns of the international order so as to fulfil national, and individual, interests. The book seeks to re-evaluate the conventional notion of Thai foreign policy of "bending with the wind" while arguing that Thaksin modified this concept to fit the changing domestic and international environments. This gives rise to crucial question: is the bending-with-the-wind policy a permanent trademark of Thai diplomacy?

5. Finally, there were visible disagreements, and thus competition, between some top diplomats at the Foreign Ministry and the Government House over foreign policy formulation. Thaksin, in his attempt to win this political game, exploited foreign policy to realize his diplomatic ambition and family wealth. He enjoyed complete control of foreign affairs during his five years

in power because of his dominance in Parliament and authoritarian style of governance. Thaksin's foreign policy is Thailand's foreign policy, as this book argues. The shape of Thailand's foreign policy was determined by Thaksin's worldview which was reconceptualized to match the thrust for economic achievements.[9]

DOMESTIC AND INTERNATIONAL ENVIRONMENT

This book addresses key goals and themes of Thaksin's foreign policy. As emphasized above, the content of Thai foreign policy is one of the two elements that were made a part of Thailand's reinvention in the Thaksin period. Before examining the fundamental goals and themes of Thailand's foreign policy, a brief assessment of the changing domestic and international atmosphere is imperative so as to understand the rationale behind certain policy formulations in the Thaksin government.

Shoring up Political Power at Home

In the domestic domain, Thaksin's rise to power was something beyond the imagination or expectation of the Thai people. Never had the Thais come across a strong civilian leader who not only found his way to power through democratic means, managing to hold onto the top position with a firm support from the grassroots, but also expressed an adamant interest in foreign affairs. In the past, strong leaders only existed in a despotic environment, with military strongmen proclaiming themselves as prime ministers, including Phibun Songkhram (1938–44 and 1948–57), Thanom Kittikachorn (1958 and 1963–73) and Sarit Thanarat (1958–63). Thaksin stands in a new league of Thai leaders. He is a civilian, of Chinese lineage, and a self-made multi-millionaire who bought his way up to the top of the political echelon.[10] The Thaksin phenomenon is a story of personal ambition as much as a tale based on the right political connections.

Who is Thaksin Shinawatra? Born on 26 July 1949, Thaksin came from a well-heeled family which owned a variety of businesses at various points in time, including cinemas, a coffee shop, bus services, a motorcycle agency, a petrol station, and a silk trading and production company.[11] Business, however, was not the only interesting subject for Thaksin. He was familiar with local politics even in his childhood. His father, Lert Shinawatra, was elected Member of Parliament (MP) for Chiang Mai, his hometown, in 1969. Thaksin's uncle, Suraphan, was also an elected MP who eventually served as Deputy Minister of Transport and Communications in 1988.[12] Thaksin himself commenced his career in the Royal Thai Police Department in 1973. In 1976, he married Pojaman, daughter of Samoe Damaphong, who was the police commander of Bangkok South at the time. Undoubtedly, this strengthened Thaksin's connection with powerful figures within the Police Department. Thaksin graduated from the Police Academy as the top student and received his doctorate in criminal justice from Sam Houston State University, Texas, in 1979. Upon returning home, Thaksin was assigned to serve in a police station in Bangkok. Also during this period, he began to venture into the business world seriously. After a couple of failed businesses, Thaksin, in 1981, started a new company that leased IBM computers to government offices. His business expanded rapidly and five years later, he secured his first government telecommunications concession — to offer paging services in a joint venture with Pacific Telesis. His successful business activities were all made possible because of concessions awarded by various government agencies, essentially as a result of his inside connections. He resigned from the police with the rank of lieutenant colonel in 1987.[13]

Having earned the title of one of Thailand's most successful businessmen, Thaksin turned to politics in 1994 as a member of the Palang Dharma Party, literally meaning "the power of justice". The party was led by Major General Chamlong Srimuang, Governor of Bangkok, a former military officer and leader of the "Young Turks" military clique, and leader of the anti-military uprising of May 1992 against military man-turned-prime minister, General Suchinda Kraprayoon. Ironically, Chamlong is today a staunch enemy of Thaksin whom he claimed has betrayed Thai democracy for his own benefit. Chamlong is one of the core members of the People's Alliance for Democracy (PAD), a coalition of royalists, Bangkok elite, factions in the military and powerful businesses, that has campaigned for the extermination of Thaksin's political legacy. But in 1994, Thaksin's political career was in steep ascent with his first ministerial portfolio coming through the same year. Palang Dharma joined in a coalition government led by the Democrat Party in the aftermath of the Black May demonstrations of 1992. Thaksin accepted the position of foreign minister (November 1994–February 1995). Duncan McCargo argued that Thaksin's term as foreign minister was a kind of trial run prior to him formally assuming the leadership of the party. But his spell as foreign minister was marred by controversy. McCargo asserted, "He was widely criticised for spending his own money to improve [the] ministry's facilities and became embroiled in a controversy over whether his monopolistic business assets rendered him constitutionally ineligible to serve in the cabinet."[14] Thaksin resigned from the post after only three months. But he returned as deputy prime minister twice, during the governments of Banharn Silpa-archa (1995–96) and Chavalit Yongchaiyuth (1996–97).

Jakrapob Penkair, Thaksin's confidant, former Minister of the Prime Minister's Office (under the Samak Sundaravej government, January–September 2008), ex-diplomat and ex-journalist, gave a different account of Thaksin's short stint at the Foreign Ministry. He said in an interview with the author that Thaksin, while at times expressing a critical view of the Foreign Ministry, admitted that Thai diplomats were well-educated and highly sophisticated.[15] Evidently, Thaksin appointed Maris Sa-ngiemphong, a high-ranking Foreign Ministry officer as one of his personal assistants. His familiarity with the Foreign Ministry provided him with new-found confidence in pursuing an active foreign policy with unfaltering back-up from certain quarters within the ministry.

Thaksin later graduated from the leader of a small party to being the head of Thailand's largest and most powerful party, the Thai Rak Thai (TRT).[16] The Democrat government, despite its seemingly clean image, struggled to improve the economic conditions that were shattered by the financial crisis of 1997. Although eventually, economic growth did return, yet the Thai public had become impatient, and there were economic costs from the Democrat policies. This impatience, in part, paved the way for the TRT to claim an overwhelming victory in the general election of 2001. Two factors need to be considered in the wake of TRT's political triumph. First, the Democrat government of Chuan Leekpai

(1997–2001) arrived in power with a mission to mend the national economy after it was torn apart by economic mismanagement of previous governments under Banharn and Chavalit. Their compliance with the economic recovery measures prescribed by the International Monetary Fund (IMF), seen as "bitter medicine" by many Thais, appeared to be the only option for Thailand at the time as a path toward recovery from the crisis. But the approval of the IMF's bailout package was largely manipulated by Thaksin. He accused the Democrat government of being unpatriotic to the motherland. He compared the loss of Thailand's economic self-control with the loss of independence.[17]

Second, Thailand in 2001 entered new political territory. Thaksin won the election with a stridently populist economic platform, now widely referred to as Thaksinomics, with the emphasis on reversing several key IMF policies adopted by the Chuan government, while aiming at producing rapid economic growth, enlarging the scale of local manufacturing known as OTOP (One *Tambon*, One Product) projects, improving rural living conditions through new subsidized loans, creating a debt moratorium for farmers and offering cheap healthcare service through the so-called "Bt30 Curing All" scheme. Surakiart Sathirathai, Thailand's foreign minister from 2001 to 2005, explained the TRT's populist programme in the context of a dual-track policy. To the new government, lessons from the financial crisis showed that a dependence on the export sector alone to achieve sustainable growth was no longer adequate. The rural sector had to be strengthened, and therefore, building the grassroots capacity to survive and thrive under globalization was mandatory.[18] Pasuk Phongpaichit argued that the Thaksin schemes were mostly about stimulating entrepreneurship by increasing the access to capital. Thaksin said, "Capitalism needs capital, without which there is no capitalism. We need to push capital into the rural areas."[19]

With the success of the campaign of his populist programmes, Thaksin and TRT members were able to monopolize Thai politics. He formed an almost one-party government, leaving the Democrats as the main opposition party. As Thaksin's time at the helm began, he turned to the reconstruction of foreign policy, and sought to shift the Foreign Ministry's paradigm of thinking. He made clear that the mission of protecting national interests and the formulation of foreign policy that reflected national interests were different entities. Thaksin acknowledged that Thai diplomats were indisputably "patriotic" and capable of safeguarding national interests. However, he doubted that they had experience and comprehension of the persistent social and economic disparity and how to formulate a foreign policy that could deal with this pressing issue.[20] The general perception of the Thai Foreign Ministry as a place of nobles and aristocrats served the political purpose of the TRT Party and its intervention in foreign affairs through the Thaksin-initiated "people-centric diplomacy". Thaksin came up with the idea of the people-centric diplomacy, purportedly to close the gap between local reality and globalization, with himself playing the role of a bridge for this connection, not the Foreign Ministry.

But how did the Thai Foreign Ministry earn the reputation of being a place for nobles and aristocrats in the first place? Thaksin painted the image of the Foreign Ministry, despite its skilled and respected background, as a "dinosaur" organization which was out of touch with the world reality and too posh to be *au fait* with the Thai poor.[21] The Ministry of Foreign Affairs has a long history. Historically, the country's foreign relations were handled exclusively by the absolute monarchs of the day. During the Kingdom of Ayutthaya (1351–1767), foreign relations were in the hands of "Krom Phra Klang", or the Treasury Department, headed by Phra Klang, equivalent to today's ministerial positions. This pattern of governing foreign relations remained throughout the early Bangkok period. In 1840, King Mongkut, also known as King Rama IV (1851–69), founded the Ministry of Foreign Affairs, which was still directly administered by the king himself. Chao Phraya Bhanuwong became the first Foreign Minister of Siam in 1871, appointed by King Chulalongkorn (1868–1910), son of King Mongkut. In 1881, Prince Devavongse Varoprakarn succeeded this position. Known widely as the father of Thai diplomacy, he reorganized and modernized the ministry to meet the nineteenth century standards.[22] Traditionally, the Thai Foreign Ministry had enjoyed a certain degree of autonomy in the decision-making process, which allowed for a technocrat-driven foreign policy. But the rise of Thaksin curtailed its autonomous power.

Thaksin aspired to transform Thailand into a regional player. To be able to accomplish his goal, he crafted an active foreign policy. In fact, a number of past political figures had long practised earlier modes of activism in diplomacy, ranging from Foreign Minister Thanat Khoman, who was a key figure in the founding of ASEAN; Prime Minister Chatichai, who transformed a battlefield in Indochina into a marketplace for Thai products; and Foreign Minister Surin Pitsuwan, whose "Flexible Engagement Policy" was a notable if somewhat controversial development in foreign relations. Indeed, both the Chavalit and Chuan governments also promoted themselves as important regional players. It is true that these examples share many similarities with Thaksin's foreign policy. All of them were bold, albeit inconsistent at times, and were pursued for a mixture of idealistic and pragmatic motives. But Thaksin pushed the envelope further by binding tightly the country's foreign policy with his domestic populist programmes. Thaksin was a master of reinventing a myriad of new political terminologies. His political slogan, "Think new, act new", a reformist emphasis on the need for considerable changes and unorthodox ways of working, was also introduced in the realm of foreign affairs. Thaksin, in a brainstorming session with senior diplomats at the Foreign Ministry, urged them to "make the almost impossible possible".[23] He also told Thai ambassadors before leaving for their missions overseas that they should be daring to "think weird" because the world had changed significantly and therefore what they might think is weird might not be weird after all. The key message laid in the courage to think outside of the convention.[24] Thaksin's intention to use foreign relations to score political points at home became the main driving force for the announcement of a new direction in foreign policy. Thailand, for the first time since the Chatichai government, promoted itself as a regional centre of gravity, particularly on mainland Southeast Asia.

Yet, a new Thailand depicted by Thaksin ran into serious political difficulties which began in 2005. The rise of Thaksin and his domination of political power posed a threat to the traditional elite who sought to eliminate him so as to maintain their power positions. Led by the PAD, the anti-Thaksin demonstrators created the condition of ungovernability, including exploiting foreign policy to achieve political goals, and provoked military intervention. They finally succeeded as the military staged a coup against Thaksin in September 2006. The internal conflict has continued into the post-coup period while Thaksin's allies took turns to hold state power;

this further infuriated the royalists. The PAD has repeatedly used foreign policy issues as a political weapon to discredit the Thaksin-backed governments, such as the dispute between Thailand and Cambodia over the Preah Vihear temple (to be elaborated in subsequent chapters). Hence, Thailand's protracted political conflict has generated a tremendous impact on the country's foreign policy.

Conducive Global Atmosphere

Thaksin's proactive foreign policy and his strategy of reassigning Thailand as a "regional hegemon" were made possible because of the conducive international environment. His arrival in power took place one decade after the Cold War (1945–91) had ended. The world in the new millennium greatly differed from that of the previous century and the chapter on the world order being dictated by ideological conflict was closed. It was the new dawn of democracy, with the United States leading the world as the supreme power. American political scientist Francis Fukuyama called this phenomenon the "end of history", where the advent of Western liberal democracy signalled the end point of mankind's ideological evolution and the final form of human government.[25] The new wave of democratization that swept across the globe was favourably responded to by Thaksin, whose rise to power was heralded much in the same way as the final phase of Thai democracy consolidation. Nominally, Thaksin was able to claim that he was a champion of democracy simply because he came to power on the basis of democratic rules of contestation, even when he actually weakened the process of democratic consolidation right at the beginning of his tenure through the strengthening of a one-party system, his co-optation of almost all the independent centres of power and authority in the domestic political process, and the state's censorship against the media.[26] The United States appeared to tolerate Thaksin's controversial style of democracy since it desperately sought allies to fight the war on terrorism in the wake of 9/11, and Thailand slotted into that role. Just as the United States tolerated the successive despotic regimes of Thailand during the Cold War because of their mutual interest in combating the threat of communism, Thaksin's abuse of democracy was not objected merely because its global attention has been on its war on terrorism.

The Force of Globalization

A decade after the Cold War also witnessed the rapidly expanding phenomenon of globalization. Globalization, in simple terms, is often referred to as a greater and better connection among people of the world in the political, economic and socio-cultural realms. Thaksin took advantage of globalization to further deepen his political power, first, in inculcating a sense of consumerism among the local people, turning on a domestic drive for higher productivity while building a greater level of materialistic dependency on the state, and second, in employing foreign policy to reach out for global business opportunities, presumably in response to the increasing needs and wider tastes of the people.[27] Thomas Friedman, however, cautioned, "Globalisation can be incredibly empowering and incredibly coercive.... It can democratise opportunity and democratise panic. While it is homogenising cultures, it is also enabling people to share their unique individuality farther and wider."[28] Thaksin adopted selective aspects of globalization, primarily as a synonym for global business that allowed nations to operate as if borders did not exist.

In the area of foreign relations, the word "globalization", under the Thaksin administration, became a commonly-heard "buzzword". Thaksin developed the notion of globalization while linking it with the necessity to adjust to a new mode of diplomacy. On several occasions, Thaksin reiterated the inevitability of embracing globalization if Thailand wanted to be recognized and successful internationally. At the "Annual Meeting of Ambassador and Consuls-General of Thailand" at the Thai Foreign Ministry on 15 August 2005, Thaksin repeated that Thailand needed to be prepared for the shifting environment resulting from globalization in four specific areas, namely the free flow of people and labour, trade and services, investment, and information and technology, and that the roles of ambassadors and consuls-general were to maintain and expand Thailand's export markets. Thaksin also highlighted the importance of concluding FTAs as well as barter trade agreements which would lead to the opening of more markets for Thailand.[29] During his interview with Maurice R. Greenberg, Thaksin even time-shifted the term "globalization" as though it had been with Thailand for centuries. He said, "Globalization is an

age-old ancestral phenomenon that has been present since the first
Goths crossed the Euphrates and the first Chinese crossed the
Yangtze."[30] In another account, Thaksin injected a sense of Asian
regionalism into the notion of globalization:

> As we are meeting today, globalization has been released from
> the box, boundaries have been blurred, and shifting to a new
> economic model will not come without political consequences.
> For this reason, East and West need to begin a serious dialogue on
> these macro-level changes and how to cope with them. Ideally,
> the West would then start paying real money for real products
> from Asia, as opposed to products farmed out for production to
> Asia, intended for consumption in the West. The West would also
> need to come up with an economic model that would hold
> employment in their own countries, for their own citizens.[31]

Meanwhile, Foreign Minister Surakiart remoulded the concept
of globalization to fit the government's foreign policy platform. He
announced, "Fully cognizant of the impacts both positive and
negative globalization have borne on Thailand and the rest of the
world, we have chosen to run a foreign policy that fully supports
domestic economic and social policy on the one hand, and projects
Thailand with a new perception in the international arena, on the
other."[32] The welcoming of globalization was indeed driven by
Thailand's economic conditions, and also reflected in Thaksin's
commerce-driven diplomacy designed to bolster the kingdom's
position to optimize the globalized climate for advancing
entrepreneurial interests. The exploitation of globalization was seen
more vividly when Thailand initiated a region-wide cooperative
framework, named Asia Cooperation Dialogue (ACD). The logic
and content of the ACD will be discussed in Chapter 3.

The Rise of China and India

Apart from the phenomenon of globalization, the new millennium
also saw the rise of two Asian powers, China and India. This
strategic shift at the regional level allowed Thaksin to formulate a
foreign policy that conveniently accommodated the growing
influence of both Asian giants, instead of having to rely on the
United States as the provider of peace and security for Thailand

as in the past. In fact, during the Cambodian conflict (1978–91), Thailand relied on China more than the United States for the guaranteeing of its national security. Various analysts have, however, interpreted Thaksin's accommodation with China and India rather differently. Some construed Thaksin's move to strengthen ties with China and India as a return of a balance-of-power policy in which counterweights are used against the U.S. influence. Some considered it as the traditional strategy of "bending with the wind", where Thailand grasped the political and economic opportunities that came with the rise of the pair to enhance its own interests. Others also likened the Thai accommodation as a policy of "bandwagoning", in which Thailand overtly sided with China and India at the same time that both were building their own exclusive spheres of influence to create a polar of power of their own.[33]

The rise of China and India broadened up a space for Thaksin to construct Thailand's foreign policy in a way that it became less restricted because of the decentralization of the international order. In other words, the emerging power of China and India, which were close friends of Thailand, proffered wider policy options for Bangkok. Thailand, in this period, was able to diversify its sources of political and economic benefits. For Beijing and New Delhi, befriending a middle-sized Thailand could help cement their status as rising powers of Asia. For example, China agreed to host the Third ACD Meeting, initiated by Thailand which already organized the first two meetings in Cha-am and Chiang Mai respectively. This made China the first member country, apart from Thailand, to play host to the ACD. Likewise, India also agreed to participate in the Thai-initiated Asian Bond Fund II, a scheme within the ACD, set up to draw on the region's financial strength to battle economic uncertainties. On Thaksin's part, he went the extra mile to please China and India because of clear advantages that would ensue. First, the new rising powers made clear that they would not interfere in Thailand's domestic affairs. A few incidents exemplified this statement. China and India refused to criticize the heavy-handed policy of Thaksin *vis-à-vis* the Muslim insurgents in the south of Thailand. The question of Thaksin's legitimacy at home was purposefully downplayed by India and China. The non-interference rule also served the rising Asian powers well. Thaksin chose not to

condemn China for the alleged violations of human rights against
its minorities on several occasions. Even when Thaksin left the
political scene, Prime Minister Samak, a self-proclaimed Thaksin
proxy, continued to uphold the non-interference principle. He
remained silent over China's brutal crackdown on Tibetan pro-
democracy protesters prior to the Olympic Games in August 2008.[34]
It was in this mutual benefit between Thailand and the two emerging
powers of Asia that boosted Thaksin's confidence to produce a
proactive foreign policy that seemed to emphasize the theme of
"Asia for Asians".

But it was not all about political benefits. The rise of China and
India also meant business opportunities for Thailand. The kingdom
signed the FTAs with both China and India in 2003. The thrust for
closer economic relations with China and India met with
encouraging response from Thaksin's commerce-driven policies
and capitalist agenda. Thaksin, in August 2006, told a group of
senior members of the Thai Foreign Ministry that today's global
economic system was defined as "capitalism". Capitalism was an
indispensable mechanism for the nation's economic success.
Democracy, despite reigning supreme in the West, could be reduced
to being only a supporting part of the national economic achievement
— no longer the core component. He emphasized that this explained
why foreign investors continued to invest in China and Vietnam in
spite of their lack of democracy. Yet, these countries enjoyed, to
different degrees, certain political stability. Capitalism, for Thaksin,
was used to describe the current international order. He even
reasoned that the 9/11 incident which caused over 2,700 deaths,
was the result of the terrorist groups' failure to catch up with the
rapidly changing world. They, therefore, chose to incapacitate the
symbol of capitalism.[35] Under the Thaksin administration, capitalism
was made an inherited trait of Thai foreign policy. The economic
rise of China, in particular, helped set the tone of Asia's international
affairs in which economic interests were prioritized at the expense
of political issues, such as the promotion of democracy and respect
for human rights. India, although democratic, has been a quick
learner in this ferociously competitive economic game. For instance,
the Indian government, in the aftermath of the state's crackdown
on pro-democracy demonstrators in Myanmar in September 2007,
pronounced its position of separating politics from economic interest

in its relations with Yangon, purportedly to protect its energy security business invested in this Southeast Asian nation.[36]

In particular, the personal cultural linkage between Thaksin and rising China was also contributory to the strengthening of his Asia-focused foreign policy. Thaksin himself illustrated one of the country's most successful Thai-Chinese leaders. It was not surprising when Thaksin set great store by China as Thailand's most important ally due to his own ancestral history. Thaksin picked China as his first destination to visit upon becoming prime minister in 2001. Beijing reciprocated the gesture in October 2003 when Thailand became the first country Hu Jintao visited as president.[37] While in China in 2005, Thaksin paid homage to his ancestors' homeland in Guangdong province. He fondly said, "When Chinese people see a Thai leader and so many entrepreneurs coming to China to pay homage to the place where their ancestors had lived, they will understand that Thais and Chinese are from one family, and they are relatives."[38] Thaksin took advantage of a surge in public positive sentiment as well as in the world's upbeat opinion about rising China. He crafted a China-favoured policy to fit domestic enthusiasm for a closer relationship with Beijing, and at the same time, acknowledged the reality in which China had become an irresistible rising power in the Asia-Pacific region.

The Region's Leadership Vacuum

As Thaksin took Thai politics by storm, with his gripping populist programmes and the unwavering support from his voters in the rural areas, Southeast Asians might have expected him to perhaps fill the region's leadership vacuum. Thaksin's emerging power in the region came at the time when ASEAN's old charismatic leaders had left the stage, with the retirement of Singapore's Lee Kuan Yew and the downfall of Indonesia's Suharto. Although Mahathir Mohamad was still Malaysia's prime minister, but he was on his way out of politics: he resigned from the premiership in 2003, more than two years after Thaksin arrived in power. Thaksin's bold foreign policy agendas, his innovative vision of the world, and his reasonable English, prompted him to flaunt his ambition of becoming the region's next leader. The gap in the region's leadership, to a certain extent, helped shore up Thaksin's global aspirations.

His creation of the Asian Bond Market was much trumpeted as Thaksin's confident move to reinstate some sense of dignity to the nation as well as the whole region that was trying to reinvent itself in the globalized world. It was also a part of redefining the Thai position in Asia.

Thaksin, in demonstrating his eagerness to represent the region, walked in the footsteps of past regional statesmen. These steps included the occasional challenge against Western hegemony, the innovative idea of constructing "Asia for Asians", and the campaign to make the Asian voice heard on the international stage — all were undertaken by Thaksin, even if some proved detrimental to the country in the long term. For example, Thaksin blasted, "The U.N. is not my father", when this international body raised questions over Thaksin's brutal war on drugs in March 2003 that led to more than 2,500 Thais being killed. He was also criticized by his critics for acting as though he was a spokesperson for Myanmar's General Than Shwe, Chairman of the State Peace and Development Council (SPDC), on numerous occasions when this Thai neighbour committed serious human rights violations against its own people, such as in the suppression of the pro-democracy movement at home. Thaksin's display of his iron-fist diplomacy served to elevate the region's position in the face of the Western-dominated international domain, albeit in a controversial manner. Ironically, Thaksin hoped that his support of Surakiart Sathirathai for the position of the United Nations Secretary-General (UNSG), despite being heatedly slated in Thailand for intricate political reasons, would help register Asia on the global map.

Apart from his outspoken personality and resolute foreign policy, his emerging leadership, especially in mainland Southeast Asia, was buttressed by the country being well positioned and centrally located in the region's political and strategic landscape. The country has enjoyed substantial military ties with both China and the United States. It has about one-eighth of ASEAN's population and one-fifth of its combined gross domestic product. John Ciorciari noted,

> He will not be able to push Indonesia and Malaysia to back his major political and security initiatives, and he will not dominate ASEAN economic expansion, but Thailand under Thaksin is well positioned to enhance its role as the leading mainland node in the

regional political system. Thaksin can also play a vocal and instrumental role in coordinating economic and security initiatives among like-minded countries inside and outside the region.[39]

NATURE AND CONTENT OF THAKSIN'S FOREIGN POLICY

This section explores key goals and themes as well as motives behind the making of Thaksin's foreign policy. It discusses the nature of such policy as featured in the many initiatives masterminded by Thaksin from 2001 to 2006. It also seeks to delve into the question of how Thaksin's foreign policy differed from that of past governments. Thaksin demonstrated that his foreign policy was designed to serve the continuity in Thailand's active interface with other countries, be they neighbours, regional partners, major powers or international organizations and non-governmental organizations (NGOs). In this process, Thaksin also personalized the country's foreign policy in order to accumulate political points and his business interests.

Key Goals and Themes

Characteristics of Thaksin's foreign policy mirrored both old and new ways in the conduct of Thai diplomacy. Certain aspects of his policy had been evident many generations before, in the supposedly astute moulding of Thai strategies in the hands of past kings and generals in the course of their interaction with the outside world. More specifically, Thaksin's foreign policy was a sharp-witted response to the shifting domestic political order as well as regional and international landscape. Some of his policy initiatives were more tangible than others and well received by his supporters in rural villages. Some were criticized for being unsustainable and corrupt because they were beset with conflicts of interest of the power-holders.

A Reflection of Domestic Policy

Thaksin's foreign policy was an annexe of his domestic policy through which the grassroots sector was strengthened, obviously for the political purpose of the ruling government. Taking the financial crisis in 1997 as a starting point, the government launched its campaign in building grassroots-capacity in order to thrive under, and take advantage of, the so-called globalization. Under the so-called dual-track policy, Thaksin sought to constitute a strong domestic foundation for the national economy, with special emphasis on advancing the grassroots activity. Accordingly, a myriad of assistance programmes was inaugurated to empower this sector of society especially with regard to increasing productivity and promoting wider access to capital. These included the revolving Village Fund and People's Bank programmes to encourage micro-credit lending to rural communities to generate income from self-employment; the OTOP scheme to enhance local entrepreneurship and productivity; new tax incentives for the SME sector; housing schemes for the poor; temporary debt suspension for farmers; and a universal healthcare programme.

For Thaksin, a proactive diplomacy was quintessential because the country could engage with the international community and search for new areas of international cooperation meaningfully. Foreign policy could also be utilized to further cement the domestic economic and social structure.[40] Describing today's world as the age of globalization helped legitimize the government's policy of expanding the local economy so as to be able to step up with the change of the international economic condition. The legitimization of Thaksin's foreign policy also included the nation's exigency to become vigorous and dynamic on the international stage, while making use of foreign affairs to create job opportunities at home, generate income and reduce the government's expenditure, as well as dealing with chronic problems, such as the growing domestic consumption of narcotics and transnational crimes. Hence, Thaksin did not only make full use of foreign policy as the basis for social and economic stability, but also a medicine to cure domestic problems arising from across borders.

The government also argued that Thailand's regional initiatives, such as the Ayeyawady–Chao Phraya–Mekong Economic Cooperation Strategy (ACMECS) and the Greater Mekong Sub-region (GMS), were launched based on the Thai good neighbourly principles of "prosper thy neighbour" and "charity begins at home". Foreign Minister Surakiart said, "To be successful with our economic growth, our neighbours must not be left neglected."[41] These programmes, according to the Thai government, offered development assistance to its neighbours on the notion of self-help and partnership. At a deeper level, Thaksin was attempting to transform immediate neighbours into marketplaces in order to support and absorb Thai merchandise produced under government schemes, for example the OTOP, even when he possessed other personal agendas. At the same time, in bringing about a better living standard in neighbouring countries, Thailand would no longer have to bear the consequences which might come with poverty and underdevelopment, like illegal workers, crimes and narcotic flows. Some joint-venture projects between Thailand and its neighbours aimed at fulfilling Thai national interests, especially for the benefits of local people in rural areas, including the search for new energy sources to fuel the nation's expanded industrialization. The existing Thai cooperation with Laos in hydropower projects and with Myanmar through the gas pipeline was used to showcase Thaksin's strategies in building close ties with neighbours and strengthening the local economy. But these strategies incited controversies too, such as the Thai piggybacking of despotic regimes in order to attain certain interests.

A Status of a Regional Player

Thaksin and his two foreign ministers, Surakiart Sathirathai and Kantathi Suphamongkhon, concocted a new face of Thai foreign policy that assigned Thailand as a dominant regional player with new agendas. The longevity of the Thaksin regime permitted a continuity of Thai foreign policy. It is also noteworthy that Surakiart served as Foreign Minister throughout the first four-year term of the Thaksin administration, and although rather unusual since cabinet posts were normally vulnerable to shifts in power within the government, helped fulfil the implementation process of the Thai foreign policy. In the past, the lack of Thai leadership in the region was due to many obstacles. Although Thailand played important roles in regional politics, such as being the frontline state in confronting the communist threat in Indochina during the Cold War, this role was to a certain degree dictated by the United States and China. Thailand was perceived by its neighbouring states, firstly as America's client state, and later China's ambivalent ally.[42] Also, throughout the Cold War, Thailand was, more often than not, dominated by successive military regimes whose worldview was built upon the consistent need to imagine enemies in order to sustain their legitimacy. Even after the end of the Cold War, political instability in the hands of civilian governments and the financial meltdown of 1997 powerfully acted as barriers for Thailand in striking a leading role in the region. But all this changed when Thaksin arrived in 2001.

Political stability, support of the Thai public and Thaksin's personal ambition made it possible for Thailand to stand tall on the regional stage. Thaksin's wealth also garnered him a certain level of respect at home and in the region. They saw in him a successful businessman and leader who could make things happen, and nothing could stand in his way. In order to increase Thailand's influence on the region, Thaksin readjusted the country's foreign policy that corresponded to the much-needed quality as a new regional player. Taking the strategic factor into consideration, Thaksin began to redefine the Thai preponderance based on the existing international order, using Thailand's economic power and the opening up of the regional economy to dominate its weaker neighbouring states. In these crude comparisons, as the United States constructing its sphere of influence in Latin America, and China in Southeast Asia, Thailand embarked upon building its own orbit of power within mainland Southeast Asia. The Thai orbit of power was materialized in Thaksin's attempt to monopolize the political economy of this sub-region. This book argues that such an attempt indicated the making of Thai hegemonization.

Since Thaksin's first year in office, he relished Thailand's new image as a donor country. He said, "Thailand will accept foreign aid, but it will not be totally obedient to foreign donors. International assistance is mutual and every nation is independent, so interference into other countries' internal affairs under the name of aid cannot be accepted."[43] Regarding the ACMECS, Thaksin hoped to show the world his visionary side, as a leader who worked to aid less developed countries (LDCs). While Thailand promoted regional prosperity, it also spread the Thai economic influence on its neighbours. Through ACMECS, Thailand offered soft loans packaged in baht, stressing its increased money power as a new leading player in this sub-region. The same strategies were also used during Thailand's participation in other sub-regional cooperation such as the GMS and BIMSTEC (Bay of Bengal Initiative for Multi-Sectoral Technical and Economic Cooperation); the latter's original name is "Bangladesh, India, Myanmar, Sri Lanka and Thailand Economic Cooperation". BIMSTEC was founded in Bangkok in 1997 under the initiative of the Chuan government, with an aim to strengthen economic ties between selected states of South and Southeast Asia.

The Thai leadership on mainland Southeast Asia was not only evident in the attempted economic domination of its neighbours. Thaksin also went ahead with new initiatives designed to stamp Thailand's supremacy on political and cultural fronts. For example, Thaksin instigated the "Bangkok Process" supposedly in order to assist the Myanmar government in reconciling with its opposition and expediting its democratization.[44] A serious assessment of Thailand's role in the Bangkok Process is essential for a measurement of Thailand's success in gauging the political impact on Myanmar, which is extensively discussed in Chapter 3. Thaksin did his part, in displaying his leadership in addressing this difficult political issue, and that he fully acknowledged the obstacles and benefits in the dealing with the leaders in Naypyidaw.

Apart from sowing the seed of Thai political eminence in the region, Thaksin sponsored an aggressive campaign on the proliferation of Thai culture in neighbouring countries which shared similar cultures and customs, such as through Thai television programmes and music, and the wide circulation of Thai currency, as was seen in Laos, Cambodia and certain parts of Myanmar. The Thaksin administration invented a programme called "Cultural Diplomacy" with the main objectives as follows:

1. Promoting active cultural diplomacy in order to support a Thai strategy of increasing international competitiveness.
2. Promoting visits to foreign countries of the prime minister and members of the Cabinet in order to reify the country's good image overseas, and as a tool to foster Thailand's trade with its partners.
3. Building trust and confidence in Thailand especially among its immediate neighbours.[45]

The subtle aim of the cultural diplomacy was to woo the region through the promotion of the supposedly superior Thai civilization, the uniqueness of Thai culture and Thai ingenuity, such as through the project "Thailand through the Lens", which celebrated the country's tourism through the photo exhibition of the Thai beautiful landscape, organized in June 2008 by the Royal Thai Embassy and the Office of Tourism of Thailand in Tel Aviv, Israel.[46] However, promoting cultural supremacy is a delicate business, and mishandling it could damage Thailand's foreign affairs. Any lack of understanding of cultural sensitivity from the Thai private sector could prove detrimental to Thai relations with neighbouring countries.

Pan-Asia Focus

One outstanding characteristic of Thaksin's foreign policy was its focus on the strengthening of Asia's stance in the world. Thaksin, on numerous occasions, repeatedly emphasized the need for Thailand to take a lead in the building of a stronger Asia based on existing sub-region and inter-sub-regional cooperation arrangements that could uplift the lives of the peoples of Asia and be beneficial to the rest of the world. Surakiart once said that his government concentrated its foreign policy on prioritizing relations and cooperation with Asia by taking an "Asian way" approach. He defined the "Asian way" as a special code of conduct that rejected confrontation and considered face-saving a serious matter. However, he defended, "But the Asian way does not mean we do not respect human rights and democracy. It does not mean we do not work together for democratization. But we have to take the Asian character into account in the conduct of foreign affairs."[47] In the election campaign of the TRT in 2000, Thaksin promised that he would turn Asia, a continent that had been torn by diversity in culture, beliefs, the level of economic development, and even race and ideology, into a continent of harmony and strength. Thaksin reasoned that with more than half of the world population and in possession of more than half of the world foreign reserves, the people of Asia deserved more than a continent of divisiveness, poverty, deprivation and degradation.[48] To its credit, TRT appeared to be the country's first political party that raised foreign affairs issues during an election campaign. For his voters, Thaksin was embarking upon constructing a greater Thailand in the eyes of the world.

Thaksin's diplomatic ambition, through the creation of a pan-Asia policy, points to certain developments in the realm of Thailand's foreign affairs. First, Thaksin, in his drive to boast his foreign policy originality, toned down the Thai role in ASEAN, but sought to invent new avenues of regional cooperation. Thaksin was not overly keen on promoting ASEAN but invested his energy in diplomacy elsewhere. He seemed to consider ASEAN as a marginal organization overburdened with bureaucratic red tape and time-consuming procedures. Although he agreed with the needed success of the ASEAN Economic Community, he impatiently pushed for several bilateral FTA negotiations.[49] It was true that Thaksin was eager to assume the role of the region's leader. But this did not necessarily mean that he was willing to prioritize ASEAN on the national agenda. There is clear evidence to support this argument. The ACD, encompassing countries from Northeast Asia to the Middle East, effectively superseded the focus on ASEAN on the Thai radar. The fact that Thaksin chose to play his Myanmar card with the launch of the "Bangkok Process" by bypassing the regional effort to promote political reforms in Myanmar, showed that Thaksin was independent and ready to grasp global attention at the expense of ASEAN's diminishing role. Also, as Thailand earned international opprobrium for the deaths of eighty-seven unarmed Muslim protesters on 25 October 2004 at the hands of police and soldiers in Tak Bai in the southern province of Narathiwat, Thaksin threatened to walk out of the Tenth ASEAN Summit in Vientiane, 29–30 November 2004, if leaders questioned the unrest which intensely concerned Muslim-majority ASEAN members, Malaysia and Indonesia.[50]

Second, far-reaching foreign policy, with a wider concentration on Asia, was formulated and supported by the Thai public because of the catastrophic impact caused by the financial crisis on Thailand's economy and its international standing. Thaksin managed to pay back the IMF ahead of time with the last instalment of the US$3.4 billion that the fund had lent the country. He spoke on television and declared "independence" against the IMF. "Today, we paid off the last batch of IMF loans, lifting the commitment to the IMF from our shoulders," said Thaksin.[51] Thailand's vulnerability in the wake of the financial crisis was relentlessly used as a tool to legitimize Thaksin's global ambitions. Other tools included the Asian Bond Fund which resulted in the pooling of reserves to establish a US$1 billion regional bond market, thus reflecting the merit of mobilizing regional funds for Asia to invigorate its own financial system and to whittle away the region's financial vulnerability.[52]

But these were not the only Asia-focused agendas in Thaksin's global ambitions. The successful APEC (Asia-Pacific Economic Cooperation) Economic Leaders' Meeting hosted by Thailand in 2003 was yet another representation of Thaksin's prophetic view of international affairs. Thailand, in 2003, was the chair of APEC. Thaksin came up with the theme "A World of Differences: Partnership for the Future". APEC, although it is certainly not exclusively "Asian", was undoubtedly a top priority for Thailand that year. The National Preparatory Committee, chaired by the Prime Minister, was set up to supervise all preparations and operations, including the provision of venues, appropriate infrastructure and accommodation, the involvement of local communities, security, communications, public relations, the provision of facilities, and the training of related personnel at event locations.[53] The APEC meeting was an exceptionally successful diplomatic event for the Thaksin government, at least for the pomp of its protocol arrangements, if not its core substance. As Thaksin gave economic diplomacy foreign policy prominence, the role of Thailand's Ministry of Commerce was accordingly enhanced. This was evident when the Commerce Ministry was assigned the lead ministry during the Thai-hosted APEC Meeting. For its day-to-day responsibility, the Commerce Ministry was instructed to expand trade and relations with neighbouring countries and to increase its capacity to support the government's policy to promote regional connectivity, a role that appeared to overlap with that of the Foreign Ministry. To conclude Thaksin's first term in office, the push to nominate Foreign Minister Surakiart for the position of the UNSG, deemed as the turn of an Asia representative according to an informal agreed regional rotation system, was prioritized as part of setting a firmer footing for Thailand in the international arena. Surakiart, in advertising his campaign, peddled the theme of "Asia for Asians", proposing to attach special importance to Asian issues, such as the crisis in

Myanmar and on the Korean Peninsula, and terrorism in South Asia and the Middle East. In the aftermath of the UNSG race, with Surakiart having to give up his nomination almost at the last minute without the full support of the permanent members of the United Nations Security Council, he still believed that, even with his loss in the competition, his mission to make Thailand heard on the international stage was fulfilled.[54]

It is noteworthy that one of the major international events during the Thaksin period was the sixtieth anniversary of King Bhumibol Adulyadej's accession to the throne in June 2006. The Thai royal family received royal visitors with accompanying entourages from twenty-five countries to watch the royal barge procession — the spectacular ceremony that was successfully organized by the interim Thaksin government. Despite being surrounded by mounting political problems, Thaksin, as a caretaker prime minister following the dissolution of parliament caused by the immense pressure from his opponents, took advantage of the golden jubilee celebration to solidify his international-oriented persona, and more importantly, to display his allegiance to the King.

Business-oriented Policy

Thaksin's foreign policy was business-oriented in both its substance and outlook. But he was not the first Thai leader who preferred economic interests to championing democracy and human rights. Chatichai launched the policy of the marketplace over a decade before Thaksin came along as part of his government searching for new sources of raw materials and potential markets for Thai products. Thaksin was a successful businessman and self-made billionaire. The implementation of a business-oriented foreign policy suited his personal predilection and fitted in well with his political dogma. The realization of his business-oriented populist programmes designed to supposedly give a better life to the Thais suggested that providing economic security would have fulfilled the basic requirement of the Thai public, and that politics should be left in the government's hands. In the realm of foreign affairs, Thaksin applied the same methodology in the making of policy, which was crafted upon the accomplishment of economic consolidation at home. His government's assertiveness in diplomacy exhibited an attitude similar to that of Chatichai since they both were civilian-based and essentially commerce-driven. Most of Thaksin's diplomatic initiatives showed a tradesman's instinct for survival as they promoted alliance-building in a cut-throat business world.[55]

To buoy up his business-oriented foreign policy, Thaksin restructured the operational mode of Thai ambassadors while assigning them a role as the country's salesman who were instructed to conduct a kind of economic diplomacy. Although the move to make ambassadors focus more on business matters began in the pre-Thaksin period, it was certainly taken further by his government. He urged Thai diplomatic representatives abroad to strive for an increase in foreign investment and tourism. In his speech, Thaksin explained what he meant by being the "country's salesman". He reiterated, "The new role of ambassador as the country's salesman does not mean that he or she will have to knock at the customer's door in order to make a direct sale. The ambassador as salesman here is someone who sells the country's good image and looks for economic opportunities abroad for Thai businesses, bearing in mind the economy of scale, economy of speed and the people's interests."[56] The thinking of the Thaksin administration was that the new economic world order required more from Thailand's diplomatic representatives. It was high time for the Thai ambassadors to come out of the Cold War and spend less time worrying about the geopolitical state of the world where Thailand had little clout or influence. For the ambassadors to succeed, merely creating goodwill and opening doors was no longer sufficient. They had to get to grips with the economic reality of the world. Krit Garnjana-Goonchorn, the Foreign Ministry's Permanent Secretary, in his endorsement of Thaksin on the mercantile role of ambassador, said, "Before, the diplomat performed as the chief functions of representation of the nation and its national interest and the negotiation in the protection and advancement of the national interest. Today, he or she has to be a strategist and manager."[57] To Krit, this was another challenge for Thai foreign policy.

A series of strategic economic programmes aimed at repositioning the country for future economic growth and greater business opportunities, as well as establishing itself to become a world leader in niche markets was unleashed. These programmes included:

1. Kitchen of the World: Centre of ready-to-eat food, tropical fruits, finest and healthiest cuisine in the world.
2. World Health Service Centre: Hub of medical tourism, alternative medical care and herbal products.
3. Detroit of Asia: Centre of pick-up production and distribution, regional centre of automobile parts.
4. Asia Tourism Capital: Centre of regional tourism, air transport hub, convention and exhibition centre.
5. Asia Tropical Fashion: Bangkok city of fashion.[58]

While business-oriented foreign policy was set in stone, supposedly for the benefits of the nation's well-being, Thaksin was condemned by his opponents of aggrandizing his family's wealth through government projects aboard. Some criticized his policy as an insidious economic plot for enriching his family's business empire. Prachyadavi Tavedikul, former Thai ambassador to the Netherlands, wrote in an open letter to the media, "Thaksin trampled upon every one of the principles of Thai foreign policy for his personal benefit." Kasit Piromya, current Foreign Minister, former ambassador to Washington and a known anti-Thaksin figure, said, "Thaksin has tailored foreign policy to be more economic oriented. His foreign visits were merely an excuse to do business while purposely ignoring sensitive issues like human rights abuses, ASEAN integration and democracy in Myanmar."[59] While it is quite standard around the world for governments to offer cheap loans to countries in order to generate business for national companies, Thaksin's exploitation of the government's tool for self-aggrandizement was an unusual exercise.

Nationalistic in Essence

Nationalism was made a part of Thaksin's political campaign, which not only echoed in the national policy but also in foreign relations. The name of his party, Thai Rak Thai, contains a passionate nationalist shade. For him, Thais must love Thais and their land. Found in his political slogans was a nationalistic catchphrase, "For every Thai". Thaksin stirred up a sense of economic nationalism which proved to be highly successful because it received firm support for two main business groups — the economic elites such as those in the agribusiness and banking magnets, and owners of small and medium-sized enterprises. Both groups, eyeing business opportunities abroad made available by the Thaksin government, had strong vested interests in supporting his nationalist agenda, hoping that it would help protect their businesses in the aftermath of the financial crisis. Thaksin himself called for the Thais to support his "geographically expansionist neo-mercantilist policy" for which he was harnessing the Thai state.[60] To a large extent, his nationalist propaganda was reminiscent of Thailand's past policy that embraced economic nationalism, especially what was seen during the country's fascist years. War-time Prime Minister Phibun Songkhram underscored such sentiment by declaring: "Thais will buy Thai and sell Thai." He urged the Thai people to work hard for the industrial and agricultural development of the country.[61]

Nationalistic characteristics of Thai foreign policy included the need for Thailand to become self-reliant and an honoured member of the international community; to have a strong-willed leader — like Thaksin — who was not afraid to be outspoken and rise up against international challenges; a people-centric focus which aimed at revitalizing the Thai economy so that the Thais could stand on a sustainable footing; and the representation of the Thai identity abroad, such as the campaign for the Thai cultural identity and Thainess. Thaksin's imposing foreign policies and the multiplying bilateral FTAs were publicized as a channel that would uplift the economic well-being of the Thais. As Thaksin said:

> There are only a few capitalist nations that become successful in the execution of their domestic programmes and foreign policy. The most important ingredient is nationalism. We, the Thais, are not really nationalistic. This government wishes to prove its nationalistic stance. For example, the conclusion of FTA with our partners must render a greater benefit to the Thai people. Some private businesses might have been negatively affected by the FTA. But the nation as a whole must win in this competitive business game.[62]

McCargo argued that nationalism was only one element in Thailand's rhetoric. A further stand was the distinction between

Asia and the West. Thaksin was often eager to include other Asians (notably the Chinese, Malaysians, Singaporeans and Indians) within his circle of reference, expanding "we" beyond the borders of Thailand, to include other vibrant Asian economies with features worthy of emulation.[63]

Evidently, the Thaksin government promoted an economic nationalism, which was targeted at achieving economic growth. It was a strict economic nationalism that wittingly sidelined other principles-based goals which were deemed by Thaksin as a distraction to the success of the national economy. Thaksin was a prolific nationalist who successfully manipulated the public sentiment to prop up the government's policy even when it jeopardized Thailand's interests abroad, such as in seeking the public support for the Thai economic dominance in neighbouring countries although this could deeply heighten mutual distrust. Thaksin also walked on a similar path of past Thai elites who claimed to adopt certain Western practices, and rejected some, for the overall benefit of the Thais. King Chulalongkorn, while taking up the modern views of the West, opposed the Western theory of democracy. Thaksin, likewise, took advantage of Western capitalism but disregarded its twin concept — democracy. The selection of certain Western practices was apparent in the formulation of Thailand's foreign policy under the Thaksin government. For instance, while claiming to acclimatize Myanmar into the regional mainstream with the introduction of a market economy and to push for political reforms with his idea of the Bangkok Process, Thaksin soon forgot about the principle of democracy as he engaged in business deals with the Myanmar junta. This political point of view, sitting on top of Thaksin's selective Western practices, revealed its dubious and hypocritical nature. It also made Thaksin's brand of nationalism a slippery thought. As another example, while embracing wholeheartedly globalization, Thaksin endorsed new items on the economic policy agenda which involved a particular mixture of protectionism, populism and nationalism denoting more emphasis on self-reliance and protection of Thai interests at the local level.[64]

The elusiveness here for Thaksin in the making of foreign policy was the dilemma of whether to open up the country to foreign money or to protect local industry, and whether to indulge in an outward-looking foreign policy or an isolationist one so as to satisfy the nationalist thrust at home. Nationalism can become an empty vessel without mass support. His foreign policy had been a story of nationalist success despite its obvious dilemmas, because he put Thai interest up against a picture of greedy foreigners, with Thaksin himself playing the role of defender of the national interest — an imaginary facade constructed by his government.

Forward Engagement Policy

Thailand's foreign policy has undergone many terminological surgeries over the decades. Being compelled to play a larger role on the regional stage, successive governments manufactured different kinds of foreign policy that covered varying arrays of objectives and served different political groups. The Thaksin government was the latest in a long line of power-holders who drew on Thai foreign policy to shore up its domestic political strength. In reinventing Thailand and divorcing himself from past policy, Thaksin unveiled his newly constructed foreign policy called the "Forward Engagement Policy" at the Thai Foreign Ministry on 12 March 2003, to replace the Democrat government's version of "Flexible Engagement". Thaksin elaborated:

> For economic recovery to be sustainable in the globalized and interdependent environment, Thailand requires a progressive foreign policy that firmly supports its domestic counterpart. We need to formulate a foreign policy that looks ahead and forward to the future while mindful of the past. We need a foreign policy that responds effectively to the rapid changes while strengthening the basic foundations. We need a foreign policy that is proactive and forward-looking. We need a foreign policy that seeks innovation opportunities while safeguarding national interests. We need a foreign policy that strengthens our existing international cooperation while further expanding to encompass new dimensions of cooperation with new partners. We need a foreign policy that accommodates differences while turning diversity into the new partnership for peace, stability and prosperity for the nation, the region and the world at large. This is what we call 'Forward Engagement Policy'."[65]

What is really the "Forward Engagement Policy"? Before delving into this concept, certain observations need to be made. The fact that Thaksin introduced his Forward Engagement Policy as a new foreign policy platform may not signify that the past government's foreign policy was no longer suitable or outdated: it may simply mean that he wanted to appear different. The Forward Engagement Policy was planted as a twin concept alongside Thaksin's domestic agenda, which evolved around a clutch of populist projects built upon the Thai inner strength. This concept was "being extrovert and supporting innovation". Thaksin's Forward Engagement Policy stands on the following objectives:

1. Connecting peoples at the grassroots to global politics
2. Building trust and partnership with neighbouring countries
3. Strengthening ASEAN
4. Strengthening the Thai economy
5. Promoting unity and consciousness among Asian nations
6. Expanding networks of partnership with all regions of the world
7. Solidifying the Thai image abroad
8. Formulating people-centric diplomacy.[66]

From this list, the Forward Engagement Policy appeared more like a general statement of multiple foreign policy objectives than a specific policy. Yet, Thaksin explained the *raison d'être* behind the construction of the Forward Engagement Policy as an attempt to tackle a major conundrum: how could Thailand reposition itself given that it was a medium-sized country in a globalized world and assert its regional leadership vis-à-vis other powerful or emerging states in the region, such as Indonesia and especially Vietnam? The Forward Engagement Policy was, for Thaksin, a reply to the urgent call for Thailand to readjust itself in order to regain interests while interacting with the outside world. It was also used to systematize the need to cultivate friendly, cooperative and constructive relationships with other countries at all levels, be they bilateral, regional and multilateral. The goals here, claimed by Thaksin, were peace, sustainable economic growth and development and shared responsibility. The philosophy was outward-looking and inclusive. The Foreign Ministry explicated in great length detailed examples of the success of Forward Engagement Policy, reflected through excellent relations between Thailand and major powers including the United States, Australia, China and India.[67]

The policy was engineered to underpin Thaksin's foreign policy agenda — the ACD and the ACMECS — and his focus on bilateral FTAs. It was described mainly as a mechanism that fostered Thailand's economic stature abroad. But because it was shaped to support some of Thaksin's ambitious worldview, his critics often perceived Forward Engagement Policy as hollow, insubstantial, and verging on neglecting certain international norms and practices.

The Forward Engagement Policy, in the mindset of Foreign Minister Surakiart, was also based on trade and informal relationships. As Thailand pursued its Forward Engagement Policy vis-à-vis the Myanmar junta, it was instantly reproached by the international community for tolerating the brutal regime in exchange for Thai economic benefits and turning a blind eye to the moribund democratization in that country. Philippine President Gloria Macapagal Arroyo told journalists that during the ASEAN Summit in Bali, Indonesia in 2004, Thaksin defended Myanmar throughout the entire meeting. The anti-junta activists quickly dubbed Thaksin's policy as "Backward Engagement", as it echoed the policy that supported the narrow economic interests of Thailand. They also slated that there was neither continuity nor sustainability in the Thai foreign policy under Thaksin.[70]

No Longer Bending with the Wind

Arne Kislenko argues that an ancient Siamese proverb likens foreign policy to the "bamboo in the wind": always solidly rooted, but flexible enough to bend whichever way the wind blows in order to survive. More than mere pragmatism, this adage reflects a long-cherished, philosophical approach to international relations, the precepts of which are very much enshrined in Thai culture and religion.[71] But was the "bending with the wind" concept a thing of the past at a time when Thaksin dominated Thailand's diplomacy? Kusuma Snitwongse suggested that Thailand in the 1990s arrived at a critical juncture, no longer bending with any prevailing wind but responding to the country's real interests. She investigated Thailand's foreign policy in this particular era from the viewpoint of a leadership dilemma: principle or profit? Which did Thai leaders choose?[72]

Kusuma's study marks a departure from previous studies elsewhere on Thailand's diplomacy that was usually defined as "bending with the wind". This description signalled how Thai leaders could shrewdly turn opportunists in times of crisis. Examples can be seen during the colonial times in which Siamese kings claimed to bend with the European imperialists to save independence. Later, the generals claimed to kowtow to the Japanese to escape from being colonized. In the Cold War period, the Thai governments also claimed to have been forced to succumb to the U.S. hegemon so as to dodge the communist threat. By doing so, the Thais had to tolerate despotic regimes at home. However, the days when Thai leaders were left with no choice but to compromise with external powers now seemed to disappear. Thaksin's assumption to power, imbued in his self-confidence and successful domestic policy, represented a sea change in Thailand's diplomatic approach. Thailand, for the first time, as portrayed by Thaksin, was able to set the direction of the wind.

Thaksin's raft of illustrious strategies in the foreign affairs effectively moulded Thailand's new image as a country willing to bend the wind.[73] This was coupled with Thaksin's powerful government and his push for rapid economic growth. By asserting itself as a major regional player, Thailand appeared eager to shift the regional balance of power to mainland Southeast Asia. But while seeking to set the wind conditions, Thaksin did not disregard the "opportunist approach" and showed no hesitation in aligning himself with prevailing powers — in this case, China — on the basis of shared benefits and mutual respect. In this period, relations between Thailand and China reached their apex. Healthy bilateral relations in all areas, ranging from political, military, economic to cultural, allowed the two countries to further develop their partnership, to the point of Beijing voluntarily assisting Bangkok in setting the wind direction.

It is important to highlight that Thailand's diplomatic ambition and its gamble in defying the prevailing wind did not derive purely from Thaksin's personal enthusiasm and his triumphant domestic policy. The changing geopolitical landscape in Southeast Asia served as a favourable factor for Thaksin. Thailand's attempted hegemonization in mainland Southeast Asia, the slow progress of ASEAN, the American preoccupation in its war in Iraq, and the rise of China and its growing influence in the region, all gave Thaksin's diplomatic prowess opportunity to intensify. However, Thaksin, in confronting the prevailing wind with confidence, often overlooked the limits of the country's real capability and bargaining power. His foreign policy occasionally verged on exhibiting arrogance, even standing against international norms and order. For example, Thaksin initially expressed an intention to remain neutral if the United States invaded a Muslim country, but of course quickly changed to full support for the U.S. war on terror. Also, he complained about the United Nations interfering in the Thai human rights situation with regard to his government's mistreatment of the suspects in the Thai war on drugs. From this perspective, Thaksin's arrogance of power seemed to damage his own assertive foreign policy. The consequences were damaging. For instance, the United Nations, the United States and some European countries expressed little interest in Thaksin's Bangkok Process. Indonesia and Malaysia continued to pass judgement on Thaksin's oppressive policy against its Muslim population. There was also a nagging mistrust among Thailand's neighbours. Thailand's attempted hegemonization of the regional politics was met by reactions of suspicion against Thailand from Cambodia and Laos. These instances confirmed that the much-publicized Thai ability to control the wind was rather sporadic and short-lived. They also induced a debate on whether Thaksin's foreign policy of manipulating the wind was genuinely independent and really free from external influences. In particular, the conflicts of interest imbued in Thaksin's foreign policy greatly diminished his ability to influence the political and economic life of his immediate neighbours. Paradoxically, this condition opened up an opportunity for these neighbours to repeatedly impose their influence on Thaksin, since they found a way to deal with his policy by capitalizing on Thaksin's own weakness.

MOTIVATIONS AND INCENTIVES

What were the motives and incentives behind the construction of Thaksin's foreign policy? This book looks at three primary motivations behind his foreign policy-making: Thaksin's personal global ambition, the attainment of national interests, and the accumulation of private interests of Thai power-holders. The focus on the latter point suggests that Thai foreign policy was from time to time arbitrarily used, just like other malleable Thai discourses, for example nationalism and nationhood, to serve its leaders' specific needs. From this perspective, Thaksin's foreign policy is often treated as a subject of deep criticism for being ephemeral and self-serving, as well as failing to fulfil certain norms related to good governance and accountability.

Thaksin's Unbounded Ambition

Extensive studies on Thaksin's personal life tend to agree on one fact: Thaksin is a self-made billionaire whose entry into national politics, and subsequently world politics, was impelled by his own unbound ambition, which, for many, could be seen as ruthless and cocky. Winning two overwhelming elections made Thaksin yet more arrogant and feel invincible.[74] Surin, currently ASEAN Secretary-General, talked of Thaksin's conceited attitude, "It is not very Thai."[75]

While serving as prime minister, Thaksin's past experience in business, in national politics, and briefly in the Foreign Ministry, to a large extent, helped mould his global vision and ambition. As a successful national leader, Thaksin commanded not only loyalty from his fellow party members but also the trust of his voters in the rural areas. These factors contributed toward Thaksin's self-belief in working to become one of Asia's most influential statesmen, and striving toward enhancing the country's international standing and the pride and dignity of the Thai people. His reinvention of Thailand as the centre of regional politics and his will power to challenge global powers and institutions — were all subsumed in his personal ambition to take on the world, just like taking on his home country. New policies invented to strengthen the immunity of the local economy, such as the Chiang Mai Initiative and the creation of the baht zone, served as a reminder of the existence of the real, brutal business world, and therefore the need of a survival plan for the country. Thaksin realized that the cure for the vulnerable local economy was to lure more foreign direct investment, thus supporting the acceleration of tariff reductions under a number of FTAs Thailand had concluded with its trading partners.

As the Chief Executive Officer (CEO) of the Thai nation, Thaksin was ambitious in his attempt to fashion a political order akin to that of Singapore and Malaysia in which one dominant party led a democratic state with a heavy hand in economic and foreign affairs. He wanted to turn Thailand into a First World nation. This seemed to signify that major powers would from then on have to deal with Thailand on an equal footing. He also took credit from the successful construction of modern infrastructure in the capital, such as sky trains, underground trains, state-of-the-art Suvarnabhumi Airport, so that Bangkok could stand shoulder-to-shoulder with other major cities in the world, although all of these projects predated the Thaksin period. In 2004, he was planning to buy an English Premier League football club, which was considered as part of his endeavour to put Thailand, as much as himself, on the world map. His dream only came true three years later. Even now out of power, Thaksin has launched a foundation for future leaders, called the "Building A Better Future Foundation", to recruit Asia's rising stars to tackle economic crises in the region and confront other pressing issues faced by developing nations – an indication of Thaksin's unbounded global ambitions.[76]

Securing National Interests

Notwithstanding all the criticisms about the way Thaksin mishandled certain international issues and complaints about his conflicts of interest, he should be given credit for promoting a foreign policy that secured certain national interests in the era of intense global competition. It was true that Thai foreign policy was largely exploited by Thaksin to meet a myriad of political purposes in the face of his opposition. But his proactive foreign policy was highly motivated as he pushed for Thailand to become a rising power on mainland Southeast Asia.

What kind of national interests were achieved during the Thaksin administration? Thaksin took full advantage of globalization, using it to revitalize the Thai economy, opening up the country to foreign investment and tourists, and finding new niche markets for innovative Thai products. In doing so, he planned to utilize foreign policy to close the gap between the haves and the have-nots, with more emphasis on the latter, deemed as his strong political supporters. The reinvention of Thailand as a donor country also aimed at fortifying ties with Thailand's immediate neighbours based on shared prosperity, ties that were plagued by bitter historical memories. The ultimate objectives were to erase the image of a Thai threat, and to turn conflict into cooperation, therefore building a peaceful environment for economic growth, especially among Thais who lived on the borderland. The ACD, an extension of a diplomacy outreach to remote parts of Asia, in particular the Middle East, not only validated the Thai leadership in the wider Asian region, but also included an economic strategy of finding and penetrating these new markets for Thai products. The concept of Thainess was merged with the promotion of tourism whereby foreign tourists were encouraged to learn more about Thai local culture, thus killing two birds with one stone: showcasing culture and encouraging tourism. In the security realm, the U.S. granting of the major non-NATO ally status was considered a long-term guarantee of Thailand's security. Thailand, in response, confirmed that it remained a steadfast ally of the United States by joining the Proliferation Security Initiative (PSI), a U.S.-led programme designed to curb trafficking in weapons of mass destruction. With this, Thai foreign policy seemed to come full circle, from serving to promote national well-being and culture and the dignity of the Thai people, to safeguarding the country's sovereignty, independence and security.

Fulfilling Private Benefits

It is naive to believe that Thaksin, like many leaders before him, would sketch his foreign policy purely for the sake of national interests. In fact, the discourse of "national interests" was rather obscure during this period since Thaksin himself openly blended business and politics to his heart's content. As the two notions — business and politics — are inseparable, so are the national and personal interests of the Thai power-holders.

Thaksin was almost coerced to step down right after he won the general election of 2001 because he was accused by the National Counter-Corruption Commission (NCCC) of concealing his immense wealth. He could have been charged with violating a rule by the Constitutional Court that required those taking up public office to declare their personal assets. He defended, "I am not corrupt. I admit I made a mistake in reporting my assets. But I am confident that this (being stripped of premiership) will not happen.

I am definitely sure I will be here as prime minister for four years."[77] In August 2006, at the height of the controversy of the Shin-Temasek deal, Korbsak Sabhavasu, a senior member of Democrat Party, launched a book, "Who Says the Rich Don't Cheat?", revealing that Thaksin concealed shares worth Bt329 million.[78] These two incidents stirred up a heated public debate on whether Thaksin took advantage of foreign policy to enrich his business empire. When he became prime minister, Thaksin might have relinquished all of his personal businesses, but he continued to be actively involved in his family conglomerates. This led to the problem of conflicts of interest that eventually, and partly, brought to an end to his premiership.

There have been allegations that pointed to Thaksin's corrupt practices through the exercise of foreign relations. When asked if he felt that foreign policy was abused by power-holders for their private interests, Tej Bunnag, former Foreign Minister and former Permanent Secretary of the Foreign Ministry during the Thaksin years, replied that he did not know if the country's policy was used to enrich anyone in particular. The ultimate goal of the Foreign Ministry, Tej added, was to get the job done, especially in the protection of national interests.[79] However, in 2007, one year after Thaksin was overthrown in a coup, the Assets Examination Committee (AEC), founded by the military government of Prime Minister Surayud Chulanont (2006–08), investigated thirteen cases in which Thaksin was accused of alleged corrupt practices. Out of the thirteen cases examined, there were four containing an international dimension that could suggest Thaksin's use of foreign policy to accumulate private interests. These include:

1. Tax evasion in the Shin Corp share sale: The AEC investigated the entire Shin Corp deal in connection with alleged tax evasion by Thaksin's children who sold the stocks to Singapore's Temasek Holdings at Bt49.25 a share via the stock market without paying tax while citing it as a market deal.
2. Excise on telecom businesses: Foreign Minister Surakiart was questioned on 13 September 2007 by the AEC about how the Thaksin government had ratified the FTA with Australia in the telecoms field.

3. EXIM Bank's soft loan to Myanmar: The AEC authorized its sub-committee to indict Thaksin for alleged graft and abuse of power relating to government-sanctioned lending to Myanmar in 2004. At Thaksin's intervention, the EXIM Bank of Thailand was ordered to increase its credit line to Myanmar from Bt3 billion to Bt4 billion. The loans were extended to finance the deal with Shin Satellite, which was then under the control of the Thaksin's family.

4. Scandal at Suvarnabhumi Airport: A translated document from the U.S. Department of State showed who was involved in the corruption in the procurement of CTX bomb scanners for Suvarnabhumi Airport.[80]

In Thailand, corruption and politicians are no strangers to each other. Thaksin's business background exposed the question whether Thai foreign policy was exercised to serve the nation's interests or those of the leaders. As Pasuk and Baker argued, "The state created the context. Thaksin found the skills to exploit it."[81] His undertaking of a modern model of diplomacy, such as the CEO ambassador with a top-down management style and the preference for an informal diplomacy based on close personal relationships between Thai and foreign leaders, further made the realm of Thai foreign affairs murky. What has kept the line between national and personal interests ambiguous is the divided sentiment among the Thais when they came to judge Thaksin's leadership style. To them, he was either the most corrupt prime minister in Thai history or a champion of the poor masses who have long been ignored by previous governments.[82] A Thaksin's supporter in Udon Thani said, "So what if he (Thaksin) is corrupt? He gets the job done."[83] Gwynne Dyer called Thaksin the "Juan Peron of Thailand", since he used his power to shift wealth and power systematically from the rich to the poor.[84] Like Thaksin, Peron was mired in scandal while ruling Argentina.

FOREIGN POLICY-MAKING PROCESS

Thaksin not only attempted to transform the face of Thai foreign policy and lift it to a new height, but also change the way it was made. He revamped the organization, making it more of, in his

own words, a business company. The revolutionized transformation
of Thailand's foreign policy and the Ministry of Foreign Affairs'
organizational management left a great divide within this state
agency. In the broader picture, Thaksin's monopoly of foreign policy
crashed head-on with the old guards of the Foreign Ministry. The
competition of hegemony in foreign affairs between the prime
minister and Foreign Ministry was visibly apparent, especially
among retired ambassadors who were in a freer position to criticize
the government.

Thaksin's Foreign Policy is Thailand's Foreign Policy

Thaksin personalized and centralized foreign policy to match his
domestic consumption, giving birth to his very own "populist
diplomacy". His personal agenda became a national agenda. It is
uncomplicated to assess why Thaksin endorsed a pro-Myanmar
regime policy. Officially, he argued that helping Myanmar reform
its economy could be the solution to its political deadlock, and this
would suit Thai economic interests in that country too. Unofficially,
Thaksin had his business fortune in Myanmar, through the
telecommunication deals with the Myanmar leaders. Abusing
foreign policy, Thaksin discursively stretched the notion of national
interests and took advantage of certain loopholes in bilateral relations
with Myanmar. Thaksin's supporters within the Foreign Ministry
admired him for his upbeat and seemingly far-sighted worldview.
However, not everyone in the Foreign Ministry shared this view.
Surapong Jayanama, former Thai ambassador, complained that
Thaksin's personalized foreign policy deliberately omitted certain
universal values, such as respect for democracy and human rights.
These universal norms must be included in its foreign policy since
Thailand is a democratic country. He also argued that Thaksin
made repeated references to globalization, yet little did he know
about its real nature and concept. Thaksin failed to understand, or
perhaps pretended not to understand, that one of the most important
features of globalization is democracy. But this trait was absent in
Thailand's foreign policy in this globalized era. Thaksin's foreign
policy, therefore, for Surapong, was thinly disguised with an outlook
of globalization when in fact its substance was rotten and corrupt.[85]
The anti-Thaksin local media often slammed the Foreign Ministry's

top echelon for collaborating with the prime minister in conducting diplomacy designed to promote his self-aggrandizement and advance his personal interest, and in doing so compromising the country's long-term national interests.[86]

This personalized foreign policy, despite being highly ambitious and goal-oriented, could prove detrimental in its execution. Thaksin, a man brimming with innovative ideas, often came up with sudden new initiatives that were executed with a total lack of preparation.[87] His exigency for engaging in FTAs negotiation with Thailand's partners was mostly driven by his own economic instinct, which dangerously overlooked Thailand's overall relationship with these partners. The troublesome U.S.-Thai FTA negotiation represents a good example in this case.[88] Thaksin was heavily criticized for surrendering to the United States' rules of the game in order to close a deal and this raised the big question of who decided what was best for whom.[89] Another drawback of Thaksin's personalized foreign policy was its lack of transparency and accountability. As an elected leader, Thaksin fully exercised his right to dictate all aspects of Thai foreign policy. This could however make it extremely difficult for Foreign Ministry officials and even the foreign minister to balance and counter Thaksin's idiosyncrasies. Under the Thaksin administration, the Foreign Ministry was compelled to play a diminished role in the decision-making process. Some top diplomats pointed out that with the waning influence of the Foreign Ministry, there were some detectable diplomatic oversights during this period.

Prime Minister Versus Foreign Ministry

I have asked the Ministry of Foreign Affairs to revamp its organization, implement reforms, and reinvent the role of today's diplomats. CEO management is already applied in some diplomatic missions abroad and will apply to all by the first of October this year. Close contacts and consultation between officers of the Foreign Ministry and officers from other ministries abroad are compulsory. The spirit of forward engagement must permeate through the entire system both vertically and horizontally. No one in this administration can lose sight of others in the process of fostering partnership and all levels of personnel must speed up implementation of partnership and coordination.[90]

Thaksin delivered the above speech at the Thai Foreign Ministry on 12 March 2003. His centralized foreign policy directly caused considerable friction between the Prime Minister's Office and some factions inside the Foreign Ministry. Customarily, the Foreign Ministry had been a custodian of strategy and process; in this, its main responsibility was to formulate and implement foreign policy for the attainment of national interests and the promotion of good relations with all countries. The Foreign Ministry officials work in "division" units and are in charge of drafting a policy in accordance with the ministry's main strategy, based on the precise calculation of the real costs and benefits, and subsequently submitting the drafted policy to their superiors in the hierarchical line of command. The drafted policy would then be approved, disapproved or revised, at the departmental and ministerial levels respectively. In this foreign policy formulation process, desk officers at the divisional level would have to be in constant consultation with members of the Thai embassies abroad so as to be able to access first-hand information and gain in-depth understanding on the situation in their host countries or groups of countries to ascertain what area of relations should be emphasized or strengthened. This intricate process allowed accuracy and pragmatism to reign supreme in Thai foreign policy. It also made Thai foreign policy credible, responsible, accountable and truly responsive to the global environment.

The Foreign Ministry often sees itself as a sole state actor that determines the country's foreign policy, as highlighted by Kusuma Snitwongse that in the old days, Thai foreign policy had been formulated independent of the public domain to the extent that the Foreign Ministry was dubbed "the twilight zone".[91] But then as now, as this book argues, its autonomous power has from time to time been challenged by forceful competition from other state actors for the ultimate jurisdiction over foreign policy. The case of Thai relations with Cambodia in the 1980s showed how multiple actors could cause confusion and add complication to foreign affairs. Whereas the Foreign Ministry, the military (with its close ties with the Khmer Rouge), and the National Security Council continued to deal with the Hanoi-backed regime in Phnom Penh strictly within the Cold War context, the Government House, run by the *Ban Phitsanulok* advisory team, preferred rapprochement based on a business-oriented policy. Some in the opposition, the academia, and the media called for a Thai alignment with ASEAN in finding a political solution in Cambodia. Here, there were at least three conflicting policies toward Cambodia.[92] Different actors attempted to manipulate foreign policy, resulting in conflict and competition in the realm of foreign policy decision-making.

During the Thaksin period, the seemingly single facet of Thai foreign policy shaped by the Foreign Ministry was declared permanently outmoded. Thaksin was now representing the face of the unitary actor in the foreign policy-making process. What followed was a centralized foreign policy with Thaksin taking over the Thai Foreign Ministry on the outset. He requested little, if any, input on decision from the Foreign Ministry, and the Government House dictated Thailand's foreign policy. All the relevant Thai agencies were under Thaksin's direct command with intent to produce a more coherent foreign policy. Thaksin shifted the foreign policy focus from enshrining abstract values, such as democracy, as stressed during the previous Democrat administration, to a more tangible outlook, as reflected in his business-oriented diplomacy. Thailand, once so economically obsessed with traditional markets like the United States and Europe, began to pay more attention to its neighbours previously deemed as backward territories. In Thaksin's days, foreign policy was drafted by business executives and run by a group of CEOs who sometimes conflated their interests with those of the nation.[93]

Thaksin formed an advisory team, similar to that seen during the Chatichai administration, led by the eccentric media veteran Pansak Winyarat, and former university professor Somkid Jatusripitak, who were behind TRT's grand domestic strategies and business-oriented foreign policy.[94] Somkid was also appointed as Deputy Prime Minister. Chockanand Bussracumpakorn revealed in his study that in setting up his advisory team, Thaksin would not allow conventional economists to attain high-level policy-making status because he was afraid that they might interfere with the approach and implementing processes. In contrast, he appointed "junior ministers", some of whom were former professors in Business Administration and Economics or successful business tycoons, to work under each minister as policy and administrative adviser. Sometimes, these junior ministers designed the policy and implemented it by themselves on behalf of the prime minister.[95]

Foreign Minister Surakiart also exercised a high degree of leadership in a series of foreign policy initiatives. Both Surakiart and Pansak were once part of an astute advisory team under the Chatichai government. Then, they were successful in riding on the global trend and moving away from traditional diplomacy. Surakiart, in particular, hoped to rekindle this can-do spirit when he reigned at the Foreign Ministry.

Thaksin's advisory team was set up to provide "intelligence" information and advise the prime minister on foreign affairs, draft a long-term foreign policy plan deemed imperative for the accomplishment of national interests, and introduce populist foreign policy ideas which were marketable both for domestic and international audiences – a parallel to Thaksin's domestic populist policy. Thaksin's advisory team and Surakiart were stage-managing Thailand's foreign policy strategies. Their firm role in the foreign policy decision-making process ignited tensions between Thaksin and the old guards of the Foreign Ministry, especially regarding the abolition of some traditional foreign policies. One of these was Thaksin's new policy direction to de-prioritize ASEAN. More importantly, Thaksin's impatience drove himself and his advisory team to bypass the cumbersome Foreign Ministry in order to save time in the quest for results.

The split in opinion concerning Thaksin's new ways of diplomatic conduct was manifest between the pro- and anti-Thaksin Foreign Ministry officials. Thaksin's defenders and close aides believed his "fast-lane diplomacy" was good for the country in an era of rapid change on the international stage. It helped raise the level of Thai competitiveness. Those in the anti-Thaksin faction criticized it for destroying the professionalism of diplomats and institutionalization of the organization. Nevertheless, they had to comply with the new paradigm, obviously for fear of retribution. Some diplomats resigned and some were transferred. As the political conflict in Thailand reached its peak in 2006, an even deeper politicization of the Foreign Ministry became more palpable. A group of anti-Thaksin officers chose to wear black in a show of support for a movement to topple the premier. In order to dismiss talk of anti-Thaksin sentiment within the ministry, Thaksin-backed diplomats in Bangkok continued to insist that there had been no significant changes in the way the foreign policy was conducted under Thaksin.[96] At this stage, it is difficult, if not impossible, to pinpoint the size of the various cliques within the Foreign Ministry that belonged to the pro- and anti-Thaksin camps. The way the power position is arranged inside the Foreign Ministry is not much different from what happens in the real political arena at the national level. Thaksin selected his supporters and placed them in top positions in the organization, thus highlighting the coexistence between political connections and access to power. Meritocracy does exist, although it is more rhetorical than practicable. Some who were not in the inner circle of power were content to paint themselves as the anti-Thaksin element. Their activities were identifiable. Some of them in the Department of East Asian Affairs were seen distributing the PAD's yellow hand-clappers to their work colleagues.[97]

It can be argued that Thaksin undertook an internal colonization of state agencies, and that he schemed to overthrow the bureaucratic polity with the introduction of changes, such as enlarging and shrinking some ministries, and by making a large number of senior appointments, promotions and transfers. The plot here was to dilute the authority of the Foreign Ministry while strengthening the power position of the prime minister and his appointees in the ministry. He announced in his weekly radio show, "This is a new era in which policy is decided by politicians. Hence, politicians have to tell people what they are going to do, what policies they have to improve things."[98] The way in which Thaksin overstepped the mark by undermining the conventional role of diplomats drew increasing flack from former ambassadors. With the support of academics and the media, they all attacked Thaksin's grip on foreign policy. Kasit once said, "Thaksin always told the Foreign Minister what to do and our foreign policy came from the Prime Minister. This was the first time for Thailand because we have always had a strong and respected Foreign Ministry."[99] At the heart of the matter is the fact that Thaksin was willing to weaken the power and authority traditionally vested in senior diplomats so that he could take control of, and perhaps manipulate, foreign policy with relative ease. Thaksin's preferred role of the Foreign Ministry was now reduced to that of an implementer of policy, often out of the loop when it came to the foreign policy decision-making process.

In defending Thaksin, his CEO scheme, first applied to provincial governors and subsequently to Thai ambassadors, was in many ways beneficial in increasing efficiency in the operation of Thai diplomatic missions abroad. Foreign affairs were being run like a business company under the CEO scheme, admitted Permanent Secretary Krit in 2006. Currently, the Foreign Ministry has some sixty CEO ambassadors around the world, all of whom are equipped with the authority and resources to carry out government policies overseas in an integrated manner with a shared vision, mission and strategy. In fact, the CEO style of management, although it was not really an innovation inside the walls of the Foreign Ministry, gave the ambassadors sole authority to govern their missions. Arguably, this could be perceived as the return of power to the top diplomats. In this, other government agencies with their representatives overseas attached to the embassies and consulates, such as commerce, agriculture, intelligence, tourism, investment and military, have to defer to the authority and direction of the CEO ambassador, under the so-called "Team Thailand". Thaksin also threatened to allow "outsiders" to become ambassadors should career diplomats prove to be ineffective. It encouraged them to raise their awareness of the changing global environment, and more importantly, take responsibility to perform to government expectations. Sceptics considered the new integrated work culture as merely complementary to the government's top-down control over state agencies. And with the pressure on the CEO ambassadors to perform as the country's merchants, they believed that it created strong antipathy towards Thaksin within the Foreign Ministry. Thitinan Pongsudhirak said, "These are dignified, prestigious positions representing the Thai state and the King. Their role has now been reduced to business and export promotion."[100]

People-centric Diplomacy

What made Thaksin's foreign policy largely different from that of previous governments was his attention to the needs of the Thai people and how to respond to them through the means of foreign policy. Whereas previous governments similarly attempted to use foreign policy to satisfy the Thais' needs, Thaksin moved one step further by clearly prioritizing foreign policy as a national agenda and popularizing it. He called it "people-centric diplomacy". The concentration here was not about the fulfilment of the people's needs alone. Thaksin claimed to have invited people's participation in the foreign policy formulation — a gesture of the government's promotion of democracy. But to what degree were the needs of the public really served? And to what extent were their voices incorporated in the country's foreign policy?

Thaksin's Forward Engagement Policy was simultaneously publicized alongside a catchy slogan, *Karn Thood Yook Mai Hua Jai Kue Prachachon*, or "New-age Diplomacy with the People at its Heart". As emphasized earlier, Thaksin's foreign policy was practised to satisfy his domestic policy — this proved the reason for the people-centric approach in Thai diplomacy. Thaksin carefully handled certain terminologies, such as preferring the term "people's interest" to "national interest". Pasuk and Baker observed that Thaksin avoided the use of harder terms, like *chart* [nation], but preferred softer terms, like *ban-mueang* [literally, home country], although the two terms mean more or less the same.[101] His attention was on the return of benefits to the people, especially at the grassroots level. Thaksin expressed his devotion to the well-being of the people who were made the "central point" in his making of foreign policy. In this process, Thaksin called for input from the people and listened to their needs so that a foreign policy could be tailored to better correspond to them.[102]

Accordingly, Surakiart kicked off the process with *Krongkarn Buakaew Sanchorn*, or "Roving Buakeaw Project".[103] Surakiart led a team of senior officials to get feedback and opinions of the people especially in the provinces along the border that had direct participation in transnational politics. The meetings usually took place at local sites such as temples, town halls, provincial schools or schools that participated in the "Young Ambassador of Virtue Project".[104] The information collected was then supposedly taken into consideration in the foreign policy formulation when appropriate. Main activities of the Roving Buakeaw Project included discussion on issues of international affairs affecting the life, such as trading and consular service, as well as roving passport services. Participants of the project were representatives from both government and private sectors in provinces, for example, members of parliament, businessmen, members of local chambers of commerce, local media, local government officials, NGOs, and interested citizens. Local people were also offered the opportunity to share their opinions through live broadcasting on local radio stations.[105] However, this project was implemented in an on-and-off fashion. Prakit Prachonpachanuk, Deputy Secretary-General of the National Security Council, opined that it should have been a regular mission to reach out to people in the provinces and get feedback from them.[106]

Diplomatic activism during the Thaksin administration did not limit itself strictly within the international realm. Consular services were also made a part of Thaksin's people-centric diplomacy. For the first time, the e-consular system was introduced as part of the government's policy that promoted the e-government system. An application or extension of validity for a passport could now be made on the Internet, which, as Surakiart confidently verified, would take only twelve minutes. Consular services were extended to the ongoing Mobile Consular Affair Project so that people in the rural areas would be able to apply and obtain a new passport within a day. The process to produce a "new generation passport" with a microchip containing biodata and signature was successfully put in place. Thailand became one of the few first countries in the world that introduced a biometric passport.[107] But, the Office of the Auditor-General (OAG) found irregularities in the Foreign Ministry's tender for a Bt7-billion e-passport project. The OAG claimed that it seemed unfair to award the project to an unqualified company and leave others unfairly disqualified, which caused the country a huge revenue loss.[108]

How should the success of Thaksin's people-centric diplomacy be measured? The fact that Thaksin won another landslide election for his second time in 2005 is in itself testimony to his seemingly successful domestic and foreign policy. During the election campaign in 2005, Thaksin came up with the slogan, "Four Years of Repair – Four years of Reconstruction" and "Building Opportunities". Under this slogan, Thaksin exploited foreign policy agendas to win the people's votes. He vowed to make Thailand ready for fierce competition in the world arena and to reclaim the country's place in the world, alongside other important domestic agendas.[109] Thailand had become more globalized. Thaksin's promotion of the Thai niche markets helped further cement the country's good business reputation in the world. Thailand, which eschewed IMF-policies under the Thaksin government, saw accelerated economic growth during the peak of Thaksin's power. Real gross domestic product (GDP) expanded by 5.4 per cent in 2002.[110] Economic growth accelerated to 6.8 per cent in 2004 and topped 7 per cent in 2005. Thaksin himself trumpeted that Thailand's FTAs with its partners engendered direct benefits to the Thai people. His foreign policy creations helped open up new markets for Thai products — an effective channel for the export of OTOP merchandise. Thaksin also claimed that good relations between Thailand and its neighbouring countries, possibly as a result of ACMECS, led to vibrant border trade between people on all sides. But this was just one side of the tale.

In real terms, a perfect Thailand fortified by Thaksin's ambition is partly an illusion that covered the unpleasant reality behind his foreign policy initiatives. Democratic consolidation in Thailand failed due to Thaksin's increasingly authoritarian way of governance. His political attitude shifted Thailand away from democracy especially on the Myanmar issue. Thaksin continued to boost his ties with the junta in Naypyidaw, which could perhaps explain the delay of political reforms in that country. The lack of a democratic element in foreign policy took its root from the crisis in domestic politics, reflected through the violation of human rights in the wake of the suppression of the Muslim minority in the south and the heavy-handed war on drugs. Every trick in Thaksin's diplomacy was used to deepen his domestic political power. On the economic front, not every Thai was happy with Thaksin's aggressive move on the FTAs. In the case of the Sino-Thai FTA, although bilateral trade volume has expanded, Thailand has continued to suffer from a trade deficit with China. Moreover, the government's claim to restore trust with its neighbouring countries through the exercise of the Forward Engagement Policy, which meant putting aside contentious topics and celebrating economic profits as well as through the practice of "cultural diplomacy", has seen little success. From 2001 to 2006, one may argue that Thaksin's good-neighbour policy yielded fruit as peace in the overall Thai-Myanmar relations was maintained. But again, one may forget that even at the peak of their close relations, skirmishes along their common border continued. Also, despite Thailand's technical and financial assistance offered to Cambodia, mutual suspicions persisted. Thaksin might not be blamed for the Thai diplomatic mission in Phnom Penh being horrendously ransacked since it was caused by Cambodia's domestic complications arising from nationalism, but his effort through cultural diplomacy failed to stop the Cambodian leaders from turning Thailand into a pawn of their own domestic political conflict. Even now that Thaksin has gone, the territorial dispute over the Preah Vihear Temple between Thailand and Cambodia refuses to subside, and haunts Thaksin's unsustainable foreign policy.

Lastly, Thaksin's harsh measures against the Muslim separatists in the south drove Thailand into conflict with Malaysia. Thaksin not only declined to apologize for the murder of unarmed protesters at Tak Bai, but further emphasized that the Thai military would intensify its campaign of repression and intimidation in the predominantly Muslim region. His statement caused disquiet in Malaysia where there was widespread sympathy among the majority Malays for the Muslim population in southern Thailand. Antagonism between the two countries was heightened by Thaksin's allegations that Malaysia's Islamic fundamentalist Parti Islam se-Malaysia (PAS) was a possible source of support for the Muslim separatists in Thailand.[111] The result was a tightening of border controls which badly affected border trade and the trust between the peoples of the two sides.

CONCLUSION

The era of Thaksin's activist diplomacy came to an end on 19 September 2006 when the military staged a coup against his government. His legacy in foreign affairs has, however, lived on. The primary objective of this book on Thaksin's foreign relations is not only to fill the gap in the studies of Thai foreign policy, but also to assess Thailand's diplomatic relations in the most stimulating, yet contentious, period in the country's recent memory. This is the first study of Thaksin's foreign policy in a comprehensive manner and through cogent analyses. Thaksin's foreign policy is in itself unique, being coloured by new initiatives that were underpinned by his monopoly of political power. The remapping of Thailand in the age of globalization quickly put his foreign policy in the spotlight — he was keen to become the region's next leader. Thaksin promoted diplomatic activism, and in this, he wanted to place Thailand at the core of the regional order, hegemonizing Thai power on mainland

Southeast Asia, where the Thai influence was wholly felt. Thailand for once seemed to no longer have to bend with the wind to gain benefits. In the latest disguise of Thailand as a regional leader, Thaksin also transformed the kingdom into a company, run by a CEO prime minister whose task was to evaluate economic costs and benefits in the conduct of diplomacy. His foreign policy initiatives, ranging from the ACMECS, ACD, FTAs, to the Bangkok Process, provided him with a channel to secure Thailand's supposed national interests. Along the way, he was accused of stoking his wealth by using state mechanisms.

Not only did the content of foreign policy change. The operational mode within the Foreign Ministry also underwent an extreme makeover. A representative of the nation and the King now became a CEO ambassador who would visit his/her customer for products demonstration. While CEO ambassadors were outfitted with more power, the role of the Foreign Ministry in the formulation of foreign policy diminished. The prime minister, his advisory team, and his chosen foreign ministers all sidelined the Foreign Ministry's officials. The Government House became enormously influential in the making of foreign policy. The transformation of the Foreign Ministry has left a deep scar of conflict between those who agreed and disagreed with the Thaksin's approach. It has also left Thailand in uncharted waters. Is Thailand from now on going all out to achieve profits or uphold principles, now that Thaksin is no longer in charge? Can Thailand have both?

The main argument raised at the beginning of this chapter — foreign policy designed to serve domestic political needs — is useful as a platform to investigate in detail the various aspects in Thailand's foreign policy, in subsequent chapters. In Chapter 2, a history of Thai diplomatic relations is examined as a foundation to understanding Thailand's present-day foreign affairs. This unveils the evolution of Thai diplomacy and how much it has changed during the Thaksin years. Chapter 3 discusses Thaksin's major foreign policy initiatives, delving into his creation of the many diplomatic acronyms, and exploring his regional and global initiatives, their aims and current status. Chapter 4 analyses Thai relations with key partners, and perhaps foes, beginning with Thailand's bordering neighbours, namely Myanmar, Cambodia, Laos and Malaysia, as well as ASEAN (as an organization), China and the United States. A brief discussion on Thai relations with Singapore, Japan and India is also included for a set of specific reasons. Throughout this analysis, the focus is on the conflicting notions of national and private interests in the conduct of Thaksin's foreign policy. Chapter 5 looks at the shortcomings and oversights of Thai foreign policy, both from the perspective of the nature of foreign policy and the intricate relations between Thaksin, Surakiart, and Kantathi on the one hand and the Foreign Ministry on the other, which engendered a huge impact on Thailand's diplomatic approaches. Evaluation and conclusion, in Chapter 6, draw the book to a close on most controversial and ambitious period in Thailand's diplomatic history.

Notes

1. Speech of Prime Minister Thaksin Shinawatra, on the topic "Forward Engagement: The New Era of Thailand's Foreign Policy", delivered at the Ministry of Foreign Affairs of Thailand, 12 March 2003. He was invited by Foreign Minister Surakiart Sathirathai to address the inaugural lecture for the Saranrom Institute of Foreign Affairs. At <http://www.mfa.go.th/web/showNews.php?newsid=5678&Q search=> (accessed 15 December 2008).
2. Thitinan Pongsudhirak, *Thai Foreign Policy under the Thaksin Government: Out of the Box for Whom*, 29 September 2004 <http://www.thaiworld.org/en/thailand_monitor/answer.php?question_id=70> (accessed 14 November 2008). Thitinan is Director of the Institute of Security and International Studies, Faculty of Political Science, Chulalongkorn University, Bangkok, Thailand.
3. Duncan McCargo, "Can Thaksin Lead Southeast Asia?", *Time*, 31 January 2005; John D. Ciorciari, "Thaksin's Chance for Leading Role in the Region", *Straits Times*, 10 March 2004; and Thitinan Pongsudhirak, "Thaksin Rising as Regional Leader?", *Korea Herald*, 13 April 2005.
4. The term "Thaksiplomacy" was invented by former ambassador Asda Jayanama, a well-known critic of Thaksin. It describes Thaksin's self-styled diplomatic approach, reflecting his business mentality and the dismissal of conventional diplomatic practices, in favour of a CEO style of work (top-down decision, shooting from the hips).
5. See Busakorn Chantasasawat, "The Burgeoning Sino-Thai Relations: Seeking Sustained Economic Security", *China: An International Journal* 4, no. 1 (March 2006): 86–112.

6. Thanong Khanthong, "Thaksin and Bush are Like Two Peas in a Pod", *The Nation*, 19 November 2004.

7. Edward Lock, "International Politics as Politics: Changing U.S. Policy Discourse", paper presented at the Oceanic Conference on International Studies, Australia National University, Canberra, 14–16 July 2004 <http://rspas.anu.edu.au/ir/Oceanic/OCISPapers/Lock.pdf> (accessed 14 December 2008).

8. See James N. Rosenau, *Linkage Politics* (New York: The Free Press, 1969). Rosenau argued that the international system shapes and determines the structures of political systems, while characteristics of political systems in turn produce the essential ingredients for an international system. This interaction has been labelled, "Linkage Politics". Also, Richard C. Eichenberg, "Domestic Preferences and Foreign Policy: Cumulation and Confirmation in the Study of Public Opinion", *Mershon International Studies Review* 42, no. 1 (May 1998): 1.

9. Surin Pitsuwan, ASEAN Secretary-General and former Foreign Minister of Thailand, once said, "Thaksin looks at the world as an extension of Thailand", in Joe Cochrane, "An Annoying Neighbour", *Newsweek International*, 21 February 2006.

10. Books on Thaksin's life include: *Thaksin: The Business of Politics in Thailand* (Pasuk Phongpaichit and Chris Baker), *The Thaksinisation of Thailand* (Duncan McCargo and Ukrist Pathmanand), *Keeping up with Thaksin* (Chirmsak Pinthong, in Thai), *Eyes on the Stars, Feet on the Ground* (Laddawan Rattanadilokchai, in Thai), and *Knight of the Third Wave* (Sorakon Adulyanon, in Thai). The first three books are known to be critical of Thaksin's style of governance.

11. Pasuk Phongpaichit and Chris Baker, *Thaksin: The Business of Politics in Thailand* (Chiang Mai: Silkworm Books, 2004), p. 35.

12. Ukrist Pathmanand, "The Thaksin Shinawatra Group: A Study of the Relationship between Money and Politics in Thailand", *Copenhagen Journal of Asian Studies* 13 (1998): 67.

13. Pasuk and Baker, *Thaksin: The Business of Politics in Thailand*, pp. 40–41.

14. Duncan McCargo and Ukrist Pathmanand, *The Thaksinisation of Thailand* (Copenhagen: Nordic Institute of Asian Studies, 2005), p. 9.

15. In an interview with Jakrapob Penkair, former Minister of the Prime Minister's Office, Bangkok, Thailand, 26 June 2008.

16. Pasuk and Baker noted that Thaksin's decision to enter Palang Dharma Party resulted in the party's destruction. Under Chamlong's original leadership, the party had stood for a cleaner and more principled politics. But in the public mind, Thaksin was a concession hunter associated with some of the most flagrant "money politicians", and

with the corrupt and discredited 1991–92 coup junta. His leadership widened the division and public bickering in the party. Pasuk and Baker, *Thaksin: The Business of Politics in Thailand*, p. 63.

17. Jeerawat Na Thalang, "PM Bangs the War Drums of TRT's Triumph", *The Nation*, 2 August 2003.

18. Speech of Surakiart Sathirathai, Foreign Minister, on the topic "Thailand: The Path Forward" at the Asia Society, New York, 30 September 2004.

19. Pasuk Phongpaichit, "A Country is a Company, a PM is a CEO", paper presented at the seminar on "Statesman or Manager? Image and Reality of Leadership in Southeast Asia", organized by the Bangkok Office of the Centre of Southeast Asian Studies (CSEAS), Kyoto University, Political Economy Centre, Faculty of Economics and Faculty of Political Science, Chulalongkorn University, Bangkok, Thailand, 2 April 2004.

20. In an interview with Jakrapob Penkair.

21. Ibid.

22. Source: Ministry of Foreign Affairs of Thailand.

23. In an interview with a Director-General at the Foreign Ministry, 27 June 2008. Thaksin made this statement on 11 August 2006.

24. Thaksin's speech on the occasion of Thai ambassadors preparing to leave for their posting overseas, at the Government House, Bangkok, 25 December 2003.

25. See Francis Fukuyama, *The End of History and the Last Man* (New York: Avon Books, 1992). Fukuyama argued, "What we may be witnessing is not just the end of the Cold War, or the passing of a particular period of post-war history, but the end of history as such: that is, the end point of mankind's ideological evolution and the universalisation of Western liberal democracy as the final form of human government."

26. N. Ganesan, "Appraising Democratic Consolidation in Thailand under Thaksin's Thai Rak Thai Government", *Japanese Journal of Political Science* 7, no. 2 (2006): 162–68.

27. Pavin Chachavalpongpun, "For the Hi-So and Lo-So, the 'Mo-So' is Surely a No-Go", *Bangkok Post*, 17 August 2009.

28. See Thomas L. Friedman, *The World is Flat: A Brief History of the Twenty-First Century* (New York: Farrar, Straus and Giroux, 2005).

29. Thaksin's speech at the Annual Meeting of Ambassadors and Consuls-General of Thailand, Ministry of Foreign Affairs, 15 August 2005. Source: Ministry of Foreign Affairs of Thailand.

30. Thaksin's interview with Maurice R. Greenberg, at the Council on Foreign Relations, New York, 18 September 2006. Greenberg is Chief Executive Officer of C.V. Starr & Co., Inc. This interview was given

one day before he was overthrown in the military coup of 19 September 2006.

31. Keynote address by Thaksin Shinawatra, Prime Minister of Thailand, at the International Business Conference on Global Economic Governance and Challenges of Multilateralism, organized by the International Chamber of Commerce of Bangladesh, Dhaka, 17 January 2004. Source: Ministry of Foreign Affairs of Thailand.

32. Speech of Foreign Minister Surakiart Sathirathai, on the topic, "Thailand: The Path Forward", New York, 30 September 2004.

33. Various scholars and analysts have interpreted Thai position vis-à-vis China differently. For example, Chulacheeb Chinwanno argued that Thailand has pursued a balanced engagement policy with external powers in order to achieve national interests. In, Chulacheeb Chinwanno, "Thai-Chinese Relations: Security and Strategic Partnerships", RSIS Working Paper no. 155, S. Rajaratnam School of International Studies, Singapore, 24 March 2008, p. 25. On the contrary, Kavi Chongkittavorn explicitly asserted that Thailand, under Thaksin, sometimes spoke on behalf of China and this may lead other ASEAN members to think that Thailand was a conduit for China's foreign policy. Quoted in Busakorn, "The Burgeoning Sino-Thai Relations: Seeking Sustained Economic Security", p. 11.

34. In August 2008, Prime Minister Samak Sundaravej, largely known as Thaksin's political nominee, declared his pro-China position in the aftermath of the brutal crackdown on the Tibetan demonstrators. See "Thai PM Proud to Host Olympic Torch", *USA Today*, 18 April 2008.

35. Interview with a Director-General at the Thai Foreign Ministry, Bangkok, 27 June 2008.

36. "Myanmar Issues a Catch-22 for India", *Economic Times*, 3 October 2007.

37. Ian Storey, "A Hiatus in the Sino-Thai Special Relation", *China Brief* 6, no. 19 (Washington D.C.: The Jamestown Foundation, 20 September 2006), p. 5.

38. "Interview: Thailand Aims to Further Enhance Thailand-China Strategic Partnership", *People's Daily*, 28 June 2005.

39. Ciorciari, "Thaksin's Chance for Leading Role in the Region".

40. Ministry of Foreign Affairs of Thailand, *Karn Thood Yook Mai Hua Jai Kue Prachachon* [New-Age Diplomacy with the People at its Heart] (Bangkok: Cyber Print, 2003), p. 19.

41. In an interview with Dr Surakiart Sathirathai, former Foreign Minister, Bangkok, 27 June 2008.

42. The Thai government had to compromise its anti-Communist stance vis-à-vis China simply because it needed Beijing's assistance in containing Vietnamese threat, in the wake of the American absence.

43. "No Change in Foreign Policy, But More Self-Reliance: Thai PM", *People's Daily*, 28 May 2001.
44. Matthew P. Daley, *Development in Burma, Testimony before the U.S. House International Relations Committee, Subcommittee on Asia and the Pacific and Subcommittee on International Terrorism, Non-proliferation and Human Rights* (Washington D.C.: Bureau of East Asian and Pacific Affairs, 25 March 2004) <http://www.state.gov/p/eap/rls/rm/2004/30789.htm> (accessed 7 December 2008). Daley is Deputy Assistant Secretary of the Bureau of East Asian and Pacific Affairs.
45. Source: Ministry of Foreign Affairs of Thailand.
46. See <http://test.mfa.go.th/web/2645.php?id=20127> (accessed 12 December 2009).
47. "Thailand Refocuses Foreign Policies to Engage Asia", *Kyodo News*, 1 March 2001.
48. Speech of Foreign Minister Surakiart Sathirathai, on the topic, "Thailand: The Path Forward", New York, 30 September 2004.
49. Speech of Kavi Chongkittavorn at the 2004 Regional Outlook Forum, organized by the Institute of Southeast Asian Studies, Singapore, 7 January 2004. He spoke on the topic, "Thaksin's Thailand: Political Unusual". Kavi is Assistant Group Editor of Nation Multimedia Group.
50. Sonny Inbaraj, "Thailand's 'Tail' Wags ASEAN 'Dog' Over Myanmar", *Asia Times*, 10 December 2004 <http://www.atimes.com/atimes/Southeast_Asia/FL10Ae03.html> (accessed 7 December 2008).
51. Wayne Arnold, "Thailand Sets Path to a Better Economy", *New York Times*, 24 October 2003.
52. Pavin Chachavalpongpun, "ASEM Forum to Boost Asian Bond Market", *The Nation*, 23 July 2003. Thaksin proposed through ASEM in 2002 a "Task Force for Closer Economic Partnership", with special emphasis on the Asian-Euro Bonds linkage, the creation of a Euro Bond Market in Asia and the use of the euro as a major currency in the region — all moves that would reduce Asian vulnerability from dollar-denominated debt instruments.
53. "Prime Minister Satisfied with Preparations for APEC 2003", *Thai Daily Digest*, 17 April 2003.
54. Interview with Surakiart Sathirathai, Bangkok, 27 June 2008.
55. Anuraj Manibhandu and Saritdet Marukatat, "Full Circle in Five Years", *Bangkok Post*, June 2002.
56. Thaksin's speech at the Annual Meeting of Ambassadors and Consuls-General of Thailand, Ministry of Foreign Affairs, 27 August 2003, in *Kham Prasai Lae Kham Banyai Khong Pon Tamruad Tree Thaksin Shinawatra Nayok Ratthamontri Lem Thi Nueng* [Speeches and Lectures of Police Lieutenant Colonel, Volume 1], Department of Public Relations, Bangkok, Thailand (n.d.), p. 101.

57. Speech by Krit Garnjana-Goonchorn, Permanent Secretary of the Thai Foreign Ministry, at the Swedish Regional Ambassadors' Meeting, Bangkok, 20 March 2006.
58. Source: The National Economic and Social Development Board of Thailand.
59. Martin Petty, "Standoff Exposes Discontent in Foreign Ministry", *Thai Day*, 26 March 2006.
60. McCargo and Ukrist, *The Thaksinisation of Thailand*, pp. 179–83.
61. Pavin Chachavalpongpun, *A Plastic Nation: The Curse of Thainess in Thai-Burmese Relations* (Lanham: University Press of America, 2005), p. 43. Also see Pisanu Sunthraraks, "Luang Wichit Watakan: Hegemony and Literature" (Ph.D. dissertation, University of Wisconsin-Madison, 1986).
62. Thaksin's speech at the Foreign Ministry, Bangkok, 11 August 2006.
63. McCargo and Ukrist, *The Thaksinisation of Thailand*, p. 183.
64. Johannes Dragsbaek Schmidt, "From Thaksin's Social Capitalism to Self-Sufficiency Economics in Thailand", paper presented at the workshop "Autochthoneity or Development? Asian 'Tigers' in the World: Ten Years after the Crisis", organized by the Working Group "Transformations in the World System — Comparative Studies of Development" under the European Association of Development Research and Training Institutes (EDAI), Vienna, 19–21 September 2007, pp. 6–7 <http://docs.google.com/gview?a=v&q=cache: ZFYJoQKNaDMJ:vbn.aau.dk/fbspretrieve/13639418/From_ Thaksin_s_Social_Capitalism_to_Self-sufficiency_Economics_in_ Thailand+thaksin+globalisation+localisation&hl=en&gl=sg> (accessed 22 August 2009). Also see Michael Kelly Connors, "Ideological Aspects of Democratisation in Thailand: Mainstreaming Localism", SEARC Working Paper Series no. 12, City University of Hong Kong, 2001, p. 4.
65. Speech of Prime Minister Thaksin Shinawatra, "Forward Engagement: The New Era of Thailand's Foreign Policy", Bangkok, 12 March 2003.
66. See <http://mfa.go.th/web/showNews.php?newsid=5678&Q search> (accessed 12 December 2009).
67. Ministry of Foreign Affairs of Thailand, *Karn Thood Yook Mai Hua Jai Kue Prachachon*, pp. 99–165.
68. Aung Zaw, "The Upside-Down World of Thaksina and Hun Sen", *Bangkok Post*, 27 October 2009). His action deeply upset the anti-SPDC movements. The exiled National Council of the Union Burma (NCUB) strongly denounced Thaksin's cosy ties with Myanmar.
69. "People and Friends of Burma Denounced Thai PM Thaksin", *Boxun*

News, 18 December 2004 <http://www.peacehall.com/news/gb/english/2004/12/200412181810.shtml> (accessed 12 December 2009).

70. "Thaksin Should be Firm with Burma", *The Irrawaddy*, 1 February 2001.
71. Arne Kislenko, "Bending with the Wind: The Continuity and Flexibility of Thai Foreign Policy", *International Journal* (Autumn, 2002): 537.
72. See Kusuma Snitwongse, "Thai Foreign Policy in the Global Age: Principle or Profit?", *Contemporary Southeast Asia* 23, no. 2 (August 2001): 189–212.
73. Presentation given by Thitinan Pongsudhirak on the topic, "Bending with the Wind: Thai Foreign Policy under Thaksin", at the Institute of Southeast Asian Studies, Singapore, 28 April 2005.
74. Thaksin won two landslide elections in January 2001 and February 2005. He also won an election in April 2006 following the dissolution of Parliament due to intense pressure from the opposition. The election was boycotted by major opposition parties which found that the positioning of the voting booths violated voter's privacy. Subsequently, the results were annulled by the Constitutional Court.
75. Cochrane, "An Annoying Neighbour".
76. "Thaksin Launches Foundation for Future Leaders", *Straits Times*, 19 November 2008. The "Building a Better Future Foundation" was official launched on 17 November 2008 with two offices, one in Hong Kong and the other in Dubai, in operation.
77. "Thailand: Premier-Elected for Softening IMF Terms", *International Press Service*, 11 January 2001.
78. "PM 'Hid Shares' That Were Worth Bt329 Million", *The Nation*, 21 August 2006.
79. Interview with Tej Bunnag, former Foreign Minister and former Permanent Secretary of the Foreign Ministry, Bangkok, 27 June 2008.
80. Phochana Phichitsiri, "Litany of Woes", *The Nation*, 19 September 2007. The other nine corruption cases are: (1) Two- and three-digit lottery, (2) Fire-fighting equipment, (3) Pojaman Shinawatra's Ratchadaphisek land purchase (Pojaman is Thaksin's wife), (4) Thaksin's practice of favouritism for vested interests, (5) Ua Athorn housing, (6) Krung Thai Bank loan, (7) Alleged tax evasion in Shinawatra Computer and Telecommunications Plc share sale, (8) Central lab project, and (9) Airport rail link.
81. Pasuk and Baker, *Thaksin: The Business of Politics in Thailand*, p. 197.
82. Daniel Ten Kate, "Thaksin's Score Card", *Asia Sentinel*, 3 July 2007 <http://www.asiasentinel.com/index.php?option=com_content&task=view&id=563&Itemid=185> (accessed 9 December 2008).

83. Nirmal Ghosh, "Thaksin Still Holds Sway up North", *Straits Times*, 22 October 2008.

84. Gwynne Dyer, "Thaksin Shinawatra Could be the Peron of Thailand", 5 September 2008, <http://www.straight.com/article-160848/gwynne-dyer-thaksin-shinawatra-could-be-peron-thailand> (accessed 9 December 2008).

85. Interview with Surapong Jayanama, former Thai ambassador to Vietnam, Portugal, Germany and South Africa. The interview took place in Bangkok, 26 June 2008.

86. "Government Must Restore Sound Diplomacy", *The Nation*, 16 October 2006.

87. Achara Ashayagachat, "Academics Slam PM's Foreign Policy Agenda: Thaksin Helping His Personal Ambitions", *Bangkok Post*, 30 September 2004.

88. In an interview with a number of former ambassadors who served during the Thaksin administration, Bangkok, November–December 2008.

89. Sajin Prachason, "Thailand-US FTA: Whatever we have to sacrifice must be sacrificed, if that helps get a better deal", Focus on the Global South, 25 April 2005 <http://www.bilaterals.org/article.php3?id_article=1753> (accessed 12 December 2009).

90. Speech of Prime Minister Thaksin Shinawatra, "Forward Engagement: The New Era of Thailand's Foreign Policy", Bangkok, 12 March 2003.

91. Kusuma, "Thai Foreign Policy in the Global Age: Principle or Profit?", p. 189.

92. Sunai, *Nayobai Tang Prathet Khong Thai: Suksa Krabuankarnkamnod Nayobai Khong Ratthaban Pon-ek Chatichai Choonhavan Tor Panha Kumphucha, Si Singhakom 1988–23 Kumphaphan 1991*, p. 74.

93. Kavi Chongkittavorn, "Tradition of Thailand's Foreign Policy is at Risk", *The Nation*, 21 March 2005.

94. His advisory team is divided into two policy planning units, *Ban Phitsanulok* and *Ban Manangkhasila*, including a legal reform committee, economic team, personal advisory team and political advisory team.

95. Chockanand Bussracumpakorn, *BID: Case Study of a Design Innovation Network Model in Thailand* (Bangkok: King Mongkut's University of Technology Thonburi, 2008), p. 5.

96. Petty, "Standoff Exposes Discontent in Foreign Ministry".

97. Telephone interview with a First Secretary at the Department of East Asian Affairs of the Ministry of Foreign Affairs of Thailand, Bangkok, 15 July 2006.

98. Thaksin's weekly radio broadcast on 27 July 2002. Quoted in Pasuk and Baker, *Thaksin: The Business of Politics in Thailand*, pp. 184–85.

99. Petty, "Standoff Exposes Discontent in Foreign Ministry".
100. Ibid.
101. Pasuk Phongpaichit and Chris Baker, "The Only Good Populist is a Rich Populist: Thaksin Shinawatra and Thailand's Democracy", Southeast Asia Research Centre Working Paper Series no. 36, City University of Hong Kong, 2002, p. 11.
102. Ministry of Foreign Affairs of Thailand, *Karn Thood Yook Mai Hua Jai Kue Prachachon*, p. 17.
103. Buakeaw means "Crystal Lotus" which is the symbol of the Ministry of Foreign Affairs.
104. "Young Ambassador of Virtue" is a project initiated by the Ministry of Foreign Affairs to celebrate His Majesty the King's 6th Cycle Birthday Anniversary. Recognizing the importance of youth as the nation's future and the significance of inculcating moral conscience in the young generation, the ministry designed this project on the following principles: (1) His Majesty the King's guidance on how to be a good, righteous and virtuous person as reflected in his addresses on various occasions, (2) Policy set forth in the 8th National Economic and Social Development Plan (1997–2001) which emphasizes the importance of human development as Thailand's main goal, and (3) ASEAN Vision 2020, shared by ASEAN member states in 1997, which gives importance to children, youth, women and the elderly, and the creation and realization of ASEAN "caring and civil societies". Source: <http://www.mfa.go.th/web/249.php> (accessed 11 December 2008).
105. Sources: <http://www.mfa.go.th/web/880.php> (accessed 11 December 2008).
106. Achara Ashayagachat, "Ministry Pledges to be More Responsive to External Needs", *Bangkok Post*, 16 October 2004.
107. Sources: <http://www.mfa.go.th/web/162.php?id=7971> (accessed 11 December 2008).
108. "Auditors Find Irregularities in Bt7-bn Billion", *The Nation*, 24 August 2006.
109. See 4 *Years of Repair for all Thais and Thailand under the Government of Prime Minister Dr. Thaksin Shinawatra (2001–2005)* (Bangkok: The Secretariat of the Cabinet). He also reiterated the success Thailand had achieved at the global stage during his first term.
110. Jephraim P. Gundzik, "Thaksin's Populist Economics Buoy Thailand", *Asia Times*, 3 August 2004.
111. John Roberts, "Thaksin Stokes Further Conflict in Southeast Thailand", <http://www.wsws.org/articles/2004/nov2004/thai-n26.shtml> (accessed 11 December 2008).

2

BAMBOO IN THE WIND
A Traditional Thai Diplomacy

Thai diplomacy is an art that has been inherited through time in the hands of kings, warriors and generals. This art is extolled as a unique characteristic of the Thai nation, mostly to the point where subsequent generations have perceived it as insuperable and flawless. This unique character of Thai diplomacy has allowed Thai elites to dominate the domain of foreign relations, without any real participation from the public. For example, during World War II, Prime Minister Phibun Songkhram declared, "When the country is in a critical situation, we have nothing to rely upon. Thus, I ask you to follow the Prime Minister."[1] The Thai state has incorporated the achievement of Thai diplomacy as part of its mission to build the nation, based on certain distinctive qualities that separate Thailand from other countries. This explains why the notion of Thailand as the only country in Southeast Asia to have never been colonized, has been much celebrated both at the state and the people levels. It connotes the intelligence of the Thai leaders and the magical art of Thai diplomacy — something, as they claimed, which is absent from Thailand's neighbours. But just as the process of Thai nation-building can be artificial and used to serve a myriad of political objectives, the conduct of Thai diplomacy can sometime be considered as arbitrary, amoral and being exploited in the same manner in order to serve the leaders' own political needs.

This chapter, firstly, explores a brief history of Thai diplomacy, from the very beginning of the supposedly first Siamese kingdom of Sukhothai, through the rise and fall of subsequent kingdoms, World War II, the Cold War, to the immediate pre-Thaksin period. It is important to note that Thai history is in itself a subject of a fierce contestation. Past and present leaders have continued to arbitrarily rewrite history to suit their political purposes. Sukhothai became Thailand's first capital even when Thailand did not exist at the time. Yet, it helped reaffirm the longevity of Thailand as a nation with such a precise boundary. Secondly, it seeks to explicate the nature and objectives of Thai foreign policy, and the techniques that were made a part of Thailand's eminent skill of diplomacy, known as the "bending with the wind" approach. The contour of this chapter is, however, not about elaborating on the details of Siamese contacts with the outside world, but rather, about investigating diplomatic practices that were exercised throughout history and their implications for the Thaksin period. Then and now, Thai leaders did not hesitate to take advantage of global conditions for their country's survival, as well as for strengthening their own power. Thaksin, in looking back to history, was eager to remould Thailand as a regional power. For him, diplomacy did not only function as a key to national survival, but also to dominate the region and to conquer the world.

CLASSIC THAI FOREIGN POLICY

Almost all textbooks on Thai diplomacy agree on the uncompromising objectives of Thailand's foreign policy. In the conduct of foreign relations, Thai leaders have sought to maintain, as far as possible, national sovereignty and territorial integrity, and to minimize external interference with the domestic system.[2] As a medium-sized state, yet aspiring to become a dominant kingdom in mainland Southeast Asia, Thailand is confined with few options in its foreign affairs. The sentiment of having to safeguard national sovereignty was fortified by successive regimes.

Thailand's escape from colonialism serves as a reminder to Thai foreign policy-makers that national sovereignty must be the ultimate goal in the conduct of diplomacy. But the concentration over the protection of sovereignty was not always a healthy sentiment. It has in the past, like now, been used to fan the feeling of nationalism. Although nationalism in itself is a product of the imagination, it has the potential of driving countries into conflict and at the same time, providing national leaders certain legitimacies at home. During the Cold War (1945–91), some despotic regimes were sustained because military leaders painted Communism as a threat to national sovereignty. The fear of losing national sovereignty, whether real or hollow, compelled the Thai public to become tolerant towards military regimes for the sake of maintaining national independence.

Because of the endless need to defend Thailand's national sovereignty, foreign policy became a state mechanism that was set up to eradicate any kind of perceived foreign threat. Siam might have been an unbound kingdom and only emerged as a modern nation-state following its adoption of the Western concept of boundary, but past kings were quick to become familiarized with the meaning and implication of sovereignty. In their understanding, the degree of national sovereignty was largely determined by the degree of foreign intervention in domestic affairs. Therefore, during colonialism in Asia when Siam had to surrender extra-territorial rights to the European powers, the legitimacy of Siamese kings was severely challenged because its national sovereignty was under threat. They were forced to urgently search for a new kind of legitimacy, by projecting Siam as a vulnerable entity which was robbed of its territories by the colonialists. During the period between 1867 and 1909, as a result of a series of bilateral treaties, Siam had ceded rights of suzerainty over western Cambodia to France, including Battambang, Sisophon and Siem Reap, as well as its vassals in the south to the British, including Kelantan, Trengganu, Kedah and Perlis. This was originally how the concept of "lost territories" came into play.[3]

The concept of lost territories was directly related to a classic foreign policy objective — to safeguard the country's territorial integrity. But as much as the Western notion of sovereignty was previously considered alien in the minds of the Thai elites, the spatial existence of Siam was even more confusing since it bore legacies of the old world politics which stood in stark contrast with that of the West. The discourse on "lost territories" was therefore at times fuzzy and troublesome. Thai historian Thongchai Winichakul remarked, "Thais have been taught their territories were lost. Every country lost territories. The idea of loss is a powerful tool used to whip up nationalism, especially in domestic politics."[4] The crisis at the Thai-Cambodian border over the territorial dispute of the Preah Vihear Temple, both in the 1960s and at present, exemplifies how nationalism casts a long shadow over the conduct of foreign relations. The need to conserve the nation's territorial integrity provided the military with a larger role in the control of foreign policy as a result of the traditional Thai concern with national security and external environment that had its roots in the pre-colonial period of Southeast Asia.[5] At a deeper level, however, the Siamese kingdom was not at all vulnerable as it portrayed itself in its fear of losing sovereignty and territorial integrity. Throughout the history, Siam attempted to create a sphere of influence over Lao and Khmer kingdoms which could be interpreted as its endeavour to have a hold over its neighbours as part of its own extended self-defence of the central plains, especially in relation to the threat in the east, as well as Siam's expansionist foreign policy and its territorial ambitions over surrounding weaker kingdoms.

Historically speaking, the maintenance of national sovereignty, independence and territorial integrity remained sanctified and acted as a compass for the country's foreign policy direction. The Thai elites might have manipulated these objectives at the same time as they scripted international politics as a dangerous space. This opened up an opportunity for them to successfully centralize foreign policy. Such objectives, in effect, reminded them that the conduct of diplomacy must not be only goal-oriented, but that it must be done in a shrewd manner by taking the country's capability and regional reality into consideration. The said consideration included changes to the international landscape, the role of policy-makers and other geopolitical factors. In recent times, Thaksin successfully shifted the national objectives to become essentially more commercialized, yet he occasionally exploited the theme of protecting economic independence and sovereignty, especially in the aftermath of the financial crisis in 1997.

Principle of Pragmatism

A number of scholars have traditionally recognized Siam, or Thailand, for its realistic foreign policy based on pragmatic principles. The uncertainties of international politics compelled the kingdom to formulate a pragmatic policy that aimed at fulfilling national interests as well as retaining its influence while dealing with foreign powers and neighbouring states. Siam's relations with China in ancient times, through the dispatch of envoys and royal gifts — as a symbol of political submission — in exchange for economic benefits reflected a high degree of realism in the kingdom's foreign policy thinking. Siam was indeed traditionally sensitive to shifts in the distribution of power. To the Siamese kings, the advent of the first Europeans at the court of Ayutthaya in the sixteenth century was an indication of a change of power and the political landscape. China no longer prescribed the regional power. The European colonialists represented a real and present danger, as well as an opportunity for the Siamese kings at the same time. Understanding foreign policy limits and constraints, Siam took on the policy of accommodation in order to appease hegemons of the day so that it could maintain its autonomy and gain other benefits, both in its relations with foreign powers and in its own internal power arrangement.

When colonialism was fully entrenched in Southeast Asia, Siam adjusted to it accordingly while observing the mistakes in the conduct of foreign policy of its neighbouring kingdoms. In the case of Burma for example, while carrying out an offensive policy against Britain, it failed to comprehend the new reality of geopolitics, its own vulnerabilities and military capacity. It finally lost its independence in 1885 after Britain annexed Upper Burma.[6] Emperors, kings and queens were stripped of their power. Kingdoms lost control over their own supposed territories. Siam, caught in the middle of this colonial politics, learned to bend with the prevailing wind dominated by European powers. As D.G.E. Hall observed, Siam entered a new era.[7] Therefore, the introduction of a new way of handling foreign affairs was imperative. Colonialism symbolized a major shift in international politics for Siam, a greater threat than any of the other traditional enemies in the past. This was due to the Europeans' superior military and technological sophistication. King Mongkut, founder of the

Ministry of Foreign Affairs, exercised his shrewd diplomatic skills, as celebrated in the historical records, in dealing with threatening European powers. Prior to the advent of colonialism, Siam was preoccupied with consolidating the kingdom, following the overthrow of the Ayutthaya dynasty by the Burmese in 1767. Siam thus pursued an isolationist policy. But the change of political surroundings, culminated during the reign of King Mongkut, urged the Siamese elites to reformulate their foreign policy in order to withstand the pressures from the outside world.

King Mongkut initiated the process of modernization. He first decided to open Siam to extensive intercourse with the West. Within a few years of his reign, he negotiated fresh treaties with most powers of the day: with Britain in 1855, France and the United States in 1856, Denmark in 1858, Portugal in 1859, the Netherlands in 1860, Prussia in 1862, Sweden and Norway in 1868.[8] But the price of complying with the international reality and the shifting balance of power was high. Siam lost the right of extra-territoriality to European powers in this process of modernization. Second, King Mongkut also commenced the modernization of Siam along the lines of the West, so that his country would be accepted in the family of nations as an equal, and so as to rid Siam of the disadvantages imposed by the treaties.[9] This mission of modernizing Siam to become more Western in its outlook continued into the reign of King Chulalongkorn, who introduced a myriad of reforms covering administration, military, laws, and monetary system, all based on those existing in the West. During his period, as Thai historians often highlight, the kingdom was able to escape colonialism because of his heartbreaking concessions of claimed Siamese territories in order to retain national independence. The modernization programmes, which appeared to lead Siam out of danger of being colonized, were part of the kingdom's adjustment to the changes in the regional order.

Thai pragmatism, based on the policy of accommodation, was also firmly upheld during World War II. But such pragmatism became the single most problematic issue in Thai foreign policy since 1932 in the way Thailand tried to be on both sides, the Allies and Axis, during the war period. It was this profound evidence of "trickiness" which led Thailand's neighbours to mistrust the country's intentions and policies.[10] This trickiness persisted in the era of the Cold War where Communism was depicted by the Thai military regimes as a new threat to national survival. They chose to align themselves with the democratic world, led by the United States, in combating Communist ideology, which was already deeply seated in Thailand's neighbouring states to the east. The United States, emerging as a superpower in post-World War II, offered security and stability to Thailand even at the cost of it tolerating totalitarian regimes in Bangkok. The new regional power game prompted Thailand to re-evaluate its foreign policy, either to become isolated and possibly to fall into the Communist trap, or to befriend the Free World and to cement its ties with America in which military aid would be guaranteed.[11] Obviously, Thailand bent with the wind again, volunteering itself as an ally of the United States in counterbalancing the Communists in Indochina. Thai leaders felt that Thailand alone would be too weak and vulnerable to endure the power of the Communists, especially as Vietnam aggressively advanced its troops in Cambodia and Laos. A call for help to the United States, and subsequently to China, seemed to echo a principle of pragmatism in the Thai approach. Bangkok also played an important role in the creation of ASEAN in 1967 to fight the spread of Communism. This pragmatic policy continued until the end of the Cold War which witnessed the victory of the democratic force over Communist ideology, and in the Asian context the Cambodian settlement in 1991. Thailand, once again, stood on the winning side, thanks to its pragmatic and flexible foreign policy.

The key understanding of Thailand's pragmatic foreign policy is that Thai leaders came to terms with their country's levels of strength, and acted eagerly in response to the reality, rather than to idealistic goals or uninhibited ambitions. They made a foreign policy based on practicality, seeing the country in terms of its history, form of government and relationship with foreign powers. This pragmatism seemed to serve one objective — to materialize the country's national interests. At the same time, however, Thai leaders used pragmatic rhetoric to deflect questions about certain foreign policy matters through a painfully complex recitation of details about the change in geopolitical conditions, which was in turn utilized to build their image as knowledgeable leaders. Thaksin employed this very same method when he supervised foreign affairs

— using pragmatic rhetoric to achieve national goals, and in the meantime painting his own image as a new generation of leader who identified himself well with current international politics.

Matters of the Elites

In retrospect, Siamese kings and generals, to a certain extent, had their hands firmly on foreign policy simply because they conceived themselves as the chief players in the field of foreign affairs and because the political system which they enjoyed maximum control over, allowed them to do so. Elite control of foreign affairs is not necessarily specially Thai: it has remained the norm in most countries, particularly those that follow the Westminister tradition which vests control of Foreign Policy largely in the hands of the executive. In the case of Siam, throughout the ancient dynasties, diplomacy had been practised strictly by monarchs and the upper classes. They were not only policy-makers, but also warriors and warfare strategists since the kingdom had consistently engaged in war with its neighbouring enemies. Members of the royal family took turns to run the Foreign Ministry, giving it a reputation of being a "playground for aristocrats". This tradition remains, as can be seen by the presence of prominent families among high officials, but intake sources are now far wider.[12]

Because members of the royal family occupied the seat of Minister of Foreign Affairs, they reported directly to the king with regard to international relations. Moreover, certain diplomatic skills, including the knowledge of world politics and the ability to speak European languages, were deemed exclusive to the upper classes. It was evident that Siamese affairs, under the absolute monarchy, were shaped by the monarchs both in the domestic administration and in the exercise of diplomacy. However, the pattern of a centralized power in the country's administration lived on even after Thailand became a constitutional democracy in 1932. The international political system, which was anarchic in itself, was conducive for subsequent leaders to take charge of the Foreign Ministry. For example, the military exploited the perceived vulnerabilities of Thailand: first, as a newly democratic state surviving in the game of ideological conflict in the aftermath of World War II;

second, as an emergent modern state which was forced to deal with the unrests at its periphery as a legacy of colonialism; and third, as a state highly susceptible to internal conflicts including the power struggle among various political factions, corrupt and incompetent civilian leaders and the threats of the Communist Party of Thailand. With all these combined, the Thai military apparently became an indispensable player in the defence of national security.[13] The military also expressed its concern about how well-equipped the Foreign Ministry was to lead Thailand in the rapidly changing world during the Cold War.[14]

Toward the end of the Cold War, however, domestic changes significantly affected the way foreign policy was traditionally formulated. The role of the military in foreign affairs was fast fading. This was owing to three main reasons. First, the political crises erupted in the 1970s and in 1992 when pro-democracy activists clashed with the military governments resulting in much bloodshed, strongly signalled a new wave of Thai democratization. Second, because of a series of political upheavals in the kingdom, the people's political consciousness was inevitably brought to life. The re-emergence of student activism and the expansion of the urban middle class served as important social forces that demanded political openness and greater transparency in the conduct of foreign policy.[15] Third, the rapid economic growth, as a consequence of an export-led growth strategy and subsequent financial liberalization adopted throughout the 1980s, called for new thinking in the approach to foreign affairs. Large business conglomerates, both in the capital and in the provinces, requested the government to fine-tune its foreign policy quickly in response to the changing international environment in the form of globalization. They preferred the government to tone down its accent on national security and to concentrate on promoting business opportunities both at home and in neighbouring countries. The civilian government of General Chatichai Choonhavan reacted favourably to the businesses' call for a reformulation of foreign policy, which also benefited the prime minister himself and his supporters who consisted mostly of businessmen. As a consequence, economic diplomacy was practised at the expense of the diminishing role of the military in foreign affairs.

In the new millennium, Thaksin was keen to reinvent Thailand's foreign policy to be even more business-oriented. Security issues were given less priority, even after the 9/11 incident when global terrorism emerged as a main agenda in many countries and certainly in Thai-U.S. relations, and even at the peak of the armed conflicts between the Thai state and the Muslim minority in the south which caused an impact on Thai-Malaysian ties. In both the Chatichai and Thaksin periods, despite the lessening military influence in politics and foreign affairs, the Foreign Ministry, while fighting for its autonomy, found itself being challenged by external security factors that came to dominate diplomacy. It was also the first time that the Foreign Ministry was openly exploited by political elites through the implementation of business-centric foreign policy.

Resilience and Flexibility

While the principle of pragmatism can be defined as a logical approach to foreign affairs and crisis, the traits of resilience and flexibility connote an attempt to strike a balance between pragmatism and principles, as seen in the Thai policy of "bending with the wind". This policy was made famous by Thai elites who pursued a conventional strategy of adjusting to whatever stance that best maintained friendly relations with the great powers and ensured the country's sovereignty and independence. Opportunism, alliance and bandwagoning are key characteristics of this policy, usually dubbed "bamboo in the wind". For example, as Arne Kislenko argued, the Anglo-French *entente* in 1904 effectively ended the rivalry between the two largest imperial powers in Southeast Asia. That put Siam in a very difficult spot, sandwiched between the British in Malaya and Burma and the French in Indochina. No longer able to play one off against the other, as they had done so well for so long, the Siamese were unable to stave off European demands. But when World War I broke out, Siam seized the opportunity to be on the winning side, which American entry in the war ensured. Siam declared war on Central Powers, while anticipating that it would give the country a seat alongside the Allies at any post-war conference, thereby undermining British and French designs.[16] Siam basically took every opportunity and risk to ride along with the direction of the wind of international politics. But was it the only reason behind the execution of this policy?

The resilience and flexibility of Thai foreign policy was buttressed by a number of factors. Likhit Dhiravegin noted, "The two main factors were Siam's geographic position as a buffer zone and the far-sightedness and ingenuity of the monarchs."[17] The location of Siam, in the heart of mainland Southeast Asia, allowed itself to be a buffer zone between the British and the French in their quest to advance their colonial objectives in this part of the world. This buffer zone precluded Siam from being colonized simply because the two European powers agreed to maintain the balance of power so that they could avoid engaging in war with one another. And Thai elites knew well how to exploit their country's geographically strategic location. Siam as a buffer zone in the colonial period was transformed into a frontline state in the Cold War era. As a frontline state, Thailand and its leaders obtained considerable benefits, including military alliance with the United States and the endurance of the Thai military regimes. In the modern day, Thailand as the centre of prosperity in mainland Southeast Asia continues to provide the country with advantages, especially in connecting itself with other economies in the region, thus making its hegemonic ambition more plausible and potential. Thaksin made full use of the location factor in constructing his business-oriented foreign policy while boosting Thailand's international standing.

The astuteness of the Thai monarchs has also been propagated by the state as one of the main criteria behind the success of Siam's foreign policy. History tells of the bravery and perspicacity of the Thai monarchs, ranging from Sukhothai's Ramkhamhaeng, Ayutthaya's Naresuan, Thonburi's Taksin, and Rattanakosin's Mongkut and Chulalongkorn, and how they sharpened their diplomatic skills in order to preserve Siam's independence. The Thai state often rationalized the role of Siamese monarchs in terms of their far-sightedness in dealing with foreign powers as well as their disheartening decision to sacrifice parts of the so-called Siamese territories so as to maintain the overall national independence. King Chulalongkorn was eulogized as the Great King because he was willing to make the necessary concessions to European powers so that Siam could escape from colonialism.[18] In this process, Siamese monarchs also learnt to select "certain things" from these European powers which they thought were good for the kingdom. For them, colonialism was a negative trait and democracy was too Westernized and modern. On the other hand, Western costumes and social etiquettes were desirable as they could be used to develop Siam into a civilized nation. However, the selective process was rather tricky and frequently served the interests of the monarchs. They looked at the European way of commanding colonies and imitated similar strategies to rule Siam.[19]

Regardless of whatever agendas the Siamese elites had in mind in their interface with foreign powers, they proved to be flexible, pragmatic and resilient to the altering balance of power. They also learned to be assertive if situations permitted and to be compliant when choices in foreign policy seemed to be inadequate. The principles of pragmatism and resilience have been passed on to the subsequent generations of Thai leaders, in designing Thailand as a bamboo that leans with the prevailing wind. But bending with the prevailing wind also induced a policy dilemma for Thailand. Because of the lack of colonial experience, and unlike its neighbouring countries, Thailand tended to entertain the politics of alliance usually with extra-regional powers instead of upholding strictly a policy of neutralism and non-alignment. Thai foreign policy depended heavily on the interests and policies of other powers, while also taking advantage of them for its own interests. Siam, or Thailand, kept up its open-door policy, despite some brief periods of isolationism, and invited external powers to compete among themselves to win over their alliance. This was a component of Siam's balance-of-power strategy. Siam realized that its survival rested on its ability to bend with the wind and its appeasement policy towards external powers, even at the expense of occasionally losing its own moral stance and principles.

A BRIEF HISTORY OF THAI DIPLOMACY

Leszek Buszynski argued that Thailand's long-established foreign policy, particularly during the Cold War era, exhibited two outstanding characteristics: one was the dominant role of the military and the other was the importance attached to external allies.[20] In fact, historical records show that Siam was always engaged in inter-state politics, seeking to assuage powers of the day, while turning unequal relationships with external powers into its own benefit and interest.

Era of the Old Capitals and the Colonial Period: Policy of Appeasement

As mentioned earlier, long before the arrival of the Europeans in Siam, China was the dominant regional power. Siam had no alternative but to cultivate amicable relations with China. Diplomatic contacts were established between the Chinese and Siamese courts in 1282. The tributary relationship lasted until at least the reign of King Mongkut before the European imperialists occupied Siam's external affairs. It was believed that King Ramkhamhaeng of Sukhothai (1239–1317), the third monarch of the Phra Ruang dynasty, paid two visits to the emperor of China; the first in 1294 while Kublai Khan was still alive, and the second in 1300.[21] His visits symbolized Siam's submission which was meant to solidify China's power position. More specifically, Siam's appeasement towards China served both the diplomatic and political purposes well. Diplomatically, China recognized the existence of Siam as an autonomous kingdom. Politically, Siam sought security and protection from the Chinese leaders while flaunting its close ties with China to fend off any aggressors from nearby kingdoms. As Sarasin Viraphol argues, "The concept that the Confucianised Manchu court allowed 'barbarian' states to participate in the material excellence of Chinese civilisation fitted the underlying Siamese assumption that intercourse with the Celestial Empire was pre-eminently commercial in character."[22] Siamese kings witnessed how some rebellious kingdoms were chastised by the Middle Kingdom and wanted to avoid direct conflict with it.

Siamese diplomacy in this period revealed a specific set of strategies. As Siam embraced an appeasement policy towards China, projected through its political obedience and the transmission of its tributes in recognition of China's supreme authority, it also exhibited its vulnerability so as not to emerge as a challenge to the Chinese emperors. Siamese kings understood that in order to sustain itself as a consolidated kingdom in the face of other rivalries in the region, amicable relations with China was mandatory because it could endow Siam with a source of security and stability. Furthermore, Siam employed its submissive diplomacy as an apparatus to enhance the economic strength of the kingdom. This tributary system progressively promoted bilateral trade between Siam and China. In fact, it was this economic benefit that became a fundamental basis of how Siam built its relations with China in subsequent periods.[23]

In the Ayutthaya period (1351–1767), relations between Siam and foreign powers continued on the basis of its appeasement policy. The emphasis was on traditional flexibility and pragmatism in the way Siamese leaders handled foreign affairs. Apart from the Chinese who had settled in the kingdom and gradually assimilated with local customs and culture, the Japanese were also present in the court of Ayutthaya, mainly as royal guards and mercenaries. Others included the Javanese, Malays, Indians, Sri Lankans and Persians. In 1511, the Portuguese arrived in Siam, paving the way for a greater influx of Europeans into the kingdom. Ayutthaya became an important trading centre controlling foreign trade with all points northward. It quickly achieved a remarkable state of prosperity. The availability of foreign technology and weaponry also made it immensely powerful among its neighbours.[24] As a hub of prosperity in this region, Ayutthaya's diplomatic ambition was further boosted by the dispatch of Siamese envoys to Europe. The first recorded visit of a Siamese envoy to Europe was in 1609 when a Siamese ambassador was received in the Hague. The connection between Siam and Europe reached its height during the reign of King Narai (1657–88) when Siamese embassies were sent twice to Versailles in 1684 and 1685, conveying the message of Siam standing equally alongside the West as a civilized kingdom.[25]

Holland and France were not the only two powers attempting to influence Siam, either through the spread of Christianity or through the monopoly of trade. The British and Spanish trading ventures and missionaries began to make their impact on Siam, and therefore posing a challenge to the Siamese kings in their ability to craft a balance-of-power policy. Ferocious competition among European powers to get Siam under their influence prompted its kings to become even more pragmatic. For instance, King Narai, while proclaiming that he was a Buddhist, gave consent to his subordinates to profess any religious faiths, instead of objecting to Christianity, which would have upset and infuriated the European powers. He was aware that European powers, France in particular, wished to draw on Christianity to force Siam's alliance.[26] Again, this was largely seen by Thai historians as proof of the Siamese monarch's good judgement, especially on how to use diplomacy to defend the interests of the kingdom. The end of the Ayutthaya period witnessed frequent wars with Burma, and eventually resulting in the sacking of this Siamese kingdom in 1767 after it had served as a main trading entrepôt for 417 years.

The Thonburi dynasty (1768–82) did not have much time to engage itself in inter-state politics, since it was beseiged by wars with its neighbours and the responsibility of consolidating the kingdom. It lasted as the so-called capital of Siam for almost fifteen years. The new kingdom, Rattanakosin, or Bangkok, was founded in 1782, and ushered Siam into a new era both through its domestic modernization and its new way of guiding diplomacy. External relations became increasingly more complicated because of the emergence of colonialism. Siam, a political entity in the Chao Phraya River, was tested while pursuing intricate relations with colonial powers. It was coerced to open itself up to free trade, to grant the right of extraterritoriality to the Europeans, to forgo outdated customs, and even to concede to the Western powers' claim of many pieces of Siam's vassals. Kingdoms nearby came under direct control of European powers. Siamese kings were convinced that avoiding close contact with Europe powers was now impossible and that resisting their pressure would lead to negative impacts on the kingdom. It was then that they renewed the traditional "bending-with-the-wind" policy. But this time, the Siamese kings faced a more serious difficulty: to bend to which prevailing wind since there was more than one power at play?

King Mongkut and King Chulalongkorn were left with a few options. They were pressed to negotiate with foreign powers because outright resistance, as seen in Burma and Indochina, would have led to direct confrontation. Siam also hoped to seek help from another power, as in appealing to Britain for assistance to apply pressure on France. But this strategy did not always work. The conflict between Siam and France over the territorial claim in Laos resulted in two French gunboats attempting to force their way up the Chao Phraya River in 1893.[27] Siam decided to open fire on them. The decision, driven by Siam's diplomatic misjudgement, almost cost the kingdom its sovereignty. Siam called upon Britain to pressurize the French, but its request was turned down because Britain was anxious to keep out of any conflict with France. The only way out for Siam was to conform to an agreement on France's terms. The colonial period therefore witnessed the kingdom's survival strategy of steering clear of forthright conflict with the Europeans, to accommodate to their needs in order to maintain the integrity of Siam, and occasionally to play one power against another while waiting to see which wind prevailed. This policy was subsequently modified in the post-World War II period where Thailand, as a new modern nation, anticipated the prevailing wind and was ready to spring to the winning side. It was known as the period of periodic opportunism.

The Wartime Period: Periodic Opportunism

The transitional period in Siam began at the end point of colonialism, the abolition of the absolute monarchy in 1932, the introduction of democracy and World War II. Siam became Thailand in 1939 because the military government claimed that this conveyed better the notion of a homogeneous Thai nation. Siam's external affairs were at this time as colourful as its domestic power struggles between competing political factions. The king no longer reigned supreme in Thailand. Neither did civilian leaders in the new democratic setting. The abrupt change of its political system did not prepare Thailand well to embrace democracy. The perilous international environment acted as a catalyst for the continuation of Thailand's centralization of political power. This time it was not in the form of absolute monarchy, but military fascist regimes. Regardless of any change in the political system, however, Thai leaders inherited the old diplomatic skill: bending with the wind.

The incident of 1893 reminded the Thai leaders that they could not rely on foreign powers in times of crisis. During World War II, the Thai state initially attempted to implement a neutral foreign policy and cease to bend with the wind — something rather unusual in the Thai diplomatic discourse.[28] Japan's aggressive imperial army was, however, too strong for Siam to oppose. The waning influence of the European powers in Southeast Asia paved the way for the Japanese army to advance its troops and turn their colonies into its own possession. To circumvent Japanese invasion and eventual occupation, the Phibun government signed a military agreement that granted rights of passage to Japan. Technically, Thailand, in signing such agreement with Japan, succeeded in saving its independence. It was perceived as a non-occupied nation, and its Army was not disarmed. Strategically, Thailand returned to the bending-with-the-wind approach, tagging along behind the Japanese when the regional situation permitted it to do so. Phibun, a fascist himself, grasped this opportunity, with Japan's blessing, to reclaim the lost territories in northern Malaya, and provinces in Laos and Cambodia, which were previously ceded to Britain and France respectively.

The fate of Thailand in the aftermath of the war was not only determined by the practical tactic of opportunism alone. It depended on luck too. The political struggle at home drove a group of Thai leaders who were residing in the United States and Europe at the time to turn against the Phibun military government. They formed the "Seri Thai" (Free Thai) movement, led by M.R. Seni Pramoj, Thai ambassador to Washington, in the United States. This was supported by Pridi Banomyong, also a prominent leader, to form an underground movement in order to set Thailand free from Japan's control. The policy of balancing powers, between the Japanese and the Allies, emerged as a shrewd solution for Thailand after World War II ended. Phibun's pro-Japanese foreign policy, as seen through its expansionist ambition vis-à-vis neighbouring countries, was rejected by the Seri Thai. The Seri Thai launched its campaign in appealing to the Allies not to brand Thailand as an enemy and to nullify any war status between Thailand and them. The United States, in providing the ground for the Seri Thai movement, decided to disregard Thailand's declaration of war and helped sway Britain not to "punish" Thailand for siding with the Japanese. As the war's end was nigh and the likelihood of Japanese defeat increased, the Phibun government was taking a new turn in its foreign policy-making. From this period until the end of the war saw Thailand working relentlessly to regain trust from the West, and even complying with certain conditions laid down by European powers, in particular Britain and France, in order that they accepted Thailand as a member of the United Nations. Those conditions included the signing of agreements that restored the disputed territories in favour of the European powers. Phibun was forced to retreat from Thai politics, at least for the time being, and to allow civilian leaders to run the country for the initial years of the post-war period.

The Cold War: From Strategic Clientelism to Equidistance

The United States came to Thailand's rescue at the end of World War II. It facilitated Thailand's pacification with Britain and France and helped secure its membership in the United Nations. The U.S. objective here was clear. The world order was now reconfigured along an ideological line, and the United States needed client states to fight against the Communists. Thailand represented itself as a major candidate in the American war against Communism within Asia's battlefield. Phibun returned as Prime Minister for the second time, in 1948. Viewing the Americans as Thailand's new best friend, Phibun did not hesitate to cultivate cosy ties with Washington. As a result, Thailand sent its troops to Korea, and aided the Kuomintang (KMT) remnants in southern China and parts of Burma in their battle against Communist Chinese on the mainland. Phibun's alliance with the United States guaranteed his country's security, as Washington provided Bangkok with generous economic and military aid. Financial and technical aid grew from US$6.5 million in 1952–53 to US$8.8 million in 1953–54; in the next fiscal year, this amount shot up to US$36.3 million.[29] Surachai Sirikrai noted:

> America viewed Phibun's strong anti-communist policy as the ideal; Thailand's strategic location was considered vital to America's containment policy. Phibun, of course, saw America's fear of communist expansion in Asia and its willingness to support his regime for his strong anti-communist cause as mutual interests. Phibun needed both American diplomatic recognition for his unconstitutional and unstable regime and military aid to strengthen his armed forces, condition dictated by internal problems.[30]

As a consequence, Phibun was wholehearted in depicting Thailand as the United States' client state. His military background earned strong support from the Thai Army for a new foreign policy that favoured the United States. The Thai army believed that close ties with Washington would further institutionalize the military in domestic politics and automatically render it authority over Thailand's foreign affairs. In 1954, Thailand participated in the Manila Pact alongside Australia, New Zealand, Britain, France, the United States, Pakistan and the Philippines in the establishment of the Southeast Asia Treaty Organization (SEATO), a new platform constructed specially to contain Communism in Southeast Asia. SEATO became a sanctuary for the Thai military regime to continue its grip on power in the name of protecting national security. Thailand therefore supported anti-Communist struggles in Indochina, thus preventing itself from becoming the last "domino" on mainland Southeast Asia. Thailand authorized the U.S. military bases that remained in the country until 1976 to back up Thai troops in the suppression of the Chinese communists initially, and subsequently the Vietnamese threat. The nature of the international order, the support of the United States for Thai military governments, and the ongoing menace posed by the Communist Party of Thailand all played their part in the enhancement of the role of the military in diplomacy. But the Foreign Ministry did not sit on the fence. The Asia-Africa Conference in Bandung in 1955 offered Thailand an opportunity to exercise its defined diplomacy with China. China, a Communist state, represented a worry. This was partly due to China's influence in Vietnam and the sheer number of Chinese residents in Thailand. At the Bandung Conference, the Thai representative was reassured by China that the latter did not have any aggressive intentions toward Thailand.[31]

At home, the military government came under criticism from the public for "getting too close" to the Americans and for its past regressive acts against the Chinese in Thailand during 1952–53 (Phibun was accused of adopting an anti-Chinese policy in order to satisfy Washington). Yet, Thailand's negative attitude toward China was not drastically abandoned. Its gradual adjustment toward Communist China, deemed as a new prevailing wind in Asia particular from the 1970s onwards, served Thailand well in a sense that it could carry on close relations with the United States but at the same time, get to know Beijing a little bit better.[32] Success came in 1975 when Thailand, under the government of M.R. Kukrit Pramoj (1975–76), normalized its diplomatic relations with China, shortly after the Communist victory in South Vietnam and the U.S. withdrawal from Southeast Asia, a move that reflected Thailand's toeing of the new U.S. line.

Ironically, SEATO, with the objective of defending member countries from the threat of Communism, consisted only of two Southeast Asian nations — Thailand and the Philippines; both were clients of the United States. Indeed, South Vietnam, Cambodia and Laos were also initially designated "protocol states" with similar protection within SEATO. Bangkok was selected as the headquarters of SEATO with Phote Sarasin, former Thai ambassador to Washington, as SEATO's first secretary-general. But SEATO went out of fashion in 1977 as it was perceived as an obvious agent of the United States and because other non-members in Southeast Asia felt uneasy over the overpowering U.S. influence. In 1967, another regional body was established under the name, "The Association of Southeast Asian Nations", or ASEAN, as an anti-Communist platform, yet, with a special focus on resolving intra-ASEAN problems as member states confronting external foes. ASEAN gave a new sense of regional identity to its founding members — Indonesia, Malaysia, the Philippines, Singapore and Thailand, bringing them together to work toward regional integration and to put aside clashing irredentist claims among themselves. ASEAN's emergence at this critical time also offered Thailand a chance to play a proactive role as a frontier state confronting Communists on mainland Southeast Asia. With Vietnam's invasion of Cambodia in 1978, Thailand renewed its partnership with the United States, as well as its strengthening ties even more intensely with China with the quick establishment of a *de facto* military alliance between the two countries.[33] This, once again, allowed the military to play a significant part in regional affairs. Meanwhile, the Thai Foreign Ministry cooperated closely with ASEAN to mobilize collective diplomatic opposition at the United Nations.[34]

From the mid-1970s until the assumption of premiership of Chatichai in 1988, Thailand favoured an equidistant foreign policy which was heavily centred on cultivating stable relations with its allies, like the United States, China and fellow members of ASEAN. Did Thailand give up totally the policy of bending with the wind? Not at all. Thailand still believed in continual adaptation to a changing global situation. Bangkok, time and again, embarked upon leaning on external powers, seeking support from its ASEAN neighbours and attaching importance to regional cooperation as the country was in the process of engineering a pragmatic foreign policy that would secure its long-term national goals.

Pre-Thaksin Omni-directional Policy

The waning of the Cold War and the conflict in Cambodia, as well as the beginning of the Chatichai government effectively led Thailand into a new epoch of diplomacy. U.S. commitment in Southeast Asia had diminished greatly. Meanwhile, China continued to rise, thanks to its successful economic development programme and its more progressive leadership. ASEAN gained a new boost as it managed to keep the Vietnamese threat in check. That, at a later stage, helped prepare Hanoi to apply for ASEAN membership in the 1990s. Chatichai supported a new look in Thai diplomacy that sought to bring foreign policy more into accord with the views of other ASEAN nations and to avoid the earlier charges made by certain members that Thailand remained a satellite of the United States. Accordingly, the government shifted its foreign policy from a firm alliance with the United States towards China and Indochina, this time mainly for economic reasons unlike in the 1970s when "security" brought them together.[35] This explains the origin of his famous marketplace policy that was endorsed by Beijing. However, Chatichai's rapprochement toward China greatly perplexed many of his ASEAN friends. Concerns in Indonesia and Malaysia at this time were more about Thailand's closeness to China, rather than the United States. Egged on by the then Army Chief Chavalit Yongchaiyuth, the Chatichai government harboured the idea of Thai hegemony on mainland Southeast Asia, harking back to the "golden land" or *Suvarnabhumi* concept of ancient Siamese empires.[36] Thailand altered its foreign policy from its previous preoccupation with the West and foreign powers, to its less powerful neighbouring countries, as a result of the shift in the regional balance of power that was slightly moving toward Indochina. The shift in foreign policy was also a response to Thailand's rapid economic growth, which was 9.5 per cent in 1987 and 13.2 per cent in 1988. This growth was related to Thailand's opening up for financial investment, development of light manufacturing exports, and financial liberalization. On top of this, economic growth was made possible thanks to Thailand's increasing trade volumes, albeit only to some extent, with its neighbours. The economic strength, in turn, allowed Thailand to formulate a regional vision for foreign policy that was realistic and tangible.[37] Moreover, the decline of the military and the security imperatives in the post-Cold War propelled the country to reassess its foreign policy philosophy. From then on, economic interests found their place in the heart of Thailand's foreign policy. It was at that moment that Thailand began to assert its influence in the Myanmar politics through the so-called "Constructive Engagement Policy".

Therefore, the pre-Thaksin period saw Thailand reaching out to various players, looking to grapple political and economic opportunities, while reassigning the country to become a hegemonic power on mainland Southeast Asia. Was it a revisit of foreign policy opportunism? Opportunism has always been a foreign policy character of Thailand. Searching for an opportunity was also common for the Thai policy practitioners in the post-Cold War era where Thailand kept on reinventing itself in the latest international setting. Chatichai announced that Thailand would pursue an independent foreign policy, and that the traditional practice of relying on external security support was slowly being removed. In an address in December 1988, he said that the age of "bending with the wind", a metaphor commonly used to describe Thailand's foreign policy, had come to an end.[38] Unfortunately, the Chatichai government was short-lived. The 1990s was marked by political turmoil as a result of the military coup in 1991 and the political violence in May 1992. Thailand was too preoccupied with domestic politics, leaving the country's earlier ambition as a regional leader unattainable. However, Thailand was not entirely without regional influence in this decade. The ASEAN Free Trade Area (AFTA) was an initiative of Anand Panyarachun, a former top diplomat who was appointed twice as prime minister during 1991–92.[39] AFTA is a trade bloc agreement by ASEAN which aims at supporting local manufacturing in the member countries. The agreement was signed on 28 January 1992 in Singapore, and its primary goals are to increase ASEAN's competitive edge as a production based in the world market through the elimination of tariff and non-tariff barriers within ASEAN, as well as to attract foreign direct investment to ASEAN. Thailand was behind the Greater Mekong Cooperation (GMC), also encompassing Myanmar, Laos and China. The GMC was designed to contribute to the development of infrastructure so that members can share their resource bases and promote the freer flow of goods and people in the sub-region. Thailand also played a significant role in the inaugural of the ASEAN Regional

Forum (ARF) in Bangkok in 1994, a security dialogue within ASEAN, as well as the Bay of Bengal Initiative for Multi-Sectoral Technical and Economic Cooperation (BIMSTEC). The BIMSTEC, founded in June 1997 in Bangkok, encompasses Bangladesh, Bhutan, India, Myanmar, Nepal, Sri Lanka, and Thailand. The objectives of BIMSTEC are to create an enabling environment for rapid economic development, accelerate social progress in the sub-region, provide assistance to each other in the form of training and research facilities, cooperate more effectively in joint efforts that are supportive of, and complementary to national development plans of member states, and maintain close and beneficial cooperation with existing international and regional organizations.[40]

From this perspective, Thailand's foreign policy priority seemed to strengthen its regional focus. However, in the bilateral context, while its relations with the United States and China remained relatively stable, Thailand also reached out to its immediate neighbours. Prime Minister Anand introduced development aid to countries in Indochina and also Myanmar in 1992. Subsequently, Thailand established a series of ministerial level joint commissions which included an important economic component and a wide range of commercial agreements with neighbours under the Chavalit and Chuan governments. This was as far as Thai ambition could go. For the most part of the 1990s, political instability, constant changes of government and the outbreak of the financial crisis weakened Bangkok's influence in the regional and international fora. The dream of emerging as a hegemon in Southeast Asia was reduced to becoming one of the region's team players in the aftermath of the economic crisis. But this was not the end road of Thailand's goal-driven diplomacy. The fully-blown globalization, the compulsion of regionalism and the new-fangled conditions of Thai politics in the millennium proved yet again that Thailand's foreign policy could be up for another reinvention. And this time, Thaksin Shinawatra, one of Thailand's most popular prime ministers, pushed Thailand even further than anyone could ever imagine.

CONCLUSION

Thailand's foreign policy objectives have been bald-faced: to maintain national sovereignty and territorial integrity. To achieve this, previous Thai elites espoused several strategies in the conduct of diplomacy, from strict neutrality to overt alliance and opportunism. Along the way, Siam acknowledged the inadequacies of its foreign policy and tried to accommodate with foreign powers in order to keep a satisfactory level of independence in conducting its diplomacy. The accommodation policy is best known as the bending-with-the-wind approach. Its logic was simple — to go with the flow of the wind, to align with hegemons of the day and to use this alliance to strengthen the power position of the Thai elites at home. From Sukhothai, Ayutthaya, Thonburi to Bangkok, Thai monarchs never shied away from playing the game of diplomacy with foreign powers. In searching for their own legitimacy, Thai kings were willing to adopt and adapt to the shifting inter-state conditions while gaining experience from mistakes made by their neighbouring kingdoms in their crude and lackadaisical dealings with the West. Because of this, they have been celebrated for their far-sightedness in the management of the kingdom's foreign relations. But the good judgement of the Thai kings was not the only recipe in the seeming success of Thai diplomacy. Thailand's strategic location proved to be an important factor that augmented its bargaining power with foreigners. Situated at the centre of mainland Southeast Asia, Thailand emerged as a buffer state in the colonial period and a forefront state in the Cold War. Dangerous as it seemed, the situation nevertheless opened the door for Thailand to forge alliances with external powers who could shield the country from the reach of enemies. The pattern of centralized political power in Thailand also played its part in the making of a continued foreign policy, as diplomacy was traditionally left in the hands of the Thai elites, be they the monarchs or military men.

But bending with the wind and consistently looking out for the right opportunities were not always positively perceived by the outside world. Thailand, playing the role of a vulnerable nation, defended its style of diplomacy as part of its surviving tactic. Therefore, at times, Thailand seemed to neglect the element of principle in its foreign policy. In times of war, Siam could only be trusted by the eventual winners, and expect harsh criticism from some of its peace-time friends.[41] Yet, Thailand was proud of its label as an opportunist, especially if this would keep the country out of danger. In modern times, economic interests have occasionally driven Thailand further away from principles.

Opportunism is still applied in the domain of foreign relations even when the international setting has changed. Thaksin, a new face of Thai opportunism, reinvented foreign policy to suit his national economic agenda, even at the expense of principles. Kavi Chongkittavorn, a prominent media commentator, criticized Thaksin's foreign policy:

> With Thaksin Shinawatra as Prime Minister in February 2001, foreign policy decision-making was turned upside-down. From foreign policy driven by the Foreign Ministry in close consultation with elected politicians as well as concerned agencies, it became a one-man show. His centrality in shaping Thai diplomacy was indisputable and nobody dared to raise any objection. He heeded no other voices. Thaksin's former Cabinet members, including former Foreign Minister Surakiart Sathirathai and retired diplomats, have already blown the whistle on Thaksin's malfeasance. Other chief articulators of Thai diplomacy took a secondary role, especially those dealing with national security questions.[42]

From 2001 to 2006, Thailand, under Thaksin, was transformed into a mini-colonialist who ventured out to conquer the region. Profits, rather than principles, were preferred, reminding the current generation of Thai elites of their yesteryears' diplomatic achievements. Thaksin, with all his political confidence, dared to set the direction of the regional wind. But was Thaksin's foreign policy sustainable and realistic? Was his diplomatic ambition a mere illusion that surpassed Thailand's existing limitations? It was certainly a new dawn of Thai diplomacy and a rather exhilarating period of the country's foreign relations. Thaksin may have regulated a new benchmark of expectation as Thailand forged its relations with external powers and its immediate neighbours. But some vital questions remained. Did Thaksin actually find a new post-Cold War foreign policy strategy? Or was it just a mere revisit of an old policy of opportunism that was repainted to cloak the new reality of the twenty-first century?

Notes

1. Thai text quoted in Thamsook Numnonda, *Fyn Adit* [Reconstructing the Past] (Bangkok, 1979), pp. 139–41. Quoted in Paul Kratoska and Ben Batson, "Nationalism and Modernist Reform", *The Cambridge*

History of Southeast Asia: From C.1800 to the 1930s, edited by Nicholas Tarling, vol. 2, part 1 (Cambridge: Cambridge University Press, 1999) p. 295.

2. Anuson Chinvanno, *Thailand's Policies towards China, 1949–1954* (Oxford: St. Anthony's College, 1992), p. 20. Also in Likhit Dhiravegin, *Siam and Colonialism (1855–1909): An Analysis of Diplomatic Relations* (Bangkok: Thai Watana Panich, 1975), pp. 78–79; and, Tej Bunnag, *The Provincial Administration of Siam, 1892–1915: The Ministry of the Interior under Prince Damrong Rajanubhab* (Kuala Lumpur: Oxford University Press, 1977).

3. In comparison to the case of lost territories of Hungary in the aftermath of World War I, the country was shorn of over 72 per cent of the territory it had previously controlled, which left 64 per cent of the inhabitants, including 3.3 million out of 10.7 million (31 per cent) ethnic Hungarians, living outside Hungary. The territory of Hungary was reduced from 325,111 sq km to 93,073 sq km and its population from 20.9 million to 7.6 million. This led to the irredentist policy of the Hungarian government in the post-war period. See George W. White, *Nationalism and Territory: Constructing Group Identity in Southeastern Europe* (Lanham: Rowman and Littlefield Publishers Inc., 2000), p. 102.

4. Thongchai Winichakul, "Preah Vihear can be Time Bomb", *The Nation,* 30 June 2008.

5. Mutiah Alagappa, *The National Security of Developing States: Lessons from Thailand* (Massachusetts: Auburn House Publishing Company, 1987), pp. 242–48. Alagappa purported that according to General Saiyud Kerdphol, Supreme Commander of the Royal Thai Armed Forces (1981–83), territorial integrity, sovereignty, independence, rights and other interests were the core values to be protected under the label of security.

6. Saw Yan Naing, "No Freedom, No Independence", *The Irrawaddy,* 4 January 2008 <http://www.irrawaddy.org/article.php?art_id =9816> (accessed 8 February 2009).

7. D.G.E. Hall, *A History of Southeast Asia* (London: Macmillan, 1955), p. 470.

8. Chula Chakrabongse, *The Twain Have Met, or an Eastern Prince Came West* (London, 1956), pp. 40–41. Quoted in Charivat Santaputra, *Thai Foreign Policy 1932–1946* (Bangkok: Thai Khidi Research Institute, Thammasat University, 1985), pp. 76–77.

9. Ibid.

10. See E. Bruce Reynolds, *Thailand and Japan's Southern Advance, 1940–1945* (New York: St. Martin's Press, 1994).

11. Daniel Fineman, *A Special Relationship: The United States and Military*

Government in Thailand, 1947–1958 (Honolulu: University of Hawaii Press, 1997), pp. 131–46.

12. Kishan S. Rana, *Asian Diplomacy: The Foreign Ministries of China, India, Japan, Singapore and Thailand* (Washington, D.C.: The Johns Hopkins University Press, 2007), p. 137.

13. Suchit Bunbongkarn, "National Security and the Contemporary Political Role of the Thai Military", paper presented at the International Conference on Thai Studies at Chulalongkorn University, Bangkok, 22–24 August 1983, p. 2. Alagappa defined the core values to be protected under the label of national security which includes the monarchy, religion, nation, democracy, regime legitimacy and security, territorial integrity, political independence, and maintenance of a favourable regional environment. In Alagappa, *The National Security of Developing States*, pp. 39–60.

14. John Funston, "Thailand's Ministry of Foreign Affairs: Managing Domestic and Global Turmoil", *International Insights* 14, special issue (1998), p. 67.

15. Ross Prizzia, *Thailand in Transition: The Role of Oppositional Forces* (Hawaii: University of Hawaii Press, 1985), pp. 80–81.

16. Adulyasa Soonthornrojana, "The Rise of U.S.-Thai Relations, 1945–1975" (Ph.D. dissertation, University of Akron, 1986), pp. 6–9. Quoted in Arne Kislenko, "Bending with the Wind: The Continuity and Flexibility of Thai Foreign Policy", *International Journal* (Autumn 2002): 539–40.

17. Likhit also argued that although Siam's geographic location as a buffer zone played an equally important part in preserving the country's independence, the country might have been divided between the French and the British had it not been for the astuteness of the monarchs. In Likhit, *Siam and Colonialism (1855–1909)*, p. 78.

18. Pavin Chachavalpongpun, *A Plastic Nation: The Curse of Thainess in Thai-Burmese Relations* (Lanham: University Press of America, 2005), pp. 35–36.

19. Thongchai Winichakul, *Siam Mapped: A History of the Geo-Body of a Nation* (Hawaii: University of Hawaii Press, 1994), p. 3.

20. Leszek Buszynski, "Thailand's Foreign Policy: Management of a Regional Vision", *Asia Survey* 34, no. 8 (August 1994): 721–22.

21. Reginald le May, *The Culture of Southeast Asia: The Heritage of India* (London: George Allen & Unwin Ltd., 1956), pp. 169–70. Quoted in Likhit, *Siam and Colonialism (1855–1909)*, p. 6.

22. Sarasin Viraphol, *Tribute and Profit: Sino-Siamese Trade, 1652–1853* (Cambridge: Harvard University Press, 1977), p. 1.

23. John K. Fairbank and Teng Ssu-yu, "On the Ch'ing Tributary System", in *Chi'ng Administration: Three Studies*, edited by John K. Fairbank and

Teng Ssu-yu (Cambridge: Harvard University Press, 1968), p. 144. In the study of Sarasin Viraphol, it was shown that King Taksin (of the Taksin Dynasty) had attempted to seek recognition from the Ch'ing court several times. He sent his envoy to China to request investiture from Peking in 1767, but the mission was turned away. Not until 1781 was Peking prepared to recognize Taksin, but unfortunately this was the last year of his reign. In Sarasin, *Tribute and Profit: Sino-Siamese Trade, 1652–1853*, p. 313.

24. See Chris Baker, "Ayutthaya Rising: From Land or Sea?", *Journal of Southeast Asian Studies*, no. 42 (1993): 41–62.

25. R. R. Palmer and Joel Colton, *A History of the Modern World* (New York: Alfred A Knopf, 1965), p. 274.

26. Donald F. Lach and Edwin J. Van Kley, *Asia in the Making of Europe: A Century of Advance*, vol. 3 (Chicago: The University of Chicago Press, 1993), p. 420.

27. David K. Wyatt, *A Short History* (New Haven: Yale University Press, 1984), p. 185.

28. See Kobkua Suwannathat-Pian, *Thailand's Durable Premier: Phibun through Three Decades, 1932–1957* (Kuala Lumpur: Oxford University Press, 1995), Chapter 5. Also see Benjamin Batson, "Siam and Japan: The Perils of Independence", in *Southeast Asia Under the Japanese Occupation*, edited by Alfred W. McCoy (New Haven: Yale University Southeast Asian Studies, 1980).

29. Thak Chaloemtiarana, *Thailand: The Politics of Despotic Paternalism* (Cornell Southeast Asia Publications, 2007), p. 157.

30. Surachai Sirikrai, "Thai-American Relations in the Laotian Crisis of 1960–1962", Ph.D. dissertation, Western Michigan University, 1979, pp. 41–42.

31. Russel H. Fifield, *Southeast Asia in United States Politics* (New York: Frederick A. Praeger, 1963), p. 246.

32. Although Phibun adopted an anti-Chinese attitude, he was forced to compromise with Beijing too. In 1956, he sent his twelve-year-old son to Beijing. He told him, "In the old days, we small nations often sent our rulers' children to China to show our loyalty and devotion to the Emperor... we could once again show to Zhou Enlai our sincere determination to improve relations and our implicit trust in China. No trust could be greater than parting with your own child... it's good to have a little living bridge between our two countries." In Sirin Phathanothai, *The Dragon's Pearl* (New York: Simon & Schuster, 1994), p. 24.

33. See details, Nayan Chanda, *Brother Enemy: The War After the War* (California: Harcourt Brace Jonanovich, 1986).

34. Rana, *Asian Diplomacy*, p. 136.
35. See Sukhumbhand Paribatra, *Beyond Cambodia: Some Thoughts on Southeast Asia in the 1990s* (Bangkok: Institute of Security and International Studies, Chulalongkorn University, 1989).
36. Thitinan Pongsudhirak, "World War II and Thailand after Sixty Years", in *Legacies of World War II: South and East Asia*, edited by David Koh Wee Hock (Singapore: Institute of Southeast Asian Studies, 2007), p. 111.
37. Buszynski, "Thailand's Foreign Policy: Management of a Regional Vision", p. 723.
38. "Thai Foreign Policy: Toward Continued Economic Prosperity," in Ministry of Foreign Affairs, *Thailand Foreign Affairs Newsletter* (August 1998), p. 3. Quoted in Ibid., pp. 723–24.
39. John Funston, "Thai Foreign Policy: Seeking Influence", *Southeast Asian Affairs* (1998): 294–95.
40. Source: <http://www.bimstec.org/about_bimstec.html> (accessed 13 December 2009).
41. See Likhit, *Siam and Colonialism (1855–1909)*.
42. Kavi Chongkittavorn, "Big Shifts Changing the Way Foreign Policy is Made", *The Nation*, 11 August 2008.

3

MAJOR FOREIGN POLICY INITIATIVES
The Making of a Hegemonic Power?

Thailand's foreign policy was under the direct dictation of Prime Minister Thaksin Shinawatra throughout 2001–06. During this period, two foreign ministers, Surakiart Sathirathai and Kantathi Suphamongkhon, were appointed to oversee the country's external affairs and to realize Thaksin's grandiose foreign policy initiatives. Whereas the former is a well-known law professor and Thailand's youngest finance minister (during the Banharn Silpa-archa government, 1995–96), the latter is a former diplomat from a respected family background. Thaksin was one of the few Thai leaders who had a clear mindset on how to express his global ambitions and put forward his foreign policy initiatives, and who also possessed a bold vision on how Thailand should play its role in the international arena. His foreign policy was designed to propel Thailand into the new century where its presence would be firmly felt within and beyond the region, and more importantly, to extend influence on mainland Southeast Asia through his economic diplomacy. It was to prioritize relations and cooperation with Asia by taking an Asian approach. Labelling it the "Forward Engagement Policy", he made known his intention to maintain good ties with neighbouring countries. Under this policy, Thailand also upheld the principle of non-intervention in its neighbours' internal affairs.[1] The evident shortcoming of this policy was that consideration for human rights and democracy seemed to be less emphasized in the conduct of foreign affairs.

Foreign Minister Surakiart made a foreign policy declaration to Parliament on 26 February 2001, underscoring five essential objectives:

1. Conduct foreign policy with an emphasis on proactive economic policy as well as other forms of diplomacy with a view to restoring and strengthening Thailand's international relations as well as seeking international cooperation in all fields.
2. Uphold the principles of security, development and international peace-building with a view to enhancing justice under the framework of the United Nations and related international organizations of which Thailand is a member.
3. Promote a more proactive role for Thailand in the international community by expanding closer international cooperation and relations between ASEAN member countries and countries in East Asia, South Asia and other regions, as well as by acting as a coordinator in pursuing cooperation for peacekeeping and prevention of international conflicts in the region.
4. Promote, preserve and protect the country's rights and national interests including those of Thailand's private sectors, Thai labourers and Thai citizens abroad.
5. Restore and strengthen Thailand's relations and developmental cooperation with its neighbours and other Asian countries expeditiously by pursuing or initiating relations and developmental cooperation in all fields, both bilaterally and multilaterally, with a view to fostering good understanding in resolving problems and sharing mutual benefits in a constructive, sincere and peaceful manner.[2]

The minister's declaration, on the surface, appeared formalistic and was not a reliable guide to foreign policy. It also seemed indifferent from that of previous governments. However, in practice, Thaksin took advantage of the new global setting to endorse an updated policy that was crafted to set the wind of regional politics. The emphasis on rebuilding ties with immediate neighbours, the making of an Asia-for-Asians policy, the weaving of partnership with other regions of the world, and the eagerness to sell the country's new look to the global market were all subsumed in Thaksin's Forward Engagement Policy. The Thai Foreign Ministry further developed the idea with more specific goals which included the promotion of peace, sustaining economic growth, and the development and sharing of prosperity. The philosophy, according to Permanent Secretary Krit Garnjana-Goonchorn, was outward-looking and inclusive. An important principle of Forward Engagement was self-help and self-reliance. The testament of this philosophy was the successful transformation of Thailand from a recipient to a donor country, especially in view of its relations with its neighbours.[3]

Thaksin's new perspective on foreign relations focused on Asia where Thailand found its strength due to its strategic location in the region, while stepping up to play the role of a regional leader.[4] The new millennium gave Asia hope in showcasing itself as a region of great interest to the rest of the world. It possessed great economic dynamism and was fast becoming the world's third most important economic region after the United States and Europe. Japan's position of economic superpower was undeniable. China and India were rising. Alongside these developments, Asia became a place criss-crossed by a number of sub-regional and regional cooperative frameworks working toward a future of sustainable development in the region. Thaksin believed that it was opportune for Thailand to become a driving force for community-building and integration in the Asian region.[5] The strategy here was for Thailand to strengthen and raise Asia's profile and voice in the international arena. However, Thaksin's enthusiasm to lead Asia was criticized by the opposition for his unrealistic foreign policy given the fact that Thailand was a mid-power country, and one among many players in the globalized world that was competing with others to reposition itself in the new international condition. Thaksin thought otherwise, convincing naysayers that the location and the size of the country could be suitably used to complete the national objective.

Thai foreign policy during this period clearly realized a significant change in the way Thailand looked at itself and the world. Firstly, in the past, Thai foreign policy was primarily formulated in response to international environment; this allowed Thailand to tilt toward the global order of the day. Thaksin, however, constructed his foreign policy according to imperative domestic economic and social agendas rather than to the existing international norms. Although his policy was "international" in its outlook, projected through the government's commitment on promoting Asian regionalism, its intrinsic quality was very much "nationalistic" and deemed a "self-serving political tool". The contradiction permeating Thaksin's foreign policy thinking subsequently emerged as the main hindrance in the Thai attempt to rebuild ties with historical enemies in close proximity. The tendency was that they perceived Thai foreign policy as insincere, highly patriotic and exploitative in favouring themselves. Thailand may have become a donor, but also aspired to be a hegemon that sought to fulfil its own interests in its conduct of diplomacy with poorer neighbouring countries.

This nationalistic foreign policy was widely admired by like-minded patriots who expressed their faith in the Thai capability and potential under the leadership of Thaksin in the making of a new Thailand. The self-centred foreign policy, engineered to feed a nationalistic thirst at home, had one clear objective: dominating the region. Foreign Minister Surakiart once said:

> Thailand has invigorated relations with its immediate neighbours which has, in turn, positioned Thailand to play a constructive role in the region. The Prime Minister and I have visited all our neighbours within these past months. We have joined hands in our shared vision with our neighbours to open borders and establish a common production base in Southeast Asia. Thailand is positioning itself to serve as a regional production base for manufacturing and agricultural goods as well as a hub for transportation networks. Indeed, from the meeting and discussions held with our foreign partners, the emerging dynamism of the region is drawing international attention to cooperation opportunities in Thailand and its linkages with the region.[6]

Secondly, Thai foreign policy was not formulated to deal with external military threats — a reminiscence of the Chatichai period. No longer was the focus on the defence of national security. Thaksin readjusted the country's worldview to one which was becoming more commercialized, which was made feasible with the opening up of the world economy. Meanwhile, he accelerated economic reforms at home so that Thailand would be able to keep pace with international changes. Thaksin, as a self-made successful businessman, strongly embraced the free-market economy, albeit selectively, as well as opened channels for mutual insider deals. At the same time, ironically, his Thai Rak Thai government also initially tapped into the nationalist sentiment of the sufficiency economy, a philosophy bestowed by the king of Thailand which promoted a more resilient and sustainable economy, something that seemed to contradict the principle of open capitalism.[7] Thaksin's populist policies succeeded in stimulating significant new growth in the economy. He spent increasing revenue undertaking a number of large-scale infrastructure projects, purportedly to reclaim Thailand's place in the economic world. In the government's policy booklet called "Four Years of Repair for All Thais and Thailand under the Government of Prime Minister Dr Thaksin Shinawatra (2001–2005)", published in 2004, major strategies in the creation of Thailand's strong role in the world's economic arena were spelt out, including the plan to develop land, air and waterway transport networks, and to seek economic opportunities with the FTA.[8]

In many ways, Thaksin emulated a traditional diplomatic approach which compelled the leaders to constantly adjust themselves to the shifting international environment. But Thaksin was not just acclimatizing himself with world conditions. He also initiated a number of high-flying foreign policies. This chapter examines five key foreign policy initiatives under the Thaksin government. They are: the Asia Cooperation Dialogue (ACD), the Ayeyawady–Chao Phraya–Mekong Economic Cooperation Strategy (ACMECS), the bilateral FTAs, the Bangkok Process, and the nomination of the Thai candidate for the position of the United Nations Secretary-General (UNSG). While the first three initiatives specifically underlined Thaksin's economic diplomacy, the Bangkok Process offered a slight hint of Thaksin's affinity of democracy, which supposedly pushed for political reforms in Myanmar. As for the post of the UNSG, Thaksin nominated Foreign Minister Surakiart to compete in the race in order to expand Thailand's profile at the international level which would complement his other foreign policy initiatives. These major foreign policy initiatives showed

Thaksin's determination to plant Thailand at the forefront of global politics. This study argues that, at the United Nations and through the ACD, Thaksin hoped to emerge as the most famous Asian leader, and that through the ACMECS, he set his sights on towering over weaker or poorer neighbours.

THE ASIA COOPERATION DIALOGUE (ACD)

The ACD was Thaksin's greatest attempt to stamp his mark on the country's external affairs. Chatichai only dreamt of turning old enemies in the immediate neighbourhood into trading partners. But Thaksin supersized his country's foreign policy ambition through the ACD in the building of the continent-wide forum, supposedly the first of its kind in Asia, with Thailand at the core of the grouping. This concept was initially raised during the First International Conference of Asian Political Parties held in Manila, from 17–20 September 2000, even before Thaksin became prime minister. Surakiart Sathirathai, deputy leader of Thai Rak Thai Party, floated the idea that Asia as a continent needed its own forum to discuss region-wide cooperation: this subsequently led to competing claims over ownership of the initiative between Thaksin and Surakiart. The idea was further developed during the 34th ASEAN Foreign Ministers' Meeting in Hanoi in July 2001. In June 2002, Thaksin officially declared the launch of the First ACD Ministerial Meeting, materializing his aspiration to constitute the missing link in Asia by incorporating Asian countries into the newly crafted "Asian Community" without duplicating other existing organizations or creating a bloc against others. A key principle was to draw strength from differences and diversity within Asia, and to transform these into gainful factors binding countries in the region together. The ACD's fundamental values were positive thinking, informality, voluntarism, non-institutionalization, openness, respect for diversity and the comfort level of member countries, and the evolving nature of the ACD process.[9] Thaksin said in October 2002 that:

> The ACD is not just a cooperation. The ACD is not just a dialogue. But, simply, the ACD is both a cooperation and a dialogue. It is a capacity-building process based on trade, economic, social and possibly political cooperation dialogues, relying upon the flexibility

and a comfort level of all its participants. Driven by positive thinking, the ACD will be an evolving, informal, and non-institutionalized, open and inclusive process. The ACD, as an Asia-wide forum, will fill in the gap of this continent's "missing link" between existing inter-regional groupings such as APEC and ASEM, and existing sub-regional groupings, such as ASEAN, ASEAN+3 [Cooperation between ASEAN and three East Asian states — China, Japan and South Korea], SAARC [South Asian Association for Regional Cooperation, encompassing Bangladesh, Bhutan, India, Maldives, Nepal, Pakistan and Sri Lanka], BIMSTEC and GCC [Gulf Cooperation Council, a regional common market with a defense planning council of countries in the Arabian Peninsula]. The ACD will create synergy among bilateral, multilateral, sub-regional and regional strategic partnerships in areas of common interests.[10]

The First ACD Ministerial Meeting was organized from 18–19 June 2002 in Cha-am, Thailand. Thaksin boasted that this first meeting was a successful event that had brought together eighteen countries representing the sub-regions of Asia, and provided a venue where they could freely discuss issues of common interest and put forward measures to enhance mutual cooperation in all areas. He also announced that participants considered the ACD as a forum that consolidated political will among Asian governments and offered opportunities for them to develop common approaches to positive issues. The ACD currently consists of thirty countries from East to West Asia. They include eighteen founding members (ASEAN countries — Brunei Darussalam, Cambodia, Indonesia, Laos, Malaysia, Myanmar, Philippines, Singapore, Thailand and Vietnam — plus Bahrain, Bangladesh, China, India, Japan, Republic of Korea, Pakistan and Qatar), four new members in 2003 (Kazakhstan, Kuwait, Oman, Sri Lanka), four more in 2004 (Bhutan, Iran, Mongolia, United Arab Emirates), two more in 2005 (Russia and Saudi Arabia), and two new members in 2006 (Tajikistan and Uzbekistan).[11] New members simply saw the benefit of using the ACD as a new social and economic network at the regional level. The main objectives of the ACD, as stipulated in its official website, are as follows:[12]

1. To promote interdependence among Asian countries in all areas of cooperation by identifying Asia's common strengths and

opportunities which will help reduce poverty and improve the quality of life for Asian people whilst developing a knowledge-based society within Asia and enhancing community and people empowerment.

2. To expand the trade and financial market within Asia and increase the bargaining power of Asian countries in lieu of competition and, in turn, enhance Asia's economic competitiveness in the global market.

3. To serve as the missing link in Asian cooperation by building upon Asia's potentials and strengths through supplementing and complementing existing cooperative frameworks so as to become a viable partner for other regions.

4. To ultimately transform the Asian continent into an Asian Community, capable of interacting with the rest of the world on a more equal footing and contributing more positively towards mutual peace and prosperity.

However, the format and modalities of the ACD are rather unclear. The ACD has been organized at ministerial level, in a retreat style and under informal setting, for the purpose of encouraging free flow of discussions. A possible theme has been put forward by the host to assist participating countries in their preparation for each annual meeting. The ACD is a process where there is no agenda, no assigned speakers, no specific topics and no joint communiqué prepared for and agreed in advance by senior officials. The host only prepares and issues a Chairman's Statement for reference.[13] "Asia Cooperation Dialogue: How to Consolidate Our Strengths?" was the suggested theme of the first historic meeting in Cha-am. One of the outcomes of this meeting was that the ministers agreed to develop two dimensions of the ACD, namely, a dialogue and a project mechanism, covering poverty alleviation, e-commerce, energy security and tourism.[14] The dialogue mechanism was invented to promote interaction and the participation of ACD ministers and government officials. The founding members collectively agreed that a continuous dialogue was imperative in the maintenance of a constant rapport, particularly between ACD policy-makers. Through the project mechanism, countries were encouraged to volunteer themselves as "prime movers" in various areas of cooperation of their choices and interests, and to progress each project for the advantage of the ACD members.

On the dialogue dimension, the ACD ministers have met annually since its inception in 2002. In between, the ACD foreign ministers also get together on the sidelines of the United Nations General Assembly every September in New York to update and inform each other on the progress of the ACD project cooperation. Member countries regard these extra gatherings as a useful avenue to strengthen a sense of familiarity among themselves and to augment the voice of Asia in the global domain. On top of these, the ACD Ambassadorial Retreats in Bangkok, having been held regularly since 2002 and usually chaired by the Foreign Ministry's permanent secretary, have also been designed to promote close consultation among members on a variety of issues of common concerns. Each ACD ministerial meeting delivers new initiatives primarily in response to the changing regional situation. A brief summary of outcomes of the ACD annual meetings is as follows:

1. The first ACD in Cha-am 2002: The inaugural meeting.
2. The second ACD in Chiang Mai in 2003: The launch of the Chiang Mai Declaration on the Asia Bond Market Development.[15]
3. The third ACD in Qingdao in 2004: The adoption of the Declaration on Asia Cooperation and the Qingdao Initiative. The Declaration provides a guideline for future cooperation in all fields among members toward building peace and prosperity in the region, whereas the Qingdao Initiative concentrates on issues of energy security through cooperation in energy-related fields, for instance, infrastructure development, exchange of information, joint exploration, alternative and renewable energies and human resource development.[16]
4. The fourth ACD in Islamabad in 2005: The endorsement of the "Guidelines for Granting the Status of ACD Partner for Development" with the objective of engaging non-ACD members and organizations in joint cooperation with member countries.[17]
5. The fifth ACD in Doha in 2006: The establishment of the ACD Energy Forum and the endorsement of the ACD Energy Action Plan to be drawn up by Indonesia and the Philippines. The ACD Energy Action Plan puts priority on promoting energy security, research and assessment on energy, energy

infrastructure development and encourages member countries to explore the possibility of re-investing revenues that accrue from the energy trade in the ACD countries.[18]
6. The sixth ACD in Seoul in 2007: The Declaration of the Seoul Information Technology (IT). The ACD ministers agreed on promoting IT development among members and addressed the issue of the digital divide in Asia.[19]
7. The seventh ACD in Astana in 2008: The launch of the initiative of Track II (non-official) participation in the ACD process. Ministers welcomed the offer of India and Iran to host the ACD Think-Tanks Network Meeting in 2008 and 2009 respectively.[20]
8. The eighth ACD in Colombo in 2009: Riding on the theme, "Spirit of Asia; Global Economic Recovery and Development Prospects", the ACD Ministers reiterated their commitment to act together to generate strong, sustainable and balanced regional growth, to reform the global governance and financial architecture and to shape regional institutions to meet the challenge of the twenty-first century. The Ministers also paid attention to the ACD Trade and Investment forum that was to be formed to encourage private sector involvement in trade and investment.[21]

Iran recommended itself to host the ninth ACD Ministerial Meeting in 2010. Kuwait will organize the tenth ACD Meeting in 2011, followed by Tajikistan in 2012 and United Arab Emirates in 2013.

Through the project mechanism, ACD members have expressed their interest and volunteered to perform as "prime movers" in the selected nineteen areas of cooperation deemed most suitable for their expertise. Ministers claimed that, for practical reasons, project cooperation should proceed on a voluntary basis and did not require a consensus from ACD countries. Details of areas of cooperation and prime movers appear in Table 3.1.

To a certain extent, in the beginning, the ACD countries demonstrated their enthusiastic participation either as prime movers or co-prime movers, while hoping to transmit their best practices to other members. For example, China was a keen prime mover in the area of agriculture and therefore played host to four activities, including the ACD Agricultural Policies Forum, held in

TABLE 3.1
Areas of Cooperation and Prime Movers of the ACD

Areas of Cooperation	Prime Movers and Co-Prime Movers
1. Energy	Bahrain, Indonesia, Kazakhstan, Qatar, China and the Philippines
2. Poverty Alleviation	Bangladesh, Cambodia and Vietnam
3. Agriculture	China, Pakistan and Kazakhstan
4. Transport Linkages	India, Kazakhstan and Myanmar
5. Biotechnology	India
6. E-Commerce	Malaysia
7. Infrastructure Fund	Malaysia
8. E-Education	Malaysia
9. Asian Institute of Standards	Pakistan
10. SMEs Cooperation	Singapore and Sri Lanka
11. IT Development	Republic of Korea
12. Science and Technology	The Philippines
13. Tourism	Thailand, Cambodia, Myanmar and Pakistan
14. Financial Cooperation	Thailand
15. Human Resources Development	Vietnam and Thailand
16. Environmental Education	Japan and Qatar
17. Strengthening Legal Infrastructure	Japan
18. Road Safety	Oman
19. Natural Disasters	Russia

Beijing from 10–12 January 2005. The meeting focused on the exchange of views and experience on agricultural policies, and the participants agreed that each would become agricultural movers for a specialized product based on their advantages. Each would also pay greater attention to future policies in facilitating trade of agricultural products among ACD members. This determination was reaffirmed during the ACD Agricultural Officials' Seminar in Beijing on 16–25 October 2006, where members shared experience on ways to expand cooperation in the area of strategic agricultural management, animal husbandry, rural economic development and agricultural information technology development. In the meantime, Japan stepped up to play a pivotal role in the area of environmental education. It already hosted three workshops on environmental education and was willing to pass on its best practices in the study of green production and green life. Foreign Minister Surakiart claimed that the available platform of the ACD allowed member countries to work closely despite bilateral conflicts at the national level.[22]

The members, particularly Thailand as a founder, attempted to keep the ACD process alive and relevant, therefore promoted new areas of cooperation that closely reflected the current regional and global situation. As the world had been encountering a shortage of energy resources in recent years, the ACD devoted more time to consultations among members looking at ways to cope with the foreseeable energy crisis. Bahrain, the Philippines, Indonesia and Kazakhstan all took turns to host the energy forum in order to highlight the importance of energy in supporting economic development and industrialization in Asia. They were aware that the ACD was composed of some of the world's major oil producers and consumers and that presented great potential to cooperate in this area.[23] A call for urgent financial cooperation, another relevant area of collaboration, was a result of the economic recession that was felt worldwide. Thailand, which suffered greatly from the 1997 crisis and thus proposed the idea of creating the Asian Bond Market in 2003, continues to campaign for the necessity of the ACD countries to ensure an environment conducive to developing Asian bond markets, especially in time of the current global economic downturn.

Asian Bond Market

During the Second ACD Ministerial Meeting in Chiang Mai in June 2003, Thaksin proposed yet another highly ambitious initiative in the area of financial cooperation through the "Chiang Mai Declaration on Asia Bond Market Development". Thaksin sold his idea of pooling financial resources among Asians in the so-called Asian Bond Market, designed to build financial stability for Asia with a more balanced financial infrastructure, thereby diversifying the risk of intermediation across a large number of institutions and market players. It was also to offer an additional source of funds, instead of being tied solely to borrowing from international financial institutions. In Thailand's Concept Paper on Asian (Regional) Bond Market Development, it states a regional financial cooperation is needed because:

1. The lack of sufficiently developed bond markets in the region has been constantly mentioned as one of the major causes leading to the 1997 financial crisis. From past experience in the region, immature debt and capital markets, to a certain extent, forced investors/borrowers to rely upon funds from external sources, in particular short-term borrowing.
2. Short-term borrowing could be destabilizing since it could lead to capital account reversals that would leave fund-receiving economies vulnerable, thanks to heavily fluctuating capital flows. Therefore, developing efficient bond markets in the region is seen to be not only a sufficient but also a necessary condition to promote a sound and stable macroeconomic environment.
3. In addition, Asian economies have accumulated substantial amount of wealth in terms of collective international reserves and a large portion of those reserves would normally be invested outside the continent. Establishing a sound and efficient Asian bond market could provide alternatives for investment of Asian economies.
4. Therefore, development of deep and liquid bond markets should be viewed as not only an enhancement to the financial development process within the continent but also a further step to promoting more integrated financial cooperation among Asian economies.[24]

Michael K. Connors argued that the Asian Bond represented an element of the Thaksin regime's response to the Asian financial crisis. Thaksin's key objective in the ACD was to ensure the materialization of an efficient Asian Bond Market in order to diminish the region's dependence on international capital flows, and to reduce the resulting vulnerability. There was no doubt that this raised a modest challenge to the region's heavy investment in U.S. bonds. Yet, for the bond market to be successful, it would have to offer the security of Western bond markets. Thus, the governance of banks and financial markets would need to undergo significant reforms in terms already desired by international markets and international financial institutions.[25] Thaksin himself reasoned that Asia possessed more than half of the world reserves which had been deposited outside Asia. Through the establishment of the Asian Bond Market, some of those reserves could be deposited in Asia and serve as financial resource to facilitate regional trade and investment. Asia's foreign reserves would contribute towards its own regional prosperity instead of being deposited and used as capital outside the region.[26]

The member countries of ASEAN+3 jointly adopted the "Chiang Mai Initiative", the first major regional financing agreement, in May 2000. The agreement strongly supported bilateral swap agreements among the member countries to pre-empt liquidity shortages and other significant financial distress in the region. It provided a much-needed boost to countries seeking region-wide swap agreements, and as of October 2003, there were thirteen swap agreements totalling approximately US$32.5 billion, or around double the number and amount before the agreement.[27] Along with these efforts, a number of specific steps designed to expand both demand and supply in the Asian Bond Market have been in the works as a way to further strengthen financial cooperation among the Asian countries. To stimulate demand, the first Asian Bond Fund was launched on 2 June 2003 by the Executive's Meeting of East Asia Pacific Central Banks (EMEAP), resulted in the pooling of reserves to establish a US$1 billion regional bond market.[28] Moreover, efforts have been underway to build a framework that can be used to support and stimulate the local bond markets throughout the region and promote cross-border trading of local currency bonds. Various studies on the feasibility of introducing a regional currency are also in the works. Studies on improving the market and institutional infrastructure for Asia's bond markets, such as proposals on pooling the region's corporate bonds and securitizing them, harmonizing the region's accounting standards, foreign exchange trading, and new settlement systems, are also gaining attention.[29] Prime Minister Thaksin claimed that the ACD provided the backbone needed to ensure that it earned the firm political support of Asian leaders for the continuation of the Asian Bond Market. He even proposed, through the Asia-Europe Meeting (ASEM) forum, the creation of a Task Force for Closer Economic

Partnership with special emphasis on the Asian-Euro Bonds linkage, the creation of a Euro Bond Market in Asia and the use of the euro as a major currency in the region—all moves that would reduce Asian vulnerability from dollar-denominated debt instruments. He saw that the use of the euro as a reserve currency and as a means of transaction in Asian financial and commercial markets would enable Europe to make a greater contribution to the development of Asia's new financial architecture, provide confidence and financial security by spreading the risks from sudden shocks.[30]

Merits and Deficiencies

Thaksin claimed that the ACD was a venue that offered a high comfort level for Asian leaders to meet on a regular basis, to get acquainted with one another, and to discuss positive approaches to potential areas of cooperation, especially economic dimensions. As a businessman, Thaksin projected ACD as a forum that would create synergy within Asia, which involved a greater flow of trade, investment, tourism, and manpower resources, and a greater utilization of modern telecommunications technology. Asian nations could make use of ACD in the interactions with the rest of the world on a more equal stance — a clear tint of Thaksin's endorsement of Asian regionalism. A stress-free ACD encourages positive cooperation and expression of views on how to consolidate Asia's strengths. In the meantime, member countries were not led to expect too much from the ACD, knowing that it was not structured to resolve outstanding conflicts in the region. The ACD was a mere forum for strengthening economic cooperation among its leaders.

Today, cooperation in non-contentious areas, such as in the field of finance, has progressed adequately despite ACD's waning momentum. With the intensifying economic recession in 2008 and 2009, cooperation in the framework of the Chiang Mai Initiative could prove valuable and beneficial in the collective response among member countries to the turmoil of global financial markets. Thailand, under the government of Somchai Wongsawat, sought to transform its bilateral agreements with ASEAN members plus three East Asian countries — Japan, South Korea and China — into a multilateral one, through the creation of a pool of reserves for an emergency credit line. This would allow members to borrow during times of abrupt massive capital outflows.[31] In the past few years since Thaksin was ousted from power, ACD activities have been few. In 2008, besides the Seventh ACD Ministerial Meeting in Astana, there were only two organized workshops; one was the ACD Workshop on Climate Change: Negotiating the Kyoto Landscape, hosted by Malaysia on 20–22 October, and the other was the Conference on Energy and Climate Change: Challenges and Opportunities, held in Bahrain on 26–27 November. In 2009, Sri Lanka played host to the ACD Ministerial Breakfast Meeting on the sidelines of the 64th United Nations General Assembly on 28 September in New York, and the Eighth ACD Ministerial Meeting in Colombo on 14–15 October; there were no other ACD activities throughout the whole year. Since Thaksin personalized foreign policy and since the ACD was purely perceived by critics as a promotional product of Thaksin's diplomatic ambitions, subsequent governments, especially those in the anti-Thaksin faction, have been disinclined to follow up the works and activities of this cooperative framework. They felt that continuing the ACD activities would have added legitimacy to Thaksin's foreign policy. This explains why the ACD is currently being left in a rather neglected state, especially as long as the Democrat Party remains in power.

Thaksin declared that the ACD was a symbol of his foreign policy success, and that it enhanced Thailand's role in the eyes of the world community and foreign investors. The Thai leadership was recognized in the ability of the Thai leaders to ride on the regional wind. In the meantime, Thailand made use of the ACD to deepen its friendship with old and new partners in Asia, a strategy that paved the way for the penetration of Thai products into these markets. It also utilized the ACD's project dimension to further develop the country's human resources, supposedly uplifting the standard of living of Thais, as much as that of their Asian fellows, and boost Thailand's potential in the increasingly competitive world. The works of the ACD also complemented Thaksin's other foreign policy initiatives, such as the ACMECS, in that the ACD strove toward building a more concrete sense of an Asian community. The picture of a pan-Asia network of cooperation, led by Thailand, was thus more tangible.[32] But does Thaksin's self-declaration of success tell the whole story behind the creation of the ACD?

As earlier mentioned, there were competing claims of ownership of the ACD. While Thaksin took credit for his self-proclaimed success of the ACD, Surakiart was believed to be the real driver behind this cooperative framework. In an interview with Surakiart, he revealed that the ACD idea stemmed from his renewed understanding of the shift of global order. Asia, at the turn of the century, was a fragmented region. Surakiart spotted an opportunity for Thailand to change in this new regional setting. As the ACD was in the making, Surakiart began lobbying for Thai neighbours' consent, including ASEAN members and in particular the CLMV (Cambodia, Laos, Myanmar, Vietnam) countries, and two Asian giants — China and India. His efforts in persuading some Asian heavyweights to embark on the Thai-initiated ACD, in Surakiart's views, was the main reason behind the success of its inaugural meeting. Today, despite being no longer in power, Surakiart strongly defends the ongoing ACD activities, and believes that ACD members are still enthusiastic about their annual meeting and other smaller-scale gatherings throughout the year. Surakiart admitted that the ACD process might eventually be forced to become less active because of Thailand's domestic situation, but the kingdom, as the founder and leader on mainland Southeast Asia, must not become passive in its diplomatic operation. Passivity would only diminish the strength of Thai diplomacy.[33]

To a certain extent, the ACD did catch international attention. But the question of whether it actually helped facilitate the progress of regional cooperation has become a continuing debate among Thai scholars, the Thai public, as well as international observers. Surakiart stood up for the ACD, perceiving it as a non-institutionalized forum that provided room for members to sit together and to discuss issues in a constructive way with a high comfort level, without having to worry about political animosity or existing conflicts. For example, the ACD presented an avenue for India and Pakistan to participate and engage with each other; and hopefully this could have led the way in improvements in their relationship.[34] But critics pointed out weaknesses of the ACD, particularly the lack of organizational structure and in upholding the principles of "no agenda", "no politics" and "no critical dialogue". Thaksin's vision of an apolitical ACD meant that the more important issues that had in the first place kept Asia apart have remained untouched, ranging from the India-Pakistan powder keg, nuclear proliferation on the Korean Peninsula and the spread of the Al-Qaeda terrorism threat in the region. So far, the ACD has issued general, unadorned statements. Khien Theeravit, one of Thailand's well-known scholars, cautioned, "Thailand does not need to spend millions of taxpayers' baht on a dialogue that has no clear objective and overlaps existing regional mechanisms. Fine, we can take it for granted that everybody likes to have cooperation, but what kind of cooperation, and how, to make it benefit all?"[35] The lack of a clear objective was one of the main reasons behind the diminishing role of the ACD, making it another "talking shop" of the region. Thaksin's diplomatic ambition was therefore called into question.

Analytically, Thaksin's policy on ACD was unsustainable because it revealed the hypocrisy of his kind of diplomacy. While Thaksin was promoting the ACD and his foreign policy reputation on the basis of international meetings and cooperation, he continued to complain about the United Nations' interference in Myanmar's domestic politics. His embrace of regionalism was only a rhetorical device addressed to the international community. Moreover, from a broader point of view, critics also had reservations about the wider eligibility of Thailand as a leader. Thailand, under Thaksin, with its shaky medium stature in international politics, poor rating in transparency, and limited press freedoms, was indeed struggling in playing a proponent of a venture that required strong and accountable leadership.[36] In reality, the initiative of the ACD was too commerce-driven in trying to bolster Thailand's position to optimize the climate for advancing business interests and Thaksin's personal drive on the world stage. The Thaksinization of the ACD therefore served short-term interests. Today, the burning spirit within the ACD is fading. First, its founding father, Thaksin, is a fugitive from Thai law. Second, the current and future anti-Thaksin governments are likely to reject his foreign policy initiative. Due to the domestic political condition, they are expected to re-prioritize the foreign policy agenda so as to justify themselves and to delegitimize Thaksin and his diplomatic content. Third, it seemed that the ACD members thus far appeared to pay lip service to diplomatic courtesy more than to strive for clear, common objectives, particularly with the lack of their political will.[37] Those who have retained their active participation in the process have been the ones in the region's periphery. They have occasionally taken advantage of the forum to put in an appearance on the regional scene.

As a consequence, the ACD has been left, since the departure of Thaksin and the Thai Rak Thai government in 2006, largely unattended. A few examples affirm its waning state. The official website of the ACD, <www.acddialogue.com>, is far from being up-to-date. The first and last ACD E-News were released in June and September 2007, respectively. The availability of key documents is scant. The Thai Foreign Ministry's official website on the ACD was last updated on 22 June 2005, even before Thaksin was removed from power. The ACD weblink has also been removed from the front page of the Thai Foreign Ministry's website. The lack of interest in the ACD has not only been felt in Thailand. It is reported that the Thai Foreign Ministry has to work extremely hard in convincing and lobbying ACD members to send representatives to attend some of its many meetings. Some meetings had to be postponed or even cancelled because of insufficient participants.[38]

THE AYEYAWADY-CHAO PHRAYA-MEKONG ECONOMIC COOPERATION STRATEGY (ACMECS)

When ASEAN leaders met at the ASEAN Plus China SARS Summit in Bangkok, I raised my concern with the three other leaders (Myanmar, Cambodia and Laos). I was glad that they shared my concern and were in agreement that the economic disparity between Thailand and her three immediate neighbouring countries must be quickly redressed. In August, the foreign ministries of the four countries met in Bangkok for the Economic Cooperation Strategy (ECS). I want the ECS to be a capacity-building initiative. The ECS should create more competitive potential, more work, more productivity, and more income. I want to see it help reduce poverty and produce sustainable development for our three neighbours.[39]

Thaksin declared the above at the ASEAN Business and Investment Summit in Indonesia in October 2003. The ECS was later rebranded "the Ayeyawady-Chao Phraya-Mekong Economic Cooperation Strategy" or ACMECS, named after the major rivers of continental Southeast Asia. The original ECS was instigated by Thaksin on the sidelines of the Special ASEAN Meeting on Severe Acute Respiratory Syndrome (SARS) between ASEAN and China in Bangkok on 29 April 2003. Thaksin envisaged the ECS as a means to narrow the economic gap between Thailand and its three neighbouring countries, to promote prosperity among them in a sustainable manner, and to complement other sub-regional efforts toward

ASEAN integration, based on the intent of building a bloc and moving ASEAN forward at a more even pace. The ECS approach stressed the need to build on comparative advantage and complementarities, and practical projects that could be quickly and efficiently implemented in such area as trade and investment, agriculture and industry, transportation linkages, tourism and human resource development.[40] Thaksin's proposal at the ASEAN SARS Summit paved the way for the meeting, in Bangkok on 1 August 2003, among foreign ministers of Thailand, Myanmar, Laos and Cambodia to discuss the concept of ECS. At this meeting, the four countries agreed to launch their first summit, which was to be hosted by Myanmar in Bagan on 12 November 2003.

At the Bagan Summit, leaders of Thailand, Myanmar, Laos and Cambodia adopted the Bagan Declaration, affirming their commitment to cooperate in five priority areas of cooperation, and endorsed the Economic Cooperation Strategy Plan of Action, under which 46 common projects and 224 bilateral projects were listed for implementation over the next ten years. The leaders also agreed to call this newly created economic cooperation framework ACMECS to give a fresh start to the process.[41] Meanwhile, the principles of ACMECS were pronounced: self-help and partnership as the ultimate objective to achieve sustainable development, including poverty reduction, in line with the United Nations Millennium Development Goals. ACMECS's objectives include:

1. To increase competitiveness and generate greater growth along the borders;
2. To facilitate relocation of agricultural and manufacturing industries to areas with comparative advantage;
3. To create employment opportunities and reduce income disparity among the four countries;
4. To enhance peace, stability and shared prosperity for all in a sustainable manner.[42]

In sum, ACMECS, as claimed by member countries, acts as a catalyst to build upon existing regional cooperation programmes and harmonize bilateral frameworks with a view to transforming the border areas of the member countries into zones of economic growth, for social progress and prosperity, and to blend local, national and regional interests for common benefits, shared prosperity, enhanced solidarity, peace, stability and good neighbourliness. ACMECS's activities are designed to be deliverable with tangible results, utilizing the comparative advantages of each country feasible and acceptable to the countries concerned, and undertaken on the basis of voluntarism, consensus, and equitable sharing of benefits. Vietnam joined ACMECS on 10 May 2004. Hanoi declared that it wanted to join hands with other ACMECS members in strengthening and expanding cooperation, friendship and solidarity at this sub-regional level.[43] A less formal reason, however, could have been that Vietnam's move was to counterbalance the Thai influence, through ACMECS, over Cambodia and Laos.

The initial five priority areas of cooperation, and one additional area, include:[44]

1. Trade and Investment Facilitation:
   - To capitalize on the comparative advantage of the countries concerned
   - To facilitate smooth flow of goods and investment for job creation
   - To create income generation and reduce socioeconomic disparities.
2. Agricultural and Industrial Cooperation:
   - To strengthen and enhance cooperation efforts in agriculture and industry by establishing and improving infrastructure facilities, joint production, marketing and purchasing arrangements, research and development and exchange of information.
3. Transport Linkages:
   - To develop and utilize transport linkages among the countries concerned
   - To facilitate trade, investment, agriculture and industrial production and tourism.
4. Tourism Cooperation:
   - To promote a joint strategy for tourism cooperation among the countries concerned
   - To facilitate tourism among member countries and from the other regions.
5. Human Resources Development:
   - To enhance capacity building of peoples and institutions
   - To initiate measures to develop a HRD strategy that is regionally competitive.

6. Public Health: (ACMECS Foreign Ministers' Meeting in Siem Reap on 5 August 2005 agreed to establish a public health sector as a new area of cooperation.)
   - To promote research and development and enhance capacity-building on public health issues.

ACMECS adopted the view that each member should volunteer to serve as coordinator in its chosen preferential areas in order to ensure satisfactory progress. In this process, all agreed to establish a working group for each sector of cooperation. Thailand volunteered to be in charge of trade and investment facilitation, and public health areas. Myanmar is responsible for agricultural and industrial cooperation. Laos oversees the transport linkages sector. Cambodia manages the area of tourism cooperation. Vietnam has put itself up to lead the human resources development field. Details of existing projects appear in Table 3.2.[45]

A Hegemonic Thailand in the Making?

Thaksin trumpeted his commitment to working closely with ACMECS neighbours in making the best use of each other's strengths and resources to enhance prosperity and stability of the peoples of the member countries. With his commitment, Thaksin offered the members technical and financial assistance through multilateral and bilateral projects under ACMECS, such as his support for early development of sister cities to connect border towns through transportation linkages and the establishment of special border economic zones. Thaksin also recognized external participation as a crucial aspect of a successful ACMECS through the exchange of expertise and resources. This allowed development partners outside the region and international organizations to contribute their technical cooperation and financial support to selected ACMECS programmes, for example, to improve transportation and telecommunication of ACMECS countries. So far, Australia, New Zealand, France, Germany, Japan and the Asian Development Bank (ADB) have shown their interest in working with ACMECS. The first meeting between ACMECS and development partners was held in Krabi, Thailand, on 1–2 November 2004.[46]

ACMECS was Thaksin's top agenda during his second term in office. This was reflected in his foreign policy statement submitted

TABLE 3.2
ACMECS's Existing Projects

Name	Section
Aviation Sector Policy Development Project	Transport/Aviation Sector
Building GIS Linkage for ACMECS Industrial Development	Industrial
Concept Paper on Fruit Tree Development Centre Project in the Northern Provinces of Cambodia	Agricultural
Concept Paper on Savannakhet Technical School Development Project	Education
Development of Road Linkages under Asian Highway (AH) Project (border area and cities along the AH or economic corridors)	Transport Linkages
Establishment of a Mechanism to Facilitate the Transfer of Standardised Production Technology	Agriculture and Industry
Establishment of a Knowledge Base on International Standards for Industrial Manufacturers in Neighbouring Countries under ACMECS	Agriculture and Industry
Establishment of Wholesale and Distribution Centre in Cambodia, Lao PDR and Myanmar	Trade and Investment
Exploration of Market Opportunities for Key Agricultural Products	Agriculture and Industry
Feasibility Study of Additional Routes and Corridors among CLMTV and Nearby Countries (or Inter-corridor Linkages)	Transport Linkages
Feasibility Study of the Cross-country Movement of Tourist Cars among ACMECS Countries	Transport Linkages
Feasibility Study of the Establishment of Road Links among Vietnam–Lao PDR–Myanmar	Transport Linkages

Feasibility Study on Cooperation in Agriculture, Particularly Cash Crops and Livestock	Agriculture and Industry
Feasibility Study on Eco-tourism and Cultural/Historical Tourism for ACMECS Tourism Industry	Tourism
Feasibility Study on the Rehabilitation of NR78 from Banlung (Ratanakiri) to O Pong Moan (Stung Treng)	Transport Linkages
Formulation of an Arrangement between and among the Governments of Five Member Countries on the Admittance of Tourism Vehicles	Transport, Tourism, Customs, Immigration, Quarantine, etc.
Human Resource Development to Support Koh-Kong Industrial Estate	Human Resource Development
Mondulkiri, Preah Vihear and Battambang Airport Upgrading and Improvement Project	Transport/Air Transport (Aviation)
One-Stop Service Arrangement at Border Gate of CLMTV Countries	Trade and Investment
Study on Facilitation of Cross Border Movements of Goods and Passengers among Laos PDR, Myanmar and Vietnam on the Route: Yangon–Meikhtila–Tarlay–Kenglap (Myanmar)–Kengkoc–Loungnamtha–Oudomxay–Deptaechang (Laos PDR)–Tay Trang–Hanoi (Vietnam)	Transport, Customs, Immigration, Quarantine
Study on Promotion of Para Rubber-based Industrial Cooperation between Thailand and Cambodia	Industry
The Setting-up of a Training Centre for Waterway Navigation Skills for the Five ACMECS Countries	Human Resource Development
Training on Enhancing the Competitiveness of the Industrial Development Planning Process of ACMECS Member Countries	Human Resource Development
Transfer of Technology and Technical Know-how of Industry (HRD)	Human Resource Development
Upgrade Inland Waterway College No. 2 into a Training Centre for Five ACMECS Countries	Transport/Inland Waterway Transport

to Parliament in March 2005. The statement attached great importance to ACMECS, being taken on as the country's flag-bearer. ACMECS replaced ASEAN as the first priority of the Thaksin administration, evident in the increasing activities within ACMECS mostly spearheaded by Thailand. Thaksin's reprioritization of the foreign policy agenda was understandable. First and foremost, Thailand's primary interest was closely intertwined with the nature of its relations with immediate neighbours. After all, Thailand shares lengthy borders with them, and at these border zones were significant economic interests as well as difficulties with regard to national security. The ACMECS, for this purpose, served as a venue for Thailand to refamiliarize itself with nearby leaders. But Thaksin aimed much higher than simply getting to know them better. He claimed to use ACMECS to build mutual trust, confidence and understanding. Past relations between Thailand and the three immediate neighbours, namely Myanmar, Cambodia and Laos, were marked by suspicion, animosity and sometimes, hatred; this stemmed from distorted history, at least on Thailand's part and the unfinished Thai nation-building process that allowed endless constructions of the faces of the enemy so that rigid regimes at home could always maintain their political legitimacy. For Thaksin, it was time to mend the negative image of these neighbours. From foes to friends and from battlefields to marketplaces, a new Thailand under Thaksin ventured into a mission of sowing the seeds of friendship, hoping that better relationships would erase existing suspicions and enmity.

Trust-building was not the only goal in Thaksin's new foreign policy design. He transformed ACMECS into a mechanism that sought to bridge the economic and development gap long obstructing the progress of the region as a whole. The Thai Foreign Ministry explained this attempt in terms of Thailand practising the "prosper thy neighbour" policy via ACMECS, based on the encouragement for capacity-building to increase competitiveness and stimulate growth in the CLMV countries. ACMECS fitted in perfectly with Thaksin's foreign policy tagline of "Forward Engagement" which also advocated the principle of partnership. The economic disparity between Thailand and the three immediate neighbours was indeed stark. Statistically speaking, the GDP of these three countries combined accounted for only 9 per cent, while Thailand alone made up 91 per cent when totalled together. From the viewpoint of Thailand's national interest, the thrust for faster economic development in the CLMV countries was part of fulfilling Thailand's own economic growth. It was a win-win formula: the neighbours would not be left neglected and at the same time, Thailand could take advantage from more prosperous neighbours to feed its own economic insatiability. Furthermore, by painting them as countries in need of Thai help and sympathy, it automatically raised Thailand's image as a benevolent and open-handed nation — the image that was crafted by Thaksin. A crucial question is whether Thailand could strike a balance between offering a helping hand to its neighbours and exploiting them. Also, how did the Thai leaders compromise between securing national interests and their own businesses in their conduct of diplomacy vis-à-vis their neighbours?

Thaksin revisited the vision of creating a *suvarnabhumi* dominated by the Thai state over its neighbouring countries.[47] The logic behind the "golden land" policy was to create a pan-Thai domination of mainland Southeast Asia. This sentiment and ambition were clearly subsumed under Thaksin's ACMECS — a reminiscence of the Chatichai period and of Phibun's attempt to restore the old parts of the Siamese kingdom.[48] For example, Thaksin set up a Bt10 billion fund for soft loans and grant aid package to be extended to the CLMV countries. But Thailand's financial assistance came with strings attached. Thaksin's soft loans and aid packages that were offered required procurement contracts to be signed with Thai firms and the currency of exchange was to be in Thai baht. Unmistakably, Thaksin was constructing a baht zone, using financial obligation to control Thai neighbours in the name of ACMECS.[49] Thaksin, during the Annual Ambassadorial Meeting in Bangkok on 27 August 2003, officially inaugurated his baht zone policy vis-à-vis immediate neighbours, and stated that Thailand would from then on offer its soft loans and financial aid in the Thai currency, not the American dollar.[50]

While ACMECS's success was in the making, Thailand's hegemonization of the region was already set. From 2003 onwards, not only did Thaksin found his own baht-dominated "kingdom", he also flooded the neighbouring markets with Thai OTOP products. The compulsion to find more markets for Thai manufacturers, especially in nearby economies, yielded an optimistic reaction to the Thaksin regime and an upbeat attitude towards his ACMECS initiative. For once, there seemed to be nothing wrong with a hegemonic Thailand exercising its power over neighbouring countries. It seemed as if Thaksin was fulfilling his duty in assuring national interest. The name of the mythical *suvarnabhumi* was purposely selected to showcase Thailand's present-day economic might in the face of poorer neighbours, to empower them with cash, and to establish itself as the centre of modern civilization, as manifested by the ultra-modernist Suvarnabhumi International Airport. Thaksin seemed to be on the path of elevating himself as another great leader who made Siam/ Thailand a hegemonic kingdom.

The Donor Image Relished

In 2001, Thaksin arrived in power with a new determination. He declared that his government would not shut the door before foreigners, but would stress more on self-reliance and make Thailand an honoured member of the international community. Thaksin said, "The international assistance is mutual and every nation is independent, so interference into other countries' internal affairs under the name of aid cannot be accepted. Thailand will accept foreign aid, but it will not be totally obedient to foreign donors."[51] Obviously, Thaksin was never short of nationalistic tricks. By standing up to the seemingly premeditated aims of foreign donors, Thaksin won general support from the Thai public for safeguarding the dignity of Thailand in the international arena. Thaksin's arrogant attitude won him more political support at home.

Not long after the Forward Engagement Policy was made public, Thaksin, in 2005, relished Thailand's latest image reinvention. He transformed Thailand from a recipient country into a donor country and took every opportunity to stress this principle in relations with neighbouring countries. The donor status, first achieved in 1992 during the Anand government, reiterated Thailand's commitment to its principle of self-reliance and burning desire to raise its regional profile. Prior to the second ACMECS summit in Bangkok in November 2005, Thaksin declared that Thailand would from then on decline donations from overseas, although in reality, the country still remained a major recipient of Japanese aid throughout the Thai Rak Thai government. He also pledged to work to help less developed countries (LDCs) in the immediate neighbourhood. The term LDCs was used for the first time to refer specifically to Laos, Cambodia and Myanmar. The LDCs became the recipients of Thai development assistance. This categorization in itself legitimized Thaksin's ACMECS and his remaking of Thailand as a donor country. Such reposition could perhaps mark a significant departure from Thailand's past foreign policy which could sometime be constrained by its unequal relations with foreign donors. ACMECS was a platform for Thailand to perform a newly-reinvented role through its financial contribution of considerable sums. The baht diplomacy was then put in place.

Immediately, the United Nations Development Programme (UNDP) issued a statement that praised Thaksin's efforts in assisting poorer neighbours.[52] It commended Thailand for seriously striving to achieve the Millennium Development Goals and even encouraging its neighbours to meet the same success. In the Foreign Ministry's report, it claimed, albeit doubtfully, that Thailand from 2001 to 2006 contributed as big a proportion of its revenue to international assistance as did the world's largest economies, including Australia, Japan and the United States. For example, in 2003, Thailand's Official Development Assistance (ODA) was estimated at US$167 million, or 0.13 per cent of the country's Gross National Income (GNI). Most of Thailand's ODA was in support of basic infrastructure development in Cambodia, Laos and Myanmar, such as the construction of roads, bridges, dams and power stations. The remainder was for technical assistance and training in the areas of education, public health, agriculture, transportation, economics, banking, finance, and science and technology.[53] As a donor, Thailand also aimed at opening up its market for imports from the LDCs. Imports from the LDCs made up 3.1 per cent of its total imports — more than any other middle-income country and more than any country in the Organization of Economic Cooperation and Development (OECD). Thailand gave LDCs favourable trade preferences on agricultural imports. Among developing countries in the region, Thailand has some of the lowest trade-weighted tariffs on imports from LDCs.[54] Moreover, Thailand's investments in the LDCs have been sizeable. It had been the largest investor in Laos accounting for about 42 per cent of total foreign direct investment during the Thaksin years. It has imported a huge amount of Myanmar's gas. The gas exports to Thailand increased from US$114.2 million in 2000 to US$1,497.4 million in 2005 and accounted for more than 80 per cent of Myanmar's exports to Thailand in 2005.[55] The kingdom has also ranked sixth in the amount of foreign investment in Cambodia. Thailand emerged as a model for developing countries. The Thai Foreign Ministry further refined ACMECS to become a platform that enabled member countries to receive financial and technical know-how and at the same time utilize their strengths and promote balanced development. ACMECS also acted as a vehicle that increased the competitiveness among members in agricultural and manufacturing industries. This in turn would create employment opportunities and reduce income disparity in the future.[56]

Perfections and Flaws

Foreign Minister Surakiart believed that trust-building was the most important contribution of ACMECS to regional peace and security. ACMECS was meant to expunge lingering suspicions between Thailand and its neighbours. Ironically, this also contradicted the leaders' intention to use ACMECS to expand the Thai influence in the immediate neighbourhood. In the past, careless expressions of Thai opinions regarding its immediate neighbours, as repeated in the local media, were the root cause of mistrust. On top of this, Surakiart also criticized Thai businesses for exploiting these resources-rich nations for their own self interests without sincerely helping them overcome economic hardship. On the part of the Thai state, previous governments used promises to gain short-term benefits but soon forgot them because of a lack of continued interest. For example, in the post-Chatichai period, the concept of marketplace seemed to quickly disappear. To regain trust, Surakiart claimed to have forged closer relationships with his counterparts at a personal level. He called upon Laos's Somsavat Lengsavad, Cambodia's Hor Namhong, and Myanmar's Win Aung, reassuring them that Thailand had no exploitation policy in the name of ACMECS, and was willing to work together with them to promote prosperity and peace in the region.[57] It is observed that the first ACMECS summit of November 2003 was perhaps the calculated response to the attack against the Royal Thai Embassy in Phnom

Penh in January the same year, which revealed the vulnerable state of Thai-Cambodian relationship based on age-old mutual distrust.

ACMECS also brought to mind the importance of the up-and-coming non-traditional issues in the region. Five mainland Southeast Asian states were long trapped in the Cold War condition whereby military conflicts defined the realm of national security. However, non-traditional issues have recently threatened to belittle the states' capacity in the way they handled this new aspect in international relations. Issues such as bird flu and the H1N1, the energy crisis, natural disasters and the spread of HIV/Aids require a collective will among members to tackle them. ACMECS opened the door for cooperation in these new fields, and not only at the state level, but also enabled collaboration with the private sector. Thaksin claimed that ACMECS represented the true face of Thai diplomatic relations with its neighbours. Of course, he was content to exploit the seeming success of ACMECS to counter criticism over what was seen as his poor handling of a string of crises, such as the conflict in the south and the alleged violation of human rights in his war on drugs campaign. On the surface, ACMECS spawned the positive message of how Thailand wished to restore a stable region based on mutual economic interests of parties involved. ACMECS was designed to meet challenges at three levels. At a national level, it generated a myriad of opportunities for Thai investors to take advantage of the relatively virginal markets in Cambodia, Laos and Myanmar. It was a boon for the Thai economy as a whole. At a sub-regional level, ACMECS supposedly provided a sense of regional belonging through close cooperation, exchange of expertise and best practices. There was an attempt to reinvent Indochina and Myanmar, once notorious ideological battlefields in the Cold War, into thriving lucrative markets. Finally at the regional level, ACMECS offered logic behind ASEAN integration. Surakiart said that ACMECS was part of an important building bloc for ASEAN which was working to achieve a single ASEAN community by the year 2015.[58]

Nonetheless, ACMECS was far from being a perfect angel. Critics saw it as a devil in disguise. They sneered at ACMECS as a mere springboard for Thaksin's launch into the international limelight. With the provision of baht loans and the strict conditions on procurement contracts, ACMECS was devised to keep Thai neighbours dependent on the country.[59] When Thaksin repositioned

Thailand to become a donor country, he declared, "Foreign aid was given (to Thailand) as an incentive and reward for allegiance. Many developing countries thus became adept at playing the game, and as a result, fell into a cycle of dependence."[60] But now, Thaksin did not seem to mind his neighbours becoming similarly dependent on Thai prosperity. At the end of the ACMECS Ministerial Meeting in Siem Reap, on 4–5 August 2005, while the consensus was on the commitment of the ACMECS principle of self-help and partnership, it was evident that member countries still wanted to use the forum to get cash and donations from Thailand.[61] Such thinking has obstructed the progress of ACMECS activities due to the lack of financial resources among the LDCs. Thaksin, in playing "big brother" vis-à-vis neighbouring countries, could have hoped to use ACMECS to influence their foreign policy in favour of Thailand. The policy of creating a Thai sphere of influence ran contrary to the concept of partnership and self-help. This explained why, until today, ACMECS projects have been progressing slowly, particularly since the departure of "big brother" Thaksin. With the current economic recession, the flow of financial assistance from Thailand to the ACMECS neighbours has been severely interrupted. Thailand as a donor country has been struggling to cope with the financial crisis too.

This image of Thailand being a donor is also troublesome. Nationalistic conditions such as lending money in Thai currency and forcing procurement contracts with Thai firms seems to suggest that Thailand's concept of international assistance had its hidden agenda. Thailand's immediate neighbours were virtually handcuffed by Thaksin's financial assistance. Projects like contract farming within ACMECS framework, which was highly commercialized with whiffs of Thai colonialism, also served geopolitical reasons. Thaksin employed such projects to thwart expanding Chinese or even Vietnamese influence in Laos, Cambodia and Myanmar, at least in the economic front. He thus promoted the donor status to boost Thailand's hegemonic viewpoint with regard to its neighbours. Inside the Thai Foreign Ministry, the debate of how Thailand should define its role as a donor was intense. Some noted that Thailand had not really ceased to receive grant aid from foreign powers as earlier declared by the Thaksin government. Furthermore, while Thaksin labelled international assistance as a cheap tactic used by developed nations to maintain their influence in the recipient countries, he also followed in their footsteps of overcoming Cambodia, Laos and Myanmar with a cash army in exchange for the Thai influence on their economic lives. It was this exploitative aspect of ACMECS that has kept the feeling of mistrust alive.

Withaya Sucharithanarugse argued that the promotion of ACMECS indeed helped enrich Thaksin's business empire in neighbouring countries.[62] To the critics, the ACMECS framework is just an insidious economic plan by Thaksin to enrich himself. Thitinan Pongsudhirak described ACMECS as being beset with conflicts of interest involving corporate concerns of the Shinawatra family and the business interests of his associates.[63] A good example was a Bt4-billion (US$120 million) soft loans package given to Myanmar's Ministry of Communications, Posts and Telegraphs under the ACMECS economic framework in early 2004 for the upgrade of its telecommunications infrastructure in which Shin Satellite won the Bt600 million concessions. Thaksin has had a long business presence in Myanmar. He has supplied satellite services to Myanmar since 1988 through his personal connection with the once-powerful General Khin Nyunt, Myanmar's former prime minister who is currently under detention. Thaksin's investment and interest in ACMECS was a perfect way for the premier to spend tax money for the sake of his companies and associates.[64] Thaksin's private businesses in Cambodia were another example of how ACMECS could be used to augment his personal wealth. Thaksin's projects such as the construction of a "modern city" near Koh Kong and the planned exploration of oil and gas in Cambodian waters were announced and confirmed by the Cambodian authorities.[65] Former diplomat Surapong Jayanama argued that Thaksin's personal diplomacy comprised Thailand when it came to managing its relations with neighbours. It explained why Thailand's past initiative on political reforms in Myanmar proved futile since the Thai leaders were not serious about Yangon's political reforms but concentrated more on economic benefits especially at a personal level.[66]

In a nutshell, ACMECS was an intelligent construct designed to parade Thai solidarity with its enemy-turned-friend neighbours. But these neighbours have remained ambivalent in their attitude toward ACMECS and Thai sincerity, even while activities within this cooperative framework are still continuing. The perception of Thailand as a regional hegemon, a neo-colonialist in the form of a financial donor, and a ruthless business entity has kept the fire of mutual suspicion burning. The attack against the Thai Embassy in Cambodia, the sporadic cultural conflicts between Thailand and Laos (mostly through Thai television soap operas that have depicted Laos as a nation of inferior culture), and the latest armed clashes between Thai and Cambodian troops over the claim of ownership of the Preah Vihear Temple in October 2008 and April 2009, all illustrate that ACMECS has not been successful in guaranteeing a better understanding between Thailand and its neighbours and among their people. Member countries had not really paid much attention to the much-publicized people-to-people aspect of ACMECS.

BILATERAL FREE TRADE AGREEMENTS

It can be said that Thaksin's foreign policy gave a high priority to a trade policy, formulated to strengthen Thailand's economic dominance. His commerce-driven foreign policy acted in response to the domestic economic needs of Thai farmers and manufacturers who were extensive supporters of the Thai Rak Thai government. Populist economic programmes, implemented to increase national productivity, were at the core of Thaksin's power strength. Foreign policy was accordingly fabricated to serve Thaksin's domestic economic imperatives. It was also drawn upon a sense of nationalism: building a rich nation to enrich the people. Thaksin revived an economic nationalism and injected it into the domain of diplomacy. Economic nationalism has been a powerful doctrine that once gave birth to a policy of protectionism during the authoritarian years of the Cold War era. This same economic nationalism was also a main motivation behind the engineering of a policy of economic imperialism during the Chatichai as well as the Thaksin administrations. Pasuk Phongpaichit argued that this notion was precisely explained in Liah Greenfeld's book, *The Spirit of Capitalism: Nationalism and Economic Growth* which Thaksin and his advisors publicly quoted on several occasions. She said, "The main message of the book is that societies which put priority on achieving economic growth to make their nation great can achieve 'economic take-off' in one or two generations."[67] The new Thailand has a new national identity. This new national identity was now redefined by Thaksin as economic achievement.

Thaksin's endorsement of economic nationalism did not necessarily spawn an inward-looking trade policy. He strongly promoted foreign investment, while strengthening economic nationalism at home through domestic capacity-building to accomplish higher economic growth. This strategy was known as Thaksin's dual-track economic policy. In many ways, Thaksin imitated similar strategies adopted by Thailand's neighbours, including China, Malaysia and Singapore. They achieved economic success with distinctive nationalism in the global environment. In this process, Thaksin was searching for the right formula of nationalism that would be a winning one for Thailand. His formula highlighted the necessity of "opening the country" and improving a national competitiveness through innovation, branding and value-added products. More importantly, economic liberalization through FTAs was made the epicentre of Thaksin's foreign policy as a key to cope with, and take advantage from, globalization while satisfying Thai businesses. At the international level, his effort in pursuing more FTAs effectively raised the level of economic competitiveness of the country. Thai mercantilism was revived. Diplomats were assigned a new role as salesmen. Thaksin stated clearly that his government would "employ FTA negotiations as Thailand's economic strategy in the field of international trade and investment".[68]

Evidently, Thaksin pushed for economic diplomacy with trade pacts as the vital ingredient in foreign policy. He promoted a leading role for Thai Trade Representatives in negotiating international trade and economic agreements, to excel the country's bargaining leverage, and preserving national economic interests.[69] Ambassadors were instructed to open up more business opportunities for Thailand. The FTAs and barter trade agreements served as a channel to open more markets for the country. Thaksin once said,

> Do you know that in four years I had travelled overseas seventy-three times? And how many times did foreign leaders visit Thailand? Ninety-nine times. I do the duty of a salesman. If I do not go off like this, how will I find new markets? I have to preserve the old markets and find new ones all the time through the use of foreign policy.[70]

The bottom line for the FTAs was to generate income and extend business opportunities. Thaksin proudly said that when his government came into office in 2001, 12.5 million Thais were living below poverty line. By the end of 2005, his government claimed to reduce the number of poor people to 7 million.[71] Thaksin's claims are however debatable and require a serious critical examination. Peter Warr argued that Thailand's economic growth had already resumed under the Democrat-led government and Thaksin benefitted from this. Recovery under Thaksin proceeded at about the same speed as Indonesia, and below that of countries such as Malaysia and the Philippines. Poverty reduction in Thailand was at a below-average rate under Thaksin. Thailand's economic gains from increased trade with neighbours were minor compared to those with traditional major trading and investment powers, for example the United States, Japan and China.[72] The Thai Foreign Ministry elaborated the rationale behind Thaksin's FTAs initiative. First, it was put forward to renew economic relationships between Thailand and its partners on a more equal basis. It was also meant to fine-tune the Thai economy so as to be able to manage the emerging multilateral trading system at the global level. The government claimed that all efforts were made to conclude FTAs that were also World Trade Organization (WTO) compatible. Second, the FTAs echoed Thaksin's broader and integral outlook of the national economy and his search for a win-win benefit with Thailand's trading partners. This outlook seemed to stand in contradiction to past economic policies which focused on exclusive products and sectors, but overlooked the whole picture of economic reality. Third, the FTAs encouraged competitiveness. Thaksin called for Thai businesses to develop their own strength and dispose of weaknesses.[73]

The FTAs were received with a mixture of great enthusiasm and wariness by both the SMEs and those in the rural areas. Together, they made up Thailand's fundamental power base. He sold the idea of the FTAs by reassuring that bilateral trade pacts would benefit smaller businesses in the export of their products to new markets. In other words, by claiming to work for this significant power base, Thaksin utilized his FTAs to justify his political objective. The emphasis on the SMEs and small business in the rural provinces represented another trick of the Thai Rak Thai government. It was to show that Thaksin had no pro-big conglomerate policy despite the fact that he himself owned major multi-billion businesses.[74] The FTAs were a construct for the poor.

The Scope of "Perd Seri"

The term *perd seri*, or liberalization, has a proximate meaning of "freedom". Thaksin used repeatedly the notion of *perd seri* to gain public support of his FTAs policy. In retrospect, Thailand was quite familiar with the idea of free trade arrangements. The country signed the first FTA with ASEAN member countries, known as the AFTA, in 1992. However, it remained a hazy subject for many Thais, and thus a challenge for the Thaksin government in the implementation of the FTAs. Thaksin explained the logic of his *perd seri* policy through the FTAs:

> Partnership in both bilateral and multilateral free trade is a vital component of our people's well-being. Thailand is committed to negotiating and making progress with comprehensive bilateral free trade agreements with several of our major trading partners, such as China, the United States, Japan, Australia, India and Bahrain. With China, we recently agreed to a bilateral tariff reduction on fruit and vegetable products to 0 per cent, to be implemented by the end of April 2003 under the Early Harvest Programme of the ASEAN-China FTA framework. The Thai-United States Consultative Joint Council has been established after the signing of Thai-United States Trade and Investment Framework Agreement last November to promote cooperation in solving problematic bilateral trade and investment issues, trade facilitation, capacity building, and liberalization. These are crucial groundwork to achieve Thai–United States FTA in the near future. The Thai-Bahrain Framework Agreement on Closer Economic partnership is expected to bring about 0 per cent tariff reduction by 2010, opening up a gateway linking Thailand to greater economic opportunities in the GCC. The Thailand–India Free Trade Framework Agreement is expected to be concluded by July this year (2003). A free trade regime does not merely create new market opportunities between the partners but can bring about closer cultural ties and understanding between peoples of respective partners through trade exchange.[75]

During the Thaksin administration, Thailand had concluded or initiated FTAs with countries including Australia, Bahrain, China,

India, Japan, New Zealand, Peru and the United States, as well as with the European Free Trade Association (EFTA) and the BIMSTEC. Details of Thai FTAs with trading partners appear in Table 3.3.[76]

Launched in 2003, the Thailand Elite Card, another commerce-oriented invention of Thaksin, conferred exclusive benefits such as discounts on spas, a fast-track line at airport check-ins and business introductions for "VIP foreigners who had high purchasing power" and wanted to buy into what promotional materials say was the world's first "countrywide country-club". Although it was unrelated to the FTAs, the Thailand Elite Card demonstrated how Thaksin made full use of the atmosphere of *perd seri*, both internally and externally, to sell Thai businesses. Costing US$25,000 each, the Elite Card promised a whole new level of service and special perks, backed by a powerful Thaksin government, based on the need of readjusting the image of Thailand as a place for high-quality tourists.[77] The Thailand Elite Card company proclaimed "for members wishing to do business in the country, it offered assistance facilitating each and every one of their needs. Whether it be a simple work permit or coordinating with the Thailand Board of Investment (BOI) or any other government agencies, it was here to help them make it happen with the right people."[78] Early targets of one million members have been revised downward since Thaksin was removed from power. To date, the card has drawn just 2,570 members, and some of those members were given their cards free as a promotional gesture. During the first few years after its official launch, opinion among Thais was divided as to whether a large enough market existed for the concept to make it viable in the long term. In 2006, the company posted accumulated losses of up to Bt1.14 billion. In January 2009, the troubled Thailand Elite Card was abandoned by the Abhisit government. The failure of the programme stemmed from the lack of transparency in its internal management as well as poor performance.[79]

Aiding Local Businesses?

Prime Minister Thaksin, in his meeting to lay out strategies on domestic and foreign policy in March 2005 at the Government House, instructed Deputy Prime Minister Somkid Jatusripitak and his chief advisor Pansak Winyarat to reset the conditions of the future FTAs in a way that would maximize the benefit to Thai

TABLE 3.3
Thailand's FTAs with Its Partners

FTA Partners	Contents
Australia (Concluded)	• Signed 5 July 2004, Came into effect 1 January 2005 • Thai tariffs on virtually all goods imported from Australia to be eliminated by 1 January 2010 • Called for liberalization of trade in goods, services, and investment, as well as for cooperation in working out obstacles to trade caused by non-tariff measures, such as restrictive sanitary and phytosanitary regulations and anti-dumping measures • Extended also to facilitation of trade in certain categories, such as customs procedures, electronic commerce, intellectual property, government procurement and competition policy • 5,000 Thai products (83.2%) get duty free access from Jan 2005, including fruits, vegetables, pick-up trucks. Meanwhile, 49.4% of Australian products get duty free access from January 2005, including big motor vehicles, fuels and chemicals. Most others by 2010, except wine (2015) beef and sugar (2020) and dairy (2025).
New Zealand (Concluded)	• Thailand and New Zealand Closer Economic Partnership (TNZCEP) was signed on 19 April 2005, and came into effect on 1 July 2005. • The agreement covers the liberalization of market access for goods, services, and investment, as well as cooperation in trade-related such as customs procedures, electronic commerce, intellectual property, government procurement, and competition policy. • Thailand has benefited from the elimination of duties on 79% of all goods imported into New Zealand, equivalent to 85% of the value of Thai products entering the country. • 54% of all imports from New Zealand, accounting for 49% of the total value of the goods imported, now enter Thailand duty free.

continued on next page

TABLE 3.3 — *cont'd*

FTA Partners	Contents
India (Concluded)	• On 9 October 2003, Ministers of Commerce of both countries signed the Framework Agreement. An India-Thailand Trade Negotiating Committee was set up to discuss details under the Framework Agreement and formulate a free trade agreement as well as to expand economic cooperation between the two countries.
	• Trade negotiations to move closer to full liberalization are still continuing and are expected to be concluded by 2010. To accelerate the realization of benefits, both countries agreed to implement an Early Harvest Scheme (EHS) covering trade in goods for eighty-four products.
	• The eighty-four items (Harmonized System [HS] code six-digit level) under the EHS included fruits (fresh mangosteens, mangoes, durian, rambutans, longans); fishery products (salmon, sardines, mackerel); electrical appliances (window/wall air-conditioners, colour TVs, ball-bearings); precious metal and jewellery; polycarbonates, and more. Tariffs on these goods were cut by 50% on 1 September 2004, 75% on 1 September 2005, and eliminated entirely on 1 September 2006.
ASEAN-China (Concluded)	• The "Framework Agreement on ASEAN-China Comprehensive Economic Cooperation" was signed by ASEAN and China on 4 November 2002 to serve as the structure and mechanism for negotiations to establish a free trade area covering trade in goods, services, and investment, as well as to affect various measures for economic cooperation between China and ASEAN.
	• Subsequently, an "Agreement on Trade in Goods of the Framework Agreement on Comprehensive Economic Cooperation between the ASEAN and China" was successfully negotiated and was signed on 29 November 2004, during the ASEAN-China Summit meeting in Vientiane, Laos.

	• Thailand and China, on 18 June 2003, signed an "Agreement on Accelerated Tariff Elimination under the Early Harvest Programme of the Framework Agreement on Comprehensive Economic Cooperation between ASEAN and China", which eliminated tariffs on goods embracing fruits and vegetables lines of products as of 1 October 2003.
Japan (Concluded)	• Negotiations for a Japan-Thailand Economic Partnership Agreement (JTEPA) began in February, 2004, and the Agreement was signed by government leaders in Tokyo, Japan, on 3 April 2007.
	• The agreement, which came into force on 1 November 2007, consists of trade in goods, rules of origin of products, trade in services, investment, as well as cooperation in nine areas and seven joint projects.
Peru	• Signed an Early Harvest Agreement in 2005, covering approximately 70% of the two countries' products.
	• Excluded from the Early Harvest will be sensitive items such as rice, sugarcane and poultry, important exports for both Thailand and Peru.
	• These have not yet come into effect since both sides are examining and adjusting the tax list of Early-Harvest products.
United States	• President Bush and Prime Minister Thaksin on 19 October 2003 agreed to negotiate a bilateral FTA.
	• Negotiations began on a comprehensive bilateral FTA in June 2004, covering investment, services, government procurement, intellectual property, as well as agriculture.
	• The sixth round of talks ended in January 2006 with all grounds covered but no deal finalized. In June 2008, Thailand sought to revive the suspended FTA, but its effort failed.
	• The moment the agreement becomes effective, tariffs of 8,100 goods, which includes wood and rubber-based products, glassware and ceramics, electronic goods, plastic products, jewellery and food, will be reduced to zero. Thailand will gradually abolish import tariffs on important goods like milk, onions, meat, corn, tea and coffee.

continued on next page

TABLE 3.3 — cont'd

FTA Partners	Contents
Bahrain	• The Thai-Bahrain FTA negotiations began in 2002. The two countries reached an Early Harvest agreement to bring down tariffs on 642 products. • Each party agreed to reduce its customs duties on goods originating from the territory of the other party by 29 December 2002 to between 0% and 3% , and to use its endeavours to reduce the customs duties for commodity tariff lines in stages to 0% by 2010.
EFTA	• The first round of trade talks with the EFTA grouping, which comprises Switzerland, Norway, Lichtenstein and Iceland, took place in May 2005, focusing on reductions in tariffs for industrial goods, the opening up of markets for agricultural goods and reductions in non-tariff trade barriers.
BIMSTEC	• On 8 February 2004, in Thailand, the ministers of economics and trade of the BIMSTEC countries jointly signed a Framework Agreement to establish a free trade area by 2012, leading to liberalization of trade in goods, services, and investment, as well as to undertake economic cooperation. • A BIMSTEC Trade Negotiating Committee was formed, with Thailand serving as Chair during the year 2004–05, to negotiate agreements for trade in goods, services, and investment under the BIMSTEC Free Trade Agreement.

consumers, even at the expense of manufacturers being put in a disadvantageous position. He said, "10,000 manufacturers may have to bear the consequences and burdens of the FTAs, but this could bring profits to 20 million consumers."[80] Thaksin saw the need to revamp Thailand's economic structure in order for the country to catch up with the mushrooming of the FTAs. Meanwhile, Thai manufacturers were required to adapt themselves to the changing business environment and invest in innovations in order to keep up with the game. The FTAs were an essential parameter in raising Thai competitiveness on the international stage. With the FTAs, Thailand would be less vulnerable as it did not have to depend on the Generalized System of Preferences (GSP) from its more powerful trading partners. While letting the plus side of the FTAs be known, the government downplayed the possibility of a trade imbalance that could be created, as this would open up an opportunity for the opposition to attack its free trade policy. In one meeting with top diplomats at the Foreign Ministry, Thaksin sought their help in explaining and publicizing the "clean" side of the FTAs to the Thai people. Thaksin was aware that the Thai public had an ambivalent attitude toward the FTAs, and might not totally trust in his government in the pursuance of the free trade arrangements.[81]

Thaksin paid special attention to the FTAs, and even moulded a foreign policy based on the promotion of trade pacts as an engine of growth. He realized that global trade was important to enhance the Thai economy both at the international and domestic levels. Thaksin viewed the FTAs as a fundamental element in the search for new markets and an increase in competitiveness. In February 2005, Thaksin set up a Special Task Force (STF) within the Ministry of Commerce. The STF was assigned to search for new markets and advise on new strategies to penetrate them. It was to forge close relations between Thai traders and potential partners in these new markets. Thaksin identified several new markets as target groups for Thai penetration, including countries in the Commonwealth of Independent States (CIS), the Middle East (Iran, Jordan, Yemen, Kuwait, and United Arab Emirates), North Africa (Morocco and Egypt), and Latin America. He also planned to conclude more FTAs with them in the future. Tasks of the STF also included the gathering of intelligence information on new markets (their product tastes, limitations and constraints in the expansion of Thai products, ways to build alliance and develop personal relationship with their trade unions and associations or trade-related agencies), the organization of brainstorming sessions between state agencies and Thai exporters, and the preparation of an "export rally" (field trip for Thai exporters to visit new markets and get to know their prospective importers).[82]

Did Thailand win or lose in the game of the FTAs? Statistics behind the Thai FTAs with Australia, India, China and Japan show a predictable picture: Thailand both won and lost some.

Within the framework of the Thai-Australian FTA, bilateral trade volume increased by 45.54 per cent during the first ten months of implementation, amounting to US$5.4 billion. However, the trade balance worsened as a result of Thai imports of Australian material goods. The deficit was at US$181 million in the same period. As for the Thai-Indian FTA, it was evident that trade volume increased, particularly for goods included in the early harvest where the volume surged by 93 per cent to US$340 million during the first year after the pact became effective. Thailand's trade balance with India improved significantly, reversing from deficit to surplus after the FTA. The impact of the Thai-Chinese FTA could be measured by the increased trade volume at 27 per cent for Thai exports and 14 per cent for those of China. However, Thailand's trade deficit with China stood at US$2 billion one year after the FTA was implemented. Julawadee Worasakyothin of the International Institute for Trade and Development concluded that one positive effect of the Thai FTAs was the increase in trade volume, and that this raised the importance of competitiveness. The FTAs have brought in huge competitors that forced some small Thai players to leave the market, they have instead created monopolies.[83] After all, Thaksin claimed that FTAs were not just purely driven by economic considerations, but the overall Thai relationships with foreign partners, including political and strategic concerns. It is essential to note here that the analysis on FTAs that relies on official statistics is made simply on the basis of trade expansion and particularly whether there was a surplus or deficit in Thailand's trade with its counterparts. This kind of analysis is limited since the FTAs are also about investment and a range of other factors. A deficit is not necessarily always negative, and can sometime quickly change depending on a variety of reasons, such as a change in consumption patterns.

The FTAs were not depicted in a positive light by Thaksin's opposition. In fact, his opponents, together with some hardline NGOs and civil societies, launched an anti-FTAs campaign that forced the Thaksin government to delay negotiations on incomplete trade pacts with certain partners. The disagreement was damning. Two main allegations against Thaksin's support of the FTAs were his exploitation of the trade pacts for his own business benefits and his willingness to break the taboo of *khai chart*, or selling the country, through offering free access to the Thai economy to powerful trading partners. This explained why the anti-FTAs campaign was launched with a tagline "Sovereignty not for sale". The suspicion of Thaksin selling national sovereignty surged because of the secretive nature of the FTA negotiations. Thai civil societies complained that the FTA negotiations were conducted out of the sight of the public, and without sufficient consultation and participation of public-interest civil society groups. Even though the government claimed to consult with people through several organized meetings, only limited groups of people had the opportunities to participate. Moreover, there was a lack of access to the draft negotiating texts in all sectors which made it difficult for the Thai public to assess the potential impacts from the negotiations.[84] They also criticized the FTAs for being a mere political device that was employed to serve only short-term benefits, especially when Thailand was searching for preferential treatment against its competitors. For example, China has not concluded a FTA deal with the United States. The success of the Thai FTA with the United States would offer the country lower tariffs for its exports and greater access to the American market, when compared to China. But it would only be a temporary advantage. Thai productivity would need to see gains to hold onto that advantage. What Thaksin did was only to open up new markets for Thai products. He did not really push for improvement in Thai productivity. This was indeed a more difficult process.[85]

The FTAs could also wipe out high-cost industries as well as smaller businesses simply because they may fail to be competitive against the invasion of cheaper foreign products. Thaksin believed that Thai FTAs with leading economies were an important Thaksinomic policy implemented to reduce the risk of over-production. Through his populist economic programmes, Thaksin incessantly promoted increase in productivity. As a result, Thai goods were over-produced. Thaksin therefore hoped that FTAs could help soak up these goods through exports.[86] Take the Thai-Chinese FTA as an example: a rapidly growing two-way trade was heavily weighted in China's favour while poor Thai farmers and manufacturers had been struggling to compete with China's cheaper products. True, China has occasionally helped absorb the leftover Thai products to reconcile the tremendous effect of their FTA, but China cannot play a generous merchant forever.[87] The FTA Watch, a coalition of public-minded academics and independent NGOs formed in 2003, also raised the issue pertaining to basic rights obligations. It says,

> FTA negotiations with developed countries in particular have an agenda that goes beyond trade in goods. They almost without fail include deregulation of investment measures, liberalization of trade in services, and implementation of competition policies. Also, trade-related intellectual property rules in FTAs risk undermining Thailand's ability to take measures to ensure access to affordable medicines. Moreover, the elimination of tariffs on agricultural goods in FTAs may have an impact on the livelihoods of small farmers, thereby affecting food security of rural communities.[88]

The anti-FTAs movement reached its peak on 8 January 2006 when several thousand Thais tried to storm the building in Chiang Mai where FTA negotiations were taking place between Thailand and the United States. The negotiations, as a consequence, were frozen. Protesters argued that under the Thai-U.S. FTA, American agricultural goods would have an advantage over Thai products, which included meat, milk, dairy products, vegetables, fruit, maize, and soya beans. Thailand would also risk losing out in terms of intellectual property rights, as well as in the telecoms, automotive and agricultural sectors. Critically, it could result in Thailand losing a certain degree of sovereign control over those important sectors of its economy, as claimed by the anti-FTAs movement. The United States could demand control of the Thai public services sector including energy, transport, and education. It could also request Thailand to open its doors to huge multinational banks like Citibank and Bank of America, thus becoming directly involved in investment, banking, insurance and currency transactions, and corporate monopoly on intellectual property rights including for seeds and drugs.[89]

Thaksin pursued an increasing number of bilateral FTAs with strategic partners which underlined the reconstruction of Thai foreign policy. He perceived trade diplomacy as essential in the strengthening of relations between Thailand and its partners. But the FTAs were not a pure economic gizmo employed to build up economic growth. They were also a political means for Thaksin to perpetuate his legitimacy based on the promotion of economic liberalism. Thaksin, however, failed to realize that using the FTAs for his own political purpose offered an opportunity for the opposition to politicize the issue and challenge his foreign policy.

THE BANGKOK PROCESS

Myanmar was on Thaksin's radar screen for at least four main reasons. First, the fact that Thailand shares approximately 2,400 kilometres of border with Myanmar automatically assigns the former as a frontline state whenever a security crisis erupts inside the latter's territory. Therefore, it seems an imperative in Thai foreign policy to seek harmony and cooperation with this neighbour although bitter history often thwarts the Thai effort. Second, all of Thaksin's foreign policy initiatives were mainly driven by his commercial motives. Promoting the issue of democracy in Myanmar would diversify the contents of his foreign policy, even when the implementation was superficial. Third, even before it joined ASEAN in 1997, Myanmar had slowly opened itself up for international trade. A resource-rich Myanmar became an attractive trading partner particularly for most ASEAN members. Thailand, too, recognized the economic significance of Myanmar and was increasingly dependent on certain commodities from it, most notably gas and oil.[90] Thus, Thaksin's Myanmar policy was to maintain a healthy bilateral relationship for the sake of Thailand's economic interests. Fourth, the desperate domestic political situation has unfailingly placed Myanmar in the international limelight. The global community has attempted through various means, such as sanctions and engagement, to convince the Myanmar leaders to seriously commence political reform, including reconciling with the opposition, releasing political prisoners and National League for Democracy (NLD) leader Aung San Suu Kyi, and holding elections with the participation of all parties concerned. Thaksin saw the opportunity to raise his international reputation. He was willing to play a broker between Myanmar and the opposition as this would lift his leadership profile at the international level. Thaksin also hoped that the Myanmar leaders would see this as a serious initiative from the Thais in helping them step into the modern era. Introducing the concept of the "Bangkok Process", Thaksin said:

For the situation in Myanmar, I'm not happy on what has happened now. I keep talking to them and even recently I went there. I'm the first leader that went to the capital, and I talked to them finally that I don't want you to isolate from international community, and I don't want the international community to isolate you. So I think you better keep the international community informed of your democratic development, including what happened to Aung San Suu Kyi, the government, the people, what about the HIV/ Aids situation, and the human rights. We worry about what is happening there. I try my best to convey the message of international community to them and convince them. And I even offered Thailand to be a place for discussion, as I call this the "Bangkok Process".[91]

A Roadmap to Nowhere

Genuinely or otherwise, Thaksin expressed his concern over the political situation in Myanmar and wanted to see political and ethnic problems in this neighbouring country resolved because of the fear of possible spillover effects considering the Thai-Myanmar geographical proximity. As part of Thaksin's much publicized foreign policy, Thailand appeared to fully support national reconciliation and democracy in Myanmar. Thaksin claimed to have tried repeatedly to convince the Myanmar leaders of the need and benefit to move forward and maintain the momentum already achieved in its political process. His endeavour saw an opportunity in the weeks after Suu Kyi was recaptured and seventy-five of her party members were killed by a pro-government mob in June 2003 during their journey up the country to meet NLD supporters. Thaksin took a bold diplomatic initiative by launching the "roadmap proposal" in the following months. The concept behind this roadmap was to outline steps to restore democracy in Myanmar and to promote its domestic political reconciliation. Thailand's proposed roadmap consisted of five stages toward political change in Myanmar. The first stage would see the release of all political prisoners from house arrest, including Suu Kyi, and the reopening of various branch offices of her NLD party. In the second stage of "confidence-building", there would be a credible investigation into the violent attack against Suu Kyi, an end to the media campaign against her, and truce agreements reached with the remaining armed opposition groups. The third stage would witness the drafting of a constitution involving the military, the democratic opposition and the ethnic groups, followed by the adoption of this document. During the fourth and fifth stages, an independent election would be held. At the end of the process, an international conference on aid for Myanmar would be organized.[92] But Thaksin's proposal of the roadmap died prematurely when it was rejected by Myanmar. Possibly, the Myanmar leaders did not fully trust Thailand. More realistically, they were not too keen to let Thailand use the roadmap as a pretext to interfere in their domestic politics. In the end, the Myanmar government, under extreme pressure from the world announced on 30 August 2003 their own roadmap for democracy. The essence of this roadmap was for Myanmar to move towards a constitutional referendum and general elections. It contained seven major steps to reform politics:

1. Reconvening the National Convention that had been adjourned since 1996.
2. After successfully holding the National Convention, step-by-step implementation of the process necessary for the emergence of a genuine and disciplined democratic system.
3. Drafting of a new Constitution in accordance with basic principles and detailed basic principles laid down by the National Convention.
4. Adoption of the Constitution through a national referendum.
5. Holding of free and fair elections for *Pyithu Hluttaws* [legislative bodies] according to the new Constitution.
6. Convening of *Hluttaws* attended by *Hluttaw* members in accordance with the new Constitution.
7. Building a modern, developed and democratic nation by the state leaders elected by the *Hluttaw*, and the government and other central organs formed by the *Hluttaw*.[93]

Thaksin covered his diplomatic misstep by saying that his idea was to show a way forward to the Myanmar leaders.[94] With the failure of the Thai-initiated roadmap, Thaksin returned with a grander project. He was aware of the shortcomings of the roadmap *à la* Myanmar, especially in its character of favouring the generals. In late September 2003, Thaksin dispatched Surakiart as his special envoy to Yangon in a bid to persuade the Myanmar leaders to come out for a retreat-styled dialogue with selected like-minded countries to further exchange views on the steps and procedure of the roadmap. Thaksin called this project the "Bangkok Process". This time, Myanmar went along with the Thai proposal, perhaps in exchange for the Thai financial assistance provided through the framework of "Economic Cooperation Strategy", the precursor of ACMECS. The first Bangkok Process meeting was held in the Thai capital on 15 December 2003 and participated by eleven countries (Australia, Austria, Italy, Germany, France, Japan, China, India, Singapore, Thailand and Myanmar), plus the United Nations Secretary-General's special envoy, Razali Ismail. It was the first time that Myanmar had sent its representatives to attend a meeting about Myanmar, and was simply undeterred, at least for now, by the principle of non-interference. At the meeting, participants were reassured by Myanmar that the Constitution-drafting National Convention would be reconvened in 2004, the NLD would be invited to join the National Convention, and the United Nations Secretary-General's special envoy would be allowed into Myanmar. But not everyone was convinced that the Myanmar government would fulfil all the assurances it made at the Bangkok Process meeting.

Prior to the Bangkok Process, Thailand insisted on Myanmar adopting an open-arms policy toward ethnic minorities in general, and particularly to begin peace talks with the remaining ethnic rebels. Thaksin even formed a team to act as a go-between for the Myanmar government and the ethnic groups so that they could narrow their differences to establish a peace dialogue. After months of shuttle diplomacy between Bangkok and Yangon, as Thaksin proudly said, Thailand managed to organize substantive peace talks between the Myanmar government and the Karen National Union (KNU), the largest ethnic rebel group, in November 2003. As a result, both sides reached a tentative ceasefire agreement on 20 January 2004.[95] One tangible success related to the Bangkok Process was the active Thai arbitration between the Myanmar regime and the KNU. Thailand has long exploited the ethnic minorities along the border, using them as a buffer zone with Yangon. But since Thaksin wanted the marketplace instead of the battlefield, the buffer zone seemed dispensable. In this view, peace-making between the KNU and the Myanmar government, through the Bangkok Process, rendered Thailand a security benefit. Thailand could also possibly regain trust from its Myanmar counterparts for not inciting the ethnic minorities along the border to clash against the regime in

Yangon. With the Bangkok Process, Thaksin's role in diffusing Myanmar's political turmoil was initially applauded by the world community. But the inaugural Bangkok Process meeting produced no substantial outcomes. Myanmar's Foreign Minister Win Aung merely outlined the concept of his government's roadmap, which was sketched by Prime Minister General Khin Nyunt, but failed to mention a timeframe.[96] To maintain the spirit of the gathering and the continued involvement of Myanmar, Thaksin proposed the second Bangkok Process meeting tentatively for 29–30 April 2004.

Myanmar kept quiet and seemed unenthusiastic about the second Bangkok Process meeting. As the proposed date of the meeting drew near, Surakiart was sent back to Yangon on 10 April 2004 to hand Thaksin's letter to the State Peace and Development Council (SPDC) Chairman Senior General Than Shwe to lobby for Myanmar's participation. Eventually, Myanmar declined the Thai invitation and the second round of the Bangkok Process never took place. This was an end to the short-lived Bangkok Process. The SPDC was unsure of the possible impact of holding the second Bangkok Process meeting before reconvening the National Convention, which, in the Myanmar leaders' view, represented the crucial first step of its roadmap. Myanmar was apparently inclined to subscribe to the thinking that it would be better to keep away from the spotlight and possible controversies and avoid any steps that might generate difficulties or create complications for the National Convention. They could have perceived the Thai-backed Bangkok Process as another kind of diplomatic measure used to compel the regime to commence political reforms too soon and too drastically. To minimize the embarrassment, the Thai Foreign Ministry stated, "The Bangkok Process was welcomed by countries concerned as well as the United Nations as a constructive effort for democratization and national reconciliation in Myanmar."[97]

Thaksin as Myanmar's Apologist?

The failure to launch the second meeting of the Bangkok Process stemmed from both the complexities within the Myanmar politics and Thaksin's dubious Myanmar policy. Myanmar, then and now, has been long ruled by the military regime. It was too ambitious to hope that Thaksin's Bangkok Process would be able to close the existing gap between Myanmar's government and its opposition. Moreover, the rift and conflict within the Myanmar leadership, which culminated in the dismissal of General Khin Nyunt as prime minister in October 2004, badly affected the entire power structure of Myanmar. Khin Nyunt, the engineer behind the seven-step roadmap, was defeated in the game of political power. His departure was a serious blow to national reconciliation and democracy in Myanmar, and therefore the Thai effort to play a brokering role in this process. Thitinan Pongsudhirak argued that Khin Nyunt's downfall bankrupted Thaksin's hitherto bilateral relationship with Myanmar, which centred on cordial ties between the respective leaders of both countries. As Thaksin had invested substantial diplomatic energy and resources in cultivating ties with Khin Nyunt, the latter's ouster was disastrous for Thailand's Myanmar policy. It also exposed the myopia and fundamental flaws of Thaksin's personalized diplomacy.[98] Since Khin Nyunt's fall from power, Thailand admitted that it was more difficult to communicate with the SPDC leaders. Thaksin was searching for new lines of communication to be established with the SPDC leadership, both for the sake of Thailand's national interest and his own businesses in the country.

Thaksin's obscure Myanmar policy served to contradict his earlier foreign policy initiatives which were aggressive, adamant and nationalistic. Thaksin's assertiveness in the conduct of diplomacy, ranging from his bold vision as an aspirant regional hegemon to his willingness to bend the wind of international politics, was compromised by his weak position vis-à-vis the generals in Myanmar. His Myanmar policy could be characterized by accommodation and appeasement. And his Forward Engagement Policy toward Myanmar was so elastic that it worked in the SPDC's favour. The reason behind his weakness was apparent. Thaksin possessed a myriad of businesses in Myanmar, most notably in the postal and telecommunications sector.[99] The overlapping of national interests with those of Thaksin's personal interests, therefore, produced Thailand's soft policy toward Myanmar. The Bangkok Process, despite its stern outlook as a forum that promoted political reforms in Myanmar, was criticized by the Thai opposition and the anti-Myanmar regime movements as a mere cover-up for certain personal interests of Thai leaders. Past Thai leaders used the politics of rhetoric to legitimize the Myanmar regime. Former Prime Minister

Chavalit once said to the Thai media that he was fully confident that the Myanmar leaders were good people and his close contact with them had shown him that they were more devout Buddhists than the Thais. They also adhered strictly to good ethics and morals, so he did not think they would stay in power forever.[100] Thaksin, similarly, in embracing the Myanmar regime, invented the Bangkok Process to outflank the West's sanctions.

Thaksin all along appeared as Myanmar's chief apologist because he seemed more anxious about his family's businesses rather than promoting democracy in this neighbouring country despite his creation of the Bangkok Process. The ongoing telecommunication services provided to Myanmar through the IPStar project and the Thai soft loan granted for the upgrading of its telecommunications technology precisely pointed to where Thaksin's interests were in his conduct of foreign policy toward Myanmar. Economic interests represented the primary necessary component of Thaksin's foreign policy toward Yangon. The Bangkok Process was one strategy used to trumpet a nominal ethical standpoint of the Thaksin government, be they democratic promotion or human rights protection in Myanmar, as well as to serve ambiguous economic interests of the Thai leaders in their interactions with its military regime. The *Irrawaddy* reported that this raised concerns about Bangkok's ability to act as an honest broker in the Myanmar's political stand-off and also questioned Thaksin's conflict of interests.[101] The Thai leaders' business mindset not only enriched the self-isolating regime with profits from its exports of natural resources and Thai investment, but also legitimized the ruthless regime of Myanmar. This, in turn, further distanced Suu Kyi and the NLD, and therefore delayed the process of political reconciliation.[102]

THE POST OF THE UNITED NATIONS SECRETARY-GENERAL

Thaksin, in his second term in office in 2005, transferred Surakiart from the Foreign Minister post to serve as Deputy Prime Minister. To many, it was a demotion. He then installed Kantathi Suphamongkhon, former diplomat, as the new Foreign Minister. The reshuffle was carried out following Thaksin's nomination of Surakiart as Thailand's candidate for the UNSG for when Kofi Annan completed his term in 2006. Thaksin claimed that transferring

Surakiart to the position of deputy prime minister would increase his chance of being selected to serve in the prestigious UNSG post. United Nations protocol suggested that it was Asia's turn to head this international body after the departure of Annan. The last Asian UNSG was U Thant from Myanmar, then known as Burma, who had served in this position from 1961 to 1971. Thaksin's endorsement of Surakiart to enter the race of the United Nations top job derived from a number of reasons. Domestically, the nomination of Surakiart for the UNSG position could be seen as an attempt to outshine the success of the Democrat Party's Supachai Panitchpakdi who had served as the Director-General of the WTO, from 2002 to 2005, and currently Secretary-General of the United Nations Conference on Trade and Development (UNCTAD). The Thai Rak Thai government wished to have its own version of this Goliath at the United Nations.

More importantly, it reiterated Thaksin's supposed fondness for multilateral diplomacy, which greatly complemented Thaksin's foreign policy platform. Surakiart himself worked passionately toward obtaining the UNSG position. He was an experienced politician, successful businessman and a highly regarded scholar with a doctorate degree in law from Harvard University, the first Thai to be able to achieve this.[103] He had also strong networks with foreign leaders while serving as Foreign Minister. Previously, Thailand's multilateral diplomacy had a low profile. It seldom took initiatives on its own at the United Nations, except after Vietnam's invasion of Cambodia in the late 1970s when Thailand, together with certain members of ASEAN, launched a campaign at the United Nations to mobilize international opinion on Hanoi's occupation of Cambodia which Bangkok perceived as serious threat to its territorial integrity.[104] Former Foreign Minister Tej Bunnag, also serving as the Ministry's Permanent Secretary during Surakiart's tenure as Foreign Minister, said that the nomination of Surakiart for the position of the UNSG, either successful or otherwise, would enhance Thailand's international profile and establish the country as a global player.[105]

While Thaksin was serving as prime minister and during the Surakiart years at the Foreign Ministry, Thailand was considerably active in conducting multilateral diplomacy. The Foreign Ministry, with Surakiart at the helm, backed the United Nations and the Millennium Development Goals and efforts to deal with certain global issues such as poverty, international terrorism, drugs, HIV/

Aids and other health threats, as well as WTO commitments. His addresses at the United Nations on numerous occasions concentrated on Thai support for the role of multilateral mechanisms to promote peace, security and prosperity. For example, Surakiart, in his speech at the 57th Session of the United Nations General Assembly in 2002, highlighted Thailand's contribution to those endeavours through forging cooperation and partnership at all levels.[106] The Thai foreign policy of endorsing multilateral diplomacy seemed to have helped prepare Surakiart to undertake the challenge of the candidacy of the UNSG position.

Surakiart Goes Global

In late 2004, news of Surakiart's application for the position of the UNSG emerged.[107] At the outset, Surakiart was not so sure about putting himself up for the chief position at the United Nations. But he felt more confident after top Thai diplomats encouraged him to enter the competition. Surakiart also subsequently received Thaksin's endorsement, with the latter believing that the effort would widen Thailand's role on the international stage.[108] But since the position of the UNSG was really about personal ambition and achievement as much as benefiting Thailand's international reputation, Surakiart took the challenge seriously, and perhaps so seriously that he irritated his enemies both within the Foreign Ministry and in the public domain. Thaksin, in displaying his support for this mission, announced Surakiart's campaign for the top job at the United Nations a national agenda. What followed was Surakiart's busy campaign agenda with scores of overseas trips to introduce himself as part of what he called a "listening tour". Surakiart managed to secure support from ASEAN, amid qualms that other outstanding figures from the grouping may also be interested in the position, such as former Singaporean Prime Minister Goh Chok Tong and Malaysia's former Deputy Prime Minister Anwar Ibrahim, now a leading opposition figure. He personally insisted on Singapore and Malaysia confirming their commitment for support for his candidacy. Finally, Surakiart was on 24 July 2006 declared the official candidate of ASEAN for the position of the UNSG.[109]

Surakiart began, as early as the beginning of 2005, his listening tour to drum up support from far-flung capitals of the world. He was the first announced candidate for the UNSG post. He exploited every opportunity to make his appearance at international gatherings and aimed to win over his voters not only from permanent members of the United Nations Security Council (The United States, Russia, the United Kingdom, France and China — collectively known as the P5), but also small and developing countries in the Middle East, Africa, Central Asia and Latin America. His agenda for the United Nations was spelt out, underscoring global good governance and democracy as the basis of his campaign strategy. He promised to work toward making the United Nations more accountable as part of the organizational management reform. He said, "I think for the United Nations to be an effective voice of democracy and human freedom, the United Nations itself must be a paragon of good governance. It has to be effective, accountable and transparent." He would also push for stricter internal oversights, independent audits, and proposed hiring a "chief operating officer" to help run the vast bureaucracy.[110] The bottom line was to make the United Nations relevant in the rapidly changing world. Surakiart elaborated on the technique of clustering the groups of supporters into three colours, namely red for those countries with candidates; yellow for those countries which had expressed a positive attitude and were considering the matter; and green for firm supporters. The colour green was again divided into various shades, namely light green for those countries which had expressed support but needed to go through internal procedures, ordinary green for countries which had expressed firm support, and dark green for countries which had not only expressed support but had also been campaigning for the Thai candidate.[111]

Surakiart made more than fifty trips abroad within the first year of his campaign, sharpening his French to impress the francophone nations on the African continent, and using his ACD networks to gain support for his candidature. This was not an easy battle. Surakiart faced serious contenders from other countries in the region, including Jayantha Dhanapala (advisor to the President of Sri Lanka), Ban Ki-moon (Foreign Minister of South Korea), Kamal Dervis (former Finance Minister of Turkey) and Shashi Tharoor (distinguished writer of India). Out of the region, his main competitors included Nirj Deva (member of European Parliament), Aleksander Kwasniewski (former President of Poland), and Vaira Vike-Freiberga (Latvian President). However, the real difficulty lay in Surakiart's own backyard. Surakiart's campaign for the position of the UNSG coincided with a critical period in which Thaksin's government was beset by a legitimacy crisis. Tens of thousands of anti-Thaksin protesters marched through Bangkok to demand Thaksin's ouster. Several former ambassadors used these rallies as opportunities to launch scathing attacks on both Thaksin and Surakiart, particularly on the government's support of Surakiart's candidature for the UNSG position. Thailand's domestic crisis and continued squabbling between Surakiart and his opponents represented major reasons behind his failure in the process of the UNSG selection.

An Unsuitable Candidate?

Surakiart once claimed that up to 130 countries offered support for his candidature.[112] But toward the end of 2006, his dream of becoming the second Asian to serve as UNSG was shattered when the United Nations, on 13 October 2006, selected South Korea's Ban Ki-moon to lead the organization. Let's begin with where it went wrong for Surakiart's campaign. It was perhaps because of the military coup that occurred in September 2006, less than a month before the name of the new UNSG was announced. But some analysts argued that the lack of clear vision was responsible for Surakiart's failure. Thitinan asserted that Thailand's approach was unclear, and that Surakiart failed to demonstrate Thai distinction, like Indonesia had done previously by showing how it was moderate, democratic and the largest Muslim country in the world when it bid for the Security Council seat.[113] He spent too much time on "getting to know" small, insignificant states in the remote regions which did not factor in the actual decision behind the selection of UNSG. When he paid a call on Singapore's Minister Mentor Lee Kuan Yew in June 2005, Surakiart was told that he only needed to win over the hearts and minds of the P5 which possessed the real power in the decision-making.[114] Early announcement of Surakiart's candidacy, although seen as his being transparent and democratic, did not necessarily contribute positively to his campaign. It permitted his enemies at home to spend time targeting his image of being an intimidating figure in the Foreign Ministry and a desolate candidate for the UNSG position. Other contenders also learnt from his campaign mistakes and used his early revelation of agenda to sound out the responses from the P5.

Geopolitical factors also acted as an obstacle for Surakiart. There was an international belief that the Thaksin government leaned heavily toward China, a sign that guaranteed U.S. rejection of Surakiart. Western diplomats, accordingly, were uncertain if Surakiart could exercise neutrality as the head of the United Nations.[115] More troubling was Thailand's credibility, which came into serious question as a result of certain policy miscalculations committed by the Thaksin regime, ranging from the extra-judicial killings of over 2,500 alleged narcotic traffickers, the bloody incidents in the deep south in the case of Krue Se and Tak Bai, to Thailand's soft policy toward Myanmar, particularly the alleged conflict of interest arising from the business interests of Thaksin's family empire. Thaksin's perceived role as Myanmar's apologist created an immense impact on Surakiart and led to questions whether his endorsement of the principles of human rights and democracy while campaigning for the United Nations top job could be taken seriously. Moreover, Thaksin's diplomatic faux pas also cost Surakiart his opportunity to emerge as a potential contender for the position. Thaksin's blunt statement of "The United Nations is not my father" summed up the perception of Thailand regarding its respect and faith in the United Nations.[116] The Thai media also reported that Thaksin urged U.S. President George Bush and British Prime Minister Tony Blair to support Surakiart's UNSG bid because he was "obedient", a term that seemed to reflect a sense of "desperation" on the part of Surakiart.[117] In many ways, this showed the intensifying rift between Thaksin and Surakiart as an ever-growing chasm, ever more apparent since the Cabinet reshuffle in 2005 which resulted in Surakiart being removed from the Foreign Minister portfolio. It is also important to point to the fact that two other Thai candidates, Surin Pitsuwan and Supachai Panitchpakdi, were much more credible figures who might easily have won U.S. backing for the post. Thaksin's preference for someone from his own circle over more qualified and popular candidates demonstrates clearly his lack of commitment to Thailand's national interest.

The coup of September 2006 seemed to cut the relationship and political alliance between Thaksin and Surakiart altogether. The media brutally slated Surakiart for his stubbornness to cling on to his candidacy even when his government was overthrown in a coup. The *Nation* reported,

> Right after the coup, Surakiart dutifully criticised the power seizure and the coup plotters, only to change his tone a few hours later. He even had the audacity to ask the coup leader, General Sonthi Boonyaratglin, to continue to back his candidacy for the United Nations top job, which the general kindly granted. Diplomats at the United Nations shook their heads in disbelief. So did the people in Bangkok, knowing full well it would cost the taxpayers several million baht more in public relations fees.[118]

A few years later, Surakiart had a chance to look back at the controversies surrounding him in his bid for the UNSG position. He told the author in 2008 that, in reality, Thaksin never genuinely supported his candidature, otherwise the former premier would not have removed him from the position of foreign minister. His taskforce team was offered a very limited budget and he was allowed up to only four staff working for his campaign. If only he had remained in the position of foreign minister, he would have been able to have approved a sizeable budget for the campaign by himself. But since he was appointed deputy prime minister, the financial plan had to be sanctioned by Thaksin. Surakiart told of the lack of sufficient financial resources as a major obstacle, particularly in investing in research and strategy for the campaign. Surakiart, on many occasions, had to spend from his own pocket for that purpose. However, it is difficult to reconcile Surakiart's complaint about the lack of a generous budget with his extensive official travels while campaigning for the position of the UNSG. Surakiart also seriously questioned Thaksin's sincerity in the support for his United Nations bid. Thaksin never instructed Cabinet members to assist in publicizing Surakiart's candidature, especially during their official visits abroad. Neither did Thaksin raise the issue of Thailand's candidature to and request the support from visiting foreign dignitaries. Foreign Minister Kantathi, likewise, failed to express his backing of Surakiart's campaign.[119]

Surakiart's calibre and determination to lead the international body was indubitable. But he had too many enemies who were willing to sabotage his campaign for the UNSG post. His personality disputes with career diplomats and his perceived nurturing of nepotism inside the walls of the Foreign Ministry created resentment among certain members of this state agency. The problem of perceived nepotism effectively separated the vast majority of officials from Surakiart's inner circle of loyalists inside the Foreign Ministry. In interviews with a number of senior diplomats, they disapproved of the way certain members of the ministry were promoted based on their loyalty to the foreign minister, rather than on the basis of strict meritocracy. This resulted in younger diplomats who were deemed devoted to the foreign minister getting promoted and reaching the executive level in a very short period of time. There was one well-known case in which a diplomat at the rank of counsellor who was recalled to Bangkok from Shanghai to work in the Office of the Foreign Minister, apparently because he "served" the foreign minister well during his visit to this Chinese city. It took him only a few years to climb up to become deputy director-general, with the blessing of the foreign minister.[120] The Jayanama family's opposition to Surakiart's campaign illustrated the personality conflicts and the problem of a growing injustice and intimidation from the top down. Jayanama was an eminent diplomat family. Surakiart's conflict with the Jayanamas could have stemmed from his transfer of two ambassadors from the family to inactive posts within the Foreign Ministry. In a mass rally in front of thousands of anti-Thaksin protesters on 15 March 2006, the retired ambassador to the United Nations Asda Jayanama blasted, "Because we had a weak Foreign Minister who responded to Thaksin as if he were his servant, we have been unable to solve any problems."[121] Asda also claimed that Surakiart parked his car outside the official residence of UNSG at night so that he could see it. "It is very embarrassing," Asda told the crowd.[122] He went on to say that Surakiart's candidature was a lost cause and an embarrassment to Thailand's international standing. Asda added, "It was silly to believe that handshakes from 127 countries amounted to formal endorsements."[123] Surakiart refuted, stating that all such accusations were lies, and threatened to file a defamation suit against Asda if such public attacks were not stopped.[124]

Thaksin's nomination of Surakiart to compete for the position of the UNSG could have simply been his final attempt to stamp Thailand's presence on the world map. It should have worked to harmonize Thaksin's other foreign policy initiatives. But Thaksin's aspiration fell short arguably because of the lack of his seriousness.

And Surakiart became the target of political vengeance. The issue of his candidature was grossly politicized. Surakiart's embarrassment might have been the short-term impact. In the long run, however, Thailand's international reputation was torn away piece by piece. With Thaksin's policy controversies, especially those pertaining to the violations of human rights, Surakiart's campaign for the UNSG position did nothing but put them under global scrutiny. The harsh attacks from Surakiart's enemies on a personal level also highlighted the fact that not only might he not be in a position to take on the United Nations' esteemed responsibilities, but Thailand was not really ready to come forward as a serious leader in multilateral diplomacy because of its internal political bickering.

CONCLUSION

Thaksin's official foreign policy evolved around an up-and-coming international order in which Asia's rise has became a great interest to the rest of the world. Asia has had immense economic dynamism and is criss-crossed by a number of sub-regional and regional cooperative frameworks working toward a future of peace, prosperity, security and sustainable development — most of which Thailand is a member. Thaksin's foreign policy was built on this notion of a thriving Asia with Thailand as a centre of its prosperity. Thaksin repositioned Thailand in the new international setting and constructed a foreign policy that aimed at dominating others, especially in the immediate neighbourhood. The end result was Thaksin's Forward Engagement Policy which was supposedly outward-looking and inclusive in nature. At the bilateral level, building strategic partnerships through trade was selected as a major theme of Thaksin's foreign policy. These partnerships were pursued through a myriad of bilateral FTAs with special concentration on external economic powers, such as the United States, Japan, China, Australia and India. Thaksin also aspired to use the FTAs to crack new markets for Thai exports. At the regional level, although his foreign policy seemed at first a bold attempt to strengthen and raise Asia's profile and voice in the international arena through the ACD and the ACMECS, in reality it served Thaksin's own ambition to fortify the status of his leadership and to reap the benefits from his immediate neighbours in the form of disguised colonization. At the global level, Thaksin showed off his affinity of multilateral diplomacy within the United Nations framework, even when he had earlier belittled it, when he nominated his deputy prime minister for the UNSG position. Also, to unveil a new multi-dimensional foreign policy, Thaksin played along with the Thai idea of peace-making in Myanmar's political crisis. He sketchily made principle, and not only profit, the latest quality of his business-oriented foreign policy.

Controversy, however, struck. Thaksin's self-proclaimed role of a regional leader was unconvincing considering his style of governance. His lack of diplomatic finesse, as well as his policies which he tended to improvise ad hoc instead of basing them on sound principles, represented a primary flaw in his diplomacy. The overwhelming Thai influence, through ACMECS, partially scared off some of the member countries. The focus here was not really the promotion of regionalism, but rather, Thaksin's self-styled nationalism which verged on hegemonization. Such a perception among Thailand's neighbouring countries lingered. The failure of Surakiart's application for the UNSG post also partly but importantly signified the lack of a legitimate principle in Thaksin's foreign policy, especially in the support of democracy and human rights. Moreover, the deliberate politicization of foreign policy issues, as in the way Thaksin exploited them to serve his domestic objectives, revealed that his diplomatic initiatives were at times hollow. They might have helped reinvent Thailand, but in which way and at what cost?

Notes

1. Interview with Dr Surakiart Sathirathai, former Thai Foreign Minister, Bangkok, 27 June 2008.
2. Policy of the government of Prime Minister Thaksin Shinawatra, delivered to the National Assembly, Bangkok, Thailand, 26 February 2001 <http://thaiembdc.org/politics/govtment/policy/54thpolicy/index_t.html> (accessed 1 May 2009).
3. Speech of Krit Garnjana-Goonchorn, Foreign Ministry's Permanent Secretary, at the Swedish Regional Ambassadors' Meeting, Bangkok, 20 March 2006.
4. Thitinan Pongsudhirak, "Thaksin Rising as Regional Leader?", *Korea Herald*, 13 April 2005.
5. Ministry of Foreign Affairs of Thailand, *Karn Thood Yook Mai Hua Jai*

Kue Prachachon [New-Age Diplomacy with the People at its Heart] (Bangkok: Cyber Print, 2003), p. 81.

6. Keynote address of Surakiart Sathirathai, Thai Foreign Minister, on the topic "Where Does Thailand Stand Now?", at the 2nd Annual Economic Review Forum, United Nations Conference Centre, Bangkok, 26 September 2001. In *Thailand's Foreign Policy, Forward Engagement: Collection of Speeches by Dr Surakiart Sathirathai, Minister of Foreign Affairs of Thailand* (Bangkok: Department of Information, Ministry of Foreign Affairs of Thailand, n.d.), p. 85.

7. Sufficiency economy was first introduced by the King in 1997. It is a middle path approach, with an emphasis on human development by putting people and their well-being at the centre of development and providing an alternative to the traditional, more narrowly focused economic growth development paradigm, suitable to U.N. development efforts to promote human development as the *modus operandi* for today's global development efforts. See <http://www.chaipat.or.th/chaipat/journal/dec00/eng/e_economy.html> (accessed 4 May 2009).

8. In this government booklet, Thaksin also revealed his plan to turn Thailand into a mini economic superpower by focusing on the following key economic areas:
   • Enhancing competitiveness
   • Extension of financial and investment opportunities
   • Directing the flow of direct foreign investment into Thailand
   • Development of human resources and development of production
   • Equipping entrepreneurs with tools
   • Promoting Thai products in the world market
   • Conducting offensives in all battlefields (in particular in joint forces with the private sector to launch full offensives in all export markets)
   • Thailand marketplace
   • Proactive diplomacy (in setting up the Thai Trade Representatives and the negotiations on trade agreements)
   • Pushing for Thailand as the centre of Asia
   In *4 Years of Repair for all Thais and Thailand under the Government of Prime Minister Dr Thaksin Shinawatra (2001–2005)* (Bangkok: The Secretariat of the Cabinet Printing Office, 2004), pp. 84–91.

9. Speech of Surakiart Sathirathai, Foreign Minister, on the topic, "Thailand: The Path Forward", Asia Society, New York, 30 September 2004.

10. Speech by Prime Minister Thaksin Shinawatra on the topic "Asia Cooperation Dialogue: The New Asian Realism" delivered at the East Asia Economic Summit 2002, Kuala Lumpur, Malaysia, 6 October

2002 <http://www.aseansec.org/13965.htm> (accessed 12 March 2009).

11. Source: Ministry of Foreign Affairs of Thailand.

12. See <http://www.acddialogue.com/about/index.php> (accessed 28 February 2009).

13. <http://www.mfa.go.th/web/977.php> (accessed 12 March 2009).

14. Kishan S. Rana, *Asian Diplomacy: The Foreign Ministries of China, India, Japan, Singapore and Thailand* (Washington, D.C.: The John Hopkins University Press, 2007), p. 150.

15. Press Release: The Second ACD Ministerial Meeting, 21–22 June 2003, Chiang Mai, Thailand. Source: Ministry of Foreign Affairs of Thailand.

16. Speech by Chinese Premier Wen Jiabao at the Opening Ceremony of the Third ACD Foreign Ministers Meeting, Qingdao, 22 June 2004, on the topic "Working Together to Promote Asian Cooperation in the New Century", <http://www.acddialogue.com/download/ministerial_meetings/203_1.pdf> (accessed 1 March 2009).

17. The 4th Asia Cooperation Dialogue (ACD) Ministerial Meeting, 6 April 2005, Islamabad, Pakistan <http://www.acddialogue.com/download/key_document/104.pdf> (accessed 1 March 2009).

18. Doha Declaration on the Occasion of the Fifth ACD Ministerial Meeting, Doha, Qatar, 24 May 2006 <http://www.acddialogue.com/download/key_document/105.pdf> (accessed 1 March 2009).

19. Chair's Statement: The Sixth Asia Cooperation Dialogue Foreign Ministers' Meeting, 4–5 June 2007, Seoul, Republic of Korea <http://www.acddialogue.com/download/ministerial_meetings/ACD%206%20Chairman%27s%20Statement.pdf> (accessed 1 March 2009).

20. The 7th ACD Declaration, Astana, Kazakhstan, 16 October 2008 <http://www.acddialogue.com/calendar/7th%20ACD%20Declaration.pdf> (accessed 1 March 2009).

21. Colombo Declaration: The 8th ACD Ministerial Meeting, Colombo, Sri Lanka, 15th October 2009 <http://www.acddialogue.com/calendar-/Colombo%20Declaration,%2015th%20October%202009.pdf> (accessed 8 January 2010).

22. Ministry of Foreign Affairs of Thailand, *Karn Thood Yook Mai Hua Jai Kue Prachachon*, p. 87.

23. See <http://www.acddialogue.com/about/index.php> (accessed 28 February 2009).

24. Asia Cooperation Dialogue: Thailand's Concept Paper on Asian (Regional) Bond Market Development <http://209.85.175.132/search?q=cache:N0JzI9ZSl_wJ:www.acddialogue.com/download/cooperation_projects/financial/50.doc+asia+cooperation+dialogue+process&cd=5&hl=en&ct=clnk&gl=sg&client=firefox-a> (accessed 12 March 2009).

25. See Michael K. Connors, "Thailand and the United States of America: Beyond Hegemony", in *Bush and Asia: The US's Evolving Relationships with East Asia*, edited by Mark Beeson (London: Routledge, 2006), pp. 128–44.

26. Speech of Prime Minister Thaksin Shinawatra, on the topic "Forward Engagement: The New Era of Thailand's Foreign Policy", delivered at the Ministry of Foreign Affairs of Thailand, Bangkok, 12 March 2003.

27. Source: Ministry of Finance of Japan. See <http://www.mof.go.jp/english/if/regional_financial_cooperation.htm#ABMI> (accessed 12 December 2009).

28. Press Statement, EMEAP (Executive's Meeting of East Asia and Pacific) Central Banks to Launch Asian Bond Fund, 2 June 2003 <http://www.emeap.org/index.asp?menu=search> (accessed 12 December 2009).

29. Oh Kap-Soo, "Promoting the Asian Bond Market", *Asian Bond Market: Issues and Prospects*, Basel: Bank for International Settlements, No. 30 (November 2006), p. 243. See also Olarn Chaipravat, *Developing the Asian Bond Market* (Singapore: Institute of Southeast Asian Studies, 2005); *Developing an Asian Bond Market: Rationale, Concerns and Roadmap*, A PECC Finance Forum Report on Institutional-Building in a World of Free and Volatile Capital Flows Stemming from the PECC Finance Forum Work 2002–2004 <http://www.pecc.org/finance/papers/ff_asianbondmarket(2004).pdf> (accessed 1 March 2009); and Barry Eichengreen, "What to do with the Chiang Mai Initiative", Asian Economic Paper, Centre for International Development and the Massachusetts Institute of Technology, vol. 2, no. 1 (Winter 2003).

30. Pavin Chachavalpongpun, "ASEM Forum to Boost Asian Bond Market", *The Nation*, 23 July 2003.

31. Deputy Prime Minister Olarn Chaipravat, one of the main engineers behind the development of the Asian Bond Market, believed that Thailand's deepened financial relations with neighbouring countries would alleviate the impact of the global financial crisis at home through the support of the Asian Bond Market. See Anoma Srisukkasem and Wichit Chaitrong, "Olarn Worried about Liquidity amid Global Squeeze", *The Nation*, 1 October 2008.

32. Ministry of Foreign Affairs of Thailand, *Karn Thood Yook Mai Hua Jai Kue Prachachon*, p. 95.

33. Interview with Dr Surakiart Sathirathai, former Thai Foreign Minister, Bangkok, 27 June 2008.

34. Ibid.

35. <http://www.fourelephants.com/current_affairs.php?sid=247> (accessed 1 March 2009).

36. Anuraj Manibhandu and Saritdet Marukatat, "Foreign Policy: Full

Circle in Five Years", *Bangkok Post* <http://www.bangkokpost.com/midyear2002/foreignpolicy.html> (accessed 1 March 2009).

37. Thitinan Pongsudhirak, *Thai Foreign Policy under the Thaksin Government: Out of the Box for Whom*, 29 September 2004 <http://www.thaiworld.org/en/thailand_monitor/answer.php?question_id=70> (accessed 7 April 2009).

38. Interview with an officer at the Office of Policy and Planning, the Thai Foreign Ministry, 27 June 2008, and with a Second Secretary at the Royal Thai Embassy, Singapore, 29 November 2007.

39. Keynote address by Thaksin Shinawatra, Prime Minister, at the ASEAN Business and Investment Summit, Nusa Dua, Bali, Indonesia, 6 October 2003. Source: Ministry of Foreign Affairs of Thailand. Thaksin also said, "ECS now involves cooperation in the areas of trade and investment facilities, industrial and agricultural cooperation, regional transport linkages, tourism and human resources development. The ESC Plan of Action must be totally feasible to implement."

40. "Foreign Ministers' Meeting of 4 Nations on Economic Cooperation Strategy, Bangkok", *Buakaew*, vol. 19 (July–September 2003), p. 14.

41. Source: <http://www.acmecs.org/index.php?id=9> (accessed 5 April 2009).

42. Source: <http://www.acmecs.org/index.php?id=10> (accessed 5 April 2009).

43. "CLMV, ACMECS summits a success, says PM", *VietNamNet Bridge*, 8 November 2008. <http://english.vietnamnet.vn/politics/2008/11/812542/> (accessed 13 December 2009).

44. Source: Office of Policy and Planning, Ministry of Foreign Affairs of Thailand.

45. Source: <http://www.acmecs.org/index.php?id=63> (accessed 5 April 2009).

46. Thailand hosted the ACMECS Special SOM (Senior Officials Meeting) and Ministerial Retreat from 1–2 November 2004 at Krabi, Thailand, with special session meetings between ACMECS members and development partners. Source: Office of Policy and Planning, Ministry of Foreign Affairs of Thailand.

47. Although the exactly location of *suvarnabhumi* was unknown, Thai government's proclamations and national museums insist that *suvarnabhumi* was somewhere on the coast of the central plain, especially at the ancient city of U-Thong. But they have not based their claims on any historical records. Recently, the Thai government named the new Bangkok airport, Suvarnabhumi, in celebration of this tradition. See *Miscellaneous Articles Written for the JSS by His Late Highness Prince Damrong* (Bangkok: The Siam Society, 1962).

48. Thitinan Pongsudhirak, "Thaksin Bends the Wind", *ISEAS Newsletter*, no. 3 (July 2005), p. 2. Also see Thitinan Pongsudhirak, "World War

II and Thailand after Sixty Years", in *Legacies of World War II: South and East Asia*, edited by David Koh Wee Hock (Singapore: Institute of Southeast Asian Studies, 2007), p. 111.

49. Ibid.

50. Thaksin's speech at the Annual Meeting of Ambassadors and Consuls-General of Thailand, Ministry of Foreign Affairs, 27 August 2003, in *Kham Prasai Lae Kham Banyai Khong Pon Tamruad Tree Thaksin Shinawatra Nayok Ratthamontri Lem Thi Nueng* [Speeches and Lectures of Police Lieutenant Colonel, Volume 1], Department of Public Relations, Bangkok, Thailand (n.d.), p. 109.

51. "No Change in Foreign Policy, But More Self-Reliance: Thai PM", *The Nation*, 28 May 2001.

52. *Global Partnership for Development: Thailand's Contribution to Millennium Development Goal 8*, Ministry of Foreign Affairs of Thailand and United Nations Country Team in Thailand, 2005 <http://www.undg.org/archive_docs/6597-Thailand_MDG_Goal_8_Report.pdf> (accessed 7 April 2009), pp. 1–2.

53. Ibid.

54. Kavi Chongkittavorn, "Thailand Relished Its New Image: Donor Country", *The Nation*, 31 October 2005.

55. Toshihiro Kudo and Fumiharu Mieno, "Trade, Foreign Investment and Myanmar's Economic Development during the Transition to an Open Economy", Institute of Developing Economies (IDE) Discussion Paper, No. 116 (August 2007), p. 14.

56. Kavi Chongkittavorn, "Thailand Relished Its New Image: Donor Country".

57. Interview with Dr Surakiart Sathirathai, former Thai Foreign Minister, Bangkok, 27 June 2008.

58. Speech of Surakiart Sathirathai, Foreign Minister, on the topic, "Thailand: The Path Forward", Asia Society, New York, 30 September 2004.

59. Don Pathan and Supalak Ganjanakhundee, "A Tale of Unrealised Global Ambitions", *The Nation*, 11 April 2006.

60. Keynote address by Thaksin Shinawatra, Prime Minister, at the International Business Conference on "Global Economic Governance and Challenges of Multilateralism, organized by the International Chamber of Commerce Bangladesh, Dhaka, Bangladesh, 17 January 2004.

61. Interview with a First Secretary at the Thai Foreign Ministry's Department of East Asian Affairs, Bangkok, 27 June 2008.

62. See Withaya Sucharithanarugse, "Concept and the Function of ACMECS", *South Asian Survey* 13, no. 2 (2006).

63. Achara Ashayagachat, "Academics Slam PM's Foreign Policy Agenda: Thaksin Helping his Personal Ambitions", *Bangkok Post*, 30 September 2004.

64. Kavi Chongkittavorn, "Thailand Relished its New Image: Donor Country".
65. Neth Pheaktra, "Koh Kong to become Second Hong Kong", *Mekong Times*, 26 May 2008.
66. Surapong Jayanama, *Karn Thood Karn Muang Maichai Ruang Suantua* [Diplomacy and Politics are not Personal Issues] (Bangkok: Siam Publishing Company, 2007), p. 141.
67. Pasuk Phongpaichit, "A Country is a Company, a PM is a CEO", paper presented at the seminar on "Statesman or Manager? Image and Reality of Leadership in Southeast Asia", organized by the Bangkok Office of the Centre of Southeast Asian Studies (CSEAS), Kyoto University, Political Economy Centre, Faculty of Economics and Faculty of Political Science, Chulalongkorn University, Bangkok, Thailand, 2 April 2004.
68. FTA Watch Group, *Thailand's Free Trade Agreements and Human Rights Obligations* (March 2005) <http://www.ftawatch.org/autopage1/show_page.php?t=22&s_id=3&d_id=3> (accessed 11 April 2009).
69. During the Thaksin years, Thailand's role in international trade negotiations and those at the WTO were described as a sort of negligence. Thai representatives to the WTO were not proactive. After all, Supachai Panitchpakdi, Director-General of the WTO, was a Democrat in the opposition.
70. Speech of Prime Minister Thaksin Shinawatra at Sanam Luang, 4 February 2005, translated by Chris Baker and Pasuk Phongpaichit. Author's copy.
71. Thaksin's interview with Maurice R. Greenberg, at the Council on Foreign Relations, New York, 18 September 2006.
72. Peter Warr, "The Economy under the Thaksin government: Stalled Recovery", in *Divided Over Thaksin: Thailand's Coup and Problematic Transition*, edited by John Funston, (Singapore: Institute of Southeast Asian Studies, 2009), pp. 153–54 and 169–71.
73. Ministry of Foreign Affairs of Thailand, *Karn Thood Yook Mai Hua Jai Kue Prachachon*, pp. 100–01.
74. Ukrist Pathmanand, *Thai Kap Asia: Karnmuang Toon Lae Khwammankong Yuk Lang Wikrit Setthakit* [Thailand and Asia: Politics, Capitals and Security in Post-Crisis Era] (Bangkok: Chulalongkorn University, 2003), pp. 30–31.
75. Speech of Prime Minister Thaksin Shinawatra, "Forward Engagement: The New Era of Thailand's Foreign Policy".
76. Sources: Department of Trade Negotiations, Ministry of Commerce of Thailand, and the Delegation of the European Commission to Thailand.
77. Somkiart Tangkitvanich, *Toon Niyom Thai Bon Naewthang Thaksinomics Lae Pontor Nayobai Karnpattana* [Thai Capitalism à la Thaksinomics

and Its Impact on Development Policy], in *Fah Daew Kan* [Same Sky] 2, no. 1 (January–March 2004), p. 94.

78. <http://www.thailandelite.com/home.php> (accessed 11 April 2009).

79. Suchat Sritama, "Thailand Elite Card Holders Reassured", *The Nation*, 17 January 2009. Also see "Playing with the Wrong Card", *The Weekend Standard*, 23–24 October 2004.

80. Source: Government House, Thailand.

81. Interview with a retired Thai ambassador, Bangkok, 27 June 2008.

82. Source: Department of Export Promotion, Ministry of Commerce of Thailand.

83. Julawadee Worasakyothin, *FTA a Year After: Does Thailand Win or Lose?*, International Institute for Trade and Development, 2006 <http://www.itd.or.th/th/node/234> (accessed 10 April 2009).

84. Somkiart, *Toon Niyom Thai Bon Naewthang Thaksinomics Lae Pontor Nayobai Karnpattana*, p. 94. Also see "Thailand's Free Trade Agreements and the Human Rights Obligations", paper prepared by FTA Watch Thailand for submission to the 84th Session of the UN Human Rights Committee, March 2005 <http://www.ftawatch.org/autopage1/show_page.php?t=22&s_id=3&d_id=3> (accessed 12 April 2009).

85. Somkiart, *Toon Niyom Thai Bon Naewthang Thaksinomics Lae Pontor Nayobai Karnpattana*, pp. 112–13.

86. Suwinai Paranawalai, *Kaeroi Thaksinomics Kapkhwamchampen Khong Thangluekthisam* [Tracing Thaksinomics: the Necessity of the Third Option] (Bangkok: Openbooks, 2004), p. 34.

87. Pavin Chachavalpongpun, *Thailand: Bending with the (Chinese) Wind?*, paper presented at the International Workshop on "East Asia Facing a Rising China", jointly organized by the East Asia Institute of Singapore and the Konrad Adenauer Stiftung, Singapore, 11–12 August 2008.

88. "Thailand's Free Trade Agreements and the Human Rights Obligations", paper prepared by FTA Watch Thailand for submission to the 84th Session of the UN Human Rights Committee, March 2005.

89. "Sovereignty Not for Sale, Say Thailand's Civil Society in Opposing the Government's Free Trade Agreements (FTAs)", FTA Watch Group <http://www.ftawatch.org/autopage1/show_page.php?t=21&s_id=5&d_id=5> (accessed 12 April 2009). Also, Charoen Khampiraphap, "Kor Toklong Karnkha Seri: Lod Phasee Lue Lod Atipatai" [Free Trade Agreements: Tariff Reduction or Sovereignty Reduction], *Kor Toklong Kedkarnkha Seri Ponkratop Ti Mee Tor Prathetthai* [Free Trade Agreements and Their Impacts on Thailand], edited by Kannikar Kittivejakul (Bangkok: Pimdee Publishing, 2004), pp. 38–39.

90. Through concessions granted through to the PTT Exploration and Production Co Ltd (PTTEP) in the Yadana and Yetagun fields in the

Bay of Bengal, Thailand is at present importing about 9 billion standard cubic feet a day and wishes to buy an additional 100 million cubic feet of gas per day to match its rising domestic demand.

91. Thaksin's interview with Maurice R. Greenberg.

92. In my interview with a First Secretary of the Royal Thai Embassy in Yangon, Myanmar, 2 December 2008. See also Priscilla Koh, "Thailand's Myanmar Roadmap under Fire", *Asia Times*, 14 August 2003 <http://www.atimes.com/atimes/Southeast_Asia/EH14Ae02.html> (accessed 13 December 2009).

93. "Mass Rally Supports Seven-Point Roadmap Clarified by Prime Minister", *New Light of Myanmar*, 20 September 2003.

94. Thitinan Pongsudhirak, "A Win-Win-Win Proposition for Thaksin", *The Irrawaddy*, 17 August 2005.

95. Source: Ministry of Foreign Affairs of Thailand.

96. "Thoughts on the Bangkok Process", *The Irrawaddy* 12, no. 3 (March 2004).

97. Kitti Wasinondh, "Thai Foreign Ministry's Continuous Thread", *The Nation*, 12 April 2006. Kitti Wasinondh was the Foreign Ministry's spokesperson at the time.

98. Thitinan, "A Win-Win-Win Proposition for Thaksin".

99. Pasuk Phongpaichit and Chris Baker, *Thaksin: The Business of Politics in Thailand* (Chiang Mai: Silkworm Books, 2004), p. 211.

100. "Burma Ties Still Good, Assures PM", *The Nation*, 24 April 1997.

101. Aung Zaw, "Thaksin's Burma Blunder", *The Irrawaddy*, 6 March 2006.

102. Pavin Chachavalpongpun, "Neither Constructive Nor Engaging: The Debacle of ASEAN's Burma Policy", in *Between Isolation and Internationalisation: The State of Burma*, edited by Johan Lagerkvist, no. 4 (Stockholm: The Swedish Institute of International Affairs, 2008), p. 216.

103. <http://www.surakiart.com/bio_e2.asp> (accessed 16 April 2009).

104. Rana, *Asian Diplomacy: The Foreign Ministries of China, India, Japan, Singapore and Thailand*, p. 154. Four years after the U.N.-brokered settlement in 1991, in which Thailand too had played a role, it welcomed Vietnam and the other Indochinese states into ASEAN.

105. Interview with Dr Tej Bunnag, former Foreign Minister and former Permanent Secretary of the Foreign Ministry, Bangkok, 27 June 2008.

106. Keynote address of Dr Surakiart Sathirathai, Thai Foreign Minister at the 57th Session of the United Nations General Assembly, New York, the United States, 17 September 2002. In *Thailand's Foreign Policy, Forward Engagement: Collection of Speeches by Dr Surakiart Sathirathai, Minister of Foreign Affairs of Thailand*, pp. 218–27.

107. Peter Heinlein, "ASEAN nations back Thai Foreign Minister as Next UN Secretary-General", *Voice of America*, 30 September 2004

<http://payvand.com/news/04/sep/1256.html> (accessed 13 December 2009).

108. Interview with Dr Tej Bunnag.

109. Source: Press Release, ASEAN Candidate for United Nations Secretary-General, 24 July 2006. Also see "ASEAN Firmly behind Thai Surakiart's Bid for Top UN Job", *Associated Press*, 20 July 2006.

110. "Thai Candidate for U.N. Sounds Reform Note", *International Press Report*, 15 December 2005.

111. Pranee Chantrakul, "Surakiart Peud Chai Kiewkap Karn Ronnarong Tamnaeng Laykhathikarn Sahaprachachart" [Surakiart Opens His Heart on the UNSG Campaign], *Kaosod*, 1 March 2006.

112. Don Pathan and Supalak Ganjanakhundee, "Thaksin's Vanishing Act: Precious Little Remains of Five Years of Foreign Policy", *The Nation*, 12 April 2006.

113. Achara Ashayagachat, "Academics Slam PM's Foreign Policy Agenda: Thaksin Helping his Personal Ambitions".

114. Author was also in the meeting.

115. See, Busakorn Chantasasawat, "The Burgeoning Sino-Thai Relations: Seeking Sustained Economic Security", *China: An International Journal* 4, no. 1 (March 2006): 86–112.

116. Supalak Ganjanakhundee, "Drug-Related Killings: Verify the Toll, Says Diplomat", *The Nation*, 4 March 2003.

117. "A Year of Thai Foreign Policy Blunders", *The Nation*, 30 December 2006.

118. Ibid.

119. Interview with Dr Surakiart Sathirathai.

120. In discussions with a number of former ambassadors, in Bangkok, during June–July 2008.

121. "Ex-Envoys Slam Foreign Policy", *The Nation*, 16 March 2006.

122. "Surakiart Embarrasses Nation by Parking Outside U.N. Sec-Gen Residence at Night: Former Ambassador", *The Nation*, 25 March 2006 <http://www.nationmultimedia.com/breakingnews/read.php?newsid=30000200> (accessed 16 April 2009).

123. "French Leader's Visit Time to Reconsider Surakiart's U.N. Bid", *The Nation*, 17 March 2006.

124. "Surakiart would File Libel Suit against Former Thai Ambassador", *The Nation*, 27 March 2006 <http://www.nationmultimedia.com/breakingnews/read.php?newsid=30000318> (accessed 16 April 2009).

4

BILATERAL RELATIONS
Tailoring of a Thaksinized Diplomacy

Prime Minister Thaksin Shinawatra divided his world of diplomacy into two zones. The first zone encompassed Thailand's immediate neighbours where primary national interests lay. The other zone included countries beyond the sub-region and great powers with whom Thailand has long woven close relations.[1] This categorization signified Thaksin's degree of interest in his engagement and interaction with them, as well as their level of significance in the eyes of Thailand. In the proximate zone, Thaksin regarded the strengthening of relations with Myanmar, Cambodia, Laos and Malaysia as his foreign policy's number-one priority. This was because of the geographical closeness, the sensitivity of security along the border, the sizeable cross-border trade, and the close and regular contacts between peoples of both sides of the frontier. These fundamental factors impelled upon Thaksin a readjustment in foreign policy that was needed to build good and friendly ties. It was a challenging task for Thaksin. A bitter history and a sense of mistrust represented the main obstacles that were faced. Formulating an amicable policy toward immediate neighbours not only served Thailand's perceived national objectives, it also accommodated Thaksin's need to provide an environment of security and economic prosperity for the Thais who lived in the borderland. With the exception of Malaysia, Thaksin promoted good neighbourliness, especially with Myanmar, Laos and Cambodia, and this benefited his voters in Thailand's north and northeast regions. Moreover, Thaksin, like Chatichai, ordered the shift of Thailand's diplomatic focus, from powers outside the region to former enemies in the neighbourhood. With a new spotlight on countries in the region, Thailand could reinvent itself as a leader with a new responsibility.

In this study, the outer zone comprises China and the United States. Thailand was at different times in the past a client state of both Beijing and Washington. Thaksin, in his determination to alter the traditional pattern of diplomatic relations with both powers, sought to become the first among equals in Chinese and American eyes. Marwaan Macan Markar wrote in 2003, "In the past, the military had a bigger voice in US policy," says Chulalongkorn University's lecturer Panitan Wattanayagorn, "but not now, after the Thaksin government was elected." Thaksin's Thai Rak Thai party was elected to power in January 2001 by a thumping majority. This ensured that for the first time since the country embarked on the road towards democracy in 1932, parliament would have the largest voice in shaping national policy. "When Thaksin came to power, he started using different approaches. One was standing up to the US," says *The Nation's* Kavi Chongkittavorn. "He is the first prime minister to have such a relationship with the US." At the same time, Thaksin has tried to cultivate new "strategic partners" rather than being completely dependent on Washington's whims. China has figured prominently in the premier's vision, which aims to be more Asian-oriented. "Thailand's foreign policy is going through a period of change; from relying on one strategic partner to having more strategic partners," says Panitan.[2] Whether the two powers really gave Thaksin special recognition is a subject of examination in this chapter. At the same time as Thaksin was revealing his newly modified foreign policy based on the concentration on immediate neighbours, his relations with ASEAN deteriorated. The region-wide crisis in 1997 and slow progress on free trade made Thaksin aware of ASEAN's limitations. Thaksin also depicted ASEAN as a Cold War-type organization, being incapable of coping with emerging issues.[3] Thaksin's attitude toward ASEAN was analogous to his view of the United Nations, as being a large, awkward and clumsy organization. Yet, he exploited his engagement with the United Nations whenever it suited him, such as in his nomination of Surakiart for the UNSG position.

One major characteristic of Thaksin's conduct of bilateral relations was his intention to obscure the line between national interest and his private interest. The goal behind the consolidation of Thailand's alliance and partnership with its neighbours and external powers might have been to fulfil national interests. However, the official goals tended to cloak the reality behind Thailand's intimate ties with these countries. National interest, despite its authoritative and sacred nature, was occasionally treated as a purely nominal objective in Thaksin's diplomatic consciousness. On this basis, it explains why his seemingly friendly foreign policy failed to win over trust from Thailand's neighbours and why it was on shaky ground. Thai relations with Myanmar, Cambodia and Laos, in particular, exemplified such complexity and ambiguity within Thaksin's foreign policy.

MYANMAR

Relations between Thailand and Myanmar have been erratic over the years, depending on the changing notions of national interests, especially on Thailand's part following its periodic change of regime types. A typical picture of Myanmar in the Thai consciousness was gloomily painted as Thailand's reprehensible enemy who destroyed its old capital of Ayutthaya in 1767. This sour part of history has been incessantly exploited by successive Thai regimes in their creation of the face of an arch enemy to justify their political existence. The arbitrary way of identifying an enemy effectively perpetuated the feeling of hatred between the two nations right to the modern day. Thailand and Myanmar established their diplomatic relations on 24 August 1948, at the time when the latter was still called Burma. Even after the normalization of diplomatic relations, Thailand continued to perceive Burma as a threat and exploited the existing bilateral problems as reasons for nurturing such perception, such as the ethnic insurgencies along their common border and the narcotic trade inside Burma. But when Thaksin came to power with his business-oriented foreign policy, Myanmar's role as Thailand's historical adversary disappeared overnight. Thaksin was more interested in promoting economic relations with Myanmar and avoided upsetting its military regime in regard to the absence of political reform in the country. In this process, Thaksin allegedly benefited from his pro-Myanmar policy to accumulate his wealth and worked with his contacts, the Myanmar generals, on business deals like the mega telecommunications projects. Thaksin's commerce-centric foreign policy met with a favourable response from Yangon whose leaders were desperate to see hard cash since they have been suffering from international sanctions. The oscillation of Thai policy toward Myanmar, from being a fierce rival to a new trading partner, had been evident for a decade since Chatichai took power in 1988 through the Democrat years from 1997 onwards. This decade witnessed a changing pattern of bilateral relationships between Thailand and Myanmar. Under the Democrat government of Prime Minister Chuan Leekpai (1997–2001), an updated version of Chatichai's "Constructive Engagement Policy" was pronounced toward Myanmar.[4] Foreign Minister Surin Pitsuwan named it the "Flexible Engagement Policy". It permitted neighbours of Myanmar to voice their concerns over the country's domestic situation, especially if it had the potential to produce negative impacts on them. Myanmar was outraged by Surin's policy. From 1997 to 2001, as a result, Thai-Myanmar relations were visibly strained.[5] This Thai policy split opinion among ASEAN members. Some slammed Surin's idea as a breach of the non-intervention principle. But Surin also gained considerable support from other ASEAN members.[6] His past performance somehow helped him attain the position of ASEAN Secretary-General.

Despite periodic armed border clashes in early 2001, the amicable era of Thai-Myanmar relations returned with Thaksin assuming the position of premier as well as coming forward as the unofficial mouthpiece of the Myanmar regime. Democracy and respect for human rights were set aside. Economic interests became an imperative determining factor in Thai-Myanmar bilateral relations under the Thaksin administration. Thaksin's visit to Yangon in June 2001, four months after he formed the government, was meant to carry Thai-Myanmar relations into a new era of friendship based on mutual trust and economic benefits. Thaksin was quick to celebrate the success of his visit as a result of both countries' conclusion of the memorandum of understanding on narcotic cooperation. However, the national agenda was not only on the mind of Thaksin. Desmond Ball noted that in the aftermath of Thaksin's visit to Yangon, the Myanmar government announced that it had leased an additional Thaksin-owned ThaiCom-3 transponder to upgrade its telecommunications transmission capacity. Thaksin, owner of Shin's ThaiCom-2 and -3 communications satellites, had provided telecommunications services to Myanmar even before he became prime minister, these including television broadcast, telephone and Internet services. Ball said, "This was perhaps the main outcome of Thaksin's visit in June to patch up Thai-Burmese ties."[7] Thaksin's new Myanmar policy was therefore contentious right at the beginning. The danger in the radical shift of Thai policy toward Myanmar, from Chuan's support for Myanmar's democracy to Thaksin's business deals, with the Myanmar generals, was that it could potentially undermine Thailand's diplomatic credibility in the long run.[8]

In 2003, Thaksin's Shin Corp, the third largest satellite operator in Asia, concluded a fresh deal with Bagan Cybertech, an internet service provider of Ye Naing Win who is the son of Prime Minister Khin Nyunt. Prior to the signing of the contract, Thaksin invited Myanmar to participate in the Economic Cooperation Strategy (ECS), a precursor of ACMECS, in which Bangkok offered Yangon generous financial assistance worth US$45 million.[9] Thaksin defended that the involvement of Myanmar in ACMECS would render greater economic benefits to Thai businesses. Of course, these included his family businesses. It was a part of bringing Myanmar into a regional mainstream, and this would aid its democratization process at home. The "Bangkok Process" was thus initiated alongside as a political platform that ran parallel with the overall business-centric foreign policy toward Myanmar. Thaksin was eager to prove his opposition's criticism wrong. Support for political change in Myanmar did not need to be antithetical to Thai economic interests in that country. And Thaksin proved this with statistics. Myanmar represented a myriad of economic benefits for Thailand, ranging from natural gas, teak, gems and precious stones, marine products, as well as low-wage Myanmar labour.[10] Significant economic interests acquired through Thaksin's new approach toward Myanmar were manifest. In 2005, Thailand was Myanmar's top trading partner, with total bilateral trade amounting to US$2.5

billion, increasing 27.2 per cent from the previous year. Thai private businesses had invested in fifty-six projects in Myanmar — totalling more than US$1.3 billion, or equivalent to 17.28 per cent of Myanmar's total foreign direct investment.[11] On top of this, Thailand's exports to Myanmar amounted to around US$1.26 billion annually. The total border trade stood at US$2.2 billion in 2005. In comparison, in the pre-Thaksin period, Thai-Myanmar total trade only amounted to US$275.91 million in 1995 and US$515.47 million in 2000.[12]

As bilateral trade was healthy and vibrant, Thaksin's family business in Myanmar was also blossoming as a consequence of the new thrust in Thai-Myanmar economic relations. Reportedly, Thaksin was involved in setting up high technology communications networks in Myanmar as part of the IPStar project, a US$350 million telecom broadband satellite.[13] This project was linked with the controversial EXIM Bank's Bt4 billion baht loan to Myanmar in 2004 within the ACMECS framework. Under ACMECS conditions, Thailand's EXIM Bank provided financial support to Thai investors and exporters under the procurement contracts granted by the Myanmar government. Thaksin's family telecom empire won major concessions and was granted the right to monopolize the supply of telecom equipment to Myanmar.[14] Clearly, Thaksin was preoccupied with shoring up his own family interests both in the form of power and money in his relations with the Myanmar government. His self interests resulted in the Thai policy of piggybacking the Myanmar regime even when the latter was accused of committing human rights violations, and continued to belittle ASEAN's credibility and reputation. Thaksin's Myanmar policy was harshly reproached by the West for lacking morality and therefore contributing to a worsening situation in Myanmar.[15] Former ambassador Surapong Jayanama argued that the Thai Rak Thai government and its business proxies gained economic benefits at the expense of their tolerance of Myanmar's ruthless regime.[16] Thaksin's trade-oriented policy vis-à-vis Myanmar failed to wield influence with the Myanmar regime because of the lack of moral principles and the conflicts of interest on the part of Thaksin. Myanmar, to a certain extent, was able to manipulate Thai policy to the regime's favour. While Thaksin claimed that Thailand was enjoying cordial economic ties with Myanmar, skirmishes between the two countries' armies, which first erupted in early 2001, continued along their common border right through 2002.[17] The Thai army, especially those stationed in the north, disapproved of Thaksin's cosy relations with Yangon. It publicly criticized Myanmar for using the Wa army to create a security crisis along the border as a bargaining chip for Thai accommodation.[18] Furthermore, Thailand had long suffered from narcotic flows from Myanmar, and the UWSA was widely believed to be behind the massive surge in illegal methamphetamine (or *yaa baa* in Thai) production in Thailand. As Thaksin declared war against drugs in 2003, he was extremely cautious not to point a finger at Yangon as a culprit.

Thaksin made public his disagreement of a sanction policy imposed against the Myanmar regime by the international community. He said in 2006, "I think better talk, dialogue is important. Whether you like me or not and whether we like you or not, if we talk, we start to understand each other. Sanctions are not working in Myanmar."[19] Thaksin's policy also compelled Thailand to abandon the buffer zone and its long-standing position of tolerating rebels who operated along its border with Myanmar. Colonel Yawd Serk of the Shan State Army voiced his disappointment over Thaksin's decision to comply with the Myanmar regime and walk out on the Shans and the Karens who had traditionally maintained close ties with the Thai Army.[20] Human Rights Watch, additionally, reported that the Thaksin government continued to repatriate Myanmar refugees living along Thailand's border, apparently to show a friendly gesture toward his Myanmar counterpart.[21] The original idea of employing foreign policy to dominate neighbouring countries proved to be ineffective in the case of Thai-Myanmar relations. In reality, Thaksin's policy was constantly shaped and influenced by Myanmar. Thaksin's final visit to Naypyidaw on 2 August 2006 was partly to reconnect the link between the Thai and Myanmar leaderships that was lost as a result of Khin Nyunt's downfall in 2004. Thaksin became the first foreign leader to visit Myanmar's new capital, Naypyidaw. This one-day visit stirred up suspicion of his other agenda and astonished the international community, as well as among the Thai Foreign Ministry officials. While Thaksin described his urgent trip as an ordinary mission aimed at persuading Myanmar not to isolate itself from the world, local and international media believed that his visit was tailored to ink his unfinished telecoms deals with the Myanmar generals.[22]

Myanmar, in the mindset of Thaksin, might have been a poorer nation, backward, and in need of Thai assistance. Yet, the reason behind numerous unsuccessful attempts to convince the regime to strive for serious political reforms was due to his flawed foreign policy. Thaksin's policy toward Myanmar was primarily self-serving, with a special emphasis on enhancing economic interests, both at the national and personal levels, but considerably soft on applying principles where necessary. This was hardly surprising since Thaksin himself, though deceptively dressed in a democratic uniform, was increasingly tilting toward autocracy. His foreign policy toward Myanmar was a mirror image of his style of governance.

CAMBODIA

Thai Historian Charnvit Kasetsiri noted,

> Among the neighbouring countries of Southeast Asia, none seems more similar to Thailand than Cambodia. Both nations share similar customs, traditions, beliefs, and ways of life. This is especially true of royal customs, language, writing systems, vocabulary, literature, and the dramatic arts. In light of these similarities, it seems surprising, therefore, that relations between Thailand and Cambodia should be characterised by deep-seated "ignorance, misunderstanding, and prejudice". Indeed, the two countries have what can be termed a "love-hate relationship".[23]

As in Myanmar's case, history plays an important, and perhaps devious, part in moulding Thai perception toward Cambodians, and vice versa.[24] Thai authorities chose to downplay certain historical facts, for example, the overwhelming Khmer cultural influence on Siam and the Thai adoption of some superior aspects of Khmer civilization. David Wyatt once said, "Ayutthaya is successor of Angkor."[25] Angkor, the seat of the Khmer empire, was destroyed by the Siamese army in 1431. Instead, this part of history that told the tragic end of Angkor was used by past Siamese monarchs and successive military regimes to champion the Thai nation and to reify a hollow Thai identity. First, Thailand today sees itself superior to its Cambodian neighbour, both as a successful consolidated kingdom and as a modern state with an advanced economy. Second, Cambodians are generally viewed as untrustworthy and traitorous; in this, they have been portrayed by the Thais as opportunists who conspired with their French master in colonial times to steal supposedly Siamese territories. To the Thais, they were taught to believe that Battambang, Sisophon and Siem Reap were Siamese territories but Siam was forced to cede them to the French. It can be argued that the ongoing territorial conflict between Thailand and Cambodia has been perpetuated by a distorted historical record. Cambodia, too, has from time to time recreated a demonic image of Thailand to satisfy its own political purposes such as during the Indochina war[26] and recently in the territorial dispute over the Preah Vihear Temple. In general, relations between the two countries have been volatile and often succumb to domestic conditions as much as to regional circumstances.

Thailand and Cambodia share approximately 800 kilometres of borders, parts of which have never been clearly demarcated. Thai support for the Khmer Rouge during the Cambodian conflict and its unconcealed antagonism towards a Hanoi-backed Cambodian regime added deeper mutual suspicions between the two countries even after the conflict was over in 1991. Prime Minister Chatichai's marketplace policy in the late 1980s was admirable as it signalled Thailand's support for peace. But Thailand's struggle in balancing its burning desire to make peace with, and the economic exploitation of, its neighbour severely discredited Thailand's foreign policy.[27] Thaksin carried with him a more determined ambition to overcome mutual mistrust and share Thai prosperity with Cambodia on a mutual benefit basis so as to avoid Thailand's earlier exploitative approach.[28] He devised his initiatives to change the pattern of Thai-Cambodian diplomatic interactions. Long years of war in Cambodia effectively legitimized the role of the Thai military in the conduct of foreign policy.[29] But in the new century, Thaksin jumped onto the front seat to steer his own form of Cambodian policy. Bilateral business cooperation was prioritized, and the first thing for Thaksin was to strengthen personal ties with Cambodia's leadership. He headed off to visit Prime Minister Hun Sen in June 2001.

After Thaksin became prime minister in 2001, he paid official and private visits to Hun Sen eight times. His strategy was straightforward: gain access to the Cambodian leadership and strengthen ties, just as he had with Myanmar's ruling leaders. In fact, these ties were forged even before Thaksin's assumption of premiership. Soon after Hun Sen retook power in a 1997 putsch, Thaksin inked telecommunications deals with Cambodia under the 35-year licence granted by Ministry of Posts and Telecommunications of Cambodia until 4 March 2028, through his company "Cambodia Shinawatra".[30] Better known as "CamShin", it was, during the Thaksin years, the second largest mobile service operator with a subscriber base of 100,000 and the fifth Internet service provider in Cambodia, and has been appointed an exclusive dealer to serve Shinawatra Satellite or SATTEL, also a Thaksin company. SATTEL has one of the largest exposures in Cambodia with a 100 per cent stake in CamShin, which has to this day provided Internet service in Cambodia under the brand "CamNet", transponder leasing and other related business services and telephone business. Revenues from sales and services of CamShin in Cambodia for 2003 was Bt4.3 billion, which was an increase of Bt607 million or 16.4 per cent from Bt3.7 billion in 2002.[31] It was undeniable that Thaksin's intimate relations with the Cambodian leadership were buttressed by the political economy of his foreign policy.

On the national front, the renewed image of Thailand as a donor promptly set a new trend in the bilateral relationship. The ACMECS was made a key platform to strengthen Thai relations with Cambodia, as well as Thaksin's family business in this country. Under the framework, forty-six common projects plus 224 bilateral projects were lined up for implementation over ten years following the first declaration. These projects mostly involved road construction, telecommunications and infrastructure development, the transfer of technology, human resources development and the exchange of working expertise between civil servants of the two countries. A bilateral Cabinet meeting was first introduced in June 2003, five months after the ransacking of the Royal Thai Embassy in Phnom Penh. Two meetings were organized back-to-back, in Cambodia's Siem Reap and Thailand's Ubon Ratchathani respectively.[32] Agreements on promoting sister cities were signed. During the first meeting of Foreign Ministers on the ECS, the precursor of ACMECS, between Cambodia, Lao PDR, Myanmar and Thailand (CLMT), held in Bangkok on 1 August 2003, a part of the discussion pertained to how to enhance cultural cooperation among member countries. Thailand and Cambodia, accordingly, agreed to carry out "sister cities programmes" to promote regular contacts among their peoples. These included Thailand's Si Sa Ket-Cambodia's Siem Reap, Surin-Oddar Meanchey, Sa Kaew-Banteay Meanchey, Chanthaburi-Pailin, and Trat-Koh Kong.[33] More activities between Thai and Cambodian provincial governors in the borderland were encouraged. On 18 June 2001, Cambodia and Thailand signed a Memorandum of Understanding (MOU) regarding the Area of their Overlapping Maritime Claims to the Continental Shelf and vowed to make use of the Joint Commission (JC) for Bilateral Cooperation, first established in 1995, to promote all areas of cooperation including the issues of border demarcation and maritime delimitation through the Joint Border Commission (JBC). On top of this, Thaksin influenced regional organizations, such as the ADB, to provide financial and technical assistance to countries in the region through frameworks like the GMS and the ACMECS, of which Thailand and Cambodia are members. Hun Sen was enthusiastic to play a part in Thaksin's projects because of the apparent political and economic interests. Vichak Visetnoi, Deputy Director-General of the Thai Foreign Trade Department, anticipated that the two-way trade value among member countries of ACMECS would increase by 50 per cent if its planned projects to promote trade and investment were completed successfully.[34]

The business-first mentality imbued within Thai-Cambodian relations served several purposes. It served as the latest avenue of cooperation where both countries could benefit directly from various joint economic projects. It supposedly helped bury their contentious history and old images of enemy, and diffuse lingering suspicions between them. More importantly, it served to neutralize the ongoing political troubles, such as territorial disputes and security issues along their common borders. But Thaksin also realized that his approach — pure business and no politics — would be successful only if he involved the Cambodian leaders who controlled most of the big businesses in Phnom Penh. Lucrative businesses owned by provincial godfathers and mafias along the Thai-Cambodian border were found to have the blessing of politicians. These businesses were an essential part of Cambodian politics. Hun Sen has been in power since 1985, making him Southeast Asia's longest serving head of government besides the Sultan of Brunei. His longevity has been sustained by the strong backing of a business community that has benefited from strong growth and political stability after decades of war. But Hun Sen's impressive record has continued to be stained by international corruption studies that rank Cambodia among the most corrupt nations in the world.[35] Sam Rainsy, a French-educated former finance minister who leads a prominent opposition party, contended that much of Cambodia's economic activity involved illegal businesses or black market operations, ranging from illicit logging, land speculation, to gambling and prostitution. Such businesses thrived, he said, because of a political system permeated with graft.[36]

Whether Thaksin's trade-centric foreign policy became an element of Cambodia's underground businesses was unclear. Yet, in looking back at the murky record, the Thai military's support for the Khmer Rouge had some business intentions. Some Thai military figures were accused by the United Nations of giving financial support to the Khmer Rouge in exchange for illegal logs, gems and priceless ancient Khmer statues. This business relationship enabled the guerrillas to continue its political course against the Phnom Penh government. L. Brooks Entwistle, who worked as a United Nations volunteer electoral supervisor for the border district of Choam Khsan in Cambodian province of Preah Vihear in 2003, revealed the existence of business ties between the Thai military and the Khmer Rouge. His account was published in the *New York Times* in 2004.[37] In the modern day, gambling dens along the Thai-Cambodian border are mushrooming. They have taken direct advantage of the openness of the Cambodian border trade partly thanks to Thaksin's business policy that promoted free flows of capital and humans across the border. The characteristics of such cross-border business activities, echoed in the blurring line between legal and illegal business, inevitably made Thaksin's personalized foreign policy and his close contacts with the Cambodian leaders questionable. After Thaksin was ousted from power, he continued to forge his alliance with Hun Sen. Their meeting in Siem Reap on 5 April 2008 centred on Thaksin's interest in a myriad of investment projects in Koh Kong province, adjacent to the Thai border. Cambodian Defence Minister General Teah Banh subsequently confirmed that Thaksin was planning large-scale investments in Cambodia with Koh Kong serving only as his first step in his business ventures in the country.[38] It was reported that Thaksin eyed Koh Kong as a prime location for his casino and entertainment complex. Besides the Koh Kong project, Thaksin also planned to develop new tourist attractions in Phnom Penh and other major cities. Hun Sen was said to be pleased with Thaksin's proposal and was keen to work with him because Thaksin was "trustworthy".[39] Thai media also reported that Thaksin offered to help the Cambodian government develop a modern town near the site of the disputed Preah Vihear Temple.[40] Members of the opposition investigated Thaksin's private businesses with Cambodia in order to find if they were benefited by his foreign policy. In the case of the Preah Vihear Temple, they accused him of selling national integrity in exchange for his economic interests in Cambodia. More recently in late 2009, as part of engineering a political plot against the incumbent Abhisit Vejjajiva government, Thaksin accepted the offer of Hun Sen to be his government's economic advisor. Both men have found a mutual enmity in Abhisit and thus worked closely to belittle his political legitimacy.

But Thaksin's merging of national interest and private business made Thailand's Cambodian policy vulnerable to the game of politics, both inside Thailand and in Cambodia. Thaksin might have believed that he was an established hegemon in his relations with Cambodia. But Cambodia never confined itself to the Thai hegemonic world. It is known that Hun Sen has long enjoyed political support from Vietnam, and therefore did not need to depend on Thailand's seeming benevolence alone. From this perspective, Thaksin's foreign policy could be seen as short-sighted. Arguably, while Thaksin explained away bilateral issues from the economic point of view, Hun Sen sought to politicize them whenever necessary or when they could be used to fulfil his legitimacy at home. The Thai embassy incident in January 2003 manifested the existing incompatibility of mindsets among Thai and Cambodian leaders. The author was caught in Phnom Penh on the night the Thai diplomatic establishment was ransacked. It was clear that Hun Sen and the army, despite their authority and capability to control the situation, chose to close their eyes to the ferocious acts against the Thai embassy, Thai businesses and even Thai nationals by the so-called Cambodian nationalists. Even CEO ambassador Chatchawed Chartsuwan had to climb over the embassy's back wall to escape from his attackers. Thaksin had tried for two hours to reach Hun Sen by phone, but it was obvious that the Cambodian leader had wanted to avoid the conversation.[41] Prior to the violent attack, Thai actress, Suvanand Kongying, hugely popular across the Thai-Cambodian border, was accused of saying that the Angkor Temple belonged to Thailand. Her alleged statement immediately stirred up a sense of resentment within Cambodia. Hun Sen angrily responded, "Suvanand was not even worth a blade of grass at Angkor."[42] However, the underlying message was not really about protecting the dignity of the Cambodian nation through the force of nationalism. A Cambodian general election was around the corner and the conflict with Thailand could have been used to favour or undermine certain political factions. The opposition party blamed Hun Sen for his plot to divert the public attention on his government's inability to wipe out corruption and its willingness to allow Vietnamese to run in the election under his party, Cambodian People's Party (CCP). From this point of view, some may argue that Thailand had done absolutely nothing to merit such a shocking violation of international law, tacitly encouraged by the Cambodian authorities, and that Thailand should not have been blamed when leaders in Phnom Penh decided to play games with the safety and security of a foreign embassy and its members.

At first, Thaksin's swift military response to the arson and looting of Thai embassy was lauded by the Thai public. He appeared on the televised media, vowing to rescue the Thais who were trapped in the Cambodian capital and to bring them home by military planes with or without Cambodia's landing permission. But this short-term solution could hardly cover the fact that there was a serious flaw in the way diplomacy with Cambodia was conducted. The Thai Foreign Ministry was told to downplay the violent incident in Phnom Penh, for the sake of diplomatic normalization with Cambodia. In fact, the Thai public had never been clearly informed of the process of compensation for the damage of Thai properties in Phnom Penh. For a seemingly ultra-nationalist leader like Thaksin, he seemed to forgive and forget rather too soon the looting on the Thai diplomatic establishment. If the violent attack symbolized the enduring feeling of hatred between the two nations, then Thaksin, in the post-crisis period, failed to address this issue seriously. What he did was to continue to exercise Thai benevolence over Cambodia through his invention of ACMECS, competing with two other regional players,

Vietnam and China. But there was never a guarantee that interwoven economic relations could serve as a catalyst for a better understanding between the peoples of the two countries. When Thaksin attended the GMS Summit in Phnom Penh on 3 November 2002, two months before the embassy attack, he drew a rosy picture of Thai-Cambodian relations. Thaksin said, "We have come a long way for a decade of cooperation. We have become closer through bilateral and sub-regional cooperation. Our close cooperation has contributed to increasing trust and confidence."[43] But did the Cambodian leadership feel the same way? A few years after the embassy inferno incident, the Thai Foreign Ministry announced, "Thai-Cambodian relations have improved and are now at a level which Prime Minister Hun Sen himself has acknowledged as the best ever".[44] Yet, the recent eruption of conflict between Thailand and Cambodia over the territorial claim of the Preah Vihear Temple in 2008 and 2009, as a result of the arbitrary use of nationalism and the political conflict between the pro- and anti-Thaksin factions, is a testament to the deep-seated disorder in their relations. It is also a reminder of Thaksin's short-lived foreign policy legacy. What seems permanent is the mutual negative image of each other.

Thaksin's hegemonic and mercantile foreign policy epitomized Thailand's domination both in the political and economic aspects in Cambodia. This was a core problem of Thai-Cambodian relations. It has led to suspicion of Thailand throughout the modern political economy of mainland Southeast Asia. The shifting Thai policy towards Cambodia, from foe to friend and back again as witnessed today, has further deepened the already frail foundation of this bilateral relationship. Thaksin's unsuccessful cultivation of trusted friendship with Cambodia was born out of his blending of national interest and personal businesses. His financial and technical assistance extended to Cambodia failed to ensure that Thailand was not viewed as an exploiter of its neighbour's resources. The embassy incident was partly a furious response to Thailand's attempted domination of Cambodia. Businessman-turned-prime minister Thaksin envisioned foreign affairs as more than a mere domain of politics, but also as a platform from which he could conduct personal business. Foreign policy that goes beyond the acceptable international norms is likely to invite trouble in the conduct of diplomacy.

LAOS

Thai-Lao relations can be traced back to the dawn of history. *Baan Pee Muang Nong,* literally translated to mean "brotherly neighbourhood", is a term commonly used to describe the inseparable ties between these two Southeast Asian nations. But Thai-Lao ties were also cast on a canvas of bitterness set during a time when Siam, in 1779, exercised suzerainty over Laos, relegating it to a status of vassalage. Through the years, Thailand and Laos have tried to overcome the memories that have plagued their interactions. In many ways, Thailand represented a traditional threat to Laos. This threat came in the form of Thai domination over Lao security and economic life, their ill-defined border, close but sensitive cultural relations, and Laos' economic dependence on Thailand. The sense of insecurity and suspicion greatly affected the shape of their bilateral relationship. The two countries established their diplomatic relations on 19 December 1950. Yet, Thailand was directly involved in the Laotian Civil War (1953–75) which was an internal war between the Communist Pathet Lao and the Royal Lao government. The manner in which Thailand intervened in Laos' domestic politics throughout this period powerfully prescribed their modern-day bilateral relations. After the Laotian Civil War ended, constant disputes concerning overlapping border erupted and led to a military wrangle in 1984 in three villages between Thailand's Uttaradit and the central Lao province of Sayabouri and more serious clashes three years later at Ban Rom Klao in Pitsanulok which Laos claimed was also part of Sayabouri. Known as the battle of Hill 1428 which indicates the height of Ban Rom Klao at 1,428 metres, the Thai-Lao armed clashes produced combined casualties of over 1,000 troops from both sides.[45] Further complicating the border situation, Thai leaders, in late 1984, accused Vietnam of meddling in Laotian affairs by pushing Laos into hostilities with Thailand. They also complained that Laos was harbouring Thai Communists belonging to a new organization called "Green Star", whose cadre numbered 2,000, and were said to be training in six insurgent camps along their shared 1,754-kilometre border.[46]

Bilateral tensions gradually subsided, though not totally eliminated, following developments in the late 1980s including the withdrawal of Vietnamese troops from Laos, the defeat of the Thai

Communist Party and Chatichai's business-oriented policy. The Thai policy of a Lao marketplace was well reciprocated by Laos' Prime Minister Kaysone Phomvihane (1975–91) who paid a visit to Thailand in 1989, the first time since his brief rapprochement with Thai Premier Kriangsak Chomanan in 1979. Although Chatichai successfully opened up the Lao economy for Thai investors, two inter-connected troubling political issues continued to decelerate the strengthening of this friendship. First, it was the issue of Laotian migrants and refugees residing in temporary Thai camps. Second, Lao and Hmong resistance groups who used the camps as bases to launch attacks against the Lao government further deepened suspicion between the two countries. In 1992, Thailand made clear of its intention to repatriate these refugees, either directly back to their homeland, through a third-country settlement programme, or to be classified as illegal immigrants and thus face deportation. Laos, in the meantime, was reluctant to welcome back the resistance groups for an apparent political reason. As for the refugees, as they had been fighting for national autonomy, they feared reprisals from the Lao authorities if repatriated. The refugee camps were finally closed down in the late 1990s, with the final remaining 15,000 Hmong refugees in Saraburi province Wat Tham Krabok who were relocated to being granted resettlement in the United States in 2003. Both sides hoped that resettlement was the end of the problem. In 2004 and 2005, however, several thousands more Hmong fled from Laos to Thailand's northern Chiang Rai and Petchabun provinces. The Thai and Lao governments claimed that they were illegal economic migrants seeking work in more prosperous Thailand. The refugees claimed they were fleeing continued persecution at the hands of the Lao government.[47] More than 4,000 ethic Hmong asylum seekers were eventually sent back to Laos in late December 2009 despite strong objectioins from the United States and rights groups who feared they would face prosecution. Back to the Thaksin's period, these problems were impeding his economic policy toward Laos. He, like Chatichai, spotted economic interests in Laos amidst ongoing conflicts and lingering suspicions. Attention was paid to the fact that Laos represented long-term economic opportunities because of its traditional policy of economically depending on Thailand. Laos, being a landlocked country, needs Thailand for its sea access and thus regional trade.

Thaksin arrived in Vientiane as he commenced his official visit to Laos on 13 June 2001. In the discussion with his counterpart, Bounyang Vorachit, Thaksin raised the issue of narcotic eradication in the Golden Triangle area. He pressed the Lao authorities for joint patrols along their common border, the Mekong River, which had become a notorious route for traffickers. He recommended the strengthening of the existing joint commissions between both countries, ranging from security cooperation (Joint Boundary Commission and General Border Committee) to bilateral trade promotion (Joint Trade Commission and Joint Trade and Investment Promotion Committee), and the setting up of necessary cooperative mechanisms designed to foster Lao development. Links between the two countries' provincial governors in the border areas were to be further cultivated. Thaksin pledged that he would not allow those with ill intentions, or *khon boh dee*, presumably referring to the ethnic insurgents along the border, to use Thai territory as a platform to attack the Lao government. The Cabinet approved on 16 September 2003 Thaksin's proposal of a review of the "blacklists" who had caused troubles in Thai-Lao relations.[48] He also supported the work of the Thai-Lao Friendship Association, founded in 1994, to promote better understanding between peoples on both sides of the Mekong. More importantly, in the area of trade and investment, Lao leaders were eager to secure Thaksin's intervention in a long-delayed US$1.2 billion hydropower electricity plan, a mega-project that would surely bring huge revenue to the country. The Electricity Generating Authority of Thailand (EGAT) and the Lao government announced their joint cooperation in constructing at least four dams in Laos, including the Theun-Hinboun Expansion Project and Nam Theun 1, as energy sources for Thailand and a source of earnings for Laos. In addition to hydropower projects, Thaksin encouraged investment in Laos' infrastructure, including an airport at Luang Nam Tha, several bridges across the Mekong and the Route 3 road project linking Thailand and China across northwestern Laos. Both countries were involved in the GMS cooperation through road networks and more efficient trade and immigration processes.[49] Laos was a member of Thaksin's ACMECS, as well as the Emerald Triangular Cooperative Framework (ETCF) that also encompasses Thailand and Cambodia in the promotion of tourism among member countries. Immediately after the first ACMECS Ministerial Meeting in Bangkok, the Inaugural Foreign Ministers' Meeting of the ETCF on Tourism was held on 2 August 2003 in Pakse, Laos's Champasak Province, to enhance the combined potential among members and promote tourism in this sub-region. Leaders hoped that cooperation would not only benefit the tourism industry, but would also generate economic growth, reduce income disparity and uplift the well-being of people at the grassroots level.[50]

In 2003, Deputy Prime Minister and Minister of Foreign Affairs Somsavat Lengsavad visited Thailand to attend the 12th Thailand-Laos Cooperation Commission Meeting. An economic agenda was principal in their discussions. The Thai state media reported that Somsavat expressed his gratitude to Thailand for providing a loan for the building of the Nan-Luang Prabang Highway, which would attract more tourists between the two countries. On this occasion, Thaksin told the Lao visitor that his government had approved a US$20 million loan, in Thai currency, for the development of Wat Tai Airport, Pakse Airport, and drainage ditches in Vientiane.[51] By 2005, Thailand and Laos fully realized the potential of their close cooperation and sustainable benefits that they expected to be accrued in the long-term. In that year, two-way trade between Thailand and Laos increased 43.27 per cent from the year before, totalling over US$1 billion. Thailand was the largest investor in Laos, with more than 100 Thai investment projects valued at US$600 million, that had already been approved by the Lao government in the electricity, transportation, telecommunications, hotel and tourism sectors.[52] The Thai injection of money into the Lao economy was, however, not solely about further solidifying bilateral ties. Thailand has always viewed Laos as a state in its sphere of political and cultural influence. Thaksin himself recognized that, despite Laos' perceived outlook of a backward nation, globalization had actually arrived in this country too. For Laos, it has long been confined within Thailand's economic domination, at least since the former regained independence in 1954, and was now striving to diversify its sources of economic wealth. The new Laos was not a passive bystander in the process. It opened itself up to eager investors not only from Thailand, but also Vietnam and China. Yet, Thaksin attempted to maintain a Thai control over Lao economic activities through his own business-centric foreign policy, which was formulated to overcome tense competition as other deep-pocketed countries, like Vietnam and China, eyed this impoverished nation.

Throughout and in the post-Cold War period, Laos has arguably remained aligned to Vietnam through a series of security agreements. Lao People's Revolutionary Party (LPRP) and the Vietnamese Communist Party (VCP) enjoyed special relations since their establishment in the 1930s. As the Cold War ended, China began to exert its influence on Laos and overwhelm this neighbour with financial and technical assistance in an attempt to pull Vientiane into its orbit. Chinese President Hu Jintao, while visiting Laos in November 2006, showered his counterpart with generous gifts including a US$12.7 million economic-technical cooperation project, debt clearance for seven projects worth US$33 million, as well as Chinese support for low-interest loans in various joint programmes. A month earlier, Nong Duc Manh, Secretary-General of the Communist Party of Vietnam, paid a visit to Vientiane, ostensibly to strengthen bilateral ties and to offset the growing Chinese influence. He reiterated his country's contribution to the Lao economy. Their two-way trade stood at US$2.2 billion from 1999 to 2005. In 2005 alone, it was valued at US$165 million, up 15.4 per cent from the previous year. Vietnam has also been a major investor in Laos with sixty-nine projects worth US$500 million, and continued to facilitate the transportation of Lao goods heading to other countries.[53] The growing influence of China and Vietnam obliged Thaksin to revise Thailand's strategy urgently in order to uphold its domination of Laos.

Thaksin's revised strategy towards Laos took account the importance of building personal relationship with top Laotian leaders, bringing Laos into the mainstream of Thai capitalism through numerous cooperative frameworks set up by the Thaksin government, as well as sweeping disconcerting issues under the rug for the sake of a good relationship. Vested interests played a crucial role in Thai-Lao relations. Thaksin's Shin Satellite had been in Laos since 1994. Originally, government-owned Entre d'Etat des Postes et Telecommunications Lao was the only telecom operator in the country. In 1994, Thaksin negotiated a deal with the Lao government and was granted a twenty-year concession to operate a Global System Mobile (GSM) network called Lao Shinawatra Telecom (LST). Thaksin even launched the service before he was officially awarded the concession. Today, Shin Satellite owns 49 per cent of government-controlled incumbent Lao Telecom.[54] CEO

Thaksin invested not less than US$400 million in Lao Telecom, which provides various services including a cellular mobile phone service, public telephone service, public switched telephone network service, international gateway service, and a paging service.[55] Economic intimacy between Thaksin and Lao leaders proved to underpin bilateral relations. Hence, Thaksin's departure from power in 2006 has shaken the foundation of this relationship. Lao Foreign Ministry Spokesman Yong Chantalangsy was reported as saying, "With Thaksin, Lao officials knew who they were dealing with. They had established clear relations. Now, there is a change in Bangkok and they want to know if it will also work well."[56]

In the meantime, Thaksin's ACMECS was made a state apparatus to cultivate ties with other members supposedly based on mutual economic benefits. Thailand's ODA to Laos was greater than any other countries in the region. From 2001 to 2004, this portion of financial assistance to Laos increased from Bt22.15 to Bt47.87 million, most of which was spent on infrastructure construction, purported to recreate Laos into a land-linked, and no longer landlocked, state.[57] The regional exposure of Laos through Thaksin's initiatives responded well to the renewed active Lao foreign policy. In fact, the building of the first and second Thai-Lao Friendship Bridge, funded by Australia and Japan in 1994 and 2004 respectively, were significant landmarks of the reconnection of two old civilizations. Thaksin played along with this theme of connecting the *baan pee muang nong*, granting financial aid for new bridges and roads between Thailand and Laos. The Boten-Houayxai Road in Laos (228 kilometres) was one of Thaksin's projects with a Thai contribution of a Bt1.3 billion loan to Laos, designed to connect Thailand's Chiang Rai with China's Kunming via Laos. Another project, the Huaikon-Pak Beng Road (50 kilometres), was to connect Thailand's Nan province with Pak Beng in Laos' Udomxai province. Thailand provided a grant of Bt252 million and a loan of Bt588 million to Laos for the construction. Both were parts of the north-south economic corridor linking Thailand, Laos and China. Other joint projects included the construction of a bridge over the Heung River (Thailand's Loei-Laos' Kanthao), with a Thai grant of Bt43 million. This bridge was opened for public use in October 2004 and aimed at facilitating border trade. The 3.5-kilometre Nongkhai-Tha Na Lang Rail Link project was to be the first railroad in Laos, running from the middle of the Thai-Lao Friendship Bridge to the suburbs of Vientiane. Thaksin approved Bt39 million and a loan of Bt138 million for this project. Moreover, he commissioned a feasibility study on the construction of a Bt20 million Mekong Bridge connecting Nakhon Phanom with Thakhek to help open the Lao interior to more foreign commerce.[58]

By promoting the physical links between Thailand and Laos under various construction projects with the former as the centre of prosperity, the idea of Thaksin's *suvarnabhumi* could not be less subtle. Already, the Thai impact has been palpable in Lao society, through the prevalent Thai cultural influence, such as Thai television programmes and music, Thai magazines and newspapers, and the wide circulation and use of Thai currency.[59] Laos tried not to become too subservient to the Thaksin rule, but to utilize its economic potential and its close relations with Vietnam and China as leverage against a Thai monopoly. Laos exploited bilateral politics, taking advantage of the existing contentious issues such as the Hmong refugees and economic migrants, certain negative perceptions of Laos in Thailand's eyes, Thailand's economic exploitative attitude, and the conflict of interest of Thai leaders in dealing with their Lao neighbour. This explained the reason behind Laos' outright refusal to take back Hmong refugees who had been living in a condition of political limbo in Thailand. The Hmong was a major diplomatic sticking point in the burgeoning economic relationship between Thailand and Laos during the Thaksin period.

More ominous was the clash between Thai and Lao cultures. The fact that the two countries shared similarities in race, language, religion and culture did not make bilateral relations simple. It was a perfect example of the "petty narcissism of small differences". The Thai-Lao Friendship Association, set up to promote better cultural understanding between peoples of the two countries, was not very successful in introducing a new era of relationship based on mutual respect. On 30 September 2005, Foreign Minister Kantathi Suphamongkhon insisted on the use of the obscure Radio Saranrom, the Foreign Ministry's radio station, to cultivate better understanding between Thailand and Laos. He also suggested the publication of guide books detailing the supposedly correct history between the two kingdoms.[60] But culture was too frequently employed at the state level to serve political objectives. Laotians often complained that their Thai neighbours constantly looked down on them.[61] This cultural ill feeling was a result of Thailand's past and present constructing of its national identity, by imaging their neighbours in a negative light and exhibiting a sense of superiority in doing so. This process of negative identification against "the others" created an insecurity complex that was ever existent.

Laotian leaders, too, were seen enforcing new symbolic elements to consolidate the ruling Communist Party's power in the globalization era. The government reconstructed its past, now extolling its Great King, Fa Ngum of the fourteenth century, as a new symbol of national achievement.[62] Ironically, the ruling Communist Party, having once abolished the monarchy, then reconstructed a royal tint as part of the nation's embodiment. The surge in Laos' cultural consciousness commanded a prominence in Lao foreign affairs. In Thailand, as much as Thaksin craved for a stronger relationship with Laos, the Thai public's awareness of Lao culture and identity was largely tangential and negligible. The recent protests among Lao leaders over a Thai television drama were testament to the cultural insensitivity that dominated the Thai psyche. In May 2006, Ministry of Foreign Affairs of Laos remonstrated the Thai sports-comedy, *Lucky Loser* or *Mak Tae Loke Talueng*, that portrayed certain aspects seen as offensive to Lao people. As a result, the release of the film was cancelled and the Thai production company had to re-edit the film and remove any references to Laos. A year later, another drama, titled *Love Song on Both Sides of the Mekong*, a love story set between a Thai and Lao couple, was released. Almost matter-of-factly, the plot, once again, denigrated Lao family values and belittled Laos' national pride (in one scene the Thai protagonist threw Laos' national flower in the dustbin). The Thai producers were subsequently forced to suspend airing the soap opera at the request of both the Thai and Lao authorities. Although Thailand may be one of Laos' closest neighbours, the historical baggage that overwhelms relations between the two countries have stood firm against commitments by both governments to move ties forward.[63] Thaksin's overemphasis on economic interests in Laos did not help rectify this negative image of the pretentiously superior Thais.

MALAYSIA

Thailand and Malaysia established their diplomatic relations on 31 August 1957. Of the four bordering states, Malaysia seemed to have been Thailand's least troublesome neighbour. Their bilateral relationship in general has been cordial, yet insipid, because both countries, especially in the past decade, possessed, at varying degrees, an advanced stage of economic and political development and their common borders are relatively peaceful. But the seemingly smooth relations were disrupted by the re-emergence of insurgency in the south of Thailand where the Muslim majority, mostly in the three southernmost provinces of Pattani, Narathiwat and Yala, has taken up arms against the Thai state. The south was never Thaksin's territory. In fact, it was known as a region hostile to the Thai Rak Thai Party.[64] Some analysts argue that the resurgence of violence by Pattani guerrilla groups indeed began in December 2001 after a number of policemen died in separate attacks in the Thai south. Over the span of seven months (December 2001–July 2002), fourteen policemen were killed. Meanwhile, the Thaksin government continued to blame the attacks on bandits and drug traffickers. The eruption of the violent conflict in January 2004 in the restive south reflected the long-standing separatist movement in Thailand, coupled with an increasing religious intolerance which was part and parcel of Thaksin's centralization policy and his employment of nationalism based on a Buddhist chauvinist attitude.[65] Thaksin, however, should not solely be condemned for the rise of Buddhist chauvinism. The monastic *sangha* and the making of Buddhism as the national religion endorsed by the monarchy all have a role to play in the monopolization of the religious space in Thailand.

In January 2004, at least a hundred armed men, believed to be Muslim insurgents, stormed the army depot in Narathiwat, stealing 300 weapons and killing four Thai soldiers. This incident triggered a series of violent outbursts in the three provinces, plus four districts in Songkhla. Two serious violent confrontations between Muslim insurgents and the Thai security forces in this same year reconfirmed the revival of irredentism in Thailand's deep south. First, the Krue Sae Mosque incident on 28 April 2004 saw brutal executions of the Muslim militants by the hand of the Thai state. More than 100 militants carried out terrorist attacks against ten police outposts across the southern provinces, and thirty-two militants retreated to the 425-year-old Krue Sae Mosque, considered the holiest mosque in Pattani. The Thai authority finally ordered an all-out assault on the mosque and all the Muslim militants were killed. Second, the Tak Bai incident, in Narathiwat province, witnessed another highly publicized tragedy when hundreds of local Muslims who protested against the detention of their fellows were also arrested. They were ordered to take off their shirts and lie on the ground. Their hands were tied behind their backs. They were later thrown by soldiers and stacked five or six deep in the trucks to be taken to an army camp. After a five-hour journey transported in this way, seventy-eight detainees were found to have suffocated to death.[66] Thaksin defended the army's action, saying that they had died because they were already weak from fasting during the month of Ramadan.

The reasons behind the rekindling of insurgency in the south are the combination of economic deprivation of the local Muslim community, political subordination and social discrimination, the rise of Islamism, the shift of government policy towards the southern conflict in the era of Thaksin, and an identity crisis in Thailand. But the unrest in the south did not only have a bearing on Thailand's domestic politics. There was also an international aspect, especially with the impact on Thai-Malaysia relations. While Thaksin, from 2001 to 2003, worked cooperatively with his Malaysian counterpart, bilateral relations from 2004 onwards were mostly shaped by the resurgence of insurgency in the Thai south. Thaksin's lack of understanding of the southern conflict, the politicization of the fragile situation, his CEO-style of dealing with the issue with his Malaysian counterpart and his desperate search for legitimacy amid heightening tensions in this far-flung region, all created a rift in the relations Thailand had with Malaysia. History has justified a role of Malaysia in the Thai southern crisis. The Patani (in Malay) kingdom was annexed to Thailand in 1902 prior to the Anglo-Siamese Treaties.[67] Remade as an alien part of a Buddhists-dominated society, the Thai Muslim minority has maintained religious and cultural links with their Muslim fellows in Malaysia. Malays in Malaysia have been sympathetic toward the plight of the Thai Muslim in the deep south. The escalating violence in the hands of Thai security agencies against them put a heavy strain on the Thai-Malaysian relations.

In August 2005, 131 Thai Muslims fled across border from the operations of Thai security forces and were given asylum in Malaysia. The Thai consulate in Malaysia's Kota Bahru reported that the asylum seekers were arrested in Kelantan. They were interrogated by the Malaysian authorities and told how the intensity of violence forced them to escape from the Thai south especially after their village head was brutally murdered. They had decided to flee in small groups of three to five people across the Thai-Malaysian border.[68] Malaysian Foreign Minister Syed Hamid Albar agreed to release them only if Bangkok could guarantee their human rights and safety. Thaksin was infuriated by his remarks. He asked the Foreign Ministry to summon the Malaysian ambassador in Bangkok to protest at the "interference in the internal affairs" of Thailand. In response, Syed Hamid said, "The government was never keen to intervene in the internal affairs of Thailand. We will not teach Thailand how to conduct its foreign policy and I ask their leaders not to tell us how to handle our foreign policy."[69] Thaksin, in the meantime, felt that he was humiliated when United Nations High Commissioner for Refugees officials interviewed the asylum seekers who were being considered for refugee status. Thaksin declared, "Our human rights standard is high. We stick to and abide by the principles and the constitution, ours being very progressive as it is."[70] Just when Thaksin thought that Thailand's foreign affairs were safely under his control and that his personalized foreign policy would serve his much needed legitimacy, the mismanagement of the conflict in the south emerged as a serious challenge to his international standing. Suddenly, Thaksin seemed ill-equipped in exercising shrewd diplomacy to lessen the southern crisis and protect Thailand's reputation abroad. The Organization of Islamic Conference (OIC) released a harsh statement condemning the Tak Bai massacre. It also slammed Thaksin for the exodus of 131 Muslim villagers who fled to northern Malaysia.[71] In 2004, Thaksin said that he would walk out of the ASEAN Summit in Vientiane if Indonesia or Malaysia raised any concerns about the south's situation. At this point, Thaksin, once a potential regional leader, was at risk of being depicted as an enemy of Muslims who make up about half of ASEAN's citizens.

Malaysia wished to cool down the bilateral tension with Thailand and proposed a dialogue with the Thai government to resolve the problem urgently. As part of this attempt, Malaysian Prime Minister Abdullah Badawi, also leader of the ruling United Malays National Organization (UMNO), together with his predecessor, Mahathir Mohamad, held informal discussion with former Thai Prime Minister Anand Panyarachun, who was the head of the National Reconciliation Commission (NRC), and reassured him that Malaysia did not support the separatist movement in Thailand. Founded in March 2005, the NRC was a product of a political compromise in

Bangkok. Prior to the establishment of the NRC, Thaksin continued to entertain the hard-line approach such as the use of martial law to curb terrorist activities. This approach no doubt further inflamed the already unstable situation. Heavily criticized for his hard-nosed measures against the Thai Muslim minority, Thaksin was compelled to seek help from the palace and the old elite to diffuse the crisis in a more subtle way. The fifty members of the NRC were therefore regarded as those outside the Thaksin power circle. They were never fully trusted by Thaksin. McCargo argued that Thaksin had created the NRC simply to neutralize his critics.[72] The opposition Democrat Party took this opportunity to put the blame on Thaksin as the cause of the conflict. Marc Askew observed that the Democrat's concern about the southern fire was primarily an issue of how to get more votes out of the government's crisis mismanagement.[73] The complexity within the Thai political domain and its impact on the issue of the southern conflict moulded Thaksin's negative attitude toward Malaysia. As much as Thaksin tried to isolate the conflict in the south, he also isolated his Malaysian neighbour. This isolation was reflected in Thaksin's policy of externalizing the cause of conflict by assigning Malaysia as a prime manipulator behind the Thai Muslim insurgents.

Thaksin claimed that the Thai military had evidence about plotted attacks by the Thai insurgents that were made on the Malaysian island of Langkawi. Such a claim reflected the traditional belief that Malaysia continued to maintain its links with southern insurgents as leverage against Thailand.[74] This allegation was immediately rejected by Malaysian Deputy Prime Minister Najib Razak. To Thaksin, separatism in the south was not solely Thailand's security problem. But what Thaksin failed to realize was that it was neither in Malaysia's interest to encourage the acts of Thai separatists against the central government. Malaysian leaders, although feeling sympathetic toward the Thai Muslims, feared that the rise of irredentism in the Thai south could stir up Islamic fundamentalism in their own country. As Malaysia was so sensitive to this issue, it explained why the 131 Thai asylum seekers who first fled into Kelantan state were quickly transferred into the neighbouring Terengganu state. Kelantan has been controlled by the Islamic fundamentalist Parti Islam se-Malaysia (PAS). PAS has been competing with UMNO for the support of the majority Muslim Malays who have intimate cultural ties with the Thai Muslims across the border.[75] John Roberts noted that the recklessness with which Thaksin provoked discontent in the south was accompanied by an apparent disregard for damaging relations with Malaysia. His administration sought to blame its neighbour for the growing intensity of the insurgency at home.[76]

Thaksin's CEO style of managing foreign relations contributed to a deepening rift between Thailand and Malaysia. Thai and Malaysian foreign ministries worked closely to ensure the success of the damage control process. Over the period of August and September 2005, efforts to alleviate the crisis that had derived from the 131 Thais crossing over to Malaysia illegally were most evident after the two countries' foreign ministries agreed on the following: (1) the conflict in the south must not give rise to bilateral conflict; (2) both sides must exchange information and monitor the situation closely; (3) both must not give wrong information to the media; and (4) both must strive toward the safe and swift return of the 131 Thais.[77] Moreover, in December 2005, with the approval of the Thai government and the King, Mahathir presided over talks between a range of insurgents and two senior Thai military figures.[78] However, Thaksin bypassed diplomatic means and procedure and instead exercised his CEO power to get things done his own way. This was mostly echoed in the way he quickly blamed Malaysia for interfering in Thailand's politics, and in his unwillingness to allow ASEAN mediation in the Thai southern crisis. While leaders in the region preferred to settle delicate issues behind the scenes, Thaksin's brash style was exercised mainly to boost nationalistic fervour at home. His domestic political dominance could have led to international hubris — a rampaging style that paid little heed to political niceties or the feelings of others. Thaksin was not the type of leader who would be willing to admit his own limitations. As in the world of business, he tended to opt for a short-cut to crisis solution. As part of finding that short-cut, Thaksin was too content to simplify the seemingly aggravated problem. During his visit to Singapore in 2005, Bhokin Balakula, Thaksin's Interior Minister, reassured Singaporean investors that the violent situation in the restive south was under the state's control. He said,

> As a matter of fact, things are not as bad as they seem. By actually going into the area, one would immediately notice that the situation is not as bad as it is portrayed. It is not the differences of language,

culture or even religion which have led to unrest. Rather, the insurgency is related to socio-psychological malaise, poverty, inadequacy of education and international-related movements.[79]

Thaksin's diplomatic style and his simplification of the conflict were the causes behind the lack of regional support for Thailand's policy towards curbing violence in the south. In the wake of Thaksin's accusation of Malaysia and Indonesia of varying support for Thai separatists, his public antics actually alienated potential allies in the fight against Muslim insurgents.[80]

Thaksin's overt concentration on making Thailand the centre of regional prosperity certainly created a vacuum in his foreign policy considerations toward the country's southern neighbour. He acknowledged that the need to re-install trust between Thailand and its old enemies, namely Myanmar, Cambodia and Laos, must be prioritized. He also understood that the attention paid to these immediate neighbours meant that business, whether legal or even shady, could be conducted to benefit Thailand and his private interests. Thaksin was therefore led to believe that he could afford to take Thailand's relations with Malaysia for granted. As it turned out, the conflict in the southernmost provinces effectively put this bilateral relationship at great risk, and imprisoned it within a specific issue. Surapong Jayanama opined that Thaksin's concern about boosting economic figures placed Thailand at odds with Malaysia and a number of Islamic nations.[81] Ironically, as Thaksin boosted economic figures, the economic well-being of southern Thais, especially in the pre-2004 period, had not improved. Fundamentally, Thaksin's foreign policy, although beautifully crafted on what seemed the basis of mutual interest, did not occasionally promote mutuality in the conduct of diplomacy or conform to international norms and practices. His foreign policy sought to overpower the Thai neighbours when necessary, had a manipulative element, and was designed to champion Thailand in the face of poorer states. Hence, Thaksin's policy was inapplicable to elucidate Thai-Malaysian relations, which, despite being relatively peaceful, required new perspectives and approaches to deal with certain issues outside the realm of economic interests.

ASEAN

ASEAN was once a foundation of Thai foreign policy. During the Cold War, Thailand relied heavily on ASEAN as much as other external powers like China and the United States. The threat of Communism in Indochina effectively dressed Thailand up as a frontline state, and therefore allowed the country to dominate ASEAN opinion in the formulation of a regional containment policy against such threat. Thai security policy now became ASEAN's security policy. In many ways, this joint exercise between Thailand and ASEAN against Communism successfully portrayed the grouping's solidarity. ASEAN members worked well together when they shared common enemies. After the conflict in Cambodia came to an end, ASEAN continued to provide Thailand with a platform for its foreign policy initiatives. In fact, the Thai newfound confidence in the conduct of an independent foreign policy transpired in the post-Cambodian conflict period. Such confidence was demonstrated by Thailand's active participation in ASEAN and Asia-Pacific multilateralism. During the Anand Panyarachun government, as Leszek Buszynski noted, Thailand's regional policy required ASEAN endorsement and had to be formulated within the framework of Southeast Asian regionalism for it to succeed.[82] For example, from 1991 to 1992, Thailand initiated the idea of an AFTA, ostensibly to enhance the grouping's economic growth as well as to raise its level of competitiveness against rising China. Thailand's proposal of AFTA signified the country's ability to adapt with the global change. The Cold War was over. The world had become more interdependent. AFTA was therefore a reflection of the salient Thai foreign policy as much as ASEAN's eagerness to face the changing global environment. Thailand was also behind the organization of a "second track" diplomacy on regional security issues, a development that led eventually to the ASEAN Regional Forum (ARF). Bangkok hosted the inaugural meeting of the ARF in 1994, a platform that promoted discussion of security-related matters.[83] Moreover, throughout the 1990s, Thailand used ASEAN to celebrate its Myanmar policy under different guises. Ranging from Constructive Engagement to Flexible Engagement, Thailand's Myanmar policy supplemented the few available approaches to deal with the stubborn military regime in Yangon. Once again, Thailand exercised its authority to "Aseanize" its policy towards Myanmar with the claim of it being a frontline state.

As one of the founding members of ASEAN, Thailand has a compulsory responsibility to ensure the maturity and success of the organization. When Thaksin became prime minister, he recognized that ASEAN was in a state of flux, beset by the financial crisis and the risk of losing its relevance in the international arena. In order to fulfil his country's obligation, Thaksin declared a policy of "reinvigorating ASEAN" based on strengthening ASEAN integration and reaching out for cooperation with actors outside the region. He came up with a new tagline "ASEAN: Regional in Focus, Global in Outlook".[84] He even announced, "ASEAN is an integral part of Thailand's foreign policy."[85] Thaksin's strategy in the resurrection of ASEAN's glorious past was to promote internal economic development and external economic relations. He supported the narrowing of the economic gap between old and new members of ASEAN, such as through the initiative of ACMECS as a supplementary framework. Thaksin also suggested closer cooperation between ASEAN and external powers, particularly the three Northeast Asian states — China, Japan and South Korea. But Thaksin's opponents saw his backing of ASEAN as being driven by his personalized foreign policy, rather than a genuine interest in ASEAN regionalism. At a deeper level, the Thai proposal to raise the developmental level among the new members of ASEAN, who happened to be Thailand's immediate neighbours, seemed to contribute more to Thailand's benefit, in terms of economic interests and for diplomatic boasting, than for ASEAN as a whole. Thaksin's urging for closer contact between ASEAN and the "+3" members was subsequently politically useful to his personalized foreign policy when he rode on the idea of the Asian Bond Market, which called for the strong involvement of China, Japan and South Korea.

Although Thaksin exhibited his leadership in ASEAN, he lacked a deeper interest in further developing this organization. For Thaksin, ACD and ACMECS replaced ASEAN as the most important foreign policy agendas. He shifted Thailand's foreign policy from promoting ASEAN to prioritizing Thai interest on mainland Southeast Asia. Indonesia, the fourth largest country in the world, has always been seen as a natural leader of ASEAN. With about one-eighth of ASEAN's population and one-fifth of its combined gross domestic product, Thailand did not have the size or demographic weight that could make it a leader of ASEAN. Unlike in the Cold War setting, Thailand would not be able to push Jakarta or Kuala Lumpur to back its political or security plans. Moreover, ASEAN itself was not Thaksin's own initiative. Thus, when Thaksin talked about raising Asia's profile and voice in the international arena, he did not include ASEAN in his foreign policy agenda. Thaksin was keen to explore new options in foreign policy, including the invention of new platforms that allowed him to shine.

As a result, ASEAN was no longer the number-one priority of Thai foreign policy, as declared to Thai Parliament by Thaksin on 23 March 2005. Thaksin instead placed great emphasis on ACMECS, as he announced:

> With regard to the strengthening of foreign relations in various dimensions, the Government shall continue to build and strengthen the good understanding and cooperation with neighbouring countries, and further expand cooperation at the levels of government, the private sector and the public, in particular, the economic cooperation with neighbouring countries under the Ayeyawady–Chao Phraya–Mekong Economic Cooperation Strategy (ACMECS) and other sub-regional frameworks in the areas of trade, investment, agriculture, industry, linkage of land-sea-air transportation networks, tourism and human resource development.[86]

The term "ASEAN" scarcely featured in his foreign policy speeches. The Foreign Ministry's ASEAN Department, despite being preoccupied all year round with countless meetings, seemed to gain little attention from top leaders. In contrast, the Department of International Economics and the Office of Policy and Planning, in charge of ACMECS and ACD respectively, were given a much wider platform to sell the prime minister's ideas to the international community. Thaksin on many occasions showed that he would not hesitate to discredit this decades-old organization if it obstructed the interests of Thailand and his own such as when it interfered in the human rights situation in its southern provinces. But his disinterest in ASEAN also caused considerable impact on the progress of ACD and ACMECS. How far his policy initiatives would go depended immensely on how far ASEAN as a group would support them. So far, Thaksin did not really talk much on how the ACD would help strengthen ASEAN integration. His objective in the ACD was indeed to promote Thai leadership at the expense of ASEAN's influence. Some ASEAN leaders even viewed the ACD as another challenge to ASEAN's claim of regional primacy.[87]

There were three main issues at the heart of Thaksin's perception of ASEAN. First, ASEAN, for Thaksin, represented the work of the old politics in Thailand. ASEAN was in the past employed to shore up certain Thai regimes. In the 1990s, the Democrat Party, Thaksin's main political rival, attached great importance to ASEAN and used it to legitimize its foreign policy. With Surin Pitsuwan as foreign minister, he repainted Thai foreign policy based on Thailand's renewed confidence in ASEAN. His Flexible Engagement Policy toward Myanmar, though criticized by certain members of ASEAN, exemplified Thailand's recognition of ASEAN's significance in dealing with such a controversial issue. Thaksin wanted to depart from the old politics. Even when Thaksin was out of power and with his proxies ruling the government, ASEAN did not rank high in Thai foreign policy considerations. After all, Surin, the current ASEAN secretary-general, is a Democrat and a Thaksin critic. The fact that the red-shirt protesters, spiritually encouraged by Thaksin while on the run from the Thai law, stormed into the meeting venue of the ASEAN+3 Summit and the East Asia Summit in Pattaya in April 2009, truly summarized the little respect Thaksin has had in this regional organization. Second, because of Thaksin's lack of interest in ASEAN, his confidence in regional mechanisms also remained at a low level. Examples can be seen in the way Thaksin handled bilateral disputes with fellow ASEAN countries. Rodolfo Severino, former ASEAN secretary-general, noted that ASEAN stood ready to intervene in any bilateral disputes if invited by the parties involved. It could have intervened in the aftermath of the Thai embassy in Phnom Penh being burned down in 2003. But Thaksin never sought assistance from ASEAN. This is also reflected in the case of the Preah Vihear Temple dispute.[88] In another account, Severino observed:

> If ASEAN were to intervene in Myanmar, it would be on account of situations that have an impact on neighbouring states. One such situation might be the flow of illicit drugs from Myanmar to other Southeast Asian countries. Another might be the burden of refugees fuelling pressures in Myanmar. In either case, ASEAN would have to take its signals from Thailand, the country that bears the brunt of Myanmar-related drugs and refugee flows. So far, Thailand has sent no such signals and seems inclined to deal with Myanmar bilaterally on both issues and to keep the rest of ASEAN out of them.[89]

Third, Thaksin's perspective of regionalism was at times erratic and unpredictable. In an interview with Surin, he explained that ASEAN was too small a stage for Thaksin. He chose to "go bigger" with the ACD. Yet, his Asia-wide initiative has proven unsustainable. Eventually, Thailand would need to refocus its foreign policy on ASEAN because this grouping always provided the best avenue for Thailand to showcase its diplomatic finesse.[90] Thaksin's concept of regionalism was fuzzy. While he acknowledged the importance of the role of the Northeast Asian states in his foreign policy, Thaksin simply overlooked the dynamism of that region that could be further promoted through new networks like the East Asia Summit (EAS) which not only encompasses China, Japan and South Korea, but also India, Australia and New Zealand. Thaksin's earlier ambivalent attitude regarding the modality of the EAS underlined his confusing viewpoint of regionalism. He was aware that the EAS could come into direct competition with his own initiative of the ACD.[91] In another example, Thaksin almost treated as insignificant the existence of the BIMSTEC which was strongly supported by the previous rival government. This was because BIMSTEC was the brainchild of former Deputy Prime Minister Supachai Panitchpakdi, another Democrat and thus another political enemy. It can be concluded that Thaksin's notion of regionalism was rigidly tied to domestic political condition in which foreign policy initiatives were locked in the game of rivalry and competition, regardless of the fact that such initiatives could really be for the good of the country. Moreover, this notion of regionalism could only be made legitimate if it served Thaksin's economic interests and enhance his international reputation and leadership.

CHINA

We are like relatives. The history of migration of the Thais: part of ancestral Thais migrated from China. Even myself. On my father's side, I am the fourth generation that migrated from China. On my mother's side, I am the third generation. I even went to China to pay respect to the tomb of my ancestors there in China. So, we are really close, and so far, the relationship between Thailand and China is very cordial.[92]

The above statement by Thaksin, delivered during an interview in New York in 2006, illustrated the ever intimate state of Thai-Chinese relations. Indeed, this bilateral relationship has been cordial since their diplomatic normalization in 1975. Throughout the latter half of the Cold War, Thailand and China formed a loose military alignment against the advancement of Vietnamese Communists in Indochina.[93] But the nature of relationship shifted after the end of the Cold War. With the rise of China as an Asian economic powerhouse, Thailand under Thaksin saw a new opportunity to engage China based on shared economic benefits. Historically, Siamese kings never failed to parade their allegiance to the Middle Kingdom which in turn brought protection and trade at little cost.[94] In the modern era, China's growing political and economic might continued to dominate Thai-Chinese relations and influence the way Thaksin manoeuvred his foreign policy toward Beijing. As a result, Thaksin had to re-traditionalize Thai foreign policy back to what Thailand had done in the past — bending with the Chinese wind, rather than trying to overcome it. Was there anything wrong in grabbing at China's coat-tails as long as it served Thailand's national interests?

Bilateral relations remained healthy between the two, thanks to the absence of territorial disputes, the firm ties between the Thai royal family and the Chinese leadership, and the well-integrated Chinese community in Thailand. Thaksin, as a model of a successful Thai-Chinese, took advantage of his Chinese ancestral roots and a new surge in public awareness about China to craft a China-favoured policy to satisfy domestic enthusiasm for a closer relationship with Beijing. A recent poll showed that more than 70 per cent of Thais considered China as Thailand's most important external influence.[95] Thaksin was not alone in bending with China to gain benefits. His predecessors and successors all walked the same path with China as they looked to the future. The difference was that Thaksin went the extra mile to please the Chinese leadership for what ultimately were purely Thai interests, be they public or private. First, during the Thaksin era, Thailand began to construct an alliance with China in a similar way as it has done with the United States. The U.S.-Thai Cobra Gold exercise — the largest in the region, lent its form and purpose to Thailand's military rapprochement with China, albeit on a much smaller scale.[96] Since the early 1980s, Thailand purchased armaments and military-related equipment under this partnership at "friendship prices", much of which effectively amounted to, in the words of Anthony Smith, "military gift aid".[97] Although some of these armaments from China were merely scrap, they symbolized close military ties between the two countries. Under Thaksin, Sino-Thai military links were among one of the most developed in the region — second only to Myanmar, China's quasi-ally. Second, the Sino-Thai FTA, the first between China and an ASEAN country, took effect on 1 October 2003. The FTA was invented to slash tariffs for fruit and vegetable flows in each other's market. Thaksin claimed that, as a result of his initiated FTA, bilateral trade reached US$3.1 billion, a 23 per cent increase in 2007 when compared with that of 2006.[98] But this claim concealed the fact that although bilateral trade volume expanded, Thailand suffered from a trade deficit with China. When Thaksin visited China in June 2005, he refuted, "Thailand may have to compete with China in some areas, but competition is not something that is a threat. Chinese products can force other countries to be more efficient and productive in manufacturing, so it is an opportunity rather than a threat."[99]

Undeniably, Thaksin was quietly sliding into China's warm, embracing arms. Most Thai Cabinet ministers, including Thaksin himself, and powerful businesses in Thailand have significant investments in China. Thailand's Charoen Pokphand (CP), one of Southeast Asia's largest companies, has been doing business in China since 1949. Bangkok Bank still has the largest foreign bank branch on Shanghai's Bund waterfront, only recently have a few other foreign banks gained token footholds on China's pre-eminent address.[100] Activities between Thai and Chinese business conglomerates were regularly conducted, with the exchange of visits and the sharing of business information. The Thai-Chinese Chamber of Commerce highlighted in its website that "all business activities must remain apolitical".[101] In the meantime, Thaksin welcomed China's soft power with arms wide open. Patrick Jory argued that since the Chinese language has been re-introduced into Thailand's schools and universities after a long period of official sanction, Chinese popular culture has been much celebrated, and imported Chinese soap operas have been highly popular.[102] Particularly during the Thaksin period, new Chinese language schools were mushrooming in Bangkok and in major cities throughout the kingdom. "Thailand has been taking the Chinese language seriously, so seriously that Thaksin asked China to send teachers," Michael Vatikiotis wrote.[103] In January 2006, China's Deputy Education Minister Zhang Xin-sheng was in Bangkok to sign an agreement to help train 1,000 Mandarin language teachers every year for Thailand. China also offered 100 scholarships for Thai students to study in China, and dispatched 500 young volunteers to teach Chinese in Thailand.[104] According to the Chinese Ministry of Education, Thai students studying in China reached 1,554, making them the sixth largest group of foreign students in the country, after South Korea, Japan, the United States, Vietnam and Indonesia.[105] "The number of Thai students studying in Chinese universities has grown six- or seven-fold within the past few years," said Tekhua Pung, director of a local Chinese-language teaching school.

Thaksin's foreign policy toward China was implemented on the basis of a win-win formula, which was not necessarily legitimate but highly practical for both sides. The key word was "respecting each other's sovereignty". To confirm this, Thaksin repeatedly expressed his one-China policy and the support for China's sabre-rattling towards Taiwan. Thaksin at one point blocked entry to the Dalai Lama and expelled members of the Falun Gong sect, which has been outlawed in China.[106] Recently, the Thaksin-backed Samak government impressed the Chinese leadership in ensuring that the Olympic torch relay passed through Bangkok, smoothly and peacefully on 19 April 2008, and stood firm that it would not tolerate the pro-Tibet, anti-Chinese regime protesters, embarrassing to both Thailand and China.[107] In return, Beijing avoided "preaching" to Thaksin on many accounts. China was silent over Thaksin's heavy-handed policy against the Thai Muslims in the south. Instead, Chinese leaders presented Thailand's case as parallel to their own difficulties in Xinjiang province where Islamic insurgency has occasionally flared up and posed as a challenge to the Chinese rule.[108] Beijing's position not to interfere in Thailand's domestic affairs generated a great sense of comfort for certain leaders who inclined themselves toward authoritarianism. Thaksin proved that, albeit not for the first time, an elected government could work hand-in-hand with Communist China. The connection between the Chinese model of "controlling development from the top" and Thaksin's style of governance is evident here. Daniel Lynch argued that "rising China" could influence the Communist Party to reconstruct global culture by inspiring actors in other Asian countries to uphold or restore authoritarian rule.[109] Thaksin's affection of a populist dictatorship could have reflected the Chinese influence.[110] Throughout his six years in power, Thaksin had upheld his governing philosophy: capitalist economy but a not-too-open political space.

Throughout that same period, Thai-Chinese relations were smooth because both Bangkok and Beijing clearly signalled that they were not interested in defending democracy or human rights. As a result, talking points on such "heavy issues" were often removed in the discussion between Chinese leaders and their like-minded Thai counterparts. But while leaders at the top echelons acted happily in regard to their seemingly peaceful relations, a sense of frustration was felt among Thai officials about China's sincerity to stop the flow of drugs and people from its southern end into northern Thailand.[111] Likewise, a rapidly growing two-way trade was heavily weighted in China's favour while poor Thai farmers and manufacturers struggled to compete with China's cheaper products. Pawin Talerngsri, Director for Agriculture and Environment at the Department of Trade Negotiations of the Commerce Ministry, confirmed that, for instance, many Thai farmers earned their living by selling garlic but were battling against cheaper garlic from China as a result of the Thai-Chinese FTA.[112] Moreover, the operation of this bilateral relationship was also very selective. It refused to deal with other serious and immediate issues such as environmental degradation, for example, as a result of dam constructions in southern China or heavy traffic in the Mekong River that was used as a transport means for Chinese products to Thailand. In Thailand, the exercise of state censorship, the top-down way of governance in the guise of a CEO style, and the weakening of civil societies were increasingly made tolerable as the Thais looked on at their Chinese friends. Some Thais expressed their disappointment and dissatisfaction toward the Chinese leaders for doing nothing but to encourage Myanmar's military regime, seen as China's own clientele state. The Chinese leaders' support extended to Myanmar simply fulfilled their self-serving interests.[113] Delivering strong economic growth while retaining rigid political control became fashionable not only in the state domain. In the private sector, centralized control is usually regarded a key to success. Greenfield Hidayat noted that Charoen Pokphand's CEO, Dhanin Chearavanont, exercised extensive political influence in securing the corporation's overseas interests. As a major investor in animal feed, agrochemicals, food processing, motorcycles, seeds and supermarkets in China, Dhanin maintained close ties with the political leadership in Beijing.[114]

Yet, numerous benefits gained from this peaceful bilateral relationship appeared to eclipse some of its intrinsic negative aspects. A close friendship between the two countries helped generate an atmosphere of cooperation beyond the bilateral context. The Chinese leaders, despite seeing themselves as a big brother, were happy to follow the lead of a smaller Thailand. Thaksin's ACD was endorsed and actively participated in by China — a symbol of China's commitment to promoting strong relations with Thailand beyond the bilateral boundary.[115] Such multilateral process lent Thailand an important mechanism to bind China into the regional framework, with China winning trust from, and proving that it was a responsible power to, countries in the region, as well as with Thailand reaping direct political and economic interests from China's regional engagement. The key point was that Thai relations with China had to reflect a strategic partnership rather than strategic competition. Also, China seemed to work closely with Thailand as both were hedging against the United States. In many ways, Thaksin's strategy was to produce a foreign policy that was less reliant on one single power, as this would restrain Thailand's conduct of diplomacy. China happened to have risen at the time Thaksin was searching to diversify his choices in foreign affairs.

THE UNITED STATES

Thai-U.S. relations, during the Thaksin period were initially difficult but became close after the 9/11 incident. This period saw the United States awarding a major non-NATO ally status to Thailand. It also witnessed gross human rights violations in Thailand which were a subject of concern of the Bush administration. Whereas economic relations have remained one of the core elements of this bilateral relationship, the FTA negotiations were derailed by domestic political factors in Thailand. The United States also had an ambivalent view on Thaksin as an emerging populist leader. Despite winning consecutive landslide elections, Thaksin was not a democratic icon in the eyes of the United States. More importantly, Thaksin's initial neutral stance regarding the American war on terror could have bankrupted the long-established military alliance between the two countries. All this took place within a period of six years of the Thai Rak Thai government.

Thailand is the oldest ally of the United States in Asia. The 1833 Treaty of Amity and Commerce set off this relationship which proved to be crucial in subsequent years when American friends were needed to pull Thailand out of dangerous situations and to help it ward off enemies. For example, the United States protected Thailand from demands of war reparations by Britain in the aftermath of World War II.[116] It also provided generous financial and military aid to Thailand in the containment efforts against Communism at the peak of the Cold War. In return, the Thai state happily cultivated an anti-Communist reputation to satisfy the U.S. government in order to justify the American aid grant.[117] This mutual benefit allowed the United States to reconstruct an anti-Communist Thai state which openly condoned the rise of militarism. Cooperative mechanisms were initiated to further cement Thailand's new image — a democratic outlook with a despotic substance, and to reconfirm Thai acceptance of U.S. hegemony. Such mechanisms included the Southeast Asia Treaty Organization (SEATO) founded in 1954 to block further Communist gains in Southeast Asia.[118] In 1962, security relations were consolidated in the Rusk-Thanat Communiqué, with special emphasis on a continued U.S. security guarantee to Thailand against Communist attacks. Even after the United States was defeated in the Vietnam War and pulled out most of its troops from the region, strong military ties were maintained even when these ties were different in character from those which preceeded them. In 1982, Thai and U.S. forces commenced annual joint training exercises "Cobra Gold", a pale shadow of the previous Thai-U.S. military relations.[119] In 1996, the Acquisition and Cross-Servicing Agreement was signed; it obliged Thailand to support the United States and its allies for military training in any untoward incident or war.[120]

With the United States' diminishing role in Asia, Washington was led to believe that the elected Thaksin government would further consolidate Thai democracy. But Thaksin was on the course of altering the traditional Thai-U.S. patron-client relationship.

Exploiting the theme of nationalism, Thaksin criticized the United States for failing to rescue Thailand in the midst of the financial crisis. Washington was also believed to be behind the IMF conditions that were seen as helping debtors by providing opportunities for foreigners to buy Thai assets at fire-sale price.[121] Thus, at first, it seemed that Thaksin was most likely to adopt an anti-American agenda. Thaksin's foreign policy assertiveness, reflected in his quest to reset the equilibrium in Thai-U.S. relations, was made possible partly because of the China factor, which was used to counterbalance the United States. But his nationalistic tone in foreign policy against the United States turned out to be more dramatic than realistic. It was dramatic because Thaksin's nationalism was manufactured purely for political reasons. Realistically, however, Thaksin fully recognized that the United States had always been Thailand's most important ally. It has still remained as the most significant trading partner. And since the international order shifted from bipolarism to multipolarism, the United States continued to play as the source of the nation's security and stability in a more unsettled global environment. On the part of the United States, its single focus on the war in Iraq allowed an adequate space for Thaksin to make use of his foreign policy as a bargaining power vis-à-vis Washington. This was hardly surprising, as Michael K. Connors argued, "The nature of U.S. hegemony required that peripheral elites were allowed the right to contest and given room to manoeuvre."[122]

What the Bush administration particularly required from Thaksin was his military support as well as a Thai anti-terrorism foreign policy that would be a foil for the U.S. campaign against terrorists. President Bush counted support from his allies as quintessential because it legitimized his policy on the war on terror and justified the U.S. military invasion of Iraq and Afghanistan. Faced with home-grown terrorists in the deep south, Thaksin found himself locked in a prisoner's dilemma, either to play the role of an obedient ally or to walk away from the U.S. request for fear that it could escalate the already tense situation. At the start, Thaksin decided to declare "neutrality" in the aftermath of 9/11, which was seen as a slap in the face for the United States. Only under heavy pressure did Bangkok subsequently dispatch an engineering corps to Afghanistan and later sent 450 troops to Karbala, Iraq, as part of the rehabilitation process there.[123] In August 2003, Thailand's cooperation with the United States' Central Intelligence Agency (CIA) led to the arrest of Riduan Isamuddin, or Hambali, former military leader of Jemaah Islamiah which has been linked with Al-Qaeda, in Ayutthaya province. The United States gave a double award for the Thai collaboration. First, in October the same year, President Bush announced Thailand's major non-NATO ally status.[124] Thailand was now eligible to participate in certain counter-terrorism initiatives, get a priority delivery of military surplus (ranging from rations to ships), access loans on equipment and materials for cooperative research and development projects and evaluations, use American financing for the purchase or lease of certain defence equipment, and receive training. Second, the U.S. government promised FTA negotiations with Thailand to further promote bilateral trade relations.

Thaksin's endorsement of the U.S. war on terror revealed a dangerous gamble behind his chosen foreign policy choices. Right after Thailand won the status of a major non-NATO ally, the Muslim community in the south staged a protest against the Thaksin and Bush governments; both aimed at toppling the regime of Saddam Hussein and further isolating the Muslim world. But Thaksin claimed to have gained more in this high-stakes gamble than what he may have lost. Statistics were used to explain Thailand's economic gains from the United States although some of these did not derive from Thaksin's policy. In economic terms, Thailand, in 2003, became the United States' twenty-third largest export market (US$5.8 billion) and its fifteenth largest supplier of imports (US$15.1 billion). The U.S. exports to Thailand increased by 20.2 per cent, while its imports from Thailand rose by 2.6 per cent. In the same year, the United States was Thailand's largest export market and the second largest investor in the kingdom, after Japan, with cumulative investments of US$20 billion. U.S.-invested firms in Thailand employed over 200,000 Thai nationals.[125] Thailand was concerned that its exports to the United States had been losing market share in recent years to countries such as Mexico and China. Thus, as Thailand justified, by eliminating the U.S. tariff and non-tariff barriers to Thai exports, an FTA could increase the competitiveness and market share of Thai products in the United States. But was this economic reason the sole determining factor that explained Thaksin's U.S.-centric foreign policy?

In many ways, from the perspective of the West, Thaksin was a troubled leader. He transformed a democratic regime into a questionable entity with a series of illegitimate policy actions. He was also accused of corruption and curbing media freedom. These vulnerabilities constrained the form and substance of his foreign policy toward countries like the United States. But the United States, too, constrained its own foreign policy with its narrow objective of winning the war on terror. President Bush said in 2001, "You are either with us or against us in the fight against terror. There is no room for neutrality in the war against terrorism."[126] Thailand and the United States found their mutual comfort level amid their perceived constraints, and therefore gave one another room for manoeuvre so long as such constraints were not too detrimental to their overall relationship. From this viewpoint, it was obvious that the United States did not intend to condemn Thaksin harshly for all the allegations against him regarding human rights abuses. Softer statements were used instead. "Washington expressed its deep concerns at the high number of deaths in the so-called war on drugs and the ongoing violence in the three provinces of Yala, Narathiwat and Pattani," the U.S. State Department had announced in March 2004.[127] Later on, Thaksin, in pushing the envelope further, called Washington a "useless friend" for its failure to defend Thailand against the U.N. report on the situation of human rights violations in his country.[128] The United States response was not forthcoming.

The level of mutual dependence and the need to satisfy each other's foreign policy imperatives represented the key that kept the Thai-U.S. relations thriving. Thaksin's support for the U.S. war on terror and its security architecture in Southeast Asia unfailingly fulfilled Bush's foreign policy. And for the rest, the United States was willing to tolerate Thaksin's other foreign policy ambitions and even his drift towards authoritarianism as long as they would not threaten Washington's interests. Thus, the United States did not oppose Thaksin's ACD initiative, the forum that excluded its participation. Washington never considered the ACD as an attempt to create a new anti-American bloc. It did not question the hegemonic intention of Thailand in proposing ACMECS. More importantly, the United States did not seem to be demoralized by Thaksin's intense courtship with China. After all, Thailand and the United States have had a comprehensive relationship covering all important areas relating to politics, economic, security, defence, education, health and human security, science and technology, sustainable development and the environment. Both have had a forum for consultation and dialogue on their bilateral relationship called the "Thai-U.S. Strategic Dialogue", a result of the joint initiative of Thaksin and Bush during their bilateral meeting in Washington D.C. on 29 September 2005. Its latest meeting was convened in November 2005 which discussed, among other matters, how to enhance military-to-military cooperation to be mutually beneficial at bilateral, regional and global levels.[129] Both also agreed to draw the Thai-U.S. Plan of Action which was to be a roadmap for moving forward the bilateral relationship. Certainly, the United States possessed one thing that China lacked — some moral authority. At the height of political tensions in Bangkok in the pre-coup period, Thaksin wrote a personal message to President Bush, dated 23 June 2006, reporting that he was being politically bullied. He said, "There has been a threat to democracy in Thailand since early this year. Key democratic institutions, such as elections and the observance of Constitutional limitations on government, have been repeatedly undermined."[130] Putting the content of his message aside, even a seemingly undemocratic Thaksin sought to get a moral espousal from the United States. Therefore, Thailand's strengthening of bilateral relations with China did not need to be a zero-sum game situation for the United States.

Overall, Thai-U.S. relations evolved greatly under the leadership of Thaksin. The shifting international order, in which the U.S. influence in Southeast Asia appeared waning due to its overwhelming engagement with conflicts in the Middle East, the scourge of terrorism, its post-9/11 trauma, and its domestic call for the return of American isolationism, remoulded Thai-U.S. bilateral relationship to become a little more of a partnership based on shared responsibilities.[131] With or without Thaksin, the United States was somehow compelled to modify its role vis-à-vis Thailand. Thaksin, as cunning as a politician can be, stepped into the character of an assertive, nationalistic leader, who dared to speak his mind before the world's superpower, the United States. In his interview in New York in September 2006, Thaksin succinctly said, "The United States is generous to provide assistance to many countries, but luckily Thailand, under my leadership, we just asked to be equal partners."[132] On the surface, the assertiveness of Thailand's U.S. policy and the transformation of bilateral relations towards a partnership effectively justified Thaksin's self-centred diplomacy. In a nutshell, however, it could also be illusive since a few flashpoints during this so-called close relationship period were simply swept under the carpet, namely the rise of "authoritarian democracy" under the Thaksin regime and the controversial issues subsumed under the FTA negotiations, including the potential loss of economic advantage of certain Thai agricultural products to the United States, and the U.S. demand of patents which could put an end to affordable medicines. But Thaksin knew too well how to please the U.S. leadership by portraying the Thai nation as *dek dee* [good boy], the term used by former Thai ambassador to Washington, Kasit Piromya, when describing Thailand's relations with the United States.[133]

THE NOT-SO-MARGINAL RELATIONS

The study on Thailand's bilateral relations would be incomplete without the analysis of Thai interactions with three other important Asian states: Singapore, Japan and India. These bilateral relations possessed their own unique characteristics and thus worthiness as a subject of discussion. In the case of Thai-Singaporean relations, the sale of Shin Corporation to Temasek Holdings in January 2006 interrupted their diplomatic links and led to the suspension of core bilateral activities. For Japan, the planned FTA, known as "Japan-Thailand Economic Partnership Agreement" (JTEPA), which eventually came into effect in 2007 after three years of negotiations, marked another milestone in this bilateral relationship. As for India, Thailand under Thaksin renewed its friendship with this rising Asian power, while assigning it as both a strategic and economic partner. This section looks briefly into each of these bilateral relations, emphasizing Thaksin's self-assured diplomacy and the intricate connection between national and private interests.

Singapore

Thailand and Singapore established their diplomatic relations in 1965, the year in which the latter was expelled from Malaysia. Singapore stood side-by-side with Thailand in leading the ASEAN campaign against Vietnam's occupation of Cambodia. Despite great differences in size and population, Thailand and Singapore share many similar qualities and worldviews. Both have been strong allies of the United States. Both have adopted market economies and democratic principles, even at different degrees and through different interpretations. Both are founding members of ASEAN and have strong economic and military links. Thaksin had a special interest in forging a more intimate friendship with Singapore, supposedly because he shared with the Singaporean leadership a business mentality and a new worldview. Successive Thai ambassadors to Singapore agreed that Thaksin and Prime Minister Lee Hsien Loong even "spoke on the same wavelength".[134] Thaksin was also the first recipient from Thailand of the Lee Kuan Yew Exchange Fellowship (LKYEF) back in 1995. The LKYEF programme invites outstanding individuals for high-level exchange visits to Singapore. The fellows are selected on the basis of their proven track record and contributions to the development of their nation, as well as in promoting international understanding and goodwill. Singapore hoped to win over future regional leaders, and Thaksin proved that the city-state had picked the right winner.[135]

Bilateral relations were strong, even prior to the arrival of Thaksin, due to the two countries' active historical interactions. King Chulalongkorn travelled to Singapore, Britain's colony, for the first time in 1871. He was the first Thai monarch ever to travel overseas, and Singapore was his first stop.[136] Thailand and Singapore have cooperated closely in various fields, especially militarily, such as in the joint air training (an air training base has been provided for Singapore in Thailand), and the annual Cobra Gold military exercise. On the economic front, Singapore ranks among Thailand's top five trading partners, and its top ten foreign investors. Solid relations have also been underpinned by existing mechanisms, namely the Prime Ministerial Retreat (The first meeting between Thaksin and Singapore's Prime Minister Goh Chok Tong took place on 10–12 January 2003), the Civil Service Exchange Programme (CSEP), first founded in 1998, and Singapore-Thailand Enhanced Economic Relationship (STEER), established in 2002. Moreover, there are over 50,000 Thai workers who are now employed in Singapore.[137] The two countries also worked closely in ASEAN. Thaksin and Prime Minister Goh, in 2003, came up with the "2+X principle" whereby two ASEAN members could embark on cooperative initiatives at a pace faster than the rest without having to wait for the group's consensus. Singapore's Foreign Minister

S. Jayakumar said during the CSEP 6th Coordinating Meeting in
Bangkok on 17 November 2003:

> At the last CSEP in Singapore, I had mentioned that during the
> ASEAN Summit in Phnom Penh, Prime Minister Thaksin had told
> Prime Minister Goh that Thailand and Singapore should do more
> and "tango" together. I am glad to report that we are already
> "tangoing" with each other. At the regional level, we have forged
> a meaningful and productive partnership as pathfinders in ASEAN
> to spur on intra-ASEAN cooperation aimed at revitalising ASEAN.
> We have cooperated to come up with the 2+X principle within
> ASEAN. We have received positive responses from several ASEAN
> countries to this initiative. This confirms the shared view of
> Singapore and Thailand that greater regional economic cooperation
> is vital for ASEAN to stay relevant in a rapidly changing global
> environment. By demonstrating the benefits of working closely
> together, I am confident that we will be able to convince the other
> ASEAN members to come on board when they are ready."[138]

In sum, Thailand under the leadership of Thaksin enjoyed
friendly relations with Singapore in all areas of cooperation.

But this close friendship was thrown into jeopardy following
the sale of Thaksin's Shin Corp to Singapore's Temasek Holdings in
January 2006. Thaksin scooped Bt73.3 billion without paying capital
gains tax, thus allowing himself to become a political target of the
anti-government protesters led by the People's Alliance for
Democracy (PAD). They accused him of selling national assets to
foreigners since Shin Corp dealt with telecommunications, deemed
as a sensitive industry to national security. The man who exploited
nationalism for his own foreign policy success was now being
burnt by the fire of the same nationalism. Since the Shin-Temasek
sale, Thai-Singaporean relations quickly drifted toward frigidity.
PAD nationalists launched the image of the "ugly Singaporean"
primarily to further delegitimize Thaksin and to tarnish the
reputation of Singapore in the eyes of the Thai public. In March
2006, the anti-Thaksin movement staged a rally in front of
Singapore's embassy in Bangkok where demonstrators burnt posters
of Prime Minister Lee Hsien Loong, torched models of Singapore
Airlines planes and its "Merlion" national mascot, as well as raised
the banner "Thailand Not For Sale".[139]

Such frigidity finally led to the official suspension of core bilateral
activities, including the CSEP and the STEER, following the deposed

Thaksin's visit to Singapore on 12–16 January 2007, four months after he was overthrown in a military coup (core bilateral activities were only resumed in March 2008 during the Samak government). Jayakumar, now serving as Deputy Prime Minister, hosted Thaksin to a private dinner since they both were long-time friends. The military-installed Surayud government protested to Singapore's government for ignoring Thailand's earlier request of embargoing Thaksin's call on Jayakumar. While in Singapore, Thaksin gave a series of interviews to the U.S. cable network CNN and the *Asian Wall Street Journal* and criticized the national policy of the Surayud government. Foreign Minister George Yeo subsequently replied to questions in Parliament, stating that there was no reason for Singapore to deny Thaksin's entry into the country since he had a valid passport and not a fugitive from Thai law. Moreover, Jayakumar could not refuse to see his old friend for a meal.[140] Thailand decided to cancel the 8th CSEP Meeting, due on 29–31 January 2007, suspend all CSEP activities and relinquish Yeo's invitation for the planned meeting. Kishore Mahbubani, former Singapore ambassador and dean of the Lee Kuan Yew School of Public Policy, told the local media, "Thaksin put Singapore in a tight spot. We tried to make his visit as low-key as possible. In some ways, Thaksin was unkind to us. It would have been better if he had done the CNN interview somewhere else."[141]

Despite the earlier strong bilateral foundation, it can be argued that both Thailand and Singapore have long been confined within an old structure in which their relations were shaped and heavily dominated strictly at the state level. At some points, they became dangerously taken for granted. In the pre-Thaksin period, bilateral relations might have seemed unruffled on the surface. At a more profound level however, new domestic and global developments produced a powerful impact on these bilateral ties. The most evident development was the rapid democratization and economic advancement in Thailand during the past decade, and more so under Thaksin, that paved the way for a more open society, the emergence of a new kind of leadership and a more active role for the civil society and the new media. Unfortunately, Singapore's leaders failed to appreciate these changes. With a change in public attitude, the Thai public has progressively become more engaged in the political process and has pushed for more influence on domestic and foreign policy. This inevitably affected Thailand's position, especially towards neighbouring countries including Singapore. As Panitan Wattanayagorn argued, "What went wrong was that Singapore simply overlooked the mounting importance of pluralism in Thailand. Both Singapore and Temasek need to do more homework on the reality and nature of Thai politics."[142]

Japan

Relations between Thailand and Japan can be traced back to the fifteenth century where a sizeable Japanese community flourished in the kingdom of Ayutthaya. Throughout the course of their long, engaging history, relations had been amicable even when they became preoccupied with other powers outside the region. Both countries establish their diplomatic relations in September 1887. During World War II, the Phibun government aligned itself with imperialist Japan, as dictated by political circumstances in the region and his innate fascist ideology.[143] But the responsibility as a political ally shifted in the post-war period following Japan's emergence as a world economic superpower. In this period, Japan played a crucial role in Thailand's economic development through trade and investment as well as open-handed financial and technical assistance, despite a temporary hiccup in 1972 when the Student Federation of Thailand launched an anti-Japanese products campaign as a result of a new rise of Thai nationalism. Warm ties were quickly resumed, in part because the two countries' royal families have been a fundamental factor underpinning bilateral relationship.[144]

Thaksin devised a two-fold strategy in regard to Thai relations with Japan. First, he sought to set a new tone in this relationship, from a donor-recipient pattern to a broad-based partnership, through the proposal of a bilateral FTA (but the donor-recipient pattern was not abolished during the Thaksin period). Second, acknowledging the status of Japan on the international stage, Thaksin hoped to earn Tokyo's blessing of his foreign policy initiatives, especially the ACD. Thaksin first visited Japan as a prime minister in November 2001. He met with his counterpart, Prime Minister Junichiro Koizumi and recommended the commissioning of a study for a "Japan-Thailand Free Trade Agreement" and an "Economic Agreement for Partnership".[145] These two initial ideas later gave birth to the negotiations of the Japan-Thailand Economic Partnership Agreement

(JTEPA). JTEPA, a free trade agreement that aimed at creating a more favourable investment and drawing additional Japanese investment in Thailand, became another ambitious step that was used to validate a Thaksinized foreign policy based on Thailand's adoption of borderless mercantilism. Prior to the JTEPA, bilateral trade had already expanded significantly during the past decades. According to Japan Trade Statistics, in 2002, trade between Thailand and Japan totalled JPY2.85 trillion (US$31.25 billion). Japan had long been Thailand's largest trading partner. Meanwhile, Thailand ranked the eighth largest trade partner of Japan. Moreover, Japan had remained the largest investor in the kingdom in terms of the number of investors as well as the amount invested. In 2002, according to Thailand's Board of Investment, the number of Japanese investors to Thailand amounted to 215, equivalent to 45 per cent of the kingdom's total number of investors.[146] Hence, JTEPA was expected to enhance trade, investment and cooperation between the two countries. Thaksin said in his visit to Japan in September 2005, "We should look at the JTEPA as a synergy of strength not as a competition between two markets. It is a long-term process that will be beneficial for both countries. I would say that the Thailand-Japan relationship is about synergizing strengths, deepening a sense of 'ownership' in our relations, and looking beyond bilateral relations."[147] But the JTEPA process was not totally rosy. Pasuk Phongpaichit noted that the process was criticized for not having sufficient transparency. While official negotiations proceeded from early 2004 to 2006 led by chief negotiators Pisan Manawapat (Deputy Permanent Secretary of Thai Foreign Ministry) and Ichiro Fujisaki (Japan's Vice Minister of Foreign Affairs), some important information, such as what Thailand could lose out in the process, was not made publicly available. Thus, the process became an issue of suspicion. Many doubted whether the agreement truly reflected Thailand's best interests, since there was no mechanism to ensure those interests were properly articulated and taken into account. Yet, everything depended on the negotiators who might have been poorly informed, or susceptible to vested interests.[148] Thaksin's preference for personal diplomacy intensified speculation of possible vested interests hidden in his endorsement of JTEPA.

One year after the departure of Thaksin, Japan and Thailand signed on the JTEPA which immediately came into effect. The total trade volume between Thailand and Japan as well as Japan's direct investment in Thailand increased noticeably after its implementation. A recent study confirmed that, in general, JTEPA improved the real GDP growth of the Thai and Japanese economies by 0.42 per cent and 0.11 per cent respectively. The percentage changes in all other macroeconomic variables similarly suggested that Thailand, as a smaller economy, enjoyed a greater positive impact than Japan, given the same magnitude of change in bilateral imports. Under the JTEPA, regional trade was facilitated and the terms of trade improved for both countries. Private and investment demands were enhanced as national incomes increased, although the reduction in public demand was unavoidable. Remarkably, in Thailand, processed agricultural products benefited the most from the bilateral partnership as outputs and exports grew by 29.58 per cent and 85.17 per cent respectively. Meanwhile, agricultural produce enjoyed a 3.08 per cent growth in output. Japan, on the other hand, expanded its production in most manufacturing sectors especially as motor vehicles and parts benefited from the 1.10 per cent and 1.81per cent output and export growth rates. Similarly, textiles, chemicals, rubber, plastic products, metal products, and machinery and equipment all clearly gained from JTEPA as their exports to Thailand increased.[149]

Japan was not only an essential trading partner for Thaksin. In drawing up the ACD, Thaksin hoped to count on Japan for its support so as to make his foreign policy initiative more credible. Japan has been an important friend-in-need for Thailand, as seen during the financial crisis of 1997. It contributed generously to the IMF rescue programme, and even went further by providing the Miyazawa Fund, a US$30 billion fund set up in 1999 as a financial package to help Asian countries that were reeling from the Asian financial crisis. This was well remembered by Thaksin who rode to power by exploiting Thailand's vulnerability during the economic crisis while Thailand was under the Democrat government. Japan itself recognized the necessity of continued engagement with Southeast Asian states, not only for its own economic benefits but also to dilute China's influence on the region. Japan was successful in securing Thaksin's support for its bid to become a permanent member of the United Nations Security Council (UNSC), a decision that irked Beijing.[150] Japan thus embraced Thaksin's proposed form of regionalism and went along with the ACD. The Japanese government offered to help develop environmental education and strengthen legal infrastructure among members of the ACD, as well as participated actively in the Asian Bond Market initiative to create more wealth in Asia from Asia's own resources. Furthermore, Japan also played a crucial part in Thaksin's ACMECS as a development partner. Japan, during the ACMECS Ministerial Meeting in Cambodia's Siem Reap, on 4–5 August 2005, praised Thailand repeatedly for such an initiative and saw ACMECS as elemental in closing the development gap between countries on mainland Southeast Asia.[151] In sum, Thaksin's foreign policy served to maintain the level of partnership between Thailand and Japan, and at the same time, accomplish his strategic and economic needs.

India

Like China, India is a rising power. Thailand's policy vis-à-vis India pointed towards Thaksin's ways and methods to bandwagon with this up-and-coming, powerful South Asian nation. Over a decade-and-a-half ago, India embarked on its "Look East" policy that marked a strategic shift in the country's perspective toward Southeast Asia and beyond. That policy has borne fruit in the form of intensifying the political dialogue, expanding trade and steadily enlarging people-to-people contacts between India and Southeast Asia, including Thailand (India and Thailand established their diplomatic ties in August 1947).[152] As the rise of India was indisputable, Thaksin, seeing Thailand as being on the rise too, renewed the old "Look West" policy, which was formulated in 1996, to cash in with the new regional reality. Thailand's old Look West policy became new. It aimed primarily at engaging, mostly economically, India and other countries in the sub-continent. Such a policy brought about the BIMSTEC and the Mekong-Ganga Cooperation (MGC) as regional mechanisms that bound countries in the region together.[153] The renewed Look West *à la* Thaksin was, however, a little different; in this, he dealt with the Indian leadership specifically on a bilateral and personal basis. In other words, Thaksin downsized the content and scope of the Look West policy to better suit his political and private objectives.

The main highlight for Thaksin's ostensible success in his relations with India was the conclusion of the bilateral FTA, the first between India and an ASEAN country. The framework agreement to establish the Thailand-India Free Trade Agreement

(TIFTA) was signed on 9 October 2003. Trade negotiations to move closer to full liberalization are still continuing, and are expected to be concluded by 2010. To accelerate the realization of benefits, both countries agreed to implement an "Early Harvest Scheme" covering trade in goods which numbered eighty-four products. The TIFTA-Early Harvest Scheme covered a three-year period from 1 September 2004 to 31 August 2006 and has now ended.[154]

In his weekly radio address in October 2003, Thaksin, following the signing of an early harvest package of the FTA and the open skies agreement with India, said, "Thailand has spent 15 years trying to negotiate an increase to 3,000 seats per month flying between Thailand and India but always failed. Now, India has opened up four cities for daily flights and 18 other cities on top of that with no limits."[155] It was expected that a bilateral FTA would see tariffs slashed to zero by 2010. Deputy Prime Minister Korn Dabarangsi boldly declared that within fourteen months, the two-way trade would double to US$2.1 billion.[156] Indian Prime Minister Atal Behari Vajpayee, during his visit to Bangkok in October 2003 to sign the FTA — the first visit in ten years of an Indian prime minister, agreed with Thaksin to expedite the implementation of the agreement, for the elimination of tariff and non-tariff barriers in the free movement of goods, capital and services within agreed timeframes. Nonetheless, bilateral relations were not limited only to trade. Thaksin intensified Thailand's security cooperation with India through joint efforts against terrorism and narcotic trafficking, and in joint naval patrols against narcotics and piracy. Besides, Thaksin offered to act as a bridge for India in its venture into Southeast Asia, and ASEAN in particular. Generally, bilateral ties seemed to be positive in all aspects. India proved once again that its Look East policy was still relevant and that Thaksin's keenness to elevate this bilateral relationship reaffirmed India's place, and power, in Southeast Asia. Thaksin gained from his Look West policy too. He was successful in courting rising India, a vast market for Thai export products, in diversifying his foreign policy options, and in bending the prevailing wind in which India was a tremendous force. But were his intimate ties with Delhi also to boost his family's business interests?

At the anti-Thaksin rally in March 2006, three former ambassadors, Asda Jayanama, Surapong Jayanama and Kasit Piromya, accused Thaksin of misusing his official overseas trips to promote the business of his family's telecom company. Asda alleged that Thaksin's three visits to India were related to a deal in which India rented the transponders of Shinawatra Satellite — an allegation which was refuted—as baseless by Foreign Minister Kantathi.[157] While the allegation remained, a recent extensive study by a Thai academic showed the possibility of Thaksin using his self-invented foreign policy to benefit and protect his family businesses and those of his affiliations. Pasuk Phongpaichit argued that the Thaksin government tried to protect its telecom businesses by not opening up the telecom industry in the country. Instead, it opened up other sectors in exchange for the liberalization of services which would benefit businesses of government politicians. An example could be seen in the Thai-Australian FTA where Thaksin opened up the Thai cattle industry in exchange for Australia's telecom and auto spare parts industries. This allowed Shin Satellite to benefit at the expense of Thai cattle farmers. She said, "The IPStar project will also benefit from FTA agreements with India and China. Shin Satellite's revenues would tremendously increase once India and China use transponders of IPStar. It was expected that IPStar's service fees from the two countries would be worth about Bt15 billion."[158]

Thaksin's Look West diplomacy was tainted by the obscurity of his foreign policy objectives and approaches. The Thai-Indian FTA might have served real national interests as well as the interest of the Shinawatra family. But other aspects of Thaksin's Look West policy did not always gratify his Indian friends. Thaksin looked beyond India when he pronounced this policy. He flirted with Pakistan too, both politically and economically. In the political realm, Thaksin was personally invited to Pakistan to participate in the ACD and took the initiative in having Pakistan inducted into the ARF. India was irked by Thaksin's cosy relations with Pakistan. Repeatedly, India had asked Thaksin to extend his support for its bid to become a permanent member of the UNSC. But Thaksin never gave a straight answer. Thaksin said,

> Thailand fully recognises and understands India's strong interest in securing a permanent seat in the UNSC. We also recognise the wishes of many other countries that want to become permanent members of the UNSC. I do hope that, whatever decision we are going to make in the near future, we can fulfil the interests of India as well as the international community at the same time.[159]

Comparing Thaksin's support for Japan's bid for the same position, India could identify a degree of manipulation in his policy towards Delhi. His new-found relations with Pakistan only intensified that deduction especially as Thaksin paid a number of visits to Pakistan and developed a close personal relationship with Pakistani Prime Minister Shaukat Aziz who, like Thaksin, was a businessman himself.

The Thaksin government claimed that the ACD would be a positive venue for rivals, such as between India and Pakistan, for the exchange of discussions, not necessarily on politics but other issues of common concerns. Thaksin led member countries to believe that this slow process of "getting to know" each other would eventually break down walls of misunderstanding between them. But such a process never came about. Thus, Thailand's aspired role as a peace facilitator between India and Pakistan was never taken seriously by the international community, nor was its volunteering role to help resolve the crisis on the Korean Peninsula. In 2006, Thailand volunteered to play an informal role to push for progress in negotiations among regional players in the six-party talks — North Korea, South Korea, Japan, China, Russia and the United States. Foreign Minister Kantathi Suphamongkhon said repeatedly that Thailand's proposed role was well received by all concerned parties. In reality, however, North Korea had an ambivalent attitude toward the Thai offer. The Thai media suggested that the government's first priority in the Korean Peninsula should be to pressure the government of North Korea to disclose the whereabouts and fate of Anocha Panjoy, a Thai lady who was allegedly kidnapped by intelligence agents from North Korea in 1978 in Macau. So far, Pyongyang has ignored repeated enquiries from the Thai government. Embassy officials in Bangkok even dismissed the kidnapping story as groundless.[160]

The credibility of Thailand in intervening in the region's major political flashpoints was let down, or compromised, by the Thaksinized foreign policy which seemed to serve a symbolic purpose rather than to attain tangible results.

CONCLUSION

Thaksin adopted a two-pronged strategy in his conduct of bilateral diplomacy. On the one hand, he invested his energy in cultivating bilateral relations with immediate neighbours and garnished them with creative ideas. Thaksin came up with a handful of new cooperative frameworks to recreate his country's sphere of influence through the process of reinventing Thailand. On the other hand, Thaksin rejuvenated the country's traditional ties with old allies, China and the United States, hoping to navigate their relationship into a new order where Thailand would hope to be treated as an equal partner. This chapter purposely omitted the discussions on Thailand's bilateral relations with other significant countries and organizations simply because they were adequately smooth and non-contentious. The reasons behind such smooth and non-contentious relations are the combination of the absence of territorial disputes and the relatively amicable ties in all areas of interactions based primarily on mutual respect and shared benefits. Thai-Vietnamese relations were stable during the Thaksin period. As a former enemy and present-day economic competitor, Vietnam was perceived in a new light by the Thaksin administration. In 2004, Thaksin proposed to his Vietnamese counterpart the first Joint Cabinet Retreat (JCR) as a main platform directing overall bilateral relations. As a result of the first JCR, the Joint Statement on the Thailand-Vietnam Cooperation Framework in the First Decade of the 21st Century was launched. Both sides agreed to set up a Joint Working Group on Political and Security Cooperation to complement the work of the Joint Trade Commission which was established in 1995. Two-way trade volume increased from US$1.3 billion in 2004 to US$3 billion in 2005. By 2007, Vietnam had become Thailand's twelfth largest investor with 153 investment projects in the kingdom worth more than US$1.54 billion.[161] Thailand's relations with Australia and New Zealand have been forthcoming, with each benefiting from the concluded FTAs at somewhat varying degrees. Thaksin's ties with Russia were strong. President Vladimir Putin became Russia's major arms salesman and sought to expand arms sales with Thailand which was well reciprocated by Thaksin.[162] In 2005, the Thaksin government agreed to buy a dozen Sukhoi-30 fighter jets from Russia worth US$500 million.[163] To show Russia's appreciation, Putin agreed to join the ACD in 2005 and volunteered to act as a prime mover in the field of natural disaster management. As for the European Union, "average" was the appropriate term to illustrate its relations with Thailand. For a globe-trotting leader like Thaksin, Europe suddenly seemed too far for Thailand's diplomatic ambitions. Thaksin made clear that the new focus in Thai foreign relations was Asia. Thus, he formulated an Asia-for-Asians policy, while downplaying Thailand's reliance on Europe like in the past. Thai-E.U. bilateral trade was good enough, with a satisfactory trade increase over the years. But this was often spoiled by the European Union's trade measures, particularly in regard to anti-dumping and countervailing duties. Besides, Thaksin was at times displeased by Europe's strong criticism on his too-convenient ties with the Myanmar generals. Yet these obstacles did not stand in the way for both sides to maintain a good relationship.

In looking at sets of bilateral relations between Thailand and its partners, confusion and inconsistency became apparent. There was no uniformity in the content of Thaksin's foreign policy. He pushed hard for economic benefits from one set of relationships, and at the same time, sought to earn international recognition from another, such as through Thaksin's Bangkok Process. What seemed to be the only pattern of uniformity in Thaksin's diplomacy was his relentless search for private interests, be they business or politics. National interests could prove peculiar in Thaksin's vocabulary. But again, he was not the first Thai leader who exploited the domain of foreign affairs to enlarge personal wealth. A lack of uniformity in Thai foreign policy has not been unusual and the "bending with the wind" approach has continually illustrated Thailand's boneless stance. A more important message must, however, be placed on the fact that the obscurity between national and private interests reached an epidemic level during the Thaksin administration. The name of the diplomatic game was profit. Thaksin reinvented Thailand as a conglomerate whereby the Foreign Ministry was required to modify its role to suit a new working environment. The outcomes were bleak. Prosperity (equivalent to inflows of money) and leadership (equivalent to power) made Thailand's relations with the outside world convincingly pleasing. They also indicated a successful foreign policy. Yet, the beauty was only skin deep. Relations built on short-sighted benefits proved to be unsustainable. The Bangkok Process has long died. The ACD is moving into a stage of inertia. The ACMECS will only last as long as Thailand continues to pump money into its less developed neighbours.

Thaksin's foreign policy was tailored to be outwardly assertive and nationalistic. Inwardly, his foreign policy was empty. His assertiveness melted away as he found his way back into the business world while engaging with leaders in the neighbourhood. A nationalist became a submissive leader. Thailand's position was often reduced to appeasement, a character that contradicted starkly with Thaksin's earlier nationalist approach, in order that certain benefits could be gained in the process, seen clearly in his dealings with the Myanmar leadership. Likewise, Thaksin's repainted Thailand was, to a certain level, only a nominally hegemonic entity. In the meantime, neighbours continued to influence Thai foreign policy and they were able to do so because they were aware of Thaksin's vulnerability in merging business and politics. Thaksin might not be totally successful in conquering and overpowering his neighbours, but was certainly effective in subduing the Foreign Ministry. That explains why Thaksin could freely adopt and adapt foreign policy to suit his own ends. Democratic Thaksin also turned back the clock to the time when absolutism ruled the kingdom. The CEO ambassadors performed like provincial governors in old Siam: domineering within their own territory but completely submissive to the central power.

Nevertheless, Thaksin's diplomacy was not only about the story of fiasco. He perceived the world as the diplomatic playground of Thailand. This world was coloured by his initiatives and positivity. Thaksin also excelled at manipulating the country's image. Thailand's hosting of the APEC Leaders' Meeting in 2003, possibly the most opulent summit ever, was praised, and is still talked about, by member countries. Bilaterally, Thaksin encouraged dialogue with his counterparts in neighbouring countries. This type of diplomacy, based on increased contacts and dialogue at the top levels, helped preserve at least a channel of communication regardless of whether it was sustainable or short-term. Thailand also obtained a considerable amount of goodwill from great powers. In new platforms like the ACD and ACMECS, they recognized Thailand's leadership through the creative initiatives aimed at closing development gaps. In fact, Thailand's participation in peace-keeping efforts under the United Nations by dispatching its personnel to Cambodia, Namibia, Sierra Leone, Bosnia and Herzegovina, and Timor Leste could be used to show the bright side of Thaksin's diplomacy. This was Thailand's involvement in its role as a responsible member of the global community. Asked if Thaksin was able to bend the wind to the benefit of the country, and perhaps his own, in the handling of bilateral relations, one could instantly give an upbeat answer, and refer to the many new acronyms recently created within the realm of Thai diplomacy. But the prevailing wind blowing the Thai way had been too fast and furious. When the dust had settled, one realized that there was little left to see, or to be remembered.

Notes

1. See, Ministry of Foreign Affairs of Thailand, *Karn Thood Yook Mai Hua Jai Kue Prachachon* [New-Age Diplomacy with the People at its Heart] (Bangkok: Cyber Print, 2003).
2. Marwaan Macan Markar, "Thaksin's Visit to Measure Ties with US", *The Irrawaddy*, 23 May 2003.
3. Thitinan Pongsudhirak, "Asia's Age of Thaksin?", *Project Syndicate*, 11 April 2005.
4. In 1992, the Thai-initiated "Constructive Engagement Policy" was conceived with the blessing of ASEAN. It was designed to help Myanmar achieve a more rapid transition toward internationally accepted behaviour and norms not only in international relations but also in tackling national economic and political issues.
5. Pavin Chachavalpongpun, *A Plastic Nation: The Curse of Thainess in Thai-Burmese Relations* (Lanham: University Press of America, 2005), Chapter 6.
6. "ASEAN Needs Flexible Engagement", *The Irrawaddy*, vol. 6, no. 4 (August 1998) <http://www.irrawaddy.org/article.php?art_id=1166> (accessed 28 December 2009).
7. "Burma Beams 'True Image' to the World", *Bangkok Post*, 31 July 2001. Quoted in Desmond Ball, *Security Development in the Thailand-Burma Borderlands*, Working Paper no. 9 (Sydney: Australian Mekong Resource Centre, University of Sydney, October 2003), p. 7.
8. "Thailand should be Firm with Burma", *The Irrawaddy*, 1 February 2001.
9. Pavin Chachavalpongpun, "Thai Position toward Burma", in *Alliances and the Problems of Burma/Myanmar Policy: The United States, Japan, Thailand, Australia and the European Union*, Asian Voices Seminar Series Transcript, (Washington, D.C.: Sasakawa Peace Foundation, 2006), p. 14. This was adapted from a paper presented at the Cosmos Club, Washington, D.C., organized by Sasakawa Peace Foundation, the United States, on 3 November 2006.
10. N. Ganesan, "Myanmar's Foreign Relations: Reaching out to the World", in *Myanmar: Beyond Politics to Social Imperatives*, edited by

Kyaw Yin Hlaing, Robert H. Taylor, and Tin Maung Maung Than, (Singapore: Institute of Southeast Asian Studies, 2005), pp. 46–47.

11. Source: The Ministry of Foreign Affairs of Thailand <http://www.mfa.go.th> (accessed 8 May 2008).

12. Source: "Country Situation Update: Burma", Southeast Asian Committee for Advocacy (SEACA), <http://www.seaca.net/_articleFiles/182/Country%20Profile%20-Burma.doc> (accessed 28 December 2009).

13. Pasuk Phongpaichit and Chris Baker, *Thaksin: The Business of Politics in Thailand* (Chiang Mai: Silkworm Books, 2004), pp. 212–13.

14. Pavin Chachavalpongpun, "Neither Constructive Nor Engaging: The Debacle of ASEAN's Burma Policy", in *Between Isolation and Internationalisation: The State of Burma*, edited by Johan Lagerkvist, Paper no. 4 (Stockholm: The Swedish Institute of International Affairs, 2008), p. 215.

15. Kavi Chongkittavorn, "Thailand has Lost its Voice and Influence on Burma", *The Nation*, 6 March 2006.

16. Surapong Jayanama, *Karn Thood Karn Muang Maichai Ruang Suantua* [Diplomacy and Politics Are Not Personal Issues] (Bangkok: Siam Publishing Company, 2007), p. 30.

17. "Armed Conflicts Report: Burma (1988: First Combat Death), *Ploughshares* (Ontario: Project Ploughshares, January 2009), <http://www.ploughshares.ca/libraries/ACRText/ACR-Burma.html> (accessed 28 December 2009).

18. In an e-mail interview with Bertil Lintner, 12 October 2007. Lintner is the author of *Burma in Revolt: Opium and Insurgency Since 1948* (Chiang Mai: Silkworm Books, 2000). For example, in 2001, the Myanmar troops reportedly assisted its close ally, the United Wa State Army (UWSA), in a bid to take control of territory held by the Shan State Army near the Thai border; this eventually triggered a full-blown battle between Myanmar and Thai security forces even when in reality both countries could have made use of the Joint Border Committee (JBC) to address their border conflict. See Aung Zaw, "Thai, Burmese Troops Clash near Tachilek", *The Irrawaddy*, 2 January 2001.

19. Thaksin's interview with Maurice R. Greenberg, at the Council on Foreign Relations, New York, 18 September 2006.

20. "Myanmar Rebel Leader Disappointed in Thai Premier's Plan to Stop Tolerating Rebels as Buffer", *Associated Press*, 9 June 2002.

21. "Thailand: Burmese Democracy Activists Targeted by Thai Government", Human Right Watch, Press Release, 29 March 2005.

22. Sophon Onkgara, "Secret of Thaksin's Burma Trip might be in the Skies", *The Nation*, 6 August 2008. Thaksin also told a similar tale

regarding his reason to visit Myanmar to the members of the Thai Foreign Ministry on 11 August 2006. Source: Ministry of Foreign Affairs of Thailand.

23. See Charnvit Kasetsiri, "Thailand-Cambodia: A Love-Hate Relationship", *Kyoto Review of Southeast Asia* 3 (March 2003).

24. Thongchai, *Siam Mapped: A History of the Geo-Body of a Nation* (Hawaii: University Hawaii Press, 1994), p. 166.

25. Charnvit Kasetsiri, "Thailand-Cambodia: A Love-Hate Relationship".

26. Sok Udem Deth, "The Geopolitics of Cambodia During the Cold War Period".

27. Sunai Phasuk, *Nayobai Tang Prathet Khong Thai: Suksa Krabuankarnkamnod Nayobai Khong Ratthaban Pon-ek Chatichai Choonhavan Tor Panha Kumphucha, Si Singhakom 1988–23 Kumphaphan 1991* [Thai Foreign Policy: A Study of Foreign Policy Making Process under the Chatichai Choonhavan Government, 4 August 1988–23 February 1991] (Bangkok: Institute of Asian Studies, 1997), pp. 109–10.

28. Ministry of Foreign Affairs of Thailand, *Karn Thood Yook Mai Hua Jai Kue Prachachon*, pp. 25–29.

29. See Puangthong Rungswasdisub, *Thailand's Response to the Cambodian Genocide*, Genocide Working Programme Working Paper no. 12 (Connecticut: Yale University, 1999). Puangthong argued, "The power of the military in Thai politics has been significantly challenged since 1973. But developments in foreign affairs in the 1980s, dominated by the Cambodia-Vietnam issue, still served to strengthen the Thai bureaucratic polity in general and the power of the military in particular. The Cambodian conflict allowed the Thai armed forces to monopolize all channels of information concerning border problems and to increase the defence budget as well as to expand its manpower. Also, for an alternative in the interpretation of the role of the military in foreign policy during the Cambodian conflict, see, John Funston, "Thailand's Diplomacy on Cambodia: Success of Realpolitik", *Asian Journal of Political Science* 6, no. 1 (June 1998): 53–79.

30. Shawn W. Crispin, "Shooting for the Stars", *Far Eastern Economic Review*, 30 May 2002, p. 32.

31. *Management's Discussion and Analysis: SATTEL*, Shin Satellite, 2003 <http://www.shincorp.com/IR/SATTEL/quarter_ssa/ssa_2003_3q_MDA.pdf> (accessed 21 April 2009).

32. Source: Ministry of Foreign Affairs of Thailand <http://test.mfa.go.th/web/2642.php?id=4269> (accessed 29 December 2009).

33. Source: Ministry of Foreign Affairs of Thailand <http://www.mfa.go.th/web/1746.php> (accessed 29 December 2009).

34. Petchanet Pratraungkrai, "ACMECS Cooperation: 50% Rise in Mekong Region Trade Expected", *The Nation*, 13 October 2005.

35. Raphael Minder, "Cambodia's Transforming Tycoon", *Financial Times*, 18 August 2008.
36. Susan Postlewaite, "Real Estate Boom in Cambodia's Capital", *Business Week*, 3 June 2008.
37. See "Thailand Wants Peace Next Door in Cambodia; Dirty Business", *New York Times*, 8 January 1994 <http://www.nytimes.com/1994/01/08/opinion/l-thailand-wants-peace-next-door-in-cambodia-dirty-business-816639.html?pagewanted=1> (accessed 29 December 2009).
38. Wassana Nanuam, "Thaksin Set to Invest Big Time in Cambodia", *Bangkok Post*, 19 June 2008.
39. Ibid.
40. Anucha Paepanawan, *Exclusive: Kanmuang Ruang Khao Phra Viharn* [Exclusive: The Political Case of Khao Phra Viharn] (Bangkok: Kleung Aksorn, 2008), in the introduction page. Anucha is a well-known journalist of *Thai Rath* newspaper.
41. Chonticha Satyawattana, ed., *Botrian Chak Khwamroonraeng Nai Kampucha* [Lessons from Violence in Cambodia] (Bangkok: Thai-Asia Studies Centre, Thammasat University, 2003), p. 19.
42. Nopporn Wong-Anan, "Temple Tantrums Stalk Thai-Cambodia Relations", *Reuters*, 20 July 2008.
43. Statement by Thaksin Shinawatra, Prime Minister of Thailand, at the GMS Summit, 3 November 2009, Phnom Penh, Cambodia. The author's personal copy.
44. Kitti Wasinondh, "Thai Foreign Ministry's Continuous Thread", *The Nation*, 12 April 2006. Kitti Wasinondh was the Foreign Ministry's spokesperson at the time.
45. Isabelle Roughol, "1980s Thai-Lao Border Conflict Bears Resemblance to Preah Vihear", *Cambodian Daily*, 24 October 2008.
46. *Laos: The Confrontational Relationship with Thailand*, The Library of Congress Country Studies; CIA World Factbook <http://www.photius.com/countries/laos/national_security/laos_national_security_the_confrontational_~42.html> (accessed 21 April 2009).
47. Brian McCarten, "Hmong Still Hinder Lao-Thai Links", *Asia Times* <http://www.atimes.com/atimes/Southeast_Asia/KA21Ae02.html> (accessed 21 April 2009).
48. Source: Ministry of Foreign Affairs of Thailand <http://www.mfa.go.th/web/2386.php?id=148> (accessed 29 December 2009).
49. McCarten, "Hmong Still Hinder Lao-Thai Links".
50. Source: Ministry of Foreign Affairs of Thailand <http://www.mfa.go.th/web/1486.php> (accessed 29 December 2009).
51. "Laos' Deputy Prime Minister Visited Thailand", National News Bureau of Thailand, 28 November 2003 <http://nntworld.prd.go.th/previewnews.php?news_id=254611270004&news_headline=

LAOS%20DEPUTY%20PRIME%20MINISTER%20VISITED%
20THAILAND&return=ok> (accessed 21 April 2009).
52. Source: Ministry of Foreign Affairs of Thailand <http://
www.mfa.go.th/web/2386.php?id=148> (accessed 29 December
2009). Also see, Pavin Chachavalpongpun, "History Matters: Sticky
Thai-Lao Ties", *Opinion Asia*, 26 February 2007 <http://
www.opinionasia.org/HistorymattersStickyThaiLaoties> (accessed
21 April 2009).
53. See Ian Storey, "China and Vietnam's Tug of War over Laos", *China
Brief* 5, no. 13 (Washington, D.C.: The Jamestown Foundation, 7 June
2005).
54. John C. Tanner, "Braced for Change", *Telecom Asia*, October 2004
<http://findarticles.com/p/articles/mi_m0FGI/is_10_15/
ai_n8563863/> (accessed 21 April 2009).
55. Source: Embassy of the People's Democratic Republic of Laos to the
United States of America.
56. "Thai PM Visits Laos and Cambodia", *Associated Press*, 15 October
2006. The report refers to the visit of military-appointed Prime Minister
Surayud Chulanont to Laos and Cambodia.
57. *Global Partnership for Development: Thailand's Contribution to Millennium
Development Goal 8*, Ministry of Foreign Affairs of Thailand and United
Nations Country Team in Thailand, 2005 <http://www.undg.org/
archive_docs/6597-Thailand_MDG_Goal_8_Report.pdf> (accessed
21 April 2009), p. 35.
58. Ibid., pp. 30–34.
59. Grant Evans, "Laos: Situation Analysis and Trend Assessment",
Writenet Independent Analysis, United Nations High Commissioner
for Refugees, Protection Information Section (DIP), May 2004, p. 9
<http://www.unhcr.org/refworld/pdfid/40c723992.pdf> (accessed
29 December 2009).
60. Taken from his keynote speech delivered at the opening of the seminar
on "Thai-Lao Media Relations", organized by the Thai-Lao Friendship
Association and the Lao-Thai Friendship Association, at Siam City
Hotel, Bangkok, on 30 September 2005. Source: Ministry of Foreign
Affairs of Thailand.
61. See Khien Theeravit, ed., *Khwamsamphan Thai-Lao Nai Saita Khong
Khon Lao* [Thai-Lao Relations in Laotian Perspective] (Bangkok:
Chulalongkorn University, 2001).
62. Colin Long, Mark Askew and William Logan, "Reshaping Vientiane
in a Global Age", in *Vientiane: Transformations of a Lao Landscape*
(London and New York: Routledge, 2007), pp. 205–206.
63. Pavin, "History Matters: Sticky Thai-Lao Ties".

64. Duncan McCargo, "Network Monarchy and Legitimacy Crises in Thailand", *The Pacific Review* 18, no. 4 (December 2005): 514. McCargo argued that the south has been dominated by officials loyal to former Prime Minister Prem Tinsulanonda, the palace and the Democrats.
65. Duncan McCargo, "The Politics of Buddhist Identity in Thailand's Deep South: The Demise of Civil Religion?", *Journal of Southeast Asian Studies* 40, no. 1 (February 2009): 11.
66. Aurel Croissant, "Unrest in South Thailand: Contours, Causes and Consequences Since 2001", *Strategic Insights* 4, no. 2 (February 2005).
67. Andrew D. Forbes, "Thailand's Muslim Minorities: Assimilation, Secession, or Coexistence?", *Asian Survey* 22 (1982): 1056–73.
68. Source: The East Asian Affairs Department, Ministry of Foreign Affairs of Thailand.
69. "Malaysia Tells Thailand not to Teach KL Foreign Policy", *Bernama*, 17 October 2005.
70. John Roberts, "Repression in Southern Thailand Fuels Diplomatic Tensions with Malaysia", *Asian Tribune*, 18 October 2005.
71. "Thailand to Explain Harsh Policies to OIC", *Islamonline.net*, 1 March 2005 <http://www.islamonline.net/English/News/2005-03/01/article06.shtml> (accessed 30 December 2009).
72. McCargo, "Network Monarchy and Legitimacy Crises in Thailand", p. 515.
73. Marc Askew, *Conspiracy, Politics, and a Disorderly Border: The Struggle to Comprehend Insurgency in Thailand's Deep South*, Policy Studies 29, East-West Centre, Washington (Singapore: Institute of Southeast Asian Studies, 2007), p. 62.
74. John Funston gave this account in his presentation on "Malaysia and Thailand's Southern Conflict: Reconciling Security and Ethnicity", at the conference on "Southern Thailand: Anatomy of an Insurgency, 2004–2009, organized by the Institute of Southeast Asian Studies, Singapore, 10–11 March 2009.
75. Roberts, "Repression in Southern Thailand Fuels Diplomatic Tensions with Malaysia".
76. Ibid.
77. Source: Ministry of Foreign Affairs of Thailand.
78. John Funston, "Malaysia and Thailand's Southern Conflict: Reconciling Security and Ethnicity". (See note 74.)
79. Speech by Bhokin Balakula, Interior Minister, to Singaporean investors, unpublished paper (2005).
80. Joe Cochrane, "An Annoying Neighbour", *Newsweek International*, 21 February 2006.

81. "Ex-Envoy Castigates Thaksin's Diplomacy", *The Nation*, 19 March 2006.
82. Leszek Buszynski, "Thailand's Foreign Policy: Management of a Regional Vision", *Asia Survey* 34, no. 8 (August 1994): 731–32.
83. John Funston, "Thai Foreign Policy: Seeking Influence", *Southeast Asian Affairs 1998* (Singapore: Institute of Southeast Asian Studies, 1998), p. 295.
84. Ministry of Foreign Affairs of Thailand, *Karn Thood Yook Mai Hua Jai Kue Prachachon*, p. 61.
85. Speech of Prime Minister Thaksin Shinawatra, on the topic "Forward Engagement: The New Era of Thailand's Foreign Policy", delivered at the Ministry of Foreign Affairs of Thailand, 12 March 2003. He was invited by Foreign Minister Surakiart Sathirathai to address the inaugural lecture for the Saranrom Institute of Foreign Affairs.
86. Policy Statement of the Government of Thaksin Shinawatra, Prime Minister of Thailand, Delivered to the National Assembly, on Wednesday, 23 March 2005 <http://thaiembdc.org/politics/govtment/policy/55thpolicy/pt-5_e.html> (accessed 30 December 2009).
87. Donald E. Weatherbee and Ralf Emmers, *International Relations in Southeast Asia: The Struggle for Autonomy* (Lanham: Rowman and Littlefield Publishers, 2005), p. 104.
88. Interview with Rodolfo C. Severino, Singapore, 31 October 2007.
89. Rodolfo C. Severino, *Southeast Asia in Search of an ASEAN Community: Insights from the Former ASEAN Secretary-General* (Singapore: Institute of Southeast Asian Studies, 2006), p. 148.
90. Interview with Surin Pitsuwan, former Foreign Minister and ASEAN Secretary-General, Seoul, 21 March 2008.
91. See Kavi Chongkittavorn, "(10+3)+(1+2)+(?+?)=Asian Identity?", paper presented at the Fourth High-Level Conference on "Asian Economic Integration: Toward an Asian Economic Community", organized by India's Research and Information System for Developing Country and Singapore's Institute of Southeast Asian Studies, New Delhi, India, 18–19 November 2005.
92. Thaksin's interview with Greenberg.
93. Sukhumbhand Paribatra, *From Enmity to Alignment: Thailand's Evolving Relations with China*, ISIS Paper no. 1 (1987): 18–19.
94. Anuson Chinvanno, *Thailand's Policies towards China, 1949–1954* (Oxford: St. Anthony's College, 1992), pp. 23–27.
95. Joshua Kurlantzick, "China's Charm: Implications of Chinese Soft Power", *Policy Brief* 47 (June 2006): 1.
96. Ian Storey argues that Sino-Thai military relations have a long way to go before they start to rival that between the United States and Thai militaries, who conduct more than forty joint military exercises every

year. In Ian Storey, "China and Thailand: Enhancing Military-Security Ties in the 21st Century", *China Brief* 8, no. 14 (July 2008): 7.

97. Anthony Smith, "Thailand's Security and the Sino-Thai Relationship", *China Brief* 5, no. 3 (February 2005): 1.
98. Source: Department of East Asian Affairs, Ministry of Foreign Affairs of Thailand.
99. "Interview: Thailand Aims to Further Enhance Thailand-China Strategic Partnership", *People's Daily*, 28 June 2005.
100. David Fullbrook, "So Long U.S., Hello China, India", *Asia Times*, 4 November 2004.
101. Source: <http://www.thaiccc.or.th/eng-main.html> (accessed 15 July 2008).
102. Patrick Jory, "Multiculturalism in Thailand: Cultural and Regional Resurgence in a Diverse Kingdom", *Harvard Asia-Pacific Review* 4, no. 1 (2000): 18–22.
103. "The Soft Power of Happy Chinese", *International Herald Tribune*, 18 January 2006.
104. Ibid.
105. Source: Ministry of Education of China <http://www.moe.edu.cn/english/international_3.htm> (accessed 13 December 2008).
106. Smith, "Thailand's Security and the Sino-Thai Relationship", p. 2.
107. "Thai PM Proud to Host Olympic Torch", *USA Today*, 18 April 2008.
108. *Xinhua* reported that local Muslims in China's northwestern Xinjiang province have waged a sputtering rebellion against the Chinese government, leading to the death toll of eight and four injured from a bombing at the height of the 2008 Beijing Olympic Games, in *Xinhua*, 10 August 2008. Seven attackers and one security guard died in the attack in which the bombers drove a tricycle laden with explosives into the yard of a police station in the remote city of Kuqa. Two police officers and two civilians were also injured, *Xinhua* news agency said.
109. See Daniel C. Lynch, *Rising China and Asian Democratisation: Socialisation to "Global Culture" in the Political Transformations of Thailand, China, and Taiwan* (Stanford: Stanford University Press, 2006).
110. Ashley Erasey, "Response to 'Cultural Clash: Rising China Versus Asian Democratisation", *Taiwan Journal of Democracy* 3, no. 1 (July 2007): 160.
111. Interview with a First Secretary of the East Asian Affairs Department, Ministry of Foreign Affairs, Bangkok, Thailand, 26 June 2008.
112. "FTAs will Hurt Small Farmers", *The Nation*, 7 May 2007.
113. Pavin Chachavalpongpun, "China's Heavy Handedness in Tibet Could Have Far-Reaching Consequences for the Country", *The Nation*, 16 April 2008.

114. See Greenfield Hidayat, "After Thaksin: The CEO State, Nationalism, and U.S. Imperialism", *The Global South* 120 (12 June 2006).

115. Interview with Surakiart Sathirathai, former Foreign Minister of Thailand, Bangkok, Thailand, 27 June 2008. Surakiart had a major role in lobbying the Chinese leaders to play host to the Third ACD Meeting.

116. See Sean Randolph, *The United States and Thailand: Alliance Dynamics, 1950–1985* (Berkeley: Institute of Southeast Asian Studies, University of California, 1986).

117. Daniel Fineman, *A Special Relationship: The United States and Military Government in Thailand, 1947–1958* (Honolulu: University of Hawaii Press, 1997), p. 97.

118. SEATO was an international organization for collective defence created by the Manila Pact which was signed on 8 September 1954. The formal institution of SEATO was established at a meeting of treaty partners in Bangkok in February 1955. Its members included Australia, Bangladesh, France, New Zealand, Pakistan, Philippines, Thailand, United States and United Kingdom.

119. Michael K. Connors, "Thailand and the United States: Beyond Hegemony?", edited by Mark Beeson, *Bush and Asia: The US's Evolving Relationships with East Asia* (London: Routledge, 2006), pp. 131–32.

120. John Funston, "Thailand: Thaksin Fever", *Southeast Asian Affairs 2002* (Singapore: Institute of Southeast Asian Studies, 2002), p. 321.

121. Kusuma Snitwongse, "Thai Foreign Policy in the Global Age: Principle or Profit?", *Contemporary Southeast Asia* 23, no. 2 (August 2001): 206.

122. Michael K. Connors, "Thailand and the United States: Beyond Hegemony?", p. 130.

123. After its troops completed a posting in Iraq with two Thai soldiers killed, Thailand eventually decided to end its operations there in September 2004.

124. The United States' Major Non-NATO Allies currently include Japan, Australia, Israel, Egypt, Bahrain, Jordan, South Korea, Argentina, New Zealand, the Philippines, Thailand, Kuwait, Morocco and Pakistan.

125. Raymond J. Ahearn and Wayne M. Morrison, *CRS Report for Congress: U.S.-Thailand Free Trade Agreement Negotiations*, Congressional Research Service, 4 February 2005, p. 7.

126. "You are either with Us or against Us", *CNN*, 6 November 2001 <http://archives.cnn.com/2001/US/11/06/gen.attack.on.terror/> (accessed 25 April 2009)

127. "Celebrating 175 Years of Thai-U.S. Relations", *The Nation*, 28 April 2008.

128. Don Pathan and Supalak Ganjanakhundee, "A Tale of Unrealised Global Ambitions", *The Nation*, 11 April 2006.

129. Source: Ministry of Foreign Affairs of Thailand <http://www.mfa.go.th/web/162.php?id=14517> (accessed 31 December 2009).
130. Thaksin's letter to President George W. Bush, dated 23 June 2006, a personal copy.
131. John Brandon and Nancy Chen, eds., *Bilateral Conference on United States-Thailand Relations in the 21ˢᵗ Century* (Washington, D.C.: The Asia Foundation, 2002), p. 10. Also see Krit Garnjana-Goonchorn, "Thai-U.S. Relations in the Regional Context", *Southeast Asian Bulletin*, Centre for Strategic and International Studies (March 2008). Krit, while publishing this article, was ambassador of Thailand to the United States.
132. Thaksin's interview with Greenberg.
133. Interview with a First Secretary of the Royal Thai Embassy, Washington, D.C., 4 November 2006.
134. Source: Royal Thai Embassy, Singapore.
135. Thitinan Pongsudhirak, "Singapore's Miscalculation", *Bangkok Post*, 23 January 2007.
136. See P. Lim Pui Huen, *Through the Eyes of the King: The Travels of King Chulalongkorn to Malaya* (Singapore: Institute of Southeast Asian Studies, 2009).
137. Pavin Chachavalpongpun, "Improving Thai-Singaporean Relations at the People Level", *The Nation*, 8 July 2008.
138. Minister of Foreign Affairs of Singapore Press Statement on the Thailand-Singapore Civil Service Exchange Programme (CSEP) 6th Coordinating Meeting, 17–18 November 2003, Bangkok, Thailand <http://app.mfa.gov.sg/pr/read_content.asp?View,3661,> (accessed 26 April 2009)
139. "Thai Protesters Burn Images of Singapore PM", *Boston Globe*, 19 March 2006.
140. Transcript of Reply by Minister of Foreign Affairs George Yeo to Question in Parliament on Thailand, 20 February 2007. Author's personal copy.
141. "Thaksin is Unfair and Unkind to Singapore: Former Singapore Envoy", *The Nation*, 17 January 2007.
142. Panitan Wattanayagorn spoke at the seminar, "Thailand's Relations with Singapore: New Direction under New Government?", at the Institute of Southeast Asian Studies, Singapore, 27 March 2007. Panitan was Professor at the Faculty of Political Science, Chulalongkorn University, Thailand. At the time of writing, he is serving in the Abhisit government as Government Spokesperson.
143. For further readings, see Direk Jayanama, *Thailand and World War II* (Chiang Mai: Silkworm Books, 2008), and E. Bruce Reynolds, *Thailand's*

Secret War: OSS, SOE and the Free Thai Underground During World War II (California: San José State University, 2004).

144. See Chulacheeb Chinwanno, "Thai Views on Japan's Role in the Region", in *Thailand, Australia and the Region: Strategic Developments in Southeast Asia*, edited by Cavan Hogue (Canberra: National Thai Studies Centre, Faculty of Asian Studies, Australian National University, 2002), pp. 119–25.

145. "Visit to Japan of Prime Minister of the Kingdom of Thailand, H.E. Pol. Lt. Col. Thaksin Shinawatra", Ministry of Foreign Affairs of Japan, 26 November 2001. Source: Japan's Ministry of Foreign Affairs.

146. "Japan-Thailand Economic Partnership Agreement Task Force Report", Ministry of Foreign Affairs of Japan, December 2003 <http://www.mofa.go.jp/region/asia-paci/thailand/joint0312.pdf> (accessed 26 April 2009).

147. "A Message from Thai PM Thaksin Shinawatra", *Japan Times*, 25 February 2006.

148. Pasuk Phongpaichit, "Impact on JTEPA on the Bilateral Relationship between Japan and Thailand", speech delivered at Symposium on Future of Japan-Thailand Economic Partnership on the occasion of the 120th anniversary of Japan-Thailand Diplomatic Relations, 1 November 2007, Hotel New Otani, Tokyo, Japan. Author's personal copy.

149. Pachara Lochindaratn, "The Evolution of Thailand's Preferential Trading Agreements with Australia, New Zealand, Japan, China and India — The CGE Approach", The Global Trade Analysis Project, Centre for Global Trade Analysis, Department of Agricultural Economics, Purdue University (10 April 2008) <https://www.gtap.agecon.purdue.edu/resources/download/3726.pdf> (accessed 26 April 2009).

150. Ian Storey, "A Hiatus in Sino-Thai Special Relationship", *China Brief* 6, no. 19 (June 2005).

151. Source: Department of International Economics, Ministry of Foreign Affairs of Thailand.

152. P. V. Rao, ed., *India and ASEAN: Partners at Summit* (New Delhi: KW Publishers Book, 2008), p. 140.

153. Mekong-Ganga Cooperation (MGC) was established on 10 November 2000 at Vientiane in the First MGC Ministerial Meeting. It comprises six member countries, namely, India, Thailand, Myanmar, Cambodia, Laos and Vietnam, and emphasizes four areas of cooperation: tourism, culture, education, and transportation linkage as a basis to build a strong foundation for future trade and investment cooperation in the region.

154. Ake-Aroon Auansakul, "Thailand-India FTA: The Impact So Far", in *International Institute for Trade and Development*, 2007 <http://www.itd.or.th/en/node/526> (accessed 6 December 2008).
155. Source: The Ministry of Foreign Affairs of Thailand.
156. Statement to the Indian Media by Prime Minister Shri Atal Behari Vajpayee at the Conclusion of his Visit to Bali and Thailand, Prime Minister's Office, 11 October 2003. In "India, Thai Ties Enter New Chapter: Thaksin", *Press Trust of India*, 11 October 2003.
157. B. Raman, "My Southeast Asia Diary I: Thai Agitation: Focus on Thaksin's Indian Visits". Paper published by Southeast Asia Analysis Group <http://www.southasiaanalysis.org/%5Cpapers 18%5Cpaper 1749.html> (accessed 27 April 2009). B. Raman is Additional Secretary (retired), Cabinet Secretariat, Government of India, New Delhi, and presently Director of the Institute for Topical Studies, Chennai.
158. "Thaksin Regime's Business Networks", *The Nation*, 26 September 2006. *The Nation* printed this article based on Pasuk's seminar on money politics held in 2005 by the Centre of Political Economy, Chulalongkorn University, Thailand.
159. "Thaksin for New Trade Links with India", *The Hindu*, 6 June 2005. This was taken from an email interview between *The Hindu* and Thaksin Shinawatra.
160. See, "Time to Rethink Position on North Korea", *The Nation*, 8 July 2006.
161. Source: Ministry of Foreign Affairs of Thailand <http://www.mfa.go.th/web/2386.php?id=273> (accessed 1 January 2010). Vietnam is also a member of ACMECS and gained benefit from Thailand's technical assistance through numerous joint projects. The friendly relations between Thailand and Vietnam served Thaksin's purpose of alleviating the intensity of competition between the two countries, especially on mainland Southeast Asia, over other two smaller states — Cambodia and Laos.
162. See Leszek Buszynski, "Russia and Southeast Asia: A New Relationship", *Contemporary Southeast Asia* 28, no. 2 (August 2006): 276–96.
163. Lyuba Pronina, "Thailand Inked Deal for 12 Fighters", *The Moscow Times*, 19 December 2005.

5

A MOOT FOREIGN POLICY
Shortcomings and Oversights

Once a foreign minister himself, Prime Minister Thaksin should not be "foreign" to diplomacy. As foreign minister for three months in 1994–95, Thaksin was busy doing his own businesses rather than practising the norms of diplomacy. During this period, Thaksin was engrossed with expanding his telecom empire and accumulating his own wealth. Ukrist Pathmanand noted that his appointment as foreign minister offered a chance for Thaksin to establish a telecommunications network in some neighbouring countries. Shin's mobile phone and pay television projects in Cambodia began during this period. Through his appointment, Thaksin was able to connect with the Myanmar military government, and became close to Khin Nyunt who at that time was the military officer working on Myanmar telecommunications issues.[1] Other studies confirm that Thaksin, in 1994, also ventured out further into the Philippines and India by extending his cable television services.[2] In this context, his professional background as a "fabulously wealthy" telecommunications magnate was not a qualification for political power with a hand on foreign policy. Foreign policy simply became an annex to his populist domestic policy.

The tale of Thaksin's unrealized global ambitions points to certain flaws in Thai foreign policy from 2001 to 2006. Some of the consequences are serious and the impact of such a flawed foreign policy has a hangover effect in the post-Thaksin era. At present, the fugitive Thaksin has continued to exploit diplomacy to justify his political course, for example, in conspiring with Cambodia's Hun Sen to delegitimize the Abhisit government. This subject will be discussed in Chapter 7. As for this chapter, oversights and shortcomings of Thaksin's foreign policy will be critically examined. A criterion would be to answer the questions posed in the Introduction in this volume: Were Thaksin's key goals in foreign policy achieved? What will be the implications and long-term consequences? What are the lessons and insights for policy-makers and the Thai public? This study concludes that five shortcomings and oversights appear to be behind Thaksin's moot foreign policy. They are: (1) Thaksin's controversial populist diplomacy; (2) the blurry line between national and private interests; (3) Thaksin's unbounded and unrealistic diplomatic ambitions; (4) radical changes in the Foreign Ministry; and (5) the question of Thailand's readiness to play a leading role in the global community.

A POPULIST DIPLOMACY

As a mirror image of the domestic populist policy, Thai foreign policy was also reconstructed as "populist diplomacy". What were the characteristics of Thaksin's populist diplomacy? His populist diplomacy rejected the bureaucratic elite and weakened the autonomy of the Foreign Ministry in favour of a personalized authoritarianism in the handling of foreign relations. Fears provoked by this new populist diplomacy helped mobilize the old guard of the Foreign Ministry, in the guise of former ambassadors, to rebuff Thaksin and his foreign policy initiatives. These ambassadors played a vital role in the anti-Thaksin campaign leading up to the coup of September 2006. Thaksin's populist diplomacy, on the surface, responded to the demands of the Thai industries that called for the government's assistance in gaining better access to the global markets as a result of Thaksin's earlier outward-oriented strategy of development.[3] In essence, his populist diplomacy was goal-oriented. It became a state mechanism that supported domestic growth, created income from overseas trading, tackled long-overdue problems along the Thai borders and maintained a good Thai image abroad. In this process, foreign policy was "localized" to serve domestic needs. Whereas in the past, foreign relations were something remote and alien in the minds of the Thais particularly in rural areas, Thaksin claimed to expose the mystery surrounding the conduct of diplomacy, and reinvent it under the name of "people-centric diplomacy". This attempt was not necessarily a bad thing, as long as the people were really offered a share in the formulation of foreign policy and the fruits of its implementation. But Thaksin's authoritarian style did not seem to allow real public participation in foreign policy-making, since the procedure only involved the vested interests of local politicians.

In practice, populist diplomacy, if handled carelessly, could cause national damage and embarrassment. Nongnuch Singhadecha defines Thaksin's populist diplomacy as an approach that promoted toughness, aggressiveness and decisive leadership in the conduct of diplomacy.[4] Populist diplomacy was sometimes crude, often extravagant, and could be used as a cover for corruption and profiteering. A part of populist diplomacy was the repeated exploitation of the notion of sovereignty in order to feed domestic consumption. It was really about grandstanding. Yet, this strategy generated long-term negative consequences on the nation's credibility and good image. In the short-term, Thaksin's popularity was sky-high. A study of Pasuk Phongpaichit and Chris Baker sums up Thaksin's application of populist-nationalist diplomacy, though it must be noted that Thaksin was not the first Thai leader who successfully proved his daring leadership:

> In early 2003, Thaksin declared Thailand would no longer take "hand-outs", meaning foreign aid and loans. In August 2003, he lashes out against UNHCR for granting refugee status to Myanmar exiles: "Nobody can violate our sovereignty. We are a U.N. member. We are not a U.N. lackey.".... In response to U.N. criticisms about human rights, Thaksin said: "We are an independent country and I would never bow to anyone. Thai people should also unite.... The United Nations does not give us rice to eat." Similarly, in reaction to the annual U.S. government report on human rights in 2003, he exclaimed: "We are a friend (of the United States), but we are nobody's lackey.... The United States should stop acting like a big brother." On the next issue of the report in 2004, he called the United States as "irritating" and "useless" friend.[5]

Nongnuch noted that most of Thaksin's speeches were crafted by his team of advisers, not by Foreign Ministry's officials. Conservative diplomats saw his fierce attack against the United Nations as ghastly diplomacy. No civilized nation would overtly denigrate this respected international body: North Korea and Myanmar were among the excepted few. Thaksin's defiance against the United Nations might have been carried out to influence Thai public opinion; at the same time, he jeopardized Thailand's position on the international stage. The message here was obvious: Thaksin was using his populist diplomacy to challenge the international order. Thaksin once said that it was alright to practise "loutish" diplomacy. He also mentioned on many occasions that what his government needed were "servicemen", not diplomats, thus underlining his penchant for a top-down administration whereby diplomats had to do as they were told by the political elite.[6]

Former Deputy Foreign Minister and former ambassador Sawanit Kongsiri (October 2006–January 2008) argued that there was nothing wrong with the prime minister stamping his authority on foreign policy formulation. After all, Thaksin was an elected leader and was therefore entitled to exercise his authority in the country's conduct of foreign relations. In this circumstance, the Foreign Ministry's role was to give advice and to offer policy options to him and his Cabinet. Sawanit acknowledged that some of Thaksin's initiatives were praiseworthy, but they were contaminated by vested interests which were in fact a part of Thai politics.[7] It was clear that, during this period, Thai foreign policy was constructed under the roof of the Government House in the hands of Thaksin's team of advisers. These advisers, however, subscribed to a different worldview from that of the Foreign Ministry. Their worldview was based on domestic imperatives and in accordance with Thaksin's populist policy which aimed at enlarging his power base through programmes that strengthened the grassroots. One could explain this worldview as a response to the rise of globalization and the new rush towards world capitalism. This was at least how the Thai public came to justify Thaksin's assertive diplomacy. But the Foreign Ministry continued to maintain its own view: endorsing traditional policy based on the country's international security concerns, rather than pushing for pure economic agendas. The collision of these two worldviews emerged as one of the fundamental flaws in Thai foreign policy.

Thaksin and his team happily confined themselves within such domestic imperatives while crafting a foreign policy. Nationally, the objective was to encourage mass production as a way to stimulate economic growth through the so-called value-creation strategy. Thaksin was serious in making use of inner strengths to build the nation's core competencies. For the first time, his government clearly declared its strategic intent to position Thailand as a world's hub both in the manufacturing and services sectors. Ranging from being the kitchen of the world, the Detroit of Asia, Bangkok city of fashion, to Asia's tourism capital, Thailand needed, more than ever, a proactive foreign policy to bolster the government's ambitions. In order to develop a global reach for that purpose, Thaksin revamped the ambassador's role on a large scale. Giving these ambassadors more power as the CEO of their own embassy, Thaksin urged them to sell more Thai products in support of his own domestic populist policy, rather than just entertaining foreign guests and building the country's good image, which to Thaksin, was an intangible exercise. In a high-level meeting between Foreign Ministry officials, representatives of selected agencies and key business figures in October 2004, prominent businessman Amarin Khoman said, "Prime Minister Thaksin's mission to turn diplomats into salesmen was a wrong policy. The ambassadors are supposed to have a better grip on political and economic situations in countries they are representing and influential enough to seek help or pressure when necessary. They already have commercial attachés to play the salesman's role." The Foreign Ministry's Deputy Permanent Secretary Pisan Manawapat defended Thaksin by saying that so far his government had proved to be the "best" government the country had ever had.[8]

Not only did domestic factors effectively dominate the way foreign policy was made, nationalism, stirred up by Thaksin, played a powerful part in Thai diplomacy. Thaksin appealed to the people's aspiration for the greatness of the Thai nation but confused them with a sense of insecurity in the way they saw Thailand's position in the world.[9] The initial outcome was the production of a nationalistic foreign policy. A nationalistic foreign policy could send out the wrong message to Thailand's neighbours and friends afar. His excessive use of nationalism in foreign policy eventually came back to hurt his diplomatic ambitions. Ostensibly, Thaksin's aggression was a part of exhibiting his nationalist impulse and presenting Thailand as a nation willing to stand up against big and small powers. The role of the Foreign Ministry was to fix Thaksin's diplomatic oversights. Moreover, at many points, nationalism à la Thaksin was purely rhetorical and bogus. He boasted that he would show no mercy to the Wa drug army operating autonomously in the Myanmar sector of the Golden Triangle and would take up the matter directly with Yangon and seek help from Beijing.[10] He also pledged to the Thai public, in a nationwide televised address, that he would demand an apology from the Cambodian government for allowing rioters to attack the Thai embassy in Phnom Penh. In both cases, it proved to be empty promises. It, however, created a short-term satisfactory result, especially in portraying Thaksin's defense of the dignity of the Thai nation.

Gimmickry was also another prominent feature of Thaksin's populist diplomacy. One example proved Thaksin's cunning use of gimmickry in diplomacy. In May 2004, Thaksin planned to pay US$115 million for a 30 per cent stake in English football club Liverpool. Pasuk and Baker noted that Thaksin initially claimed that the Liverpool purchase would help upgrade Thailand's football league. Thai youth would then be inspired to kick drugs and kick a ball. Liverpool branding would help sell Thailand's OTOP goods all over the world. Over-enthused sports journalists dreamed of Thai players in the Liverpool team. Hopeful entrepreneurs imagined Thai brand names emblazoned across Liverpool jerseys during global telecast. Six years earlier, Thailand was being crushed by globalization. Now, Thailand could buy a highly symbolic global brand.[11] The opposition, however, suspected that Thaksin was trying to deflect attention from the breakout of violence in the south a month earlier. Eventually, the purchase collapsed; it was accused by some law academics of being unconstitutional. Although Thaksin's scheme of owning a famous English football club was still in the planning stage, it successfully grabbed the Thai public's attention. Moreover, his unfulfilled deal with Liverpool made headlines across the world. This at least was strident public relations for the new-age Thai diplomacy.

Yet, such gimmickry was evidently exercised to serve Thaksin's agenda rather than to really enhance the country's good image and reputation. Three years after his first bid to own Liverpool, and one year after his departure from the premiership, Thaksin once again used football to play politics. It was reported in June 2007 that Thaksin steadily built up his shareholding in and lodged a US$164 million takeover bid for Manchester City through his U.K. Sports Investments. Sven-Goren Eriksson was named manager of the Premier League club.[12] While Thailand was under military rule, Thaksin's purchase of Manchester City made breaking news across the globe. He signed up three young Thai footballers for the club, declaring it as a "historic" day for Thai football. At the glitzy signing ceremony in Bangkok, Thaksin sent his video message to his supporters, turning the event into a launching pad against the military regime. Critics immediately slated Thaksin for exploiting the football platform for his own political revenge — a smart move in soccer-crazy Thailand. For Thaksin, possessing Manchester City appeared to be an effective way of keeping in touch with the soccer-loving Thai public.[13] But the man who pledged to act as a role model for Thai youth through football decided to sell his Premier League club in October 2008. During his ownership period which lasted a little over a year, Thaksin failed to provide evidence of his football club actually helping develop Thailand's football league. He also failed to attest that his ownership of Manchester City helped in kicking the habit of drug addiction among the Thai youth. In fact, Prime Minister Samak had to turned to adopt extreme measures to improve the drug situation in the second war on drugs campaign in April 2008.

NATIONAL INTERESTS VERSUS PERSONAL PROFITS

Thaksin was undoubtedly a successful businessman. His slogan of "country is a company and prime minister is a CEO" hints strongly at the profit-driven objective.[14] Part of Thaksin's downfall was because he never drew clearly the line between national and private interests. In fact, he intentionally left this line blurry, so that certain private benefits could be reaped in obscurity. It would spark a public outrage in most other places in the world if leaders treated their country like a company while seeking to accumulate interests of their own. Unlike in Thailand, Thaksin played both roles; and for the period of six years in power, he was accused of using state office to enrich his family company. While the line between national and personal interest was ambiguous, Thaksin evaded public scrutiny by presenting himself as the saviour of the poor. He claimed to have been the champion of the have-nots. Those who supported Thaksin in far-flung regions admitted to the fact that Thaksin might have been corrupt. But they asked: who else in Thailand was not corrupt? Locals cared little about how Thaksin got things done. In 2003, one Thai local told a foreign media outlet, "So what if he is corrupt? He gets the job done."[15] This was the basis of Thaksin's social contract with the poor.

The success of the Thai Rak Thai Party and Thaksin's overwhelming election winning were partly made possible because of the strong support from giant conglomerates which aimed at dominating state power so as to control the national economy as a way to build some business immunity.[16] Thaksin's Shin Corporation was one of those companies which sought to hold sway over the economy through its direct access to politics. While in power, Thaksin's government issued several economic policies which directly benefited listed firms with close connections to the prime minister and Cabinet members. The policies also benefited and protected businesses of the politicians and their affiliates. Such policies included tax privileges, deduction of concession fees, creating barriers of entry for business rivals, and delaying policies which could affect businesses of the Thaksin network.[17] Pasuk points out that there were at least three economic policies implemented to complement Shin Corp in its venture into foreign markets. First, his government transferred the business risks of Shin Satellite from the firm to the Finance Ministry by instructing the Export-Import Bank of Thailand to grant a controversial twelve-year-term soft loan of Bt4 billion to the Myanmar government. Second, he attempted to protect his telecom businesses by blocking the telecom industry in the country. In the meantime, he set conditions of the FTA in the way that it encouraged liberalization of services, which could be beneficial to his telecom business in a given FTA counterpart of Thailand, even if he had to open up other sectors in the Thai industry in exchange. Third, as Thaksin's Shin Corp planned to invest in Air Asia, a major low-cost airline in Southeast Asia, he was particularly enthusiastic about concluding open-sky agreements with Thailand's trading counterparts since, as Pasuk noted, they would allow Air Asia to explore new domestic and international routes overlapping those of Thai Airways International. As a result, Air Asia gained income growth worth Bt3 billion at the end of 2005, compared with the shrinking income of the national carrier. It was alleged that Thai Airways International was forced by the government to make way for Air Asia.[18]

Thaksin's control of state office to shore up his personal business power seemed to emerge as a norm in Thailand. The Jungrungreangkit family, Thaksin's close business ally, had been Thailand's leading auto-parts manufacturer for vehicles and motorcycles. They enjoyed advantages from Thaksin's "Detroit of Asia" policy drive. Following the signing of the Thai-Australian FTA, the Jungrungreangkit family became the second group to benefit from the agreement after Thaksin's telecom empire.[19] This happened at the time Suriya Jungrungreangkit served as Industry Minister in the Thaksin Cabinet. The prime minister's telecom business had a strong presence in almost every country in the region, ranging from Myanmar, Laos, Cambodia and India. But the more Thaksin abused his political power for private economic gains, the more Thailand became politically handcuffed by it, which was reflected in the country's crippled diplomacy vis-à-vis those neighbours. Thaksin was reluctant to raise irritable matters with countries with which he had business deals. As a result, they were put aside. His regime lacked moral authority as a basis to conduct a moral foreign policy. So when Thaksin reinvented Thailand's foreign policy based on his thrust of becoming the new leader of mainland Southeast Asia, he also reconstructed Shin Corp as the embodiment of the nation's economic entity.

Neighbours learnt of Thailand's weak point: a country being run as a company with Thaksin as the ruling CEO preoccupied with making Shin Corp a global success. These neighbours definitely enjoyed ample benefits from Thai investments under the emblem of Thaksin's Shin Corp. And they never hesitated to politicize such investments to serve their own purposes. The more fundamental message was, however, that the weakness in the Thai political system that permitted business profits of leaders to supersede national interests greatly hampered the state's sincerity, if any, in the strengthening of bilateral ties. With remaining bitter memories between Thailand and old enemies in the neighbourhood, the same weakness also further impeded the national efforts to create goodwill and regain trust from them. In an interview, former Foreign Minister Surin Pitsuwan argued that to a certain degree, neighbours felt that Thailand was practising a hegemonic policy. Having the eyes on economic interests at all cost without any cushions, such as the support of people-to-people diplomacy, left Thailand in a very dangerous position indeed. He also said that extreme mercantilism engendered a new kind of diplomacy that did not care about equity. It was a kind of diplomacy that was tailored specially for the interest of certain groups with political connection.[20]

Conflict of interest can be used to describe the state of Thai diplomacy during the Thaksin years. It also reported that Thaksin's objective in visiting Nagpyidaw on 2 August 2006 was to discuss "old and new investments" with the Myanmar government. Thaksin was anxious to explain to the Myanmar generals regarding the sale of his Shin Corp to Singapore's Temasek Holdings. His IPStar project in Myanmar was not yet a done deal. The building of IPStar ground stations on high mountains in Myanmar was not yet completed. Thus, Thaksin's visit could have been to sort out the complications.[21] Over the period of six years, Thaksin seemed to have mixed official and unofficial visits to foreign countries. Several shopping trips to Singapore just preceding the sale of Shin Corp were also interpreted as economic diplomacy on behalf of his family rather than the country. Former Ambassador Kasit Piromya, a controversial figure himself, dismissed Thaksin's official visits as a pretext to carry out his personal businesses.[22]

UNBOUNDED AND UNREALISTIC DIPLOMACY

Thaksin has always been an ambitious and competitive man. He successfully rose to the top echelon in the world of business thanks to his untamed ambitions and his well-connected political friends. Thaksin was also well educated. Yet, his opponents agreed that they did not see in him a leadership quality. Snoh Thienthong, a veteran politician, gave his personal account of Thaksin when he talked of the prime minister's lack in mature leadership. Snoh said,

> If you want to know what Thaksin is up to, you have to understand what kind of person he is, because the characteristic and the self of Thaksin dictate the behaviours of power usage and Thaksin's administration which, as a whole constitute Thaksin regime, which has both the system of administration of power and (unlawfully) earning benefits coinciding together. Thaksin has educational qualifications but lacks of a mature leadership. He has no leadership particularly at national level. He has no experience in administration of the bureaucratic system. Although he used to work as a police; it was not long. He spent spare time with his personal business. He was a gambler and careless. He used to have problems with his business when he had to cash some cheques and was sued for bouncing cheques. He prefers doing business management as a quick thinker and a quick doer with marketing as a tool.[23]

The ambition to drive Thailand ahead of other nations resulted in the engineering of new policy initiatives. With the encouragement of his Deputy Prime Minister Somkid Jatusripitak, Thaksin was eager to propel Thailand into the future. In 2005, the Thaksin government officially pronounced its strategy to transform Thailand into a "First World" nation. But exactly how to lift Thailand into the First World and what kind of First World Thailand wished to become were never clearly defined. Somkid did spell out ways to earn the status of a First World nation, such as by strengthening the grassroots economy, reducing poverty, building innovation capacity among small and medium enterprises, as well as financing the government's mega-investment programmes and supporting bilateral FTAs.[24] But these were merely one aspect of being in the First World league. Thaksin and Somkid deliberately paid no attention to the elimination of corruption, the promotion of good governance and political transparency, as part of the new First World Thailand they wanted to establish. Thaksin's idea of graduating Thailand from Third to First World nation was impressive and ambitious. In fact, it was perhaps too ambitious considering the existence of certain Thai political cultures that ran contrary to those in the Western world, such as cronyism and nepotism. Ironically, it was these "cancerous" political cultures that were consistently nurtured by Thaksin throughout his six years in power. The appointment of General Chaiyasit Shinawatra as the army commander-in-chief in 2003 exemplified Thaksin's conflicting ideologies. Chaiyasit, who remained in this position for about a year, was proved incompetent. He is Thaksin's cousin.

His lack of meticulousness was spotlighted in his steering of diplomacy. Thaksin's tendency to go for "megaphone diplomacy", a term used by the Thai media, reduced the country's diplomatic corps, including two of his foreign ministers, to a bunch of "repairmen" who were left to pick up the pieces and fix missteps caused by the prime minister himself. In fact, Thai diplomats, were given the many titles, ranging from salesmen, servicemen to repairmen. When asked if Thaksin's outspokenness affected his work, Foreign Minister Kantathi insisted, "It is part of the dynamism of this government."[25] Former ambassador Asda Jayanama, however, begged to differ. He believed that having a prime minister who was active in foreign affairs was not inherently bad, pointing to the late Chatichai Choonhavan and Kriangsak Chomanan. He also emphasized that these were men well versed in diplomacy and foreign affairs. "The same cannot be said of Thaksin," Asda added.[26] The challenge for the foreign minister as well as members of the Thai diplomatic corps was how to keep up with Thaksin's every whim and imagination. Yet, arguably, Thaksin's megaphone diplomacy became part of a political intent. Bluntness and ruthlessness, proved to be highly effectual in the business world, were grafted onto diplomacy. Thaksin's megaphone diplomacy operated hand-in-hand with his populist diplomacy in a way that it manifested Thaksin's strong leadership. On top of this, Thaksin emphasized a very informal and personal way of conducting international relations. On 11 August 2006, Thaksin told top diplomats at the Thai Foreign Ministry to exercise "diplomacy with a personal touch", meaning the forging of bilateral relationships based on personal acquaintances. He urged them to pay more attention to results rather than processes. Thaksin said, "My mission was to give a face-lift to the out-of-date bureaucratic system. Diplomats must be willing to adapt to a new working environment, or else Thailand would fail."[27] So, the ambition here was to celebrate results at the expense of processes. In Thaksin's mindset, Thai bureaucracy had long been imprisoned by processes. Thaksin's new paradigm was based on new work ethics. In the current global setting, processes had to be brief and quick with clear direction and objectives. Personal relationship with foreign leaders was imperative. Thaksin claimed that this also allowed Thai leaders to showcase its human side to the outside world. He recommended that official visits should be organized only once, followed by a working visit, corridor meetings, or even phone calls, since informal discussions were considered more frank and fruitful than the formal ones. It was a part of Thailand creating international networks of its own.[28]

The ACD, the ACMECS, the Bangkok Process, the FTAs and the nomination of Surakiart for the position of the UNSG were all highly ambitious projects. But Thaksin's dream of ruling the world, through his ostentatious diplomatic initiatives, was marred by his ignorance of the national capacity. These projects were mostly designed to accomplish mere short-range goals. At the national level, Thaksin did not create, or restructure, a system that would sustain Thailand's leading role abroad. Limitation of budget, insufficient manpower, and the lack of capacity-building and training among ministry officials to cope with new demands of the government greatly affected foreign policy execution on the part of the ministry. It is true that the national budget for the Foreign Ministry from 2001 to 2006 increased each year: from Bt3.7 billion in 2001, Bt4.3 billion in 2002, Bt4.6 billion in 2003, Bt5.3 billion in 2004, Bt5.6 billion in 2005, to Bt6.3 billion in 2006. But this budget portion constitutes only 0.5 per cent of the overall national budget.[29] At the same time, the Defence Ministry was allocated a budget twenty times bigger than that of the Foreign Ministry, even when Thaksin declared the use of hard power obsolete and deprioritized national security. In 2003, the year the ACMECS was born and one year after the founding of the ACD, the Foreign Ministry's staff strength was 1,576, of whom 946 were diplomats, and the rest were support staff. Almost half of the diplomats served in Thai missions abroad. At the time, the overseas network consisted of 59 diplomatic missions (57 bilateral embassies and 2 permanent missions), plus 21 career consulates. In 2006, the total number went up to 1,606, of whom 990 were diplomatic officials. This number has not changed significantly up to the year 2009. Considering the country's profile and Thaksin's up-and-coming, extravagant foreign policy initiatives, this network was small. There were sixty-seven foreign countries maintaining resident embassies in Bangkok, meaning that the Thai overseas network was unusually much smaller than what it hosted at home.[30] The Ministry's Policy and Planning Office has been in charge of the ACD matters which, during the Thaksin period, were supervised by fewer than three officials. These three officials were in constant contact with thirty members of the ACD. The CEO ambassadors were caught up with internal administration inside their embassies. Some of them were preoccupied with opening the door for the export of Thai products to fulfil Thaksin's "economy of speed". Routine responsibilities prevented the CEO diplomats from stepping back and looking at the bigger picture of Thailand's foreign affairs.

When Thaksin reinvented Thailand based on his diplomatic ambitions as some sort of regional power, he located the country at the centre of the universe. By doing so, Thaksin overlooked other geopolitical factors, traditional diplomacy that has made Thailand a prominent state in ASEAN, and the realization of the scope of national capability in pursuing certain initiatives. Undoubtedly, Thailand, due to its medium size, could play a non-threatening, leading role in the region. But at what degree did Thailand possess its bargaining power? Was it viable for Thailand to spend its energy in cultivating ties with countries in remote regions where mutual interests could hardly be established? Through the ACD, did Thailand have enough resources to expand its influence that covered as far as the Middle East and Central Asia? What kind of justified interests could Thailand gain from its support of Tajikistan and Uzbekistan in becoming members of the ACD in 2006? Were there any Thai economic interests in these two Central Asian states? If yes, what were they exactly? Would it not have been more justifiable for Thaksin to cement stronger ties with old allies? How well did Thailand really know, say, Singapore or Malaysia? As for the ACMECS, could Thai economic and technical assistance to its less developed neighbours in the region be translated into a new level of mutual trust? Did Thailand pay adequate attention to encouraging more bilateral contacts at the people level, rather than to just opening their doors for Thai OTOP? Was Thaksin ready to stand on principles, when he dealt with the Myanmar regime, and walk a little further away from pure benefits? In the Bangkok Process, was Thaksin's brand of democracy really a democracy that could lead the light for Myanmar's political reforms? Was Thaksin prepared to wake up the Thais' awareness in regard to advantages and disadvantages of the FTAs? How could he prove that the FTAs were not another political device to serve certain legitimacies of the government? Lastly, how could he restore his faith in the international organizations as he was endorsing Surakiart for the top position at the United Nations?

These hard-to-swallow questions point to one fact: Thaksin was driving his diplomacy way above the national limits. The intention to bend the prevailing wind was reduced to certain pretensions in the conduct of diplomacy. What began as a bold insinuation, such as standing to break the wind of the international order, turned out to be a mere spectacle put on to entertain audiences at home and abroad.

RADICAL SHIFTS IN THE FOREIGN MINISTRY

The Foreign Ministry is one of the oldest state agencies of Thailand. Under the absolute monarchy, its role was of great magnitude especially in crafting policies that sought to instil national pride. Earlier, the study highlighted that Foreign Ministry had in the old days enjoyed a considerable degree of autonomy. It tended to stay above politics and, if possible, avoided being manipulated by regimes of varying guises, ranging from the most despotic to the democratic ones.[31] The nature of its responsibility — dealing mostly with the outside world — put it a good distance from money politics at home. This was at least in the past. The ability to switch sides according to the direction of the wind, known as the bamboo policy, is believed to be one of the main contributing factors behind the Thais' escape from colonialism. Such achievement perpetuated the reputation of the Thai Foreign Ministry in the eyes of the Thais and their political elites. This belief has lived on.

Inside the Foreign Ministry, a major reorganization took place in the 1990s. Five regional departments were created in 1992, covering: European Affairs; American and South Pacific Affairs; East Asian Affairs; South Asia, Middle East and African Affairs. A separate Department of ASEAN Affairs handles regional coordination, although bilateral political work in Southeast Asia is handled by the East Asian Affairs Department. Every department has three or four divisions, each headed by a director. Six functional departments cover other tasks: Consular; Protocol; International Economic Affairs; Treaties and Legal Affairs; Information; and International Organizations. The Thailand International Development Cooperation Agency (TICA) is in charge of external aid.[32] The permanent secretary is assisted by three to four deputy permanent secretaries. Each is assigned to oversee the following clusters: the four regional departments; the functional departments plus ASEAN; and the administration plus consular affairs.

The recruitment process can be described as gruelling. Candidates are required to endure up to three rounds of examinations: paper, oral, and field-trip examinations. In the paper examination, all aspects of diplomacy, including international politics, international law, international economy and linguistic proficiency are the main parts of a three-hour test. Candidates are obliged to write essays and summarize texts in Thai and English, plus one other language. The successful candidates are called back for an oral examination at the Foreign Ministry. The examiners, consisting of the permanent secretary, his deputies and directors-general, usually pose questions to, and seek opinion from the candidates related to general and specific knowledge on international politics, instructing them to reply either in Thai or English, or other foreign languages. Potential candidates are shortlisted to enter the final phase of recruitment. Normally, the finalists are taken to a resort-style location for the final examination which combines the tests of *saviour-vivre* skills, social manners and team spirit. Such a demanding recruitment process helps screen highly-qualified candidates and adds to the much celebrated Foreign Ministry image. These newcomers often take leave to further their studies overseas after a few years of work experience. In 2000, of a total number of diplomatic officers, 100 held qualifications at the level of Ph.D. — much higher than the foreign service norm.[33] Because of the high prestige of the Foreign Ministry vis-à-vis other state agencies and its relative isolation from political intervention, most Thai diplomats tended to pursue a career in the ministry. Thailand, therefore, has a large pool of experienced foreign policy practitioners from which it could draw.[34]

This explains why there has been no practice of appointing non-career ambassadors, except only rarely from 1960 to 1975.

By dint of its long history of existence, its close connection with the royal family, and its stature that attracted well-educated candidates, the Foreign Ministry has always been perceived by the general public as a place of the elite. The definition of the Foreign Ministry as an elitist agency is confirmed by the numbers of aristocratic and influential families in its ranks. They were at one time the epitome of the Foreign Ministry. At present, most officials are no longer from the aristocracy. Still, they come from a privileged social background. But possessing perfect qualifications is not always positive. It could come across as being conservative and resistant to change. Jakrapob Penkair, former Minister of the Prime Minister's Office and former Government Spokesperson, said that, as the world environment has changed, the Foreign Ministry had refused to shift its work paradigm accordingly. This became its major roadblock in realizing policy objectives.[35] This was how Thaksin came in to fill the gap. Thaksin's mission was to revolutionize the Foreign Ministry with a new paradigm of working and thinking. Jakrapob reflected Thaksin's thoughts on the necessity to make a radical change within the Foreign Ministry. He said that based on democratic principles, the Foreign Ministry should not be given authority in the formulation of foreign policy in the first place. This was the role of the head of (elected) government. Yet, traditionally, it enjoyed power and leadership in foreign policy decision-making to the point of it taking its role for granted. Jakrapob also said that, in the past, the foreign minister could only be considered "good and efficient" if he left the decision-making authority to the Foreign Ministry. Its aristocratic image had so far prevented the ministry's officials from serving the real needs of the Thais. In Jakrapob's words, "Only do the *khun nang* [nobles] make foreign policy, not the *phrai* [serfs, commoners, low-class]."[36] Jakrapob's assertion, while upsetting many conservative diplomats, rightly points to the fact that the growing democratization in Thailand was spearheading a radical headway inside the Foreign Ministry. Diplomats were expected to come to terms with a new political condition even at the expense of their own autonomy.

Thaksin's new paradigm for the Foreign Ministry was a business paradigm. Top-down administration, centralization of power, and normalization of cronyism were characteristics of his approach. Thaksin strategically assigned his "own people" in the ministry, as his eyes and ears, to complete the process of state power monopolization. At first, some wondered why Thaksin appointed Preecha Laohapongchana as Deputy Foreign Minister during the second period of his administration. Preecha, a former Deputy Minister of Industry, had close relations with Thaksin. Furthermore, the CEO ambassadors became a major component of Thaksin's absolute control of the Foreign Ministry. It is true that the CEO system might have led to a greater integration of Thai state agencies abroad, and thus permitted the ambassadors to tailor some sort of unified stance, under "Team Thailand", while conducting diplomacy. But the centralization of power through the CEO system only empowered the Thaksin regime in which little space was left for the bureaucrats to voice their policy concerns or initiatives. The government looked at this argument from a different angle. To Thaksin, Thai embassies did not have a reputation for a proactive style in the past. But now, under his leadership, they were called upon to perform to a higher standard under the rubric of the CEO ambassador.[37]

The CEO regime was officially in operation from October 2003. Jakrapob defined the concept of CEO as the making of an integrated system and goals-oriented process. The focus of CEO ambassadors shifted from two "Ms" (money and manpower) to one "M" (management), based on the assumption that "good management" led to a solution for every problem. Jakrapob also characterized the new role of CEO ambassadors: to know how to manage and be an efficient manager; to reduce individualism and learn how to work with others; to support both profit-oriented and non-profit activities; to promote a sense of Thai comradeship abroad; and to represent the Thai state and the king.[38] In fact, since 2002, the CEO programme was applied on a pilot basis in six embassies — Brussels, Beijing, New Delhi, Tokyo, Vientiane and Washington. By the end of 2003, it was extended to all missions. Running parallel with that of the CEO governors at provincial level, the CEO ambassadorial programme mandated close consultation between Foreign Ministry and other state agencies posted abroad. These other agencies were required to report directly to the ambassador. Embassies held periodic Team Thailand meetings to plan strategy, set annual targets and follow up pending assignments. "Key performance indicators" served as benchmarks for the team and to evaluate the envoy.[39] Some embassies were more enthusiastic than others. The Foreign Ministry's website provided a space for embassies to advertise their Team Thailand activities and to compete among themselves for the spotlight.

The collision between the old and new paradigms at first seemed minor. Like modernity crashing with tradition, a sense of resistance was felt especially among senior ambassadors who perceived the introduction of the CEO system as a radical change that had been forced upon the Foreign Ministry. Despite being granted absolute power within their jurisdiction abroad, some ambassadors believed that such power was only a small compensation for the loss of overall control of foreign policy which was now firmly in the hand of the Prime Minister.[40] Traditionally, the stationing of Thai officials in the diplomatic missions abroad contributed to the gathering of first-hand analysis of situations in their posted countries and realistic policy recommendations as valuable inputs in the foreign policy formulation. Some wondered if such activities were no longer valuable since new foreign policy initiatives were born out of Thaksin's ambitions. The resistance inside the Foreign Ministry against the CEO paradigm also originated from the shift in foreign policy content. The Foreign Ministry was known to have upheld a conventional worldview without engaging the public or private sector. In the past, the difficulty of changing its attitude toward embracing unregimented capitalism erupted following Chatichai's proposal of the marketplace policy in the Thai relations with Cambodia. Chatichai's team of advisors chose to bypass the Foreign Ministry's recommendations which, to them, very much echoed the Cold War nostalgia.[41] In the Thaksin period, the real content of Thai foreign policy was business-like in essence. But this was not the reason behind the denunciation of Thaksin's CEO foreign policy.

The apprehension here was the manner in which Thaksin and his cronies merged their own interests with those of the country. If this was the case, what the Thai ambassadors were striving for might not be the national interests, but the personal interests of the political leaders. The overemphasis on economic diplomacy, to some top diplomats, was not only demeaning, but also potentially eclipsing other significant factors and objectives, such as the protection of national dignity and sovereignty, and the obligation to promote regional stability and cooperation. The polarization within the Foreign Ministry was evident between the pro-Thaksin faction and the rest. Those who opposed Thaksin's domination of the Foreign Ministry feared that the conventional foreign policy could be swallowed up by the new commerce-driven paradigm. They also feared the increasing politicization of the Foreign Ministry since foreign policy had already been exploited to serve domestic political purposes. In fact, like Chatichai, Thaksin successfully broke the ministry's traditional rule of non-political intervention. His appointment of a new position, Thailand Trade Representatives (TTR), in 2001, could be viewed as a direct political interference in the Thai Foreign Ministry. The TTR office, an imitation of the Office of the United States Trade Representative (USTR), was an additional arm to promote Thai trade abroad. Thaksin appointed Prachuab Chaiyasarn, former Foreign Minister, as President of the TTR office, supported by two other representatives, Kantathi Suphamongkhon (to be reassigned as foreign minister in 2005) and Gornpot Asavinvichit, former Deputy Commerce Minister. From 2001–2004, each was assigned tasks geographically, with Prachuab in charge of Russia and the Commonwealth of Independent States (CIS) markets, Kantathi the European markets, and Gornpot the Asia and Middle East markets. It had its office in the Office of the Secretariat of Prime Minister. During Thaksin's second term in office, Prachuab remained as the President of the TTR. Thaksin replaced Kantathi and Gornpot with Sompong Amornwiwat, former Minister of the Prime Ministerial Office (to become foreign minister in the Samak administration), who oversaw the Europe, West Asia and Africa markets, and Pravich Rattanapian, at the time serving as Minister of Science and Technology, who was responsible for the North and South America and Australia and New Zealand markets. Prachuab revealed that the TTR dealt with more than 100 countries around the world, worked out strategies to penetrate markets, acted as coordinators, and cooperated closely with the private sector and government agencies.[42] But this mission, to a large extent, bypassed both the Foreign and Commerce Ministries. More importantly, all representatives who enjoyed the same status as Ministers, had some kind of political connection with Thaksin. Critics saw this as

a part of Thaksin's game of power distribution and political award
to his cronies. Hence, the TTR's mission might have been to
campaign for Thai economic activities abroad, but its real
significance was to strengthen Thaksin's political network. (The
current Democrat government followed in Thaksin's footsteps
by resurrecting the TTR Office in May 2009, appointing Kiat
Sithi-amorn, former Director of the Chamber of Commerce, as
its President, and Thammasat University's lecturer Suthad
Setboonsarng and former Deputy Minister for Public Health
Vatchara Pannachet as trade representatives.)

An equally important factor affecting the shift within the Foreign
Ministry appeared to be the role of the foreign ministers and their
relations with diplomatic officers. Indeed, the intricate relationships
among Thaksin, Surakiart and Kantathi have up until now shaped
and divided opinions among Thai diplomats regarding the issues
of the organizational revamp and the new direction of foreign
policy. Foreign Minister Surakiart possessed a unique personality.
He came across as an unrivalled minister in terms of his perfect
educational background, and at the same time, was also an
intimidating figure for many Foreign Ministry officials. Surakiart
demanded the highest working standards from officials. He was
also very much fixated on meticulous and detailed protocol.
Punctuality and neatness were the ultimate requirements in his
world of protocol. Indeed, such requirements effectively
differentiated Surakiart from Thaksin who claimed to prefer a
drama-free diplomacy. Subsequent clashes between Surakiart
and some senior ambassadors led to several stirring incidents.
Retribution became the name of the game. Surakiart ordered the
transfer of members of the Jayanamas, an influential family within
the Foreign Ministry, allegedly due to personal conflicts. The
Jayanamas eventually hit back with a forceful anti-Surakiart
campaign during his bid for the position of the UNSG. Asda
Jayanama called Surakiart a third-rate politician, clumsy, bungling
and lacking a brand name.[43] The *Bangkok Post* reported intensifying
fears of a wider purge aimed at ensuring subservience inside the
Foreign Ministry:

> Indicative of the climate of insecurity that has descended on the
> Foreign Ministry, reports were rife but unconfirmed yesterday
> that... Thai ambassadors in Vienna, Brussels, Phnom Penh and

Rangoon were cited as other targets of the purge many saw as propelled by petulance and a hankering for complete control of the office. Ambassador Somkiati Ariyapruchya reportedly displeased Foreign Minister Surakiart Sathirathai for being late to meet him at Vienna airport last week. A career diplomat, Somkiati has one more year to serve before mandatory retirement. Surapong Posayanonda, ambassador to the European Commission in Brussels, is said to have irked the Minister by speaking critically of the government's understanding of Thai-European trade issues at a meeting of regional envoys. Chatchawed Chartsuwan, the ambassador to Cambodia, is expected to be transferred to Poland, apparently because he informed Prime Minister Thaksin Shinawatra before the Foreign Minister of the anti-Thai riots in Phnom Penh in late January. The Minister was then visiting Egypt, and the Prime Minister himself called ambassador Chatchawed in Phnom Penh for information on the situation. The transfer of Apiphong Jayanama, Director General of the Americas and South Pacific Affairs Department, and his deputy, Isorn Pokmontri, could complicate matters today, when plans for the Prime Minister's visit to the United States next month are to be discussed. Reportedly, the two had upset Foreign Minister Surakiart by acting without his prior consent. Apiphong recently received the Iraqi ambassador who was expelled from Sri Lanka. Isorn reportedly had responded to a call from Pansak Winyarat, the PM's chief adviser, for an update on preparations for the Prime Minister's coming trip. This reportedly annoyed the Minister, whose relations with Pansak have been cool since the Minister had to him as chief adviser to former Prime Minister Chatichai Choonhavan in the late 1980s.[44]

Surakiart did not only fall out with diplomats. His alliance with Thaksin was on the brink of breakdown the day the prime minister replaced him with Kantathi at the Foreign Ministry. Surakiart grumbled that Thaksin was not sincere in the endorsement for his nomination for the UNSG position, citing the stingy budget provided for the assignment and Thaksin's subsequent lack of interest in the support for the campaign.[45] At the Foreign Correspondents' Club of Thailand (FCCT) in December 2007, Surakiart stressed that there were many things he was not happy about in the Thaksin government, but did not add any details.[46] The sign of enmity became clear when Surakiart gave testimony to the Assets Scrutiny Committee (ASC) regarding to the Bt4 billion loans granted to

Myanmar to buy the IPStar satellites from Shin Satellite. Surakiart reportedly told the ASC that Thaksin instructed him to approve a Bt1 billion increase in the loan amount from the original Bt3 billion loans. Surakiart insisted that he opposed the provision of the loan because this would be in breach of the Bagan Declaration barring Thailand from lending for telecom development to prevent conflicts of interest on the part of Thaksin whose family owned the country's largest telecom business at that time and even suggested to the Myanmar leaders to take a loan from China instead.[47] In December 2009, Surakiart told the Supreme Court in Bangkok that Thaksin requested the cabinet to take a "lenient" stand towards the Myanmar junta when it asked for a reduction of interest rate on the loan from 5 per cent to 3 per cent on the ground that the Laotian and Cambodian governments got soft loans from Thailand at the rate of 2 per cent per annum.[48]

In another side of the relationship, the Thai media sensationally told the story of a bitter rivalry between Surakiart and Kantathi since both aimed for the same Cabinet portfolio. *The Nation* wrote, "Ministry officials were caught between a young, wet-behind-the-ear minister and an experienced politician."[49] The newspaper also commented:

> While Kantathi was hopping around the world, back home Surakiart successes in getting the cabinet to appoint his trusted aid and friend, Sorajak Kasemsuwan to the post of the Foreign Ministry's Vice Minister. Furious, Kantathi was not lost for words upon learning about this development. But when he returned to Bangkok, his lips were sealed…. While Surakiart may have got away with the stunt, it turned the Ministry into a laughing stock. Sorajak might have got the position as the Vice Minister, but he did not have the guts to go into the Ministry.[50]

To conceal the ongoing rift, Kantathi, in charge of lobbying for Surakiart for the UNSG position, told reporters, "Surakiart is a highly qualified candidate who will continue to receive Thailand's backing, and that of the 130 countries that have pledged their support."[51] But Kantathi himself was not free from troubles at work. His first challenge was to emerge from Thaksin's shadow and undertake his duty with a certain degree of independence. Asda analysed that the problem with Kantathi was because he was not in full control of the Foreign Ministry since he did not have too many loyal officials around him and in key positions. Some officials still acted as if Surakiart was still the foreign minister.[52] In general, Kantathi was criticized for being an inactive foreign minister. Certain reasons justify such criticism. First, he was unfortunate to have taken over the post from Surakiart. Surakiart, having been in the position for a full four-year term, left a considerable influence not only on the ministry's officials, but also in the way diplomacy had been conducted under his reign. Second, all the flagship policies were implemented during the Surakiart era. Surakiart seemed to have left big shoes for Kantathi to fill in terms of catching up with the success he had made during his four-year stint at the Foreign Ministry. Third, some diplomats openly expressed their disappointment in Kantathi, also a former diplomat with a profound familiarity of diplomacy and protocol, who failed to come to the rescue whenever Thaksin went off the deep end. Fourth, Kantathi's tenure at the Foreign Ministry coincided with a critical period of Thai politics. Thailand's foreign policy was tainted by lip service as diplomacy came to a standstill because of domestic problems. No major foreign policies were executed during this period. As part of attacking Thaksin's foreign policy, anti-Thaksin forces grabbed Kantathi's performance by the throat and held Thailand's foreign relations hostage for much of his time at the Foreign Ministry. His opponents criticized his globe-trotting as lacking in substance. It was reported that from February to September 2006, Kantathi paid visits to over twenty countries. In September alone, were it not for the coup, he would have travelled to eleven cities in eight countries and almost every continent. His visit to the United States where he held a discussion with Secretary of State Condoleezza Rice in July 2006 stirred much controversy as Kantathi, on his part, struggled to justify a real objective behind this trip. He said, "It was simply a visit in response to an invitation from Rice."[53]

It can be said that the Foreign Ministry became distraught and disillusioned by Thaksin's power and policies. The personality conflicts between and among many actors, ranging from Thaksin, his two foreign ministers, to former ambassadors, have greatly diminished, more than any other periods in history, the morale and spirit of the ministry's officials. The deep division is not only found in the domain of national politics, but also under the roof of the Foreign Ministry. Thaksin's top-down administration also spurred resentment among the conservatives inside the ministry who felt that new practices accompanying his personalized diplomacy went over their heads. Definitely, the restructuring of the Foreign Ministry under the Thaksin regime was not the first time it has seen change in its history. But what Thaksin did in regard to revamping the Foreign Ministry was somehow large-scale, and perhaps the most radical in the eyes of some of its members.

WAS THAILAND READY TO CONQUER?

Setting aside Thaksin's uninhibited foreign policy ambitions, a more serious question is whether Thailand, in its current state, could really become the region's leader in its own right. Two levels of analysis are required in accessing Thailand's capability, strength and leadership during the Thaksin period: global and national. At the international level, Thailand under Thaksin competed vigorously with a number of players to reach the top spot in the region. Within Southeast Asia, Indonesia, the world's largest Muslim state, has long been ASEAN's natural leader. Particularly, Indonesia has in recent years emerged as a re-born democratic entity after years of deep political turmoil. The successful political transition in this post-Suharto era has further strengthened its democratization process as well as economic growth. Both Malaysia and Singapore have also stepped up their game by using ASEAN to strengthen their regional leadership, with the former maintaining its ASEAN-centric foreign policy as reflected in its firm support of ASEAN's role in the driver's seat in regional cooperation, and the latter concentrating more on materializing ASEAN integration and the making of the ASEAN Community. Thailand, one of ASEAN's founding members, was a recognized leader of the grouping especially during the Cambodian conflict. From 1997, the Democrat government of Chuan Leekpai sought its leadership in ASEAN as a supplement to its own implementation of foreign policy. In the new millennium, ASEAN suddenly became too small a stage for Thaksin to show off his leadership. Thailand may have over the years enjoyed steady economic growth, but it was not the only Southeast Asian state which had reached the next level of economic development. In its own way and at its own pace, Vietnam proved to possess enormous potential in turning itself into a regional economic powerhouse. Already, there has been talk about Vietnam competing for a leading role in ASEAN against Thailand and Indonesia.[54] The level of competition for a regional leadership has been an all-time high.

In a wider context, the rise of China and India has practically overshadowed most nations in the region. The discussion of Thailand's competition with rising China and India is more suitable only within the context of mainland Southeast Asia. Since the end of the Cold War, China and India have tried hard to extend their influence and successfully made strong inroads into Indochina and Myanmar, hoping to take economic advantages from them, either in securing the sources of energy, or turning them into an economic gateway to lower Southeast Asia, partly to reduce their own dependency on maritime trade. Thaksin's invention of ACMECS was arguably a nuanced response to the growing influence of China and India in its immediate neighbours. In other words, ACMECS was presumably set up to dilute the Chinese and Indian domination of Thailand's bordering neighbours, a zone Thaksin also claimed under Thai supremacy. For example, Thaksin's contract farming programme in Laos was said to be initiated to offset similar projects between Laos and China. Contract farming is a system for the production and supply of agricultural or horticultural products under forward contracts between producers/suppliers and buyers. The essence of such an arrangement is the commitment of the cultivator to provide an agricultural commodity of a certain type, at a time and a price, and in the quantity required by a known and committed buyer, typically a large company.[55] Currently, Laos produces corn, soybeans and cardamom under contract farming for export to China.[56] Meanwhile, Laos was seeking to reduce its dependence on Thailand and reaching out to China as well as Vietnam to help rejuvenate the moribund economy. This was where China and Thailand's tug of war over Laos began.

Was Thailand from 2001 to 2006 ready to lead Southeast Asia? The country's steady economic growth alone does not automatically confer leadership status. The business-centric foreign policy seemed to reflect more of Thailand's domestic needs than its hunger to play a leading economic role in the region. Thailand's donor status failed to erase a sense of suspicion in the perspective of its counterparts. This was because Thai assistance came with strings attached. In the ACD, having more members should not be naively construed as the country's achievement in influencing a wider Asian region. The geography of the ACD is too large. The level of economic development and the cultural composition among ACD members are too diverse. And the fact that Thaksin presented the ACD as some kind of Asia-for-Asians platform conveyed a message of racism, the existing clash of civilizations and a return to the divisive "Asian values" debate — issues that are highly sensitive and therefore downplayed in the Western world. With all these reasons combined, Thaksin's sprawling footprint on the Asian region through the ACD has been gradually fading. Member countries have become less enthusiastic about this cooperative framework. The rest of the world appears to have forgotten altogether that the ACD still exists. In sum, Thailand's shaky stature in international politics raised the question of its eligibility to claim a leading role in the region, particularly mainland Southeast Asia. But what shattered Thailand's dream to become a serious contender as a regional leader was its own worsening domestic political situation that has literally decimated its hope at the international level. Thai diplomacy had been chained up by its domestic crisis.

Thaksin fought a political war in his own backyard from 2005 and it critically damaged his diplomatic efforts. His abuse of democracy and eagerness to set against the old establishment instigated severe responses from the royalists. They were terrified of Thaksin's sole domination of political power, a domain traditionally influenced by the palace, as well as his control over the country's foreign affairs. In de-legitimizing the government, not only did the royalists, led by the PAD, accuse Thaksin of arrogant, despotic practices, but they also exploited his foreign policy to create friction with Thai neighbours. The PAD charged Singapore's Temasek Holdings of conspiring with Thaksin to take over Thailand in the aftermath of the Shin-Temasek deal.[57] The PAD also allowed anti-Thaksin former ambassadors to front the campaign against the nomination of Surakiart for the UNSG job. Even when Thaksin was ousted from power, the PAD continued to disparage his friendly policy toward Cambodia as a Thaksin ploy to do business with the Cambodian leaders. In doing so, the PAD stirred up a sense of nationalism against Thaksin and Cambodia, using the disputed Preah Vihear Temple as a backdrop for its campaign. A series of books entitled *Ru Than Thaksin*, or *One Step Ahead of Thaksin*, was launched by anti-Thaksin scholars and social critics. The books emphasized the dark side of business that was used to drive the Thaksin government at the expense of democracy. They also argued that Thaksin's embrace of democracy was merely a rhetorical tool addressed to the international community.[58] Thaksin's political behaviour strongly suggested that he was not really fond of democracy. Poor ratings in transparency, limited press freedom, rampant corruption and an emerging culture of business mixed with politics tarnished the reputation of the country and smashed into pieces Thaksin's ambition to command the region. Thaksin's maltreatment of the minority Muslims in the south and his endorsement of the extra-judicial killings of suspected narcotic traffickers expunged the possibility of Thailand taking a leading role in the region especially as a proponent of democracy and human rights protection.

Ultimately, a more fundamental question emerges: were the Thai people ready to stand behind their leaders in exercising leadership through a responsible diplomacy? Did Thaksin's populist diplomacy successfully arouse the Thais' consciousness in what was going on in the world and the country's role in it? Thaksin attempted to make diplomacy tangible: he hosted a weekly radio programme, since taking office in 2001 until 2006, using it as a channel to forge a better understanding of, and to correct misinformation about his administration and foreign policy among his supporters in the rural areas. For example, he appealed to the Thai people to help the government promote APEC in 2003, to play a good host to foreign guests, as well as to comprehend how and why APEC was important for Thai interests. Through his radio programme and his addresses on television, or even in town halls in small remote villages of Thailand, Thaksin talked about the ACD, what kind of English textbooks he read and what he actually did when he visited foreign countries. But there was a thin line between Thaksin opening the window of the people's consciousness about the world, and elevating himself as the ultimate leader who knew a lot more than his subordinates. As a justification of this argument, Thaksin's speeches mostly conveyed a tone of "preaching" rather than "sharing" his worldview. He once said, "We must change the way we work. If we are unsuccessful, the whole country could go down the drain. Look at the glorious past of Angkor. It is one of the world's Seven Wonders. But there is nothing else left to admire."[59] Thaksin's high concentration on domestic politics, as part of the strengthening of his power base in the rural provinces, somehow denotes an inward strategy. Even when he bombarded the Thai public with international acronyms and repeated use of English in his Thai speeches, the degree of exposure to international diplomacy among Thai people remained rather limited. Thaksin's construction of a foreign policy that strictly answered to domestic needs further confirmed the fact that his kind of diplomacy was not designed to arouse the Thais' awareness of international politics or to encourage their critical responses to it. Instead, he imposed upon the Thai public to look at the world only through his own lens.

CONCLUSION

> I am convinced that under the present global environment, there is no consensus or unanimity regarding which political or economic theories are "correct". Therefore, it is unlikely that any single approach would be appropriate for and applicable to every country and society. No single thought, no single theory can work for everyone. There is no "one-size-fits-all" cure for the problems for the world. Therefore, it is essential for us to help one another in finding innovative and constructive ways to co-exist and cooperate with one another in order to perform the duties that our peoples have entrusted to us.[60]

This keynote speech of Thaksin, delivered in Bangkok in 2002, depicted a beautiful picture of Thailand playing the role of a charming leader who offered hope and optimism. But an exquisite speech does not necessarily lead to pragmatic substance. Indeed, the content in this speech was principally contradictory to the logic behind Thaksin's grand policy initiatives. What Thaksin had done in his capacity as the chief of policy formulation from 2001 to 2006 was to force a one-size-fits-all strategy upon its neighbours. In his view of regional politics, he believed that all nations needed one thing: prosperity. To forge amicable relations with them, "money talk" must be prioritized. And he assumed that this money-oriented recipe could be applied to all kind of relations Thailand had with the outside world. Even when armed conflicts erupted along the border, leaders in Bangkok were still convinced that "prosperity" could cure the existing misunderstandings between the two states. This type of one-sided Thaksinized diplomacy created a dangerous illusion in the way Thailand was managing its relations with its neighbours.

There are five major shortcomings and oversights in the way Thai diplomacy was put into effect during the Thaksin period. His diplomacy contained a mixture of vices: arrogance, short-sightedness, self-aggrandizement, toe-stepping and face-slapping, and falsehoods. Thaksin misused foreign policy with impunity to reinforce his political power and personal wealth. It was also used arbitrarily to feed his unrealistic ambitions. Diplomacy turned even more complicated when politicians took over the Foreign Ministry, transforming it into a factory that produced policy based on their quirky initiatives. When things seemed to go wrong in the hands of political leaders, the Foreign Ministry was brought in to whitewash the nation's blemished reputation. During the Thaksin years, the Foreign Ministry was, to the highest degree, politicized. Those closer and subservient to benevolent leaders got the reward. Those opposed to them suffered transfer and retribution. These practices were a setback to Thai diplomacy. How could Thaksin win over traditional enemies in the neighbourhood when he could not even win over his enemies at home?

Notes

1. Duncan McCargo and Ukrist Pathmanand, *The Thaksinisation of Thailand* (Copenhagen: Nordic Institute of Asian Studies, 2005), p. 31.
2. Pasuk Phongpaichit and Chris Baker, *Thaksin: The Business of Politics in Thailand* (Chiang Mai: Silkworm Books, 2004), p. 49.
3. Thaksin's populist diplomacy functioned hand-in-hand with his domestic populist programme. For details on Thaksin's populism see Pasuk Phongpaichit and Chris Baker, "Thaksin's Populism", *Journal of Contemporary Asia* 38, no. 1 (February 2008): 62–83.
4. Nongnuch Singhadecha, "Pon Saehai Rairaeng Khong Karnthood Prachaniyom" [Disastrous Implications of Populist Diplomacy], *Matichon*, 19 October 2005.
5. Pasuk and Baker, *Thaksin: The Business of Politics in Thailand*, p. 141.

6. Nongnuch, "Pon Saehai Rairaeng Khong Karnthood Prachaniyom".
7. Interview with Sawanit Kongsiri, Yangon, Myanmar, 23 June 2008. Sawanit is former ambassador to Australia, China and Vienna, former Deputy Foreign Minister in the Surayud government, and currently Assistant Secretary General for External Relations for the Thai Red Cross Society.
8. Achara Ashayagachat, "Ministry Pledges to be More Responsive to External Needs", *Bangkok Post*, 16 October 2004.
9. Pasuk Phongpaichit, *Thailand Under Thaksin: A Regional and International Perspective*, Core University Project, Centre for Southeast Asian Studies, Kyoto University, Japan, 6–8 September 2004, p. 3. The author's own copy.
10. Don Pathan and Supalak Ganjanakhundee, "A Tale of Unrealised Global Ambitions", *The Nation*, 11 April 2006.
11. Pasuk and Baker, *Thaksin: The Business of Politics in Thailand*, p. 244.
12. "Thaksin Completes Man City Buyout", 6 July 2007 <http://news.bbc.co.uk/1/hi/business/6277502.stm> (accessed 30 April 2009).
13. "Is Thaksin Using Football to Play Politics" <http://www.sgclub.com/singapore/thaksin_using_football_36229.html> (accessed 1 May 2009).
14. See Bidhya Bowornwathana, "Thaksin's Model of Government Reform: Prime Ministerialisation through 'a Country is my Company' Approach", *Asian Journal of Political Science* 12, no. 1 (June 2004).
15. Nirmal Ghosh, "Thaksin Still Holds Sway up North", *Straits Times*, 22 October 2008.
16. Yos Santasombat, "Power and Personality: An Anthropological Study of the Thai Political Elite", Ph.D. dissertation, University of California Berkeley, 1985, p. 196.
17. "Thaksin Regime's Business Networks", *The Nation*, 26 September 2006. This piece of news report was based on Pasuk Phongpaichit's seminar on money politics held in 2005 by the Centre of Political Economy, Chulalongkorn University, Thailand.
18. Ibid.
19. Ibid.
20. Interview with Surin Pitsuwan, former Foreign Minister and currently ASEAN Secretary-General. The interview was conducted in Seoul, South Korea, on 21 March 2008.
21. Sopon Ongkara, "Secret of Thaksin's Burma Trip might be in the Skies", *The Nation*, 6 August 2006.
22. Martin Petty, "Standoff Exposes Discontent in Foreign Ministry", *Thai Day*, 26 March 2006.
23. Quoted in Pleaw See Ngern, "Uttaprawat Badsop Thaksin Maethap Daeng" [Disreputable Biography: The Red Army Chief Thaksin],

Thai Post, 26 March 2009 <http://pad.vfly.net/en/497/thaksin-pojaman-sanoh-perceptions/> (accessed 31 May 2009).

24. Speech of Deputy Prime Minister and Finance Minister Somkid Jatusripitak on the topic "Competing for the Future with Winning Strategies", held at the Plaza Athenee Hotel, Bangkok, 26 July 2005. The author's own copy.

25. Don Pathan, "Megaphone PM Tests Kantathi's Diplomacy", The Nation, 1 November 2005.

26. Ibid.

27. Interview with a Director-General at the Thai Foreign Ministry, 27 June 2008.

28. Ibid.

29. Source: Bureau of the Budget, Thailand.

30. Kishan S. Rana, Asian Diplomacy: The Foreign Ministries of China, India, Japan, Singapore and Thailand (Washington D.C.: The Johns Hopkins University Press, 2007), p. 137. Rana stated that in 2000, the number of resident foreign embassies in Bangkok was fifty-one; the increase of the past six years is testimony to growth in the country's importance.

31. Pavin Chachavalpongpun, "A Sad State of Affairs at the Thai Foreign Ministry", Bangkok Post, 2 March 2009.

32. Rana, Asian Diplomacy, pp. 139–40.

33. Ibid., p. 145.

34. John Funston, "The Role of the Ministry of Foreign Affairs in Thailand: Some Preliminary Observations", Contemporary Southeast Asia 9, no. 3 (December 1987): 232.

35. Interview with Jakrapob Penkair, Bangkok, 26 June 2008.

36. Ibid.

37. Thaksin's speech at the Annual Meeting of Ambassadors and Consuls-General of Thailand, Ministry of Foreign Affairs, 27 August 2003, in Kham Prasai Lae Kham Banyai Khong Pon Tamruad Tree Thaksin Shinawatra Nayok Ratthamontri Lem Thi Nueng [Speeches and Lectures of Police Lieutenant Colonel, Volume 1], Department of Public Relations, Bangkok, Thailand (n.d.), p. 95.

38. Jakrapob Penkair, Khon Lahlok Diew Khan: Aek-akkarachathood CEO [In a Different World: CEO Ambassadors], Phuchadkan, 5 September 2003.

39. Rana, Asian Diplomacy, p. 147.

40. Interview with a number of former and current ambassadors, Bangkok, June–December 2008.

41. See Sunai Phasuk, Nayobai Tang Prathet Khong Thai: Suksa Krabuankarnkamnod Nayobai Khong Ratthaban Pon-ek Chatichai Choonhavan Tor Panha Kumphucha, Si Singhakom 1988–23 Kumphaphan 1991 [Thai Foreign Policy: A Study of Foreign Policy Making Process

under the Chatichai Choonhavan Government, 4 August 1988–23 February 1991] (Bangkok: Institute of Asian Studies, 1997).
42. "Trade, Trade and More Trade for the TTRs", *The Nation*, 18 July 2005. Prachuab emphasized, "We're not trade negotiators but trade-facilitators working on behalf of the Thai government. We have to create a smooth trade and investment atmosphere in both bilateral and multilateral talks.
43. See "French Leader's Visit Time to Reconsider Surakiart's UN Bid", *The Nation*, 17 February 2006; Robert T. McLean, "Change is Slow at Turtle Bay", *The American Spectator*, 18 April 2006; and Achara Ashayagachat, "Backing Sought for Surakiart: U.N. Post to be Raised during Chirac Visit", *Bangkok Post*, 17 February 2006.
44. "Transfers Fuel Fears of a Purge", *Bangkok Post*, 16 May 2003.
45. Interview with Surakiart Sathirathai, Bangkok, 27 June 2008.
46. "Surakiart Sathirathai at the FCCT", *Bangkok Pundit*, 11 December 2007 <http://bangkokpundit.blogspot.com/2007/12/surakiart-sathirathai-at-fcct.html> (accessed 8 January 2010).
47. Ampa Santimatanedol, "Surakiart Testifies He Opposed Burma Loan", *Bangkok Post*, 1 May 2007.
48. Usa Pichai, "Thaksin Wanted Leniency Towards Burmese Junta", *Mizzima*, 23 December 2009 <http://www.mizzima.com/news/regional/3198-thaksin-wanted-leniency-towards-burmese-junta.html> (accessed 2 December 2010).
49. "A Year of Thai Foreign Policy Blunders", *The Nation*, 30 December 2006.
50. Ibid.
51. Martin Petty, "Too Much Diplomacy for Surakiart", *International Herald Tribune*, 16 February 2006.
52. Don, "Megaphone PM Tests Kantathi's Diplomacy".
53. "A Year of Thai Foreign Policy Blunders", *The Nation*.
54. Shaun Narine, *Explaining ASEAN: Regionalism in Southeast Asia* (Boulder and London: Lynne Rienner Publishers, 2002), p. 113.
55. Jayati Ghosh, "Is Contract Farming Really the Solution for Indian Agriculture?", MacroScan, 15 May 2007 <http://www.macroscan.com/cur/may07/cur150507Indian_Agriculture.htm> (accessed 4 January 2010).
56. See Anthony M. Zola, *Contract Farming for Exports in ACMECS: Lessons and Policy Implications*, a paper presented at the meeting on "Investment, Trade and Transport Facilitation in ACMECS", Bangkok, Thailand, 13 March 2007. Author's own copy.
57. "PAD Tells Singapore to Exit Deal or Face Boycott", *The Nation*, 8 March 2006.

58. See Asda Jayanama, "Karnthood Yuk Thaksin: Thaksiplomacy" [Diplomacy in the Thaksin Era], in *Ru Than Thaksin* [One Step ahead of Thaksin], edited by Chermsak Pinthong (Bangkok: Khor Kid Duai Khon, 2004).

59. Speech of Thaksin Shinawatra on the topic "Thailand in a New Context of Competition on the Global Stage", at the meeting "Leadership Development: Managing Changes", at Impact Muangthong Thani, Nonthaburi Province, 16 August 2003. In *Kham Prasai Lae Kham Banyai Khong Pon Tamruad Tree Thaksin Shinawatra Nayok Ratthamontri Lem Thi Nueng* [Speeches and Lectures of Police Lieutenant Colonel, Volume 1], p. 3.

60. Keynote speech by Thaksin Shinawatra at the 2nd International Conference of Asian Political Parties, Bangkok, 23 November 2002. In *Thai Politics: Global and Local Perspective*, edited by Michael H. Nelson, King Prajadhipok's Institute Yearbook no. 2, 2002–2003 (Nonthaburi: King Prajadhipok's Institute, 2004), p. 595.

6

CONCLUSION
A Rickety Reinvention

This concluding chapter seeks to answer the question posed at the beginning of this book: Did Thaksin successfully construct a post-Cold War foreign policy strategy? If yes, was it effective? And how did it shape the face of Thai diplomacy? The Thaksin period was one of the most intense periods of Thai diplomacy. Thaksin and his foreign ministers embarked on revolutionizing the way Thai diplomacy was conducted, and changed habits of past centuries and the content of the country's traditional foreign policy. A sea change in Thai foreign policy coincided with the shift in the role of the Thai Foreign Ministry. In many ways, the less autonomous Foreign Ministry should be held up as a positive model in any thriving democratic society. Thaksin thus questioned why Thai foreign policy should be the rightful purview of bureaucrats. His perspective of foreign policy was a "twin brother" to his domestic policy. Thaksin's self-styled diplomacy was proactive, aggressive and confident. It contained a sense of nationalism − practising diplomacy supposedly for the interests of the Thais. Also known as populist diplomacy, Thaksin claimed to place people at the core of his foreign policy. His strategy was two-fold: adopting a nationalistic foreign policy and raising the country's international profile. But critics saw this as a collision between the nationalist and internationalist approaches. Such a collision caused confusion among Thailand's neighbours. More importantly, Thaksin's assertive diplomacy occasionally came across as self-serving: promoting personal economic interests and domestic political gains. This generated a negative impact on his regional leadership aims.

Foreign Minister Surakiart rationalized that at the beginning of the millennium, the global political and economic landscape had changed tremendously and that it was necessary for Thailand to fine-tune its foreign policy orientation accordingly. One of the foreign policy initiatives was to urgently narrow the gap between the more and less economically developed states in the region. Thailand was eager to bridge the gap of development through its initiation of the ACMECS. The emphasis of Thailand's donor status also served this purpose of assisting its neighbours reach a higher level of development. Surakiart also implemented Thaksin's vision of turning Asia's diversity into advantage. This was the rationale behind the construction of the ACD.[1] In doing so, Thaksin and Surakiart together began the process of elevating Thailand's role in the wider Asian region, and more specifically, shifting the Thai concentration to mainland Southeast Asia. The refocus of Thai interest on mainland Southeast Asia seemed to reflect certain new conditions at the time. Thailand's traditional policy was largely infatuated by its involvement in superpower politics. Thaksin diminished the Thai reliance on the West, namely the United States and Europe, while exploring economic interests closer to home. Thaksin's shift of policy direction to mainland politics also revealed the fact that Thailand was in a difficult position to influence maritime states in Southeast Asia. Thaksin hoped that a preponderance of Thai influence on mainland Southeast Asia would pave the way toward Thai supremacy over its immediate neighbours. Then, the rise of Thailand's regional power would enhance its role in the international arena.

The above foreign policy direction was part of Thaksin's axiom of "thinking out of the box". By thinking out of the box, Thaksin set up his own rules of diplomacy, such as the obligations attached to the baht loans, handcuffing his neighbouring recipients. The goal had been to celebrate Thailand's economic interests abroad at the expense of its political role, such as the promotion of democracy.

But along the way, the Thai economic policy was sullied by conflicts of interest involving Thaksin's private businesses and those of his political allies. So when Thaksin personalized Thailand's foreign policy, many wondered if it was to benefit the country or his personal agenda. Thaksin's attempt to sideline the Foreign Ministry also raised questions about the real content of his personalized foreign policy. It is therefore imperative to reassess Thaksin's foreign policy outlook in the following pages to draw a conclusion on whether his reinvention of Thailand was a success or otherwise.

THAKSINIZED DIPLOMACY: SUNRISE OR SUNSET?

To establish whether Thaksin's diplomacy was a compelling tool for exploring a new post-Cold War foreign policy strategy, this book aims to answer a set of questions, revolving around the notion of national interests, Thaksin's concept of economic diplomacy, Thai hegemonization and the sustainability of his foreign policy. On the surface, Thailand's foreign policy in the Thaksin period was impressive and ambitious. Thaksin embarked on creating a golden age of foreign policy where Thailand's poorer neighbours followed his lead. He forged the country's relations with the United States and China. Thaksin even dared to challenge the international order traditionally based on the old Western world, and introduce a new world by leading Asia through the ACD. At a deeper level, however, his foreign policy was problematic. His self-centred foreign policy failed to strengthen the regional focus. The emphasis was not on cooperation with neighbours in the region, but verged on dominating them. Thaksin's regionalism through his endorsement of the ACD and the ACMECS was also troublesome. It was designed to enshrine Thaksin's leadership at the expense of achieving real significant results.

Foreign Policy Performance

Thailand lives side-by-side with its historical enemies. New domestic conditions allowed Thaksin to fashion a different approach and outlook on foreign policy from the ones once upheld by his predecessors. Thaksin's personal choices in foreign policy, driven by his overwhelming success of domestic agendas, were made out of a "can-do" spirit in his conduct of diplomacy, even when it went beyond the nation's recognized shortcomings. Bureaucratic politics and the traditional security-oriented foreign policy of the Thai Foreign Ministry were treated with less significance. Thaksin's worldview was large-scale, unbounded and motivated. He looked at the world with Thailand at its centre. He created a foreign policy that emphasized economic exploitation of Thailand's neighbours. Thai political culture and its state-constructed national identity also had an influence on Thaksin's foreign policy. Thaksin further concretized the general belief among Thais that Thailand has always been a great nation led by great leaders. The ability to switch alliances was a proud character among the Thais. Thaksin manipulated such factors, using them to swing public attitude toward a normalization of the leaders' domination of foreign relations in the interest of the country.[2] The rise of Thaksin and his business-oriented foreign policy also eclipsed the role of the military in diplomacy. It was a new era of Thai foreign policy never to have been influenced by the military and concerns of national security. With all these combined, Thaksin felt that he could afford to become more independent from international institutions, and to use foreign policy to define the regional order, rather than the other way round.

In the process, Thaksin rewrote the history of Thailand's foreign relations. The eagerness to compose a new history, now with Thailand at the epicentre of the region, overrode the endeavour to promote certain principles deemed quintessential to its bilateral relations with old enemies, such as mutual respect and shared benefits. Thaksin's foreign policy came across as a ruthless, cut-throat business regime aimed at exploiting neighbours even when it was accompanied by heightened mutual distrust. This book has shown earlier that even at the peak of seemingly good relations between Thailand and its neighbours during the Thaksin years, mutual suspicions still remained. Thaksin stated that CEO ambassadors were tasked to accomplish national interests in the countries of their responsibility. "In the name of capitalism, economic interest was the ultimate objective. The winners in this game were those who achieve this in the craftiest way," said Thaksin.[3] Thaksin's imposing diplomatic ideas, built on favourable domestic conditions, were put forward to convince the Thai public of the tremendous performance of his foreign policy, mostly justified by the number of Thai-hosted international meetings, the admission of new members (into the ACD for example), the number of planned cooperative projects (of both the ACD and the ACMECS), and the amount of money Thailand granted to its neighbours. He was also popular among some of his admirers in ASEAN. Simon Tay, Chairman of the Singapore Institute of International Affairs, once said, "I think ASEAN does need leadership, it does need a Thaksin."[4] Nevertheless, the performance of Thai foreign policy should not be assessed based on numbers and statistics alone. The sustainability of foreign policy initiatives and their actual contributions to the country's foreign relations as a whole must also be taken into consideration. On this basis, the fading strength of some of Thaksin's initiatives and the remaining inimical attitude between Thailand and its neighbours are testimony of a botched foreign policy. One of the main reasons behind the seemingly flawed foreign policy was Thaksin's maltreatment of the notion of national interests.

National Interests Compromised

Previous studies on Thai foreign policy tend to focus on achieving national interests as the main objective and driving force behind the conduct of Thai diplomacy. For example, Arne Kislenko, while appreciating the continuity and flexibility of Thai foreign policy which he called "bending with the wind policy", argued that Thailand has consistently crafted a cautious, calculated foreign policy and jealously guarded its independence. Indeed, it has occasionally gone to extraordinary lengths to preserve it.[5] His argument signifies that Thai leaders deemed national interests as the most important agenda in their foreign policy. Thaksin's foreign policy behaviour, however, raised doubts as to whether national interests remained the most desirable objective in his conduct of diplomacy. The political economy of Thaksin's foreign policy, with its concentration on making economic profits, stirred up debate on whether the private interests of certain personalities in government occasionally superseded national interests. For the sake of this observation, this book has highlighted earlier that the interaction between national interests and those of the prime minister must be given prominence. His family's investments in the telecom business in neighbouring countries, including his Sattel's CamChin in Cambodia, Lao Shinawatra Telecom in Laos, Sattel and Bagan

Cybertech in Myanmar, and his IPStar broadband satellite which has been marketed in a number of ACD/ACMECS countries, certainly obscured the line between national and private interests.

Thaksin's network of elites were active in particular business domains, namely in telecommunications, construction and finance. It is apparent that the state apparatus was not powerful and unable to contest the leader's self-serving foreign policy in which the practice of pursuing national policy for personal purposes was normalized.[6] While promoting Thai investments abroad through a series of foreign policy initiatives, Thaksin was also conducting his family's business with foreign counterparts. The work of Pasuk Phongpaichit disclosed that since Thaksin took office as Prime Minister in 2001, his government implemented several economic policies, which directly benefited and protected businesses of certain politicians and their affiliations. As an example, the Chearavanont family, a close ally of the Shinawatra, gained considerable profits from its chicken and prawn exports through a number of FTA contracts. Also, the family's telecom business expanded at a rapid pace especially after Shin Corp was sold to Temasek Holdings of Singapore.[7] In fact, the making of a confusing line between national and private interests is nothing new in Thai politics. Throughout the past decades, relations between Thailand and Myanmar have been based on personal interests between Thai politicians and generals in Yangon.[8] Thai politicians hoped to exploit this resource-rich country, through the logging business, gems trade and even business based on cheap labour, under the pretext of a policy of acclimatizing Myanmar into the region's economic mainstream. The difference in the Thaksin era was that Thaksin systematized the exploitation of foreign policy for personal consumption through the amendment of certain rules and regulations. His initiatives sought to put a legitimate face on a variety of dubious business ventures in neighbouring countries.

Thaksin carefully rationalized each of his foreign policy ideas, using the notion of "nation interests" to gain support from the Thai public in acquiring economic benefits, strengthening the country's international relations, and showcasing the Thai leadership in regional and global affairs: all were linked to his domestic populism. On the surface, Thaksin seemed to fulfil some of the objectives of his foreign policy. He put Thailand at the forefront of international politics, for a variety of reasons. The ACD, regardless of how much progress it has made over the years, was the first-ever attempt to incorporate most countries in Asia into one entity. The launching of the ACMECS also responded to the national agenda of revitalizing Thailand's influence on mainland Southeast Asia. His support for the FTAs partly satisfied the local economic needs in gaining advantage from international mechanisms. Increased trade volumes between Thailand and its FTA counterparts were testimony to a seemingly successful foreign policy. But such success should not shroud the fact that this same national interest was also abused by leaders to accumulate private gains. It would be naive to justify Thaksin's foreign policy based on a normative analysis in which the nation only strives for national objectives.

In reality, while serving as prime minister and doing international business at the same time, Thaksin seemed to equate national interests with his personal aggrandizement.

Bending the Prevailing Wind?

This book seeks to re-evaluate the traditional notion of Thailand's bamboo policy, which was described as the ability to bend with the direction of the wind in order to accomplish a national mission. Thaksin was definitely not the kind of leader who would take orders and appear submissive in the conduct of diplomacy. His bold domestic policies, such as the war on drugs campaign, proved his aggressive mindset. This tough image may have been one factor earning him an unprecedented second term in office as prime minister. But Thaksin's audacity not to follow the international wind of politics should not simply be translated as the capacity to dictate the prevailing wind.

Was Thaksin successful in setting wind conditions favourable to Thai interests? It is essential to examine fundamental factors that could be used to justify the Thai position in regional politics. First, geography plays a crucial role in Thai foreign relations, in particular in Thaksin's foreign policy. Thaksin took advantage of Thailand's strategic location to craft a foreign policy that hegemonized the kingdom in the face of its neighbours in the region. Thaksin envisioned a host of regional economic development programmes with Thailand as the regional hub. In ambitious projects like the ACD, Thaksin celebrated the country's strategic geography as a bridge between Southeast Asia and Northeast Asia, and a gateway for ASEAN to the Middle East and Central Asia. In the ACD, while much published emphasis was on the necessity to convert Asia's diversity into collective advantage, Thaksin never failed to nominate Thailand as the centre of access and economic development in the wider Asian region. Such confidence was further boosted by the country's economic growth under his regime. His proposal of the Bangkok Process also underscored the importance of the geographic factor. Thailand possessed a legitimate concern over the political situation in neighbouring Myanmar. The Myanmar issue has long been internationalized. The Western world had relentlessly exerted its influence on the political development in Myanmar. Thus, the Thai involvement could set a new level of leadership in the handling of such a difficult and politically sensitive issue. Regardless of its failure, the Bangkok Process initiative reminded political observers of the government's cunning use of local geography to publicize its foreign policy globally.

Second, whether Thaksin actually bent the prevailing wind depended on the extent to which he was prepared to become bold and authoritative in the implementation of foreign policy. In retrospect, one of the outstanding characters of the bamboo policy was the demonstration of a great flexibility and pragmatism in the conduct of diplomacy. By toughening up Thailand's position towards larger powers, Thaksin exercised his will to break free from international norms and practices, as well as from the occasionally languid foreign policy as seen in the past. However, as evident, Thaksin's toughness was largely superficial in its content, and more of a political device designed to entertain the domestic audience. Thaksin's trust in the United Nations, shown through the nomination of Surakiart for the UNSG position after insulting the organization in the media, signified the plasticity of his tough foreign policy. In reality, not only was Thaksin unable to command the direction of the wind, he was seen to have been conspicuously timid and passive in his interactions with the country's immediate neighbours. The bottom line was that Thaksin hoped to maintain business connections with them.

Third, opportunism was another hallmark of Thailand's bamboo policy. Past Thai leaders consistently searched for opportunities to make new friends and enemies as the world environment changed in order to preserve the nation's independence and sovereignty.

Was Thaksin an opportunist in his management of foreign relations? Opportunism in the traditional sense in Thai foreign policy is usually defined as a quest for an escape from precarious situations. In Thaksin's diplomatic point of view, opportunism meant different things and served different purposes. Thaksin grasped opportunities available within the regional or global order, turning them to the country's advantage, or even exploiting them for domestic political reasons. He also chose to take on certain opportunities while disregarding some of them that could threaten his political position both at home and on the international stage. An economic expansionist policy was the outcome of his response to the global economic opportunity that came with globalization. The emergence of multipolarity also represented another opportunity for Thaksin to catch up with the hegemonic world of the West. Thaksin was eager to prove that smaller, less powerful Asian states could work together toward building a polar of its own. Such opportunity permitted Thaksin to experiment with his brand of regionalism through the ACD.

Where did Thaksin's diplomacy stand as far as the traditional policy of bending with the wind was concerned? His flamboyant personality and innate egoism cast a long shadow over his personalized foreign policy. On the international stage, Thaksin was a fine actor who appeared to be daring to modify his country's position from "going with the flow of the prevailing wind" to "setting a new order". Behind the scene, his business interests hindered his ambition. He was obliged to reconstruct a timid foreign policy as he mixed personal business with diplomacy. The old bamboo policy may have no longer been desirable in the eyes of Thaksin since he embarked on a new process of reinventing Thailand and reinventing himself as a prominent regional leader. But what has remained intact, since Siam's old days up to Thailand's modern era, is the adoption of the accommodation approach in Thai foreign policy.

The Question of Sustainability

Thaksin's foreign policy initiatives were unsustainable owing to a number of reasons. First, the fact that Thaksin remoulded foreign policy on the basis on his business philosophy and turned ambassadors into CEOs suggested his preference to conduct diplomacy in a snappy and result-oriented manner. In other words, the objective was to gain immediate profits, rather than investing energy and anticipating long-term rewards. A business mentality can, however, generate negative consequences. David Levine argues that businessmen often imagine themselves to be in a paranoid situation. Surrounded by competitors desiring his market share, caring nothing for his welfare or even survival, indeed hoping to destroy that which he values most, the business mentality adopts characteristic that could be called paranoid.[9] The narcissistic side of a business mentality leads to the interpretation that it is all about the single-minded pursuit of self-interest. Thaksin's creation of business-oriented foreign policy based on a paranoid construction of the world, expressed not the power of his country in the global community, but rather its weakness. Prapat Thepchatree noted, "CEO diplomacy was the wrong medicine since the root cause of the problem was the central government."[10] Thaksin's Forward Engagement Policy, whose goals were to promote economic growth and development as well as shared prosperity, was particularly weak in its political aspect. Ultimately, it failed to enhance Thailand's capacity to play an all-round role in regional and world affairs. Foreign policy is by nature multi-dimensional. For Thaksin to restrict it in within the narrow business domain, therefore, reduced its significance and longevity. This justifies the unsustainable state of Thaksin's foreign policy.

Moreover, it was also untenable because of the conflicts of interest that effectively erased the principled aspect of foreign policy. Thaksin tying his business gains with national interests cut short the life of his foreign policy initiatives. Foreign policy became so personalized and self-serving that it was no longer valid once its architect was out of power.

Practicality is also a fundamental factor in assessing foreign policy. The ACD has remained an ill-structured organization with a lack of defined agendas. The creation of the ACMECS on the idea of Thai hegemony, likewise, proved highly problematic. ACMECS members did not need to rely solely on Thai prosperity. Thaksin clearly underestimated the worldview of his neighbours and believed that Thai domination of the region was an undeniable phenomenon.

Lastly, the current political crisis in Thailand where political enemies have sought to undermine and de-legitimize Thaksin effectively put his foreign policy legacy to rest. Political revenge in Thailand has reached its critical phase whereby opponents are willing to employ any tactic to annihilate their counterparts. The PAD had campaigned for the resignation of Thaksin since 2005. One year later, its wish came true as the military staged a coup against his government. But Thaksin's departure has not ended the political confrontation. Up until now, the PAD and the Abhisit government have continued to blame Thaksin's foreign policy, which they claimed diminished Thailand's reputation for the sake of his business bottom-line. Accordingly, the Abhisit administration has paid less attention to Thaksin's foreign policy initiatives, on the argument that holding on to Thaksin's legacy would have meant legitimizing his foreign policy, even if some of his diplomatic initiatives were well thought out if executed properly and without vested interests.

CONCLUSION

Let's begin where Thaksinized diplomacy should be praised. His conduct of foreign policy was indeed in line with the overall policy championed by the Thai Rak Thai government which received an overwhelming mandate from the Thai public through democratic means. His ambition, through the engineering of grand foreign policy projects, caught international attention and helped facilitate the evolution of regional cooperation. These projects were designed to maintain national sovereignty and promote national interests. Thaksin himself made use of nationalism to formulate a more independent foreign policy, such as shifting Thailand's role from recipient to donor country, and to re-map the political landscape by locating Thailand at the centre of the region. The latter mission was to showcase Thai leadership, and in particular, the leadership of Thaksin as the face of a new Asian statesman.

Was a post-Cold War foreign policy strategy successfully constructed during the Thaksin years? The many diplomacy setbacks, as a result of Thaksin's miscalculations, missteps, and even misbehaviour, lead many to conclude that his new-found strategy could be erroneous. Yet, in any case, Thailand under Thaksin experienced a taste of leadership. Not often did Thailand emerge as a leading actor in the region. The experience was, however, too short-lived, rocky, dramatic and overly sensational. The final product of Thaksin's malfunctioning foreign policy points to one fact, that is, his mission of reinventing Thailand was more complex, elusive and difficult to manipulate than he had previously imagined.

Notes

1. Interview with Surakiart Sathirathai, Bangkok, 27 June 2009.
2. In Nikolaos Zahariadis, *Emotion and Manipulation in Comparative Foreign Policy* (New York: Peter Lang, forthcoming). Zahariadis' analysis used for the Thai case is extracted from his paper prepared for presentation at the annual meeting of the 2005 International Studies Association, Honolulu, Hawaii.
3. In his speech delivered at the Thai Foreign Ministry, 11 August 2006.
4. Joe Cochrane, "An Annoying Neighbour", *Newsweek International*, 21 February 2006.
5. Arne Kislenko, "Bending with the Wind: The Continuity and Flexibility of Thai Foreign Policy", *International Journal* (Autumn, 2002): 537.
6. For a detailed analysis on this subject, see John P. Heinz et al., eds., *The Hollow Core: Private Interests in National Policy Making* (Cambridge: Harvard University Press, 1993), pp. 262–312.
7. "Thaksin Regime's Business Networks", *The Nation*, 26 September 2006. This piece of news report was based on Pasuk Phongpaichit's seminar on money politics held in 2005 by the Centre of Political Economy, Chulalongkorn University, Thailand.
8. See details in Pavin Chachavalpongpun, *A Plastic Nation: The Curse of Thainess in Thai-Burmese Relations* (Lanham: University Press of America, 2005).
9. David P. Levine, *Normative Political Economy: Subjective Freedom, the Market and the State* (London and New York: Routledge, 2001), p. 89.
10. Achara Ashayagachat, "Ministry Pledges to be More Responsive to External Needs", *Bangkok Post*, 16 October 2004. Prapat, a former diplomat, is currently Thammasat University's Director of the Centre for International Policy Studies.

7

EPILOGUE
The Post-Thaksin Foreign Policy

The military coup toppled the government of Prime Minister Thaksin Shinawatra on 19 September 2006. Naming itself the Council of National Security (CNS), the new military regime claimed to have undertaken the coup for a number of justifiable reasons. These included: the lack of political confidence among the Thais and the impasse caused by political differences; a drastic increase in disunity among the Thai people; signs of rampant corruption, malfeasance and widespread nepotism; interference into national independent agencies, crippling their ability to function properly and to effectively solve the nation's problems; and evidence of words and actions which were proven to be against the very foundation of Thailand's democracy with the king as Head of State.[1] In the domain of foreign relations, the CNS confirmed the country's international commitment, as follows:

1. Thailand's reaffirms adherence to the United Nations Charter and remains committed to obligations under international treaties and agreements, under the basis of equality of states.
2. Thailand's foreign policy will remain unchanged. The existing relationship between Thailand and other countries shall continue to be fostered and enhanced.

3. Thailand's international economic policy, including multilateral trade negotiations and free trade agreements, will be continued.[2]

In reality, an unchanged foreign policy sent out a confusing message. Continuity could imply that Thaksin made no mistakes in foreign policy. Since the military coup, Thailand has had no new foreign policy initiatives. Protracted political crisis as a result of a fierce power struggle between the royalists and the pro-Thaksin movement has kept successive governments occupied with having to fight for their political survival, and therefore seeing no sense of urgency in developing foreign policy. The Thai Foreign Ministry was put in ever more awkward positions as it had to defend different governments with different political ideologies. The organization has been preoccupied with repairing the country's image and reputation, largely tainted first by the military coup and second by the political bickering at home. The mission to restore the good image of the country has become a routine job for the Thai Foreign Ministry officials. It has left them with no space or time to initiate any new foreign policy programmes. The contrast between Thaksin's diplomatic assertiveness and that of his successors is immensely stark. In the post-Thaksin era, Thailand has seemed to let other players in the region take a leading role. Critics have however worried that such an attitude would further damage the standing of Thai diplomacy. Thailand was chairman of the ASEAN Standing Committee (from July 2008 to December 2009). ASEAN members thus expected Bangkok to navigate the organization, especially at a time when the grouping is celebrating the launch of its charter, and toward the realization of an ASEAN Community, by 2015 based upon three pillars — security, economic, and socio-cultural communities. Meanwhile, Thailand's borderlands have turned dangerously restive. Its territorial conflict with Cambodia over the overlapping claim of ownership of the land adjacent to the Preah Vihear Temple has threatened Thai national sovereignty. The Myanmar issue has continued to challenge the Thai leadership. Thailand, as frontline state, has been under the close scrutiny of the global community in regard to its Myanmar policy.

While there has been no clearly defined foreign policy during the post-Thaksin era, successive governments have continued to play with the fire of nationalism to earn political legitimacy.

Immediately after the ouster of Thaksin, the military government under Surayud Chulanont proposed the toughening of the Foreign Business Act (FBA) as a direct response to the sale of Shin Corp to Temasek Holdings. The government sorted out the definition of foreign companies, the question of management control and the list of protected professions and investment sectors — a great leap forward from the previous era of Thaksin when rules and regulations of foreign investment were largely lax. But nationalism was not an exclusive tool of the government. The PAD also exploited nationalism to create friction between Thailand and its neighbours, even when the real aim was to de-legitimize the pro-Thaksin government. The contentious Preah Vihear Temple was made a perfect nationalist device for the PAD due to lingering mutual distrust between Thailand and Cambodia. Foreign affairs have become much politicized by various political players both in the pro- and anti-Thaksin factions. In the meantime, the domestic political conflict has escalated as a result of Thaksin's continued political involvement from abroad, and his enemies' patient attempt to annihilate him and his political legacy. With the Democrat Party in power now, a known Thaksin's political rival, the Foreign Ministry has been tasked to exercise its diplomatic muscle to achieve the extradition of Thaksin, sentenced in October 2008, from wherever he is residing. The responsibility was even more pressing following the violent demonstrations in Bangkok on 13 April 2009 during which the pro-Thaksin red-shirt supporters clashed with the security forces. Thaksin was accused of inciting violence and destabilizing the Thai state. More recently, the conflict between the Abhisit government and Cambodia's Hun Sen, which derived from the latter's refusal to extradite Thaksin, has further complicated the conduct of Thai diplomacy. The Foreign Ministry has been entrapped by domestic vengeance between two political powers camps.

Since the ouster of Thaksin, Thailand has had four governments; one military rule, two Thaksin-backed regimes and one royalist government. It is evident that some of Thaksin's legacy has lived on, and that each successive regime has continued to treat foreign policy as an extension of its own domestic policy in order to maintain power and at the same time to undermine its opponents. Such politically motivated foreign policy, like during the Thaksin days, has not always served Thailand's national interests, but rather those of the power-holders.

SURAYUD CHULANONT: AN ETHICAL DIPLOMACY

Thaksin was not the only master of reinvention. The military reinvented itself after it seized power from an elected government by sugar-coating its image in righteousness and ethics. The mandate of the military, as it claimed, was to cleanse the dirt in Thai politics caused by Thaksin and his cronies.[3] Thus, the mission of the military government was held to be legitimate. The leader of the CNS, General Sonthi Boonyaratglin, installed General Surayud Chulanont, as prime minister, perceived to be ethical figure. Surayud was a former Army Chief and a Privy Councillor. He was well respected by the Bangkok elite and middle-class Bangkokians. The military's propaganda tactic, based on the depiction of Thaksin as an authoritarian demon versus Surayud as a royalist angel, seemed to function effectively in the domain of foreign affairs. The United States was quietly sympathetic toward the coup. It was legally obliged to suspend military support programmes worth around US$24 million annually, but it did not halt the annual joint military exercises "Cobra Gold".[4] The European countries and China maintained good relations with the military-installed government. ASEAN members sealed their lips on the return to military rule in Thailand, with the exception of Singapore whose leader, Prime Minister Lee Hsien Loong, called the military takeover a "setback" for Thai democracy.[5]

Sonthi and Surayud appointed two former ambassadors, Nitya Pibulsonggram and Sawanit Kongsiri, as Foreign Minister and Deputy Foreign Minister respectively.[6] The choice of career diplomats could have signified the return of authority back to the Foreign Ministry. To differentiate himself from the previous regime, Surayud declared the implementation of *karn thood khunna dharma*, or ethical diplomacy. Surayud said, "I would like to see greater balance given to the social and ethical side of our development.... The current domestic imperative will not make us shy away from our commitments as a responsible member of the international community."[7] It is easy to understand the logic behind his ethical diplomacy, a concept similar to the previous ethical foreign policy of Britain's Tony Blair during his first term in office when Robin Cook was foreign secretary. In sanctifying his diplomacy, Surayud automatically reproached that of Thaksin. He demonized certain diplomatic practices of Thaksin, such as the pursuit of private interests while in office and making personal profits out of official policy. From then on, Thai foreign policy would be transparent, accountable and ethical.

The foreign policy priorities of the Surayud administration included addressing the political problems and the conflict in the deep south. In the first undertaking, as Nitya said, the government hoped to restore international confidence in the country's political integrity and economic vibrancy.[8] This was done through countless visits to foreign countries by Prime Minister Surayud, active participation in international conferences and gatherings, and official publications containing supposedly correct information about the domestic political situation. As part of proving its proactive diplomacy, the government produced a foreign policy that promoted cooperation and strengthened friendship with countries in the region, supported ASEAN integration, elevated the role of Thailand in the United Nations, and increased the country's level of economic competitiveness.[9] In his mission of restoring peace in the south, Surayud paid an official visit to Penang, Malaysia, in August 2007, and held talks with Malaysian Prime Minister Abdullah Badawi. Malaysia agreed to help strengthen Islamic banks in southern Thailand to stimulate its economic life, train a new generation of entrepreneurs among the Thai Muslims, provide scholarships for students and training for teachers in the Thai south, and boost education links between the Muslims of the two countries.[10] This new approach of seeking Malaysia's assistance to heal the insurgency-wrecked south was designed to improve Thailand's ties with Kuala Lumpur that were strained during the Thaksin years from 2004 onwards. It also reflected an aspect of ethics. Earlier, Surayud condemned the hard-nosed measures adopted by the Thaksin regime in dealing with the southern conflict. In November 2006, in his answer to a question about the government's tough approach towards the residents of the Muslim-majority southern provinces, Surayud made an emotional plea to them, and offered a public apology for the deaths of at least eighty-five people during and after a demonstration in Tak Bai two years ago. He later said in an interview, "I have come here to apologize to you on behalf of the previous government and on behalf of this government. What happened in the past was mostly the fault of the state."[11]

Fixing Thaksin's diplomatic faux pas and illegitimate practices was also a demanding business of the Surayud government. Because

Thaksin took advantage of the loopholes in Thai business regulations, as apparent in his sale of Shin Corp to Singapore's Temasek Holdings without paying tax, the Surayad government proposed to amend the FBA 1999 so that the existing legal gaps could be closed in order to increase transparency and good governance. There have been two major ways to circumvent the FBA, that is, by using voting rights and having nominees. Through these arrangements, foreigners could engage in businesses which were regulated in the FBA without applying for a licence.[12] But the proposal of the amendment came under fire as it was criticized by business communities at home and abroad. They argued that the amendment of the FBA would hurt Thailand's global competitiveness based on the fact that one of the reasons why Thailand had been so successful in attracting foreign investments over the years was that its framework regulating foreign investments was more open than that of its neighbours. Any changes to the FBA, to them, would diminish Thailand's competitive advantage. Moreover, the changes would impact on the existing foreign-run companies operating in the kingdom and would go against market realities in a world that had become increasingly integrated with an undeniable free flow of capital.[13]

The Surayud government also realized that despite numerous cooperative programmes Thailand had with its immediate neighbours, such as through ACMECS and bilateral technical and financial assistance projects, their relations remained shaky and sullied with lingering suspicion. Scandal and corruption allegations, such as the controversial Bt4 billion loan for Yangon as part of the ACMECS in which Thaksin appeared to have a conflict of interest, were scrutinized by the military-installed Asset Examination Committee. Using ethics as a guiding light while pursuing a new relationship, Surayud wanted to regain trust from the Thai neighbours and to erase Thailand's exploitative image crafted by Thaksin and his cronies. Foreign Minister Nitya called for a meeting of Thai ambassadors and consuls-general in neighbouring ACMECS countries at the Foreign Ministry on 17–19 January 2007. The main purpose of the meeting was to assess the current relations between Thailand and its neighbours with regard to problems, and obstacles and policies in all aspects including political, security, economic and social dimensions. In particular, Nitya stressed that the aim was to build a better understanding so as to achieve mutual benefits by way of providing a clear future direction.[14] Nitya, however, did not mention the exercise of the CEO-ambassador system as part of his government's ethical diplomacy.

The CEO-ambassador was not the only Thaksin legacy that was abandoned by the military junta. Yet, throughout its rule of thirteen months, the Surayud government was never clear about which of Thaksin's foreign policy initiatives should be maintained. In his speech at the Foreign Correspondents' Club of Thailand in November 2006, Surayud revealed his diplomatic standpoint, highlighting the need to solidify his country's relationship with ASEAN members as well as with the international community. He omitted Thaksin's grand acronyms in his speech, including the ACD and the ACMECS.[15] He even watered down the enthusiasm for the FTAs, raising the importance of the concept of "sufficiency economy", which was the brainchild of the King. In the sufficiency economy, Surayud saw a philosophy of balancing essential economic elements with the way the Thais conducted their daily lives. But he insisted that his government's adoption of such a concept would not necessarily turn Thailand economically inward. Time and again, Surayud wanted to distance his government from the past Thaksin regime which celebrated aggressive business practices and thus blatantly ignored the royal concept.

Despite dressing itself in an ethical guise, the Surayud government was not free from criticism and diplomatic pretension. First, the so-called ethical diplomacy was never clearly defined. It was ironic that the military government seizing power in the most unethical manner would care to construct an ethical diplomacy. As in the Thaksin period, Surayud's moral foreign policy looked impressive but lacked substance. Its supposed pro-democracy stance failed to change in the country's position toward Myanmar. His government was criticized for helping Myanmar withstand increased international condemnation and its worsening human rights situation which was debated by the United Nations Security Council.[16] In the aftermath of the state crackdown on pro-democracy protesters on the streets of Yangon in September 2007, Surayud was mute on the crisis in this neighbouring country, a position in absolute contrast to that when he served as an army commander from 1998 to 2003.[17] On the part of the Foreign Ministry, Thai policy toward Myanmar remained status quo. Kavi Chongkittavorn stated that the reasons why Thailand has walked its cats backwards could be because of unfinished business deals and other concessions which involve some powerful Thai politicians from the previous government who still have a strong connection inside the Foreign Ministry. "These people do not want to abandon the pro-Burmese policy and their concessions", Kavi wrote.[18] In defending itself, the Foreign Ministry asserted that the period of the interim administration offered Thais an opportunity to reflect on what was best for the country. A Foreign Ministry official noted, "Some say it is a period for 'soul-searching' in connection with the country's domestic agenda."[19] Thus, a silent foreign policy was considered part of the soul-searching by the military-backed Surayud government.

Two years after leaving the premiership, in January 2010, the perceived ethical Surayud became the target of the red-shirt members who protested over his alleged illegal land ownership on the Khao Yai Thiang mountain in Sikhieu district of Nakhon Ratchasima. They red-shirts also complained about the practice of a double standard endured by the current Abhisit government by not taking legal action against the Privy Councilor's possession of forest reserve land.[20]

SAMAK SUNDARAVEJ: AN ERRATIC APPROACH

Samak led a new political entity, the People's Power Party (PPP), a reincarnation of the Thai Rak Thai Party that was disbanded because some of its members were charged with electoral fraud. Samak was a self-proclaimed puppet of Thaksin. His PPP won the post-coup election comfortably and formed the government in late January 2008. Samak, known for his sharp tongue, was a veteran politician, former Bangkok governor, and possessed a personal connection with the palace. However, the fact that he was Thaksin's political nominee provoked the anti-Thaksin PAD to stage a months-long campaign against his government. In this process, the PAD sought to discredit his government's foreign policy to the detrimental extent of inciting conflicts with neighbouring countries.

The Preah Vihear Temple

The dispute between Thailand and Cambodia over the area surrounding the Preah Vihear Temple, known in Thai as *Phra Viharn*, was purposely intensified by the anti-government agents. Thailand lost the Preah Vihear Temple to Cambodia in 1962 after both countries took their overlapping claim to the International Court of Justice (ICJ). The issue had been dormant for over forty years but was revitalized by the self-nominated nationalist PAD who took advantage of the dispute in its attempt to remove the government from power. Earlier, the Samak government agreed to endorse the Cambodian request to the United Nations Educational, Scientific and Cultural Organisation (UNESCO) to have the temple listed as a "World Heritage" site. Foreign Minister Noppadon Patama, former personal lawyer of Thaksin, went on to conclude a Joint Communiqué with Cambodia's Deputy Prime Minister Sok An in Paris on 22 May 2008, reaffirming full Thai support for the inscription of the Preah Vihear Temple on the World Heritage list. Upon returning home, Noppadon was greeted by furious PAD nationalists at Bangkok International Airport. They called him a traitor. The PAD claimed that the government ceded 4.6 square kilometres of disputed land near the temple to Cambodia in exchange for business concessions for Thaksin.[21] The PAD's nationalistic rhetoric, employed to hurt the image of the government, also severely impaired diplomatic ties between Thailand and Cambodia and opened the wounds of mutual hatred between the people of the two countries.

Samak's foreign policy toward Cambodia followed in the footsteps of Thaksin: forging personal ties with the Cambodian leaders while encouraging more Thai investments in the country. Samak chose to pay an official visit to Cambodia, on 3–4 March 2008, the first country after his government was formed. But Samak's overt enthusiasm about strengthening ties with Cambodia was ill-received by his political opponents. His visit to Phnom Penh was widely publicized by the PAD as a preparation for possible business deals between Thaksin and Cambodian leaders. This was coupled with a number of cases involving the transfer of government bureaucrats in charge of Cambodian issues without good explanation, including the transfer of the secretary-general of the National Security Council and the director-general of the Department of Treaties and Legal Affairs of the Ministry of Foreign Affairs. On 14 May 2008, Foreign Minister Noppadon and Somchai Wongsawat, Deputy Prime Minister and Thaksin's brother-in-law, were invited to preside alongside Cambodia's Hun Sen over the opening ceremony of the newly renovated 152-kilometre National Highway 48 and a 1,560-metre concrete bridge. The road was built with Bt1 billion in financial assistance from Thailand that was initially designated to facilitate the transport of goods from Cambodia to Laem Chabang port in Chonburi through Trat. During this visit, Noppadon admitted to have met with Cambodian Deputy Prime Minister Sok An and discussed the development of a joint management plan for the Preah Vihear Temple.[22]

As the PAD continued to fan the flame of nationalism against the government, the Administration Court stepped in and ruled that Noppadon's Joint Communiqué with Cambodia was unconstitutional because it was not given parliamentary approval as required under section 190 of the Constitution.[23] Meanwhile, Sondhi Limthongkul, one of the core leaders of the PAD, proposed a radical solution to the conflict. He said,

> A commission must be set up to invite Cambodia to bilateral negotiations. If the dispute cannot be settled, Thailand would, temporarily adhering to the ICJ's ruling, mobilise Thai troops, push Cambodians back from Thai territory, and formally inform Cambodia that, apart from the Preah Vihear temple, the surroundings belong to Thailand, and Thailand would pay any price to protect its sovereignty, even at the cost of war.[24]

Put under tremendous pressure, Noppadon resigned on 10 July 2008 from the position of Foreign Minister. His resignation did not end the Thai-Cambodian conflict. Indeed, it marked the beginning of a new surge in their mutual antagonism. The bilateral dispute became more violent as it was blown out of proportion and control was lost.

The Southern Fire

Samak showed little interest in tackling the conflict in the restive south. It took him three months after becoming prime minister to visit the southern provinces. Samak started badly by reiterating Thaksin's initial claim that deaths at Tak Bai were accidental, caused by weakness due to fasting. Throughout his premiership, he made only few comments on the topic and handed matters over to army chief General Anupong Paojinda.[25] In March 2008, Samak visited Indonesia as part of his introductory tour and held talks with

President Susilo Bambang Yudhoyono. Because Indonesia was the world's largest Muslim-populated country, Samak reckoned that its stance on the unrest in southern Thailand would have an influence on the opinions of members of the OIC. Yudhoyono, in response, told Samak that he was willing to help explain to other Muslim countries the nature of the violence in Thailand's southern provinces, and to give them a better understanding of the situation.[26] One month later, Samak made an official visit to Malaysia. Among other issues, Samak sought to increase mutual understanding of the Muslim issue in Thailand, and to strengthen bilateral relations that had recovered during the Surayad administration. Prior to his visit to Kuala Lumpur, reports surfaced that he would consider asking his counterpart for the repatriation of five suspected secessionists held captive in Malaysia. Given the political situation in Malaysia at the time and the kind of dilemma facing Abdullah Badawi, Samak's request would have been untimely and inappropriate. He was forewarned of the sensitivities involving the issue, especially with Thailand having to seriously study the demands of the Muslim insurgent, and with Malaysia needing to identify with Malay problems in the Thai south or it would lose ground to the Parti Islam Se-Malaysia (PAS). Discreet diplomacy was therefore preferred.[27] In the end, Abdullah reassured Samak of his close cooperation and support both bilaterally and in the OIC.

It seemed that the main impediment in tackling the southern crisis was in fact caused by the Samak government's erratic policy. The inconsistency of Thai policy regarding the south further complicated the nature of the problem. Interior Minister Chalerm Yoobamrung said that his government was considering granting some degree of self-rule to Muslim-majority provinces that had long been hit by bloody insurgency unrest. "I want to reaffirm that autonomy is possible," Chalerm emphasized.[28] The next day, Samak wrote off Chalerm's proposal, saying that it could be dangerous and could get out of hand. But Samak himself was not short of controversy. Before his trip to Indonesia, Samak blamed foreign militants for instigating the insurgency movement in the southern provinces, another interpretation of the crisis which strongly opposed the previous Thai position that saw insurgency as a home-grown problem. Samak said, "Other people are staging attacks on our soil. We have concluded that our people are not doing this kind of thing. But I don't want you (media) to say anything about

Indonesia and the Philippines. We must preserve good relations. Let me visit the region first and I will tell you more later."[29] Just as the government appeared to endorse a renewed approach in dealing with the insurgents by keeping a channel of communication open, it changed its position in a matter of weeks. Samak subsequently ruled out peace talks with the southern rebels. In reality, both Surayud and Samak were equivocal about negotiating with southern insurgents. Such mixed signals confounded and worried its Islamic neighbours about the unbalanced Thai policy toward peace-making in the troubling south.

Return of a Thaksinized Diplomacy

Samak and his Foreign Minister Noppadon breathed some life into Thaksin's foreign policy. In March 2008, the Samak government announced its foreign policy in Parliament. The draft portions of its foreign policy initiatives were a rehash of those under the two previous Thaksin governments. The Foreign Ministry was instructed to expand its efforts, with the help of the Commerce Ministry, to research and identify new markets for Thai exports. The country's priority was to rehabilitate the sagging economy caused by ongoing political wrangling and to increase confidence in trade and investment. It was clear that Thailand's relations with neighbouring countries followed a similar pattern to the diplomatic and economic engagement as was practised by Thaksin from 2001 to 2006.[30] While Samak was Thaksin's nominee in the way he became prime minister, Noppadon was Thaksin's close aide. Noppadon, in particular, had a tendency to act on Thaksin's behalf while he was seeking refuge abroad. The PAD argued that maintaining Thaksin's business interests in neighbouring states was indeed a major foreign policy agenda of Noppadon. The PAD said, "Thaksin put Noppadon in the Foreign Ministry for a reason".[31] The Foreign Ministry was once again dragged into the circle of political combat. Thai diplomats were wary of the possibility in which Noppadon mixed his own agenda with national interests. Local media posed two crucial questions: with foreign affairs in the hands of Noppadon, would the entire direction of foreign policy be driven by Thaksin in exile?[32] And, could Noppadon show in sustained and tangible ways that he was the spokesperson of Thai foreign policy, not Thaksin's personal policy? As a way of answering the questions, Noppadon, after assuming the Foreign Ministry portfolio, immediately returned a diplomatic passport to Thaksin, revoked during the Surayud administration. This, to a certain extent, helped vindicate the corruption allegations against Thaksin and his family members.

What followed was the glorification of some of Thaksin's old policies toward neighbours in the region. Thailand under Samak and Noppadon reconciled with Singapore after a year of estranged relations that had been affected by Thai domestic politics. Singapore, once the target of attack of the PAD in the aftermath of the Shin-Temasek deal, was known to have had close relations with Thaksin. The coup-makers accused Singapore of eavesdropping on the army's conversations, as a consequence of the sale of Shin Corp's telecommunication assets to Temasek. The rapprochement with Singapore during the Samak administration was meant to reject such allegations on behalf of Thaksin. Samak visited the city state on 19 March 2008. The foremost outcome was the resumption of two cooperation programmes: the Thailand-Singapore Civil Service Exchange Programme and the Singapore-Thailand Enhanced Economic Relationship. Noppadon, a few weeks earlier, gave an interview to the *Straits Times*, "My feeling is we should not allow internal politics to affect our international relations with other countries. That's how I see what happened, and it affected Thailand's stature in the international community and jeopardized our economic, social and political opportunities in the world."[33]

The most striking resemblance among the three men, Thaksin, Samak and Noppadon, concerning their views on regional affairs, was their identical foreign policy toward Myanmar. Promotion of democracy never made it to the top of Samak's foreign policy agenda. This can be easily explained considering Thaksin's existing economic interests in Myanmar. Noppadon did not hesitate to manipulate the sacred principle of "non-intervention" institutionalized by ASEAN and apply it to his Myanmar policy. He told reporters in February 2008 that democracy in Myanmar was "an internal affair". He said, "We are not a headmaster who can tell Myanmar what they should do. We have to respect their sovereignty."[34] On 14 March 2008, Samak paid a visit to Naypyidaw for the first time as prime minister. He held discussions with Chairman of the SPDC, General Than Shwe, and Prime Minister Thien Sein. The talking point was on boosting cooperation in natural gas and hydropower resources. Samak insisted that he would not raise the issue of democracy and minorities.[35] Some Western governments hoped that Samak's newly elected government would put across its critical view to the leaders in Naypyidaw on democratization especially after the army's crackdown on the pro-democracy demonstrators in September 2007. This would help recover Thailand's democratic image in the wake of the military coup. They were left disappointed. In late April 2008, Thien Sein accepted Thailand's invitation to visit Bangkok, apparently for the purpose of strengthening business ties. On this occasion, Samak made a number of controversial statements. First, he said that Thailand opposed Western sanctions on Myanmar. Second, that Thailand had not attempted to pressure Myanmar to move towards democracy. His government viewed such action as interference in Myanmar's internal affairs. Third, Samak approved the continued house arrest of Suu Kyi. He remarked, "They are not releasing her, but they will not interfere with her. They will put her on the shelf and not bother with her, which is unacceptable to foreigners. We think it is okay if she is put on the shelf, but others admire her because of it."[36] Analytically, Samak supported the Myanmar regime possibly because he was naturally sympathetic to the junta, but for somewhat different reasons to Thaksin. As an ultra-rightist conservative, Samak sided with authority, respected military might, and despised human rights perspectives. This however produced the same outcome — a Thai policy that piggybacked the junta. The bilateral relationship had the potential to worsen the situation in Myanmar. In addition, with Samak's support, the Myanmar military junta could feel ever more confident of its ability to overcome international sanctions.

Staying in power a little over seven months, Samak hardly had time or energy to develop a defined foreign policy. Thailand, from July 2008 onwards, assumed the chairmanship of ASEAN. Yet, under Samak's fragile government, Thailand's political illness thwarted its ASEAN leadership. The years 2008 and 2009 were special for both ASEAN and Thailand. It was the period in which the ASEAN charter was to be ratified and implemented. Thailand had its chief at the ASEAN Secretariat, Surin Pitsuwan. There were many opportunities through which Thai leadership could be exercised and recognized, such as stepping up its initiative in responding to the global financial crisis which reached its peak in 2008.[37] But ASEAN, under Samak, operated on autopilot and was beseiged by the Thai political crisis. Domestically, Samak encountered a series of mass protests which culminated in the seizure of Government House by the PAD in August 2008. In terms of overall foreign policy, Samak emulated Thaksin's diplomatic strategy which aimed at enlarging Thailand's influence over the neighbouring countries. By dint of his close connection with Thaksin, Samak's foreign policy was heavily condemned by the anti-Thaksin coalition for lacking in transparency. Exactly because Samak's foreign policy was essentially business-focused, this allowed the PAD and the opposition party to question its accountability and inflame the issue of continued conflicts of interest. The Foreign Ministry had drifted into the mainstream of the political war. A significant change in foreign policy, from ethical diplomacy back to mercantilism, set great hurdles for the Thai officials in terms of having to remodel a policy platform to match different political environments.

Samak was ordered to resign from the premiership on the grounds that he violated Article 267 of the military-drafted Constitution of 2007 which prohibits Cabinet members from holding any position in a partnership, a company or an organization carrying out business with a view to sharing profit or income, or from being an employee of a person or company. Samak was found guilty because he hosted a culinary television show after he had assumed office in late January 2007. Although his resignation was not directly brought about by the months-long demonstrations spearheaded by the PAD, they were likely to have influenced the decision of the Constitutional Court in disqualifying Samak's premiership on a seemingly insignificant charge. The pro-Thaksin movement condemned the politicization of the Constitutional Court and its perceived representation as the voice of the royalists.[38]

Samak passed away on 24 November 2009 of liver cancer, at the age of seventy-four.

SOMCHAI WONGSAWAT: SAY HELLO, WAVE GOODBYE

The PPP, holding the majority of the Lower House, nominated Somchai Wongsawat to replace Samak. Somchai was another controversial figure being Thaksin's brother-in-law. He married Yaowapha who is Thaksin's younger sister. The Somchai government ruled a disconcerted Thailand for just over two months (18 September–2 December 2008) and had to fight the political storm stirred up by the PAD. During this period, Somchai's devotion was purely on securing his political survival. There were no new diplomatic activities. Foreign policy was virtually ignored. He appointed Sompong Amornwiwat to oversee foreign affairs despite the fact that the latter had little experience in diplomacy.[39]

In his policy statement of the council of ministers delivered at the National Assembly on 7 October 2008, Somchai pronounced the essence of his foreign policy. It aimed at strengthening friendly relations with countries in the region, particularly neighbouring countries and ASEAN. It sought to promote cooperation in support of Thailand's efforts to resolve the situation of the southern border provinces. The Somchai government also ensured that Thailand would play a constructive role in international organizations, in particular the United Nations. At the same time, it would work to enhance confidence in Thailand on the world stage and cultivate people-to-people contact with foreign countries. Protection of Thai nationals and Thai workers abroad and of their interests also remained a priority.[40] But like Samak, Somchai was caught up in the midst of a political face-off with the PAD whose leaders accused him of being another proxy of Thaksin. His ten weeks as prime minister were engulfed by a long political battle with the anti-government protesters who continued to occupy the Government House. On 7 October 2008, they blocked the Parliament entrances to prevent Somchai and his Cabinet from delivering policy statements. This led to a brutal head-on collision between the demonstrators and the police force which resulting in the death of two members of the PAD. But the crisis reached its apex when the PAD seized Suvarnabhumi International Airport from 25 November to 3 December 2008, an operation which cost the Airports of Thailand more than Bt350 million in losses, and in addition to this, there was a Bt500 million loss per day for Thai Airways International (THAI). ACM Narongsak Sangkhapong, the acting president of THAI, stated that the airline's cargo department lost Bt438 million per day while the catering department suffered a loss of Bt10 million per day.[41] Somchai met with the same fate as Samak when the Constitutional Court dissolved his PPP on the charge of vote-buying committed by one of its members, Yongyuth Tiyapairat. He was accordingly forced to resign from the premiership on 2 December 2008. The court also prohibited him and the PPP's executive members from politics for five years.

In reassessing Somchai's foreign policy direction, it was apparent that he stressed the obligations Thailand had with the outside world. But Thailand's performance as the chair of ASEAN was far from being efficient or sufficient. Foreign Minister Sompong flew to New York in September 2008 to chair an informal meeting of ASEAN ministers. He was expected, after having assumed the post of foreign minister ten days before, to lead discussions about ASEAN restructuring and the preparation of its summit that was due, at the time, to take place in December 2008. But the collapse of the Somchai government resulted in the postponement of the ASEAN Summit until the arrival of the new government. Apart from the ASEAN issue, Somchai was heavily beleaguered by the ongoing Preah Vihear Temple dispute between Thailand and Cambodia that had been intensified by the PAD. As a chair of ASEAN, Thailand refused to allow ASEAN to referee its conflict with Cambodia despite the existence of the provisions on bilateral dispute settlements as indicated in the ASEAN charter. Foreign Minister Sompong told U.N. Secretary-General Ban Ki-moon in New York that Thailand and Cambodia would settle the matter on a bilateral basis.[42] To be fair to Somchai, he might not be responsible for Thailand's failure to use the new and untested, and at that point unratified, charter provisions for ASEAN dispute resolution since there was no reason to believe that any other recent Thai governments, including the present one, would be willing to go down a route that could be readily portrayed by political enemies as undermining national sovereignty. Meanwhile, a spirit of Thaksin's foreign policy was rekindled. Sompong strongly supported the third summit of ACMECS, held in Hanoi, Vietnam, on 4–7 November 2008, reaffirming the Thai commitment to its less developed neighbours through financial and technical assistance. Keeping up appearances, Prime Minister Somchai broke away from the tumultuous politics at home and flew to Lima, Peru, to participate in the Asia-Pacific Economic Cooperation (APEC) Summit on 22–23 November 2008. Somchai took this opportunity to pay an official visit to Peru where he explored a possible bilateral FTA with his counterpart — a move that also reflected the legacy that Thaksin left behind.[43]

The political crisis was no longer limited within the domestic realm. It had far-reaching implications on Thailand's foreign affairs. The role of the Foreign Ministry was crucial particularly following the closure of Thailand's airports. Some U.S. congressmen warned that Thailand could slip into becoming a failed state.[44] Cambodia suggested that Thailand should give up its chairmanship of ASEAN due to its prolonged turmoil.[45] Thailand might then be on par with Myanmar, whose government had been forced to relinquish its chairmanship in 2006 because of its legitimacy crisis. Unable to cope with the increasing political violence, the Somchai government decided to postpone the ASEAN Summit to March 2009. At the same time, exiled Thaksin threw Thailand into the international limelight further as he continued to manipulate politics from his base overseas. The PAD and the opposition party exploited Somchai's relation with Thaksin to disqualify his government's internal and external policy. The Foreign Ministry was tasked to repair the country's global image. But the real challenge came from the profound political division inside the Foreign Ministry. In October 2008, Kittiphong Na Ranong, Thai ambassador to Vietnam, challenged the headquarters' instruction on how to explain to foreigners in a way that would play down the fatal incident of 7 October 2008 in which the police used excessive force against PAD protesters. Kittiphong wrote in his memoir to the Foreign Ministry, "Explaining something untrue would only discredit the image of the Foreign Ministry. This will cause a long-term negative impact on other responsibilities of Thai diplomats. Trust and credibility is the most important quality of the Foreign Ministry. Without it, our diplomats will face many difficulties in achieving national interests".[46] His memoir was later leaked to the Thai media. Such deep internal division, effectively hampering the country's foreign policy, has lasted into the current period of Prime Minister Abhisit Vejjajiva.

ABHISIT VEJJAJIVA: THE FRAGILITY CONTINUES

The Thai political squabbling has continued between the royalists and the pro-Thaksin faction. This time, under Prime Minister Abhisit Vejjajiva, it has turned even more violent and bloody. Abhisit, leader of the Democrat Party which remained as the opposition throughout the Thaksin, Samak and Somchai periods, gained a parliamentary upper hand when the Constitutional Court disbanded the PPP and barred its executive members from politics. Newin Chidchob, a one-time Thaksin's ally, decided to defect from the disbanded PPP and offered support to his former rival, Abhisit, to form a new government led by the Democrat Party. His "Friends of Newin" group comprising thirty-seven elected members of parliament threw their votes behind Abhisit for the premiership, possibly under the influence of the military.[47] The Thaksin political faction and the red-shirt protesters were enraged by the new power arrangement which they believed was stage-managed by the military.[48] Forty-four-year-old Abhisit is one the youngest prime ministers Thailand has produced. He was born in Newcastle, England, and received his education from Eton School and Oxford University. He has perfect mastery of the English language and appears comfortable in putting across his views on global politics.

But his tenure as prime minister has been inundated by the incessant political conflict at home. His choice of foreign minister made his administration a vulnerable target of the pro-Thaksin supporters. He picked Kasit Piromya, former ambassador, renowned anti-Thaksin figure and sympathizer of the PAD, as foreign minister. It is an open secret within the Foreign Ministry that the relationship between the two men came to an end soon after Thaksin broke an earlier promise to promote Kasit to serve as his personal advisor after the latter returned to Thailand from his post as the ambassador to Germany. Thus, Kasit's foreign policy was coloured by his deep animosity towards Thaksin and his political proxies. In the anti-Thaksin operation and the crusade to remove Samak and Somchai from power, Kasit was a regular speaker at the PAD rallies and accused Thaksin of abusing foreign policy to enrich his companies.[49] His most controversial statement was when he referred to the PAD's seizure of Suvarnabhumi International Airport as "good fun". He said, "I enjoyed the PAD demonstration as the food and music there were good."[50] Thus, Kasit's new role as foreign minister struck a wrong chord with the pro-Thaksin faction right from the beginning. At the Foreign Ministry, Kasit took his words seriously when he earlier said that he wanted to cleanse his former office and uproot those serving the Thaksin regime once he became Foreign Minister. The *Bangkok Post* reported that Kasit was anticipating the outcome of the investigation undertaken by the National Anti-Corruption Commission (NACC) regarding four Thai Foreign

Ministry officers — Virasakdi Futrakul, Permanent Secretary; Krit Kraichitti, Director-General of the Department of Treaty and Legal Affairs; Pisanu Suvanajata, Deputy Director-General of the Department of East Asian Affairs, and; Chirdchu Raktabutr, Director of the Boundary Division, Department of Treaty and Legal Affairs — who had a hand in the unconstitutional signing of the communiqué endorsing Cambodia's successful listing of the Hindu Preah Vihear Temple as a World Heritage Site.[51] But as the verdict was later disclosed, they were spared from indictment in a corruption and negligence of duty case. Regarding the reshuffle inside the Foreign Ministry, according to the *Bangkok Post*, Kasit brought back the perceived anti-Thaksin and outspoken diplomat Kittiphong Na Ranong from Vietnam to head the East Asian Affairs Department. Virachai Palasai, a key negotiator in the Preah Vihear territorial dispute who was transferred by Noppadon from the Treaties and Legal Affairs to the International Economic Affairs Department and then moved back during the brief term of Tej Bunnag to head the legal department again, would be given more responsibility.[52] For Kasit, the Foreign Ministry's number-one priority is to protect the integrity and reverence of the royal institution. This new priority could have deepened further the political fault line in the Foreign Ministry. It is undeniable that some diplomats have been sympathetic toward Thaksin and/or the red-shirt movement. But by doing so, they have been automatically perceived as anti-monarchy.[53] Such gross categorization could increase the level of suspicion between some diplomats and the foreign minister, or even among diplomats themselves. Polarization in the Foreign Ministry has the potential to generate an impact on Thailand's foreign policy.

Setting aside Kasit's personal hurdles in his responsibility at the Foreign Ministry, Thailand has had another urgent task to complete: to rebuild the country's international credibility after the closure of Thai airports and the fatal clash between the PAD protesters and the police force. In his first few days in office, Abhisit already talked about the need to regain foreign investors' confidence in the Thai economy quickly and revive an active foreign policy which, to him, had been in hibernation for too long. His participation in the G-20 Summit in London in early April 2008 where he met and discussed with world leaders, while assuring them of the Thai political situation and available economic opportunities, provided him with an important platform to exercise his diplomacy. Prior to his London trip, Abhisit managed to organize the 14th ASEAN Summit, from 27 February to 1 March 2009, in Hua Hin, despite being threatened by the red-shirt protesters of possible interruption. The summit marked a new chapter for ASEAN following the entry into force of the ASEAN Charter in December 2008. Under the theme "ASEAN Charter for ASEAN Peoples", the Abhisit government put forward the underlining theme of ASEAN in a new era with people at the heart of cooperation. On 1 March 2009, ASEAN Heads of State and Government signed the Hua Hin Declaration on the Roadmap for an ASEAN Community (2009–2015) as a guideline for the materialization of the regional community. At the end of the meeting, Abhisit set a new date for the ASEAN+3 Summit and the East Asia Summit in April 2009, hoping that the success he achieved at Hua Hin would continue to shine in the upcoming event.

Foreign Policy Trend

Abhisit has reinstated ASEAN as the cornerstone of Thai foreign policy. Democracy and respect of human rights, long-claimed trademarks of the Democrat Party, feature prominently in Abhisit's foreign policy. Abhisit also learned from the mistakes of Thaksin, especially in turning foreign policy into a machine that promoted private interests, and in making an unrealistic and unsustainable foreign policy that focused solely on Thai domination. Abhisit once said that the prevalent corruption in the Thaksin regime severely tarnished the reputation of the country.[54] The Democrat's "Flexible Engagement Policy" could also be rekindled as it would allow Thailand to voice concern over its neighbours' problems. In fact, without any formal announcement of the return of such a policy, Thailand under Abhisit has already called for an end to Myanmar's opposition leader Aung San Suu Kyi's detention upon her term of house arrest expiring at the end of May 2009. Kasit said, "As the period for the detention is about to come to an end, we hope that there is no more detention". But the Myanmar military junta decided to try Suu Kyi on 18 May 2009, after John Yettaw, an American citizen, swam across Inya Lake to her residence in Yangon.[55] Thailand, as Chair of ASEAN, issued a statement on 19 May 2009, voicing "grave concern" over the unfolding political situation in this country. U.S. Secretary of State Hillary Clinton later came out to praise Thailand's stance on Myanmar.[56] But this new Thai position has led Thailand to face an intense reaction from Myanmar's regime. In June 2009, the Myanmar army, or the *tatmandaw*, launched a series of attacks against the Karen National Union (KNU) along the Thai-Myanmar border. The KNU territory has long been treated as a buffer zone for Thailand. The launch of attacks was indeed to create instability and extreme disorder at the border zone.

Also, Thailand's friction with Cambodia over Preah Vihear Temple, fuelled by the relentless use of Thai nationalism, has seriously challenged Abhisit's leadership skills. In fact, the Cambodian issue has hit hard at Kasit more than anyone else in the Thai Cabinet. Before he became foreign minister, Kasit himself was a master at stirring nationalism. On 14 October 2008, Kasit, the shadow deputy prime minister of the Democrat Party at the time, appeared on the televised political talk show *Khom Chut Leuk* and insulted Cambodian Prime Minister Hun Sen. He called Hun Sen a *kui*, a derogatory term meaning a tramp, a vagrant or a gangster, and believed that Hun Sen did not want good relations with Thailand. He speculated that Hun Sen was a *khikha*, or slave, of Thaksin. These disparaging terms were used against Hun Sen in order to satisfy the nationalistic need of the PAD and the Democrat Party.[57] After Kasit became foreign minister, and during the no-confidence motion against his government in March 2009, he continued to make unflattering remarks about Hun Sen. Kasit called him a *nakleng* (in this context possibly meaning a bully or ruffian). When put under diplomatic pressure, Kasit subsequently apologized. But he defended himself by saying that his terminology had been misunderstood. To him, *nakleng* could also be interpreted as tough guy, big-hearted man or sportsman.[58] This sparked widespread discontent among pro-Thaksin members of parliament. Puea Thai Party, the latest reincarnation of the Thai Rak Thai and the People's Power Party, told their parliamentarians that Kasit was not fit for the foreign affairs portfolio because he had created enemies.[59] Hun Sen responded to Kasit, asking, "What if I insult your King? What would you say if I insulted your Prime Minister and your ancestors? I'm not angry with you, but please use dignified words."[60]

Thus, Thai-Cambodian ties, obviously a flashpoint in Thai foreign relations, will continue to occupy the Abhisit government as well as the Thai Foreign Ministry. So far, the bilateral tension has shown no sign of subsiding. In late March 2009, about 100 Thai troops briefly entered contested territory near the Preah Vihear Temple. Hun Sen immediately threatened to use force to drive away the intruders. Eventually, his threat became real when the two countries' troops clashed again on 3 April 2009, leaving two Thai and two Cambodian soldiers dead and several injured.[61] This was not the first time deadly armed clashes occurred along their common border. In October 2008, Thai and Cambodian troops briefly engaged in the exchange of rifle and rocket fire as a result of their imminent territorial dispute. In May 2009, Cambodia demanded that Thailand pay more than US$2 million in compensation for damage caused by the fighting on the border the previous month.[62] The diplomatic awkwardness did not only take place at the border, Hun Sen had confronted the Thai leadership through the pages of Thai and foreign media. First, he doubted if Thailand could fulfil the obligation as ASEAN Chair because of its uncontrollable domestic situation. Later, Cambodia's government spokesman Khieu Kanharith said it would be costly and difficult for Hun Sen to attend the summit that was moved from Bangkok to Hua Hin.[63] It has also been speculated in Bangkok that Cambodia might have issued Thaksin a passport after his Thai passports, first diplomatic and second ordinary, were revoked for the second time by the Abhisit government.[64] Such speculation has remained unconfirmed.

The other thorny issue in the domain of Thai foreign relations is the Thai treatment of the Rohingya refugees. In late January 2009, the Rohingya refugees were intercepted off the coast by the Thai Royal Navy after fleeing their native Myanmar. It was alleged that the Thai military mistreated the Rohingya refugees by towing them out to sea in boats with no engines, and little or no food and water provided.[65] The allegation could reconfirm that Thailand's human rights situation is in trouble, especially looking back to Thaksin's war on drugs and his harsh measures against the Thai Muslims in the south. The Abhisit government attempted desperately to resurrect the country's reputation as a guardian of human rights. It allowed the U.N. High Commissioner for Refugees (UNHCR) and the NGOs to investigate the incident, and agreed to discuss the issue during the ASEAN Summit in Hua Hin. However, the final chairman's statement did not offer solutions specifically to the Rohingya situation. Abhisit said, "We refer to illegal migrants in the Indian Ocean since the term is wider, covering more groups of people, not only the Bengali or Rohingya people. Now the issue will be on the regional agenda. Thailand will no longer be a defendant in the eyes of the world community."[66]

The Pattaya Saga[67]

In order to prove that he was able to restore some sense of normalcy back to Thai politics and to improve the image of Thai leadership in the region, Abhisit went ahead with the hosting of the ASEAN+3 Summit and the EAS, on 10–12 April 2009 in Pattaya, Chonburi province. The red-shirt protesters threatened to disrupt the summit if Abhisit did not resign from the premiership and General Prem Tinsulanonda from the presidency of the Privy Council, a body of appointed advisors to the King.[68] Prem was accused by the red-shirt members of masterminding the military coup of September 2006. Abhisit defied the threat and assigned Deputy Prime Minister Suthep Thaugsuban to oversee the security arrangement at the Pattaya Summit. But his government failed to calm the situation and to curb the terrorist acts of the angry red-shirt protesters. They managed to intrude into the meeting venue, the Royal Cliff Beach resort, and forced the government to cancel the summit. Some ASEAN+3 leaders had to be evacuated by helicopters. The successful raid of the meeting venue brought about the question as to why the security agencies were reluctant to block the rioters. The fact that the military and the police suddenly seemed impotent in handling the red-shirts casts doubt on their alliance with the government. Witnesses reported that the military and the police sat on the fence as the red-shirts and the pro-government blue-shirts clashed. Wearing dark blue T-shirts saying "Protect the Institution (the monarchy)", members of the blue-shirts are believed to be Interior Ministry volunteers and canvassers for the Bhum Jai Thai party whose leader is Newin Chidchob. The blue-shirts have the clear objective of opposing the red-shirts and protecting the government.[69] They even used the police force to shield themselves again the red-shirts. In the aftermath of the Pattaya saga, the inability of Prime Minister Abhisit to deal with the mobs raised the question of whether he should step down. The red-shirts succeeded in ruining the image of the government and in tarnishing the country's reputation. This alone would justify Abhisit's resignation.[70] But his leadership was rebuilt in a matter of days following the violent and bloody uprising in Bangkok on the Thai New Year's Day, 13 April 2009. Despite the presence of the state of emergency, the red-shirts staged mass protests on the day, and even attempted to physically attack the prime minister and some of his Cabinet members. They virtually closed down Bangkok, destroying government properties, and clashing with local residents who felt they were affected by the red-shirts' violent demonstration. This led to at least two Bangkok residents being killed in the shootings committed by red-shirt members.[71] This time, Abhisit gave direct policy guidelines to security officers involved in the operations. Their objective, as claimed by Abhisit, was to restore peace and order, and to exercise utmost restraint and avoid any use of force. He adopted persuasion tactic and mobilized the army, while repeatedly asking demonstrators to give up and go home; and this was done through the televised media. His intention was to underscore the transparency of the operations and there were no reports of deaths committed by the security forces.

Thailand, initially having rescheduled the ASEAN+3 and the East Asia Summits to be held on 13–14 June 2009 in Phuket, had to be postponed again because, as Kasit confirmed, the new dates conflicted with the ASEAN leaders' individual engagements. A more important issue was in fact related to security concerns among leaders of the participating countries.[72] The two summits were finally organized on 23–25 October 2009 in Cha-Am and Hua Hin, ten months later than originally planned without interruption from anti-government protesters.

The Worsening Thai-Cambodian Relations[73]

In the latest twist in Thai-Cambodian relations, Prime Minister Abhisit rekindled the nationalistic impulse by requesting UNESCO to review the World Heritage status of the contentious temple when the UNESCO committee met in Spain in late June 2009. Abhisit's decision was made not long after he returned from a one-day visit to Phnom Penh, on 12 June 2009, where he met and discussed ways to alleviate the border conflict with Hun Sen. Abhisit's motives to revive Thailand's objection to UNESCO seem to have derived from two main reasons. First, Abhisit realized that his popularity had dropped significantly according to the Bangkok University poll conducted during the second week of June 2009. The poll showed that his government scored only 4.06 out of 10 after six months in office, slipping from the 5.42 points it received after one month in office.[74] To regain his government's popularity, Abhisit chose to exploit Thai patriotism through Thailand's renewed objection to the temple's status with UNESCO. Second, Thailand was in the process of holding two by-elections in Sakon Nakhon and Si Sa Ket provinces on 14 and 28 June 2009 respectively. These by-elections were crucial as they could be taken as an indicator of the level of success of the Democrat-led coalition government in winning the hearts and minds of the voters in Thaksin-dominated provinces. Abhisit might have thought that his struggle with UNESCO for the recognition of putative Thai interests could have scored him some political points. As it turned out, not only did his coalition government lose the two by-elections to the Thaksin-endorsed Puea Thai party, his objection to the listing of the Preah Vihear as a World Heritage site fuelled the flames in the already fragile Thai relations with Cambodia.

Angrily, Cambodian Foreign Minister Hor Namhong challenged the Thai objection, "Cambodia welcomes Thailand militarily, diplomatically, internationally, or through peaceful negotiations. I heard that the second Thai commander on the border put his troops on alert and I would like to tell them that Cambodian soldiers are also on alert".[75] The provocative response from Cambodia prompted Abhisit to rephrase his former statement. He later stressed that his objection against the listing of the Preah Vihear was a matter between Thailand and UNESCO, not between Thailand and Cambodia.[76] Currently, UNESCO still disregards the Thai proposal that the grounds of the disputed temple should be placed under joint Thai-Cambodian maintenance. Receiving only a cold response from UNESCO, the PAD rekindled its protests against Cambodia near the Preah Vihear temple in Si Sa Ket province on 19 September 2009. Up to 100 PAD members tried to march to the disputed area but met with unexpected resistance from Si Sa Ket villagers. The PAD protests spun out of control. As a result, the PAD demonstrators clashed with villagers and police, causing a number of casualties. The Abhisit government was forced to declare martial law after the PAD protesters broke through barricades to reach the military-controlled area. Intensifying Thailand's fragile domestic politics,

Hun Sen reciprocated to the PAD's provocation by announcing, "If they (Thais) enter again, they will be shot." He publicly ordered troops along the border to fire against civilian or military "invader enemies" who illegally entered Cambodia.[77]

In October 2009, General Chavalit Yongchaiyuth, former prime minister (November 1996–November 1997) and former army chief, agreed to take on the chairman of the opposition Puea Thai Party. By accepting this position, Chavalit seemed to declare himself the enemy of the traditional elite and the defender of Thaksin's interest. His role has so far intensified the stress in relations between Thailand and Cambodia. On 21 October 2009, Chavalit paid a one-day visit to Phnom Penh at the height of bilateral tension. The retired general's visit brought back the inflammatory remark by Hun Sen who expressed how he felt Thaksin was unfairly treated by the Thai government and that he would offer one of his luxurious mansions to receive Thaksin if the latter wanted refuge in Cambodia,[78] and would not extradite him. A few days later during the ASEAN Summit in Hua Hin, Hun Sen further provoked Thai patriots by announcing that Thaksin would be appointed as his government's economic advisor. The appointment was made official by virtue of a Royal Degree in the Cambodian capital on 4 November 2009. The fact that Cambodia's cabinet and King Sihamoni endorsed the appointment of Thaksin unveils that Hun Sen's plot, in collaboration with Thaksin in discrediting the Abhisit government, was well planned. Thaksin immediately thanked Hun Sen and accepted the offer, through his Twitter account.

The Cambodian leader carried on releasing contentious statements to disparage the Thai government and question its legitimacy. Hun Sen compared Thaksin with Nobel laureate Aung San Suu Kyi, leader of the National League for Democracy of Myanmar. He said on behalf of his wife, Bun Rany, "Though I am not Thai, I am hurt by what has happened to him. My wife even cried on learning about it and has an idea to build a home for Thaksin to come and stay honourably." Furthermore, Hun Sen also offered his support to the red-shirt protesters in Thailand. He stated, "This is just moral support from me. As one million Thai people of the red-shirt group support Thaksin, why cannot I, as a friend from afar, support Thaksin?"[79] Hun Sen's offensive move sorely raised the political temperature in Thailand and was once again inflated by the Democrat and PAD nationalists. The PAD condemned Hun

Sen for interfering in Thailand's internal affairs and impugning its judicial system. Maj-Gen Chamlong Srimuang, one of the PAD's leaders, accused Thaksin of treachery in using a neighbouring nation to push his personal political agenda in Thailand.[80] Meanwhile, the government adopted harsher diplomatic measures against Cambodia this time. On 6 November 2009, The Thai Foreign Ministry recalled its ambassador to Phnom Penh to protest against Cambodia's official appointment of Thaksin. It also decided to review all bilateral agreements with Cambodia and pull out of maritime talks, which would have covered potential rich supplies of oil and gas in a disputed area of the eastern Gulf of Thailand. Cambodia retaliated by recalling its ambassador to Bangkok and accused Bangkok of overreacting. So far, while border trade has continued as usual with no restrictions on Thais visiting Cambodia, the situation along their common border has been tense. The Thai military, exploiting the notion of national security and nationalism, has depicted a deadly scenario of a possible new round of armed clashes. It built 340 bunkers in two schools and several villages in Si Sa Ket near the site of the Preah Vihear as a sign of unease that has swept across this border town.[81]

Portraying Thailand as a nation under attack by the enemy, the Abhisit government regained some popularity due to the decisive reaction to Thaksin and Hun Sen's actions, thus demonstrating that nationalism was once again politically useful. According to the ABAC (Assumption University) Poll conducted from 25 October to 5 November 2009, Abhisit's popularity had almost tripled from 23.3 per cent in September 2009 to 68.6 per cent in the latest poll; this was due to the increase in support for the government in the aftermath of Hun Sen's attack on the Thai judicial system and the appointment of Thaksin.[82] Countering the rise of Abhisit's popularity in Thailand, Thaksin paid a visit to Cambodia on 12 November 2009 at the invitation of Hun Sen and gave a lecture to Cambodian government officials. He later travelled to Siem Reap to play golf with the Cambodian leader and met with a group of Puea Thai members and red-shirt supporters with intent to irritate the Abhisit administration. On top of this, Hun Sen deepened the degree of "awkwardness" in his relations with Thailand by arresting a 31 year-old Thai engineer, Sivarak Chutiphong, an employee of Cambodia Air Traffic Services, on the charge of spying on Thaksin for Thailand.

The Puea Thai Party has stepped up its political game and vowed to bring Sivarak home safe and sound. It took advantage of the existing frosty relations between Abhisit and Hun Sen which led to a delay in the legal process. The captive's mother, Simaluck, told the media that she was tired of Abhisit's lack of sincerity and seriousness in rescuing her son. She thus decided to seek help from the Puea Thai. Chavalit said that he was confident that Sivarak would receive a pardon from the Cambodian government if convicted, and emphasized that the Puea Thai was not trying to "steal the show" from the government.[83] Since the Puea Thai and Cambodia have joined forces in contesting Abhisit's legitimacy and his kind of nationalism, Hun Sen took every opportunity to label the Abhisit's government as his country's enemy, just like Abhisit and the PAD earlier nominated the Cambodians as Thailand's enemy. Hun Sen said, on 1 December 2009, "I am not the enemy of the Thai people. But the prime minister (Abhisit) and the foreign minister (Kasit) look down on Cambodia extremely. Cambodia will have no happiness as long as this group is in power in Thailand".[84] To intensify the political game, Hun Sen, apparently at the request of the Puea Thai, released the imprisoned Sivarak following the royal pardon granted by King Sihamoni on 11 December 2009. And the conflict between the Abhisit government and Hun Sen continues.

THAKSIN: THE GUILTY VERDICT

On 26 February 2010, in a historic anti-graft case, the majority of the nine Supreme Court judges voted to confiscate Bt46.37 billion of Thaksin's Bt76.6-billion of frozen assets. The guilty verdict undoubtedly legitimized the military coup of 2006 that ousted Thaksin's elected government. It took the Thai authorities more than three years to reach a verdict. Although the Supreme Court would return some assets back to Thaksin, especially the portion that had belonged to him and his family before his premiership, the guilty verdict failed to please his red-shirt supporters who have continued to accuse the Bangkok elites of nurturing double standard and social injustice. The Supreme Court's Criminal Division for Political Office Holders delivered seven rulings in the cases involving abuses of power by Thaksin to benefit Shin Corp; these were (1) holding shares of Shin Corp through nominees (2) conversion of telecom concession fees into excise tax (3) reduction of revenues paid to the Telephone Organisation of Thailand (TOT) for prepaid mobile-phone service (4) amendment to the mobile-phone roaming contract (5) IPStar Satellite (6) amendment of the concession contract to reduce Shin Corp's shares in Shin Satellite, and (7) the loan to Myanmar.[85]

The case of soft loans offered to Myanmar obviously shows how foreign policy was exploited in the hands of Thaksin. The Supreme Court ruled unanimously that Thaksin abused his power by providing Bt4 billion to the Myanmar government to upgrade its telecom infrastructure. Of this amount, Myanmar spent Bt600 million purchasing broadband Internet from Shin Corp and Shin Satellite then under the Shinawatra family's control. The guilty verdict was clear. Thaksin had not only executed policies that benefited his family business, but also took advantage from the country's foreign policy to accumulate personal wealth. While other corruption cases may confirm that Thailand's domestic politics have always been a vulnerable domain easily manipulated by corrupt politicians, the case of the soft loan to Myanmar testifies that foreign affairs, too, have remained a murky realm dominated by the power holders. Thaksin was not the first Thai leader who abused foreign policy for private gain. Under the Chatichai Choonhavan administration, a number of Thai politicians also exploited his "from-battlefield-to-marketplace" policy for self-aggrandisement while they interacted with the Myanmar regime.

From this perspective, Thaksin would not have been so successful in taking advantage of foreign policy had the Thai foreign policy-making process been a transparent and accountable one. In other words, as this study argues, the making of Thai foreign policy has traditionally been a closed process. This state agency, dubbed by Kusuma as a "twilight zone", created the perfect environment whereby Thaksin exercised his skills to exploit it. Most scholars agree the Foreign Ministry has all along been reluctant to expose foreign policy decision-making to greater public scrutiny. Such a mentality has led to the building of a protective wall within the ministry itself against public interference. Some Thai diplomats believe that opening themselves up to the public would cost them their control of foreign policy. Here, the core issue lies in the fact that "openness" as a concept and practice in Thai governance has remained largely overlooked. This is why "transparency" has been treated as insignificant in foreign policy formulation. Occasionally, the conduct of Thai diplomacy has been dictated by the personal motives and intentions of the leaders. Thaksin makes Thai diplomats realize that national interests may not always be the ultimate goals in Thai foreign policy.[86]

THE FOREIGN MINISTRY: WHAT NEXT?

The Foreign Ministry has undoubtedly fallen into the pit of political conflict. The current political situation sees two main opposing political factions, one that supports former Prime Minister Thaksin and the other that, to a certain extent, represents the Bangkok elite, exploiting the Foreign Ministry and using it as a tool to put their political messages across, as in the case of Noppadon and the Preah Vihear conundrum. Consequently, the Foreign Ministry has been dragged into a seemingly endless, vicious political game that has tainted its reputation deeply and diminished its relative independence in the conduct of diplomacy. To this day, the prestigious ministry remains hostage to ongoing political battles. The United Front for Democracy against Dictatorship (UDD) has in return been demanding that Foreign Minister Kasit resign because of his previous association with the PAD. The demand signifies the latest attempt by the UDD to politicize the Foreign Minister's portfolio.

In retrospect, the Foreign Ministry was able to operate independently of the public domain because it dealt directly with external affairs. But all this changed when Thaksin became prime minister and began his domination of the Foreign Ministry.[87] As a democratically elected government, it was aware of the overwhelming power of the bureaucrats, and thus sought to limit the authority of the Foreign Ministry especially on foreign policy-making. However, democratizing the Foreign Ministry and politicizing it are two separate things. Today, Thailand is entering a new international political landscape with full-blown globalization, threats of terrorism, the urge for regionalism and, now, the global economic recession which has begun in 2007. Hence, the ministry needs more than ever, a conducive political condition to deal with many of these burning issues. But it has been hamstrung by political tussles at home. The Foreign Ministry could have utilized its human resources much better. It is, however, not easy because there is a considerable number of officials who increasingly disagree with the political ideology endorsed by the current foreign minister and his government's regime. A deep political division within the walls of the ministry could be the answer as to why Thai foreign policy has reached a state of inertia. Political conflicts and internal disagreements have prevented this state agency from formulating long-term foreign policy strategies. The Foreign Ministry, therefore, is missing the opportunity to boost Thailand's image overseas by adopting a more proactive approach and assertive stance.

In this ending note, the future of the Thai Foreign Ministry, at this critical time in Thai politics, seems rather dim. Thaksin's rise to power in 2001 brought about so many promises in regard to the making of a better and more powerful Thailand in the eyes of outsiders. Through countless foreign policy initiatives, the Thais might have hoped for a glorious Thailand after their long passage with Thaksin. Yet, the flaws imbued in his foreign policy proved that Thaksin's vision of foreign affairs was troublesome. The engine that drove his foreign policy ambition occasionally sputtered, thus diminishing the credibility of Thailand's diplomacy. Unfortunately, this negative trend is likely to continue.

Notes

1. Guideline for Thai Missions Abroad on the Current Situation in Thailand, as of 21 September 2006, Ministry of Foreign Affairs of Thailand. Personal copy.
2. Ibid.
3. *Thailand: Calming the Political Turmoil*, Policy Briefing, Asia Briefing no. 82 (Bangkok and Brussels: International Crisis Group, 22 September 2008), p. 2.
4. Duncan McCargo, "Thailand: State of Anxiety", in *Southeast Asian Affairs 2008* (Singapore: Institute of Southeast Asian Studies, 2008), p. 351. Quoted in ibid., p. 9.
5. "Singapore PM Defends Shin Deal", *The Nation*, 7 October 2006.
6. Supalak Ganjanakhundee, "Retired Diplomat Nitya to Retain Foreign Policy", *The Nation*, 10 October 2006.
7. Address by General Surayud Chulanont at the Foreign Correspondents' Club of Thailand, Grand Hyatt Erawan Hotel, Bangkok, 7 November 2006. Personal copy.
8. *Phon Ngan Daan Karn Tangprathet Khong Rattaban Pol-Ek Surayud Chulanont, Tulakhom 2549–Mokkarakhom 2551* [Foreign Policy Performance of the Surayud Chulanont Government, October 2006–

January 2008], Ministry of Foreign Affairs of Thailand (Bangkok: Aroon Printing, 2008), p. 4.

9. Ibid.
10. "Thailand Gets Malaysia's Help to Develop its South", *Straits Times*, 23 August 2007.
11. Don Pathan, "Surayud Apologises for Government's Abuses in South", *The Nation*, 3 November 2006.
12. Source: The Foreign Business Act Amendment: Q&A, Ministry of Commerce, 22 January 2007.
13. Michael Doyle, "Does Thailand Want Foreign Investment?", *The Nation*, 21 September 2007. Doyle is an American attorney specializing in Thailand's business law.
14. "Foreign Minister Chaired a Meeting of Thailand's Ambassadors and Consuls-General in Neighboring Countries", *Bua Kaew* (December 2006–January 2007), p. 18.
15. Address by General Surayud Chulanont at the Foreign Correspondents' Club of Thailand, Grand Hyatt Erawan Hotel, Bangkok, 7 November 2006.
16. Kavi Chongkittavorn, "Burma: Thai Diplomacy's Biggest Travesty", *The Nation*, 4 December 2006.
17. Kavi Chongkittavorn, "Thai Diplomacy an Utter Failure over Past Year", *The Nation*, 26 November 2007.
18. Kavi, "Burma: Thai Diplomacy's Biggest Travesty".
19. Arjaree Sriratanaban, "Continuity, Opportunity for Diplomacy", *The Nation*, 10 October 2006. Arjaree is an official at the Foreign Ministry's Information Department.
20. Red Shirts End Rally at Vacation Residence of Gen Surayud, *Bernama*, 12 January 2001 <http://www.bernama.com/bernama/v5/newsworld.php?id=467788> (accessed 12 January 2010).
21. "Thai PM's Foes Throw Nationalist Temple Tantrum", *Reuters*, 25 June 2008.
22. <http://antithaksin.wordpress.com/2008/10/16/preah-vihear-for-koh-kong-and-natuaral-gasoil/> (accessed 1 April 2009).
23. Thiradej Iamsamran and Ram Indaravichit, *Thodsalak Khadi Prasat Phra Viharn: Wiwatha Guru Sudyod Haeng Thosawad* [Decoding the Phra Viharn Temple Case: Opinion of the Guru, The Best of the Decade] (Bangkok: Matichon Publishing House, 2008), pp. 62–63.
24. "Sondhi Limthongkul's Solution to the Preah Vihear Dispute", *Prachathai*, 2 August 2008 <http://www.prachatai.com/english/news.php?id=732> (accessed 29 March 2009). On 28 July 2008, Sondhi Limthongkul, leader of the PAD, took to the stage at about 9 p.m. to address the crowd rallying near Government House in Bangkok, and proposed the mentioned way-out to the crisis.

25. John Funston, *Conflict in Southern Thailand: Causes, Agents and Trajectory*, The Islam, Syari'ah and Governance Background Paper Series 2 (Melbourne: Melbourne Law School, 2008), p. 20.
26. "Thai PM on Official Visit to Indonesia", *Bernama*, 27 March 2008.
27. "Thai-Malay Ties Best Served by Diplomacy", *The Nation*, 25 April 2008.
28. "Muslim Self-rule Possible, Says Thai Minister", *Straits Times*, 13 February 2008.
29. "Foreign Militants behind Unrest in South: Thai PM", *Straits Times*, 8 March 2008.
30. Kavi Chongkittavorn, "Thaksin Doesn't Deserve That Red Passport", *The Nation*, 12 February 2008.
31. <http://antithaksin.wordpress.com/2008/10/16/preah-vihear-for-koh-kong-and-natuaral-gasoil/> (accessed 1 April 2009).
32. Kavi, "Thaksin Doesn't Deserve That Red Passport".
33. Normal Ghosh, "About that Spat with Singapore Last Year...", *Straits Times*, 7 March 2008.
34. Wai Moe, "Will Thailand Create a Friendly Burma Policy?", *The Irrawaddy*, 7 February 2008.
35. "PM Samak to Visit Myanmar for Energy Cooperation" <http://enews.mcot.net/view.php?id=3259> (accessed 17 May 2009).
36. Pavin Chachavalpongpun, "Economic Trumps Politics: Thai-Myanmar Relations", *Straits Times*, 5 May 2008.
37. K. Kesavapany, "ASEAN in Disarray?", *Straits Times*, 29 October 2008.
38. For further details, see Andrew James Harding, "A Turbulent Innovation: The Constitutional Court of Thailand 1998–2006", unpublished conference paper, 2007 <http://works. bepress.com/andrew_harding/2>.
39. Supalak Ganjanakhundee, "Sompong Faces Twins Tasks in New York", *The Nation*, 29 September 2008.
40. Policy Statement of the Council of Ministers, delivered by Prime Minister Somchai Wongsawat to the National Assembly, 7 October 2008. Personal copy.
41. "Thai Losing US$14m a Day During Airport Siege", 27 November 2008 <http://www.aviationrecord.com/Home/ArticlesPages/tabid/58/articleType/ArticleView/articleId/1645/categoryId/26/Thai-losing-US14m-a-day-during-airport-siege.aspx> (accessed 17 may 2009).
42. Amrit Rashmisrisethi, *U.N. Chief: Thai-Cambodian Conflict Resolved Bilaterally*, National News Bureau, Public Relations Department of Thailand, 30 September 2008 <http://www.thaindian.com/newsportal/thailand/un-chief-thai-cambodian-conflict-resolved-billaterally_100101687.html> (accessed 17 May 2009).

43. "Thailand and Peru Plan FTA Talks" <http://enews.mcot.net/view.php?id=7424> (accessed 17 May 2009).
44. Pavin Chachavalpongpun, "Conflict Leaves Nation's Reputation Abroad in Tatters", *Bangkok Post*, 12 December 2008.
45. "Cambodian Prime Minister Doubts Thai Ability to Chair ASEAN", *Deutsche Presse-Agentur*, 15 September 2008.
46. Prasong Visuth, "Kuen Tamnieb Torraraj" [Becoming Tyrant], *Matichon Online*, 10 October 2008 <http://www.matichon.co.th/news_detail.php?newsid=1223646263&catid=01> (accessed 7 January 2010). Kittiphong is currently Director-General of the East Asian Affairs Department, Ministry of Foreign Affairs.
47. "Some Members of Newin's Faction Present at Democrat's Press Conference", *The Nation* <http://www.nationmultimedia.com/search/read.php?newsid=30090340&keyword=friends+of+newin> (accessed 18 May 2009).
48. "Poll Point to Public Backing for Abhisit", *The Nation*, 12 January 2009. Also see Nonoy Oplas, "Killing in Thailand during the Military Crackdown", 16 April 2009 <http://funwithgovernment.blogspot.com/2009/04/killings-in-thailand-during-military.html> (accessed 18 May 2009).
49. Martin Petty, "Standoff Exposes Discontent in Foreign Ministry", *Thai Day*, 26 March 2006.
50. "Kasit: Airport Closure just Good Fun", *Bangkok Post*, 24 December 2008.
51. "Chong Por Por Chor Cheud Samak 27 Rattamontri Kadhi Khao Phra Viharn 20 Singhakhom" [NACC Charges Samak's 27 Ministers Involved in the Preah Vihear Case, 20 August], *Matichon*, 18 August 2009 (accessed from news.sanook.com website on 7 January 2010).
52. "Kasit Makes Minor Changes to Reshuffle List at the Foreign Ministry", *Bangkok Post*, 27 December 2008.
53. My discussions with a number of Thai diplomats from the ranks of First Secretary to Director-General, from January–May 2009.
54. Abhisit Vejjajiva, *Karnmuang Thai Lang Ratthapraharn* [Post-Coup Thai Politics] (Bangkok: Khor Kid Duai Khon, 2007), pp. 57–58.
55. Supalak Ganjanakhundee, "Thailand Urges Burma to End Aung San Suu Kyi's Detention", *The Nation*, 18 May 2009.
56. "U.S. Praises Thai Stance on Suu Kyi", *The Nation*, 19 May 2009.
57. See Kasit's interview at <www.youtube.com/watch?v=_UCi-mgmIDs>.
58. "Here, It's all Here in the Dictionary", *Bangkok Post*, 4 April 2009.
59. "Kasit Bears Brunt of Criticism", *Bangkok Post*, 21 March 2009.
60. "Cambodia's PM Hun Sen may Misunderstand Thai FM", *The Nation*, 31 March 2009.

61. Wassana Nanuam, Thanida Tansubhapon and Prasit Tangprasert, "Thailand Shuts Tourist Spots after Fatal Clashes", *Bangkok Post*, 4 April 2009.
62. "Cambodia Tells Thailand to Pay Border Damages", *Bangkok Post*, 12 May 2009.
63. "Cambodia likely to Miss ASEAN Summit", *Bangkok Post*, 10 January 2009.
64. "Prawit Visits Cambodia, Not Talk about Thaksin's Passport", *The Nation*, at <http://www.nationmultimedia.com/breakingnews/30101505/Prawit-visits-Cambodia-not-talk-about-Thaksin%27> (accessed 18 May 2009).
65. "The Rohingya, Thailand and ASEAN", 28 January 2009 <http://www.otherperspectives.com/2009/01/28/the-rohingya-thailand-and-asean/> (accessed 19 May 2009).
66. "14th ASEAN Summit Thailand 2009", *Hua Hin Today*, 2 March 2009.
67. For an excellent discussion of the Pattaya saga, see Michael J. Montesano, "Contextualising the Pattaya Summit Debacle: Four April Days, Four Thai Pathologies", *Contemporary Southeast Asia* 31, no. 2 (August 2009): 217–48.
68. Apart from Prem, the red-shirt protesters also requested former Prime Minister General Surayud Chulanont and Chanchai Likhitjittha to resign from the Privy Council. See "Red-Shirts Demand PM, Surayud, Chanchai to Resign", *The Nation*, 8 April 2009.
69. Piyanart Srivalo, "Newin Shows his Hand as Blue -Shirt's Boss", *The Nation*, 12 April 2009.
70. Pavin Chachavalpongpun, "Thai Power Drama Enters its Most Dangerous Stage", *The Straits Times*, 13 April 2009.
71. "Thai Police Probe Reports of Red-Shirt Death", *AFP*, 16 April 2009. Several media outlets, local and regional, also reported and confirmed the death of two Thai local residents who were shot by the red-shirt protesters.
72. "ASEAN Summit Postponed for the Second Time", *Bangkok Post*, 13 May 2009.
73. This section is taken from the author's paper on "Temple of Doom: Hysteria about the Preah Vihear Temple in the Thai Nationalist Discourse", in *Legitimacy Crisis and Conflict in Thailand*, edited by Marc Askew (Chiang Mai: Silkworm Books, 2010).
74. "Poll: Thai Coalition Government Fails Six-Month Exam," MCOT News, 22 June 2009 <http://enews.mcot.net/view.php?id=10447> (accessed 5 July 2009).
75. "Cambodia Rebukes Thailand, Cambodia Information Centre, 20 June 2009 <http://www.cambodia.org/blogs/editorials/2009/06/cambodia-rebukes-thailand.html> (accessed 8 January 2010).

76. Pradit Ruangdit and Manop Thip-Osod, "Deputy PM Gets Hun Sen Task". *Bangkok Post*, 21 June 2009).
77. "Hun Sen Orders Army to Shoot Thai Trespasses", *Agence France-Presse*, 29 September 2009.
78. Veera Prateepchaikul, "Gen Chavalit: Mediator or Divider?", *Bangkok Post*, 27 October 2009.
79. Veera Prateepchaikul, "Does Hun Sen Want to Play in our Political Sandbox?", *Bangkok Post*, 26 October 2009.
80. "PAD Condemns Hun Sen", *Bangkok Post*, 6 November 2009.
81. Marwaan Macan-Markar, "Thai-Cambodian Tension Gives Rise to Schools with Bunkers", *The Irrawaddy*, 25 November 2009.
82. The poll was conducted between 25 October and 5 November 2009, and involved 3,709 people, aged 18 and up, in 21 provinces. By region, support for the Abhisit government was 88.2 per cent in the South, 68.9 per cent in the Central, 68.8 per cent in Bangkok, 64.6 per cent in the North, and 53.1 per cent in the Northeast. See "Souring Public Support for the Government", *Bangkok Post*, 6 November 2009.
83. "Chavalit: Accused Spy will be Pardoned", *Bangkok Post*, 5 December 2009.
84. "Hun Sen Slams Abhisit, Kasit Again", *Bangkok Post*, 1 December 2009.
85. "Seven Ruling in Abuse-of-Power Cases that Benefited Shin Corp", *The Nation*, 27 February 2010.
86. Pavin Chachavalpongpun, "Little Light Penetrates Foreign Ministry's Murky Walls", *Bangkok Post*, 8 March 2010.
87. Pavin Chachavalpongpun, "A Sad State of Affairs at the Thai Foreign Ministry", *Bangkok Post*, 2 March 2009.

BIBLIOGRAPHY

Abhisit Vejjajiva. *Karnmuang Thai Lang Ratthapraharn* [Post-Coup Thai Politics]. Bangkok: Khor Kid Duai Khon, 2007.

Achara Ashayagachat. "Academics Slam PM's Foreign Policy Agenda: Thaksin Helping His Personal Ambitions". *Bangkok Post*, 30 September 2004.

_____. "Ministry Pledges to be More Responsive to External Needs". *Bangkok Post*, 16 October 2004.

_____. "Backing Sought for Surakiart: U.N. Post to be Raised during Chirac Visit". *Bangkok Post*, 17 February 2006.

_____. "New Approach to Burma, Says Noppadon". *Bangkok Post*, 26 February 2008.

Adulyasa Soonthornrojana. "The Rise of U.S.-Thai Relations, 1945–1975". Ph.D. dissertation, University of Akron, 1986.

Ahearn, Raymond J. and Wayne M. Morrison. "CRS Report for Congress: U.S.-Thailand Free Trade Agreement Negotiations". Congressional Research Service, 4 February 2005.

Ake-Aroon Auansakul. "Thailand-India FTA: The Impact So Far". *International Institute for Trade and Development*, 2007. <http://www.itd.or.th/en/node/526>. Accessed 6 December 2008.

Alagappa, Mutiah. *The National Security of Developing States: Lessons from Thailand*. Massachusetts: Auburn House Publishing Company, 1987.

Ampa Santimatanedol. "Surakiart Testifies He Opposed Burma Loan". *Bangkok Post*, 1 May 2007.

Amrit Rashmisrisethi. "U.N. Chief: Thai-Cambodian Conflict Resolved Bilaterally". National News Bureau, Public Relations Department of Thailand, 30 September 2008. <http://www.thaindian.com/newsportal/thailand/un-chief-thai-cambodian-conflict-resolved-billaterally_2100101687.html>. Accessed 17 May 2009.

Anoma Srisukkasem and Wichit Chaitrong. "Olarn Worried about Liquidity amid Global Squeeze". *The Nation*, 1 October 2008.

Anucha Paepanawan. *Exclusive: Kanmuang Ruang Khao Phra Viharn* [Exclusive: The Political Case of Khao Phra Viharn]. Bangkok: Kleung Aksorn, 2008.

Anuraj Manibhandu and Saritdet Marukatat. "Full Circle in Five Years". *Bangkok Post*, June 2002. <http://www.bangkokpost.com/midyear 2002/foreignpolicy.html>. Accessed 1 March 2009.

Anuson Chinvanno. *Thailand's Policies towards China, 1949–1954*. Oxford: St. Anthony's College, 1992.

Arjaree Sriratanaban. "Continuity, Opportunity for Diplomacy". *The Nation*, 10 October 2006.

Arnold, Wayne. "Thailand Sets Path to a Better Economy". *New York Times*, 24 October 2003.

Asda Jayanama. "Karnthood Yuk Thaksin: Thaksiplomacy" [Diplomacy in the Thaksin Era]. In *Ru Than Thaksin* [One Step ahead of Thaksin], edited by Chermsak Pinthong. Bangkok: Khor Kid Duai Khon, 2004.

Askew, Marc. *Conspiracy, Politics, and a Disorderly Border: The Struggle to Comprehend Insurgency in Thailand's Deep South*. Policy Studies 29, East-West Centre, Washington. Singapore: Institute of Southeast Asian Studies, 2007.

Baker, Chris. "Ayutthaya Rising: From Land or Sea?". *Journal of Southeast Asian Studies*, no. 42 (1993).

Ball, Desmond. "Security Development in the Thailand-Burma Borderlands". Working Paper no. 9. Sydney: Australian Mekong Resource Centre, University of Sydney, October 2003.

Batson, Benjamin. "Siam and Japan: The Perils of Independence". In *Southeast Asia Under the Japanese Occupation*, edited by Alfred W. McCoy. New Haven: Yale University Southeast Asian Studies, 1980.

Beasley, Ryan K., Juliet Kaarbo, Jeffrey S. Lantis and Michael T. Snarr, eds. *Foreign Policy in Comparative Perspective: Domestic and International Influences on State Behaviour*. Washington D.C.: CQ Press, 2001.

Bidhya Bowornwathana, "Thaksin's Model of Government Reform: Prime Ministerialization through 'a Country is my Company' Approach". *Asian Journal of Political Science* 12, no. 1 (June 2004).

Brandon, John. and Nancy Chen, eds. *Bilateral Conference on United States-Thailand Relations in the 21st Century*. Washington, D.C.: The Asia Foundation, 2002.

Busakorn Chantasasawat. "The Burgeoning Sino-Thai Relations: Seeking Sustained Economic Security". *China: An International Journal* 4, no. 1 (March 2006): 86–112.

Buszynski, Leszek. "Thailand's Foreign Policy: Management of a Regional Vision". *Asia Survey* 34, no. 8 (August 1994).

_____. "Russia and Southeast Asia: A New Relationship". *Contemporary Southeast Asia* 28, no. 2 (August 2006).

Chanda, Nayan. *Brother Enemy: The War After the War*. California: Harcourt Brace Jonanovich, 1986.

Charivat Santaputra. *Thai Foreign Policy 1932–1946*. Bangkok: Thai Khadi Research Institute, Thammasat University, 1986.

Charnvit Kasetsiri. "Thailand-Cambodia: A Love-Hate Relationship". *Kyoto Review of Southeast Asia* 3 (March 2003).

Charoen Khampiraphap. "Kor Toklong Karnkha Seri: Lod Phasee Lue Lod Atipatai" [Free Trade Agreements: Tariff Reduction or Sovereignty Reduction]. In *Kor Toklong Kedkarnkha Seri Ponkratop Ti Mee Tor Prathetthai* [Free Trade Agreements and their Impacts on Thailand], edited by Kannikar Kittivejakul. Bangkok: Pimdee Publishing, 2004.

Chockanand Bussracumpakorn. *BID: Case Study of a Design Innovation Network Model in Thailand*. Bangkok: King Mongkut's University of Technology Thonburi, 2008.

Chonticha Satyawattana, ed. *Botrian Chak Khwamroonraeng Nai Kampucha* [Lessons from Violence in Cambodia]. Bangkok: Thai-Asia Studies Centre, Thammasat University, 2003.

Chula Chakrabongse. *The Twain Have Met, or an Eastern Prince Came West*. London, 1956.

Chulacheeb Chinawanno. "Thai Views on Japan's Role in the Region". In *Thailand, Australia and the Region: Strategic Developments in Southeast Asia*, edited by Cavan Hague. Canberra: National Thai Studies Centre, Faculty of Asian Studies, Australian National University, 2002.

_____. "Thai-Chinese Relations: Security and Strategic Partnerships". RSIS Working Paper, no. 155. Singapore: S. Rajaratnam School of International Studies, 24 March 2008.

Ciorciari, John D. "Thaksin's Chance for Leading Role in the Region". *Straits Times*, 10 March 2004.

Cochrane, Joe. "An Annoying Neighbour". *Newsweek International*, 21 February 2006.

Connors, Michael K. *Ideological Aspects of Democratisation in Thailand: Mainstreaming Localism*. SEARC Working Paper Series no. 12. Hong Kong: City University of Hong Kong (2001).

_____. "Thailand and the United States of America: Beyond Hegemony". In *Bush and Asia: The US's Evolving Relationships with East Asia*, edited by Mark Beeson. London: Routledge, 2006.

Corrine Phuangkasem, *Thailand's Foreign Relations, 1964–80*. Occasional Paper No. 74. Singapore: Institute of Southeast Asian Studies, 1984.

Crispin, Shawn W. "Shooting for the Stars". *Far Eastern Economic Review*, 30 May 2002.

Croissant, Aurel. "Unrest in South Thailand: Contours, Causes and Consequences Since 2001". *Strategic Insights* 4, no. 2 (February 2005).

Daley, Matthew P. "Development in Burma, Testimony before the U.S. House International Relations Committee, Subcommittee on Asia and the Pacific and Subcommittee on International Terrorism, Non-proliferation and Human Rights". Washington D.C.: Bureau of East Asian and Pacific Affairs, 25 March 2004. <http://www.state.gov/p/eap/rls/rm/2004/30789.htm>. Accessed 7 December 2008.

"Developing an Asian Bond Market: Rationale, Concerns and Roadmap". A PECC Finance Forum Report on Institutional-Building in a World of Free and Volatile Capital Flows Stemming from the PECC Finance Forum Work 2002–04. <http://www.pecc.org/finance/papers/ff_asianbondmarket(2004).pdf>. Accessed 1 March 2009.

Direk Jayanama. *Thailand and World War II*. Chiang Mai: Silkworm Books, 2008.

Don Pathan. "Megaphone PM Tests Kantathi's Diplomacy". *The Nation*, 1 November 2005.

———. "Surayud Apologises for Government's Abuses in South". *The Nation*, 3 November 2006.

——— and Supalak Ganjanakhundee. "A Tale of Unrealised Global Ambitions". *The Nation*, 11 April 2006.

——— and Supalak Ganjanakhundee. "Thaksin's Vanishing Act: Precious Little Remains of Five Years of Foreign Policy". *The Nation*, 12 April 2006.

Doyle, Michael. "Does Thailand Want Foreign Investment?". *The Nation*, 21 September 2007.

Dyer, Gwynne. "Thaksin Shinawatra could be the Peron of Thailand". <http://www.straight.com/article-160848/gwynne-dyer-thaksin-shinawatra-could-be-peron-thailand>. Accessed 9 December 2008.

Eichenberg, Richard C. "Domestic Preferences and Foreign Policy: Cumulation and Confirmation in the Study of Public Opinion". *Mershon International Studies Review* 42, no. 1 (May 1998).

Eichengreen, Barry. "What to do with the Chiang Mai Initiative". *Asian Economic Paper*. Centre for International Development and the Massachusetts Institute of Technology 2, no. 1 (Winter 2003).

Erasey, Ashley. "Response to 'Cultural Clash: Rising China Versus Asian Democratisation". *Taiwan Journal of Democracy* 3, no. 1 (July 2007).

Evans, Grant. "Laos: Situations Analysis and Trend Assessment". Writenet Independent Analysis, United Nations High Commissioner for Refugees, Protection Information section (DIP), May 2004. http://www.unhcr.org/refworld/pdfid/40c723992.pdf>. Accessed 29 December 2009.

Fairbank, John K. and Teng Ssu-yu. "On the Ch'ing Tributary System". In *Chi'ng Administration: Three Studies*, edited by John K. Fairbank and Teng Ssu-yu. Cambridge: Harvard University Press, 1968.

Fifield, Russel H. *Southeast Asia in United States Politics*. New York: Frederick A. Praeger, 1963.

Fineman, Daniel. *A Special Relationship: The United States and Military Government in Thailand, 1947–1958*. Honolulu: University of Hawaii Press, 1997.

Forbes, Andrew D. "Thailand's Muslim Minorities: Assimilation, Secession, or Coexistence?". *Asian Survey* 22 (1982).

"Foreign Ministers' Meeting of 4 Nations on Economic Cooperation Strategy, Bangkok". *Buakaew* 19 (July–September 2003).

Four Years of Repair for All Thais and Thailand under the Government of Prime Minister Dr Thaksin Shinawatra (2001–2005). Bangkok: The Secretariat of the Cabinet Printing Office, 2004.

Friedman, George. "Foreign Policy and a President's Irrelevance". *The Straits Times*, 9 February 2008.

FTA Watch Group. *Thailand's Free Trade Agreements and Human Rights Obligations* (March 2005) <http://www.ftawatch.org/autopage1/show_page.php?t=22&s_id =3&d_id=3> Accessed 11 April 2009.

Fukuyama, Francis. *The End of History and the Last Man*. New York: Avon Books, 1992.

Fullbrook, David. "So Long U.S., Hello China, India". *Asia Times*, 4 November 2004.

Funston, John. "Thailand's Ministry of Foreign Affairs: Managing Domestic and Global Turmoil". *International Insights* 14, special issue (1998).

_____. "Thai Foreign Policy: Seeking Influence". *Southeast Asian Affairs* (1998).

_____. "Thailand's Diplomacy on Cambodia: Successes of Realpolitik". *Asian Journal of Political Science* 6, no. 1 (June 1998).

_____. "Thailand: Thaksin Fever", *Southeast Asian Affairs 2002*. Singapore: Institute of Southeast Asian Studies, 2002.

_____. *Conflict in Southern Thailand: Causes, Agents and Trajectory*, The Islam Syari'ah and Governance Background Paper Series 2. Melbourne: Melbourne Law School 2008.

_____, ed. *Divided over Thaksin: Thailand's Coup and Problematic Transition*. Singapore: Institute of Southeast Asian Studies, 2009.

Ganesan, N. "Myanmar's Foreign Relations: Reaching out to the World". In *Myanmar: Beyond Politics to Social Imperatives*, edited by Kyaw Yin Hlaing, Robert H. Taylor, and Tin Maung Maung Than. Singapore: Institute of Southeast Asian Studies, 2005.

_____. "Appraising Democratic Consolidation in Thailand under Thaksin's Thai Rak Thai Government". *Japanese Journal of Political Science 7*, no. 2 (2006).

Ghosh, Jayati. "Is Contract Farming Really the Solution for Indian Agriculture?" MacroScan, 15 May 2007. <http://www.macroscan. com/cur/May07/cur150507Indian_Agriculture.htm>. Accessed 4 January 2010.

Ghosh, Nirmal. "About that Spat with Singapore Last Year...". *Straits Times*, 7 March 2008.

_____. "Thaksin Still Holds Sway up North". *Straits Times*, 22 October 2008.

Global Partnership for Development: Thailand's Contribution to Millennium Development Goal 8. Ministry of Foreign Affairs of Thailand and United Nations Country Team in Thailand, 2005. <http://www.undg.org/ archive_docs/6597-Thailand_MDG_Goal_8_Report.pdf>. Accessed 7 April 2009.

Gundzik, Jephraim P. "Thaksin's Populist Economics Buoy Thailand". *Asia Times*, 3 August 2004.

Hall, D.G.E. *A History of Southeast Asia.* London: Macmillan, 1955.

Harding, Andrew James. "A Turbulent Innovation: the Constitutional Court of Thailand 1998–2006". Unpublished conference paper, 2007 <http://works.bepress.com/andrew_harding/2>.

Harris, Nick. "Liverpool Close on Deal with Thai PM". *The Independent*, 11 May 2004.

Heinlein, Peter. "ASEAN Nations Back Thai Foreign Minister as Next Secretary-General". *Voice of America.* 30 September 2004. <http:// payvand.com/news/04/sep/1256.html>. Accessed 13 December 2009.

Heinz, John P. et al., eds. *The Hollow Core: Private Interests in National Policy Making.* Cambridge: Harvard University Press, 1993.

Hidayat, Greenfield. "After Thaksin: The CEO State, Nationalism, and U.S. Imperialism". *The Global South* 120 (12 June 2006).

Inbaraj, Sonny. "Thailand's 'Tail' Wags ASEAN 'Dog' Over Myanmar". *Asia Times*, 10 December 2004 <http://www.atimes.com/atimes/ Southeast_Asia /FL10Ae03.html> (accessed 7 December 2008).

Jakrapob Penkair. "Khon Lahlok Diew Khan: Aek-akkarachathood CEO" [In a Different World: CEO Ambassadors]. *Phuchadkan*, 5 September 2003.

Jeerawat Na Thalang. "PM Bangs the War Drums of TRT's Triumph". *The Nation*, 2 August 2003.

Jory, Patrick. "Multiculturalism in Thailand: Cultural and Regional Resurgence in a Diverse Kingdom". *Harvard Asia-Pacific Review* 4, no. 1 (2000).

Julawadee Worasakyothin. *FTA a Year after: Does Thailand Win or Lose?"*. International Institute for Trade and Development, 2006. <http://www.itd.or.th/th/node/234>. Accessed 10 April 2009.

Kate, Daniel Ten. "Thaksin's Score Card". *Asia Sentinel*, 3 July 2007. <http://www.asiasentinel.com/index.php?option=com_content &task=view&id=563&Itemid=185>. Accessed 9 December 2008.

Kavi Chongkittavorn. "Tradition of Thailand's Foreign Policy is at Risk". *The Nation*, 21 March 2005.

_____. "Thailand Relished its New Image: Donor Country". *The Nation*, 31 October 2005.

_____. "(10+3)+(1+2)+(?+?)=Asian Identity?" Paper presented at the Fourth High-Level Conference on Asian Economic Integration: Toward an Asian Economic Community, organized by India's Research and Information System for Developing Countries and Singapore's Institute of Southeast Asian Studies, New Delhi, India, 18–19 November 2005.

_____. "Thailand has Lost its Voice and Influence on Burma". *The Nation*, 6 March 2006.

_____. "Burma: Thai Diplomacy's Biggest Travesty". *The Nation*, 4 December 2006.

_____. "Thai Diplomacy an Utter Failure over Past Year". *The Nation*, 26 November 2007.

_____. "Thaksin Doesn't Deserve that Red Passport". *The Nation*, 12 February 2008.

_____. "Big Shifts Changing the Way Foreign Policy is Made". *The Nation*, 11 August 2008.

Kesavapany, K. "ASEAN in Disarray?". *Straits Times*, 29 October 2008.

Kham Prasai Lae Kham Banyai Khong Pon Tamruad Tree Thaksin Shinawatra Nayok Ratthamontri Lem Thi Nueng [Speeches and Lectures of Police Lieutenant Colonel, Volume 1] Department of Public Relations, Bangkok, Thailand (n.d.).

Khien Theeravit, ed. *Khwamsamphan Thai-Lao Nai Saita Khong Khon Lao* [Thai-Lao Relations in Laotian Perspective]. Bangkok: Chulalongkorn University, 2001.

Kislenko, Arne. "Bending with the Wind: The Continuity and Flexibility of Thai Foreign Policy". *International Journal* (Autumn 2002).

Kitti Wasinondh. "Thai Foreign Ministry's Continuous Thread". *The Nation*, 12 April 2006.

Kobkua Sawannathat-Pian. *Nayobai Tangprathet khong Rattaban Phibun Songkhram 1938–1944* [Thai Foreign Policy under the Phibun Songkhram Government 1938–1944]. Bangkok: Thai Khadi Research Institute, Thammasat University, 1989.

_____. *Thailand's Durable Premier: Phibun through Three Decades, 1932–1957*. Kuala Lumpur: Oxford University Press, 1995.

Kratoska, Paul and Ben Batson. "Nationalism and Modernist Reform". *The Cambridge History of Southeast Asia: From C.1800 to the 1930s*, edited by Nicholas Tarling 2, part 1. Cambridge: Cambridge University Press, 1999.

Krit Garnjana-Goonchorn. "Thai-U.S. Relations in the Regional Context". *Southeast Asian Bulletin*. Centre for Strategic and International Studies (March 2008).

Koh, Priscilla. "Thailand's Myanmar Roadmap under Fire". *Asia Times*, 14 August 2003. <http://www.atimes.com/atimes/Southeast_Asia/EW14Aeoz.html>. Accessed 13 December 2009.

Kudo,Toshihiro and Fumiharu Mieno. "Trade, Foreign Investment and Myanmar's Economic Development during the Transition to an Open Economy". Institute of Developing Economies (IDE) Discussion Paper, No. 116 (August 2007).

Kurlantzick, Joshua. "China's Charm: Implications of Chinese Soft Power". *Policy Brief* 47 (June 2006).

Kusuma Snitwongse. "Thai Foreign Policy in the Global Age: Principle or Profit?". *Contemporary Southeast Asia* 23, no. 2 (August 2001).

Lach, Donald F. and Edwin J. Va Kley. *Asia in the Making of Europe: A Century of Advance* 3. Chicago: The University of Chicago Press, 1993.

Levine, David P. *Normative Political Economy: Subjective Freedom, the Market and the State*. London and New York: Routledge, 2001.

Likhit Dhiravegin. *Siam and Colonialism (1855–1909): An Analysis of Diplomatic Relations*. Bangkok: Thai Watana Panich, 1975.

Lim, P. Pui Huen. *Through the Eyes of the King: The Travels of King Chulalongkorn to Malaya*. Singapore: Institute of Southeast Asian Studies, 2009.

Lintner, Bertil. *Burma in Revolt: Opium and Insurgency Since 1948*. Chiang Mai: Silkworm Books, 2000.

Lock, Edward. "International Politics as Politics: Changing U.S. Policy Discourse". Paper Presented at the Oceanic Conference on International Studies, Australia National University, Canberra, 14–16 July 2004. <http://rspas.anu.edu.au/ir/Oceanic/OCISPapers/Lock.pdf>. Accessed 14 December 2008.

Long, Colin, Marc Askew, and William Logan. "Reshaping Vientiane in a Global Age". In *Vientiane: Transformations of a Lao Landscape*. London and New York: Routledge, 2007.

Lynch, Daniel C. *Rising China and Asian Democratisation: Socialisation to "Global Culture" in the Political Transformations of Thailand, China, and Taiwan*. Stanford: Stanford University Press, 2006.

Macridis, Roy. *Foreign Policy in World Politics*. New Jersey: Longman, 1991.

Markar, Marwaan Macan. "Thaksin's Visit to Measure Ties with US". *The Irrawaddy*, 23 May 2003.

_____. "Thai-Cambodian Tension Gives Rise to Schools with Bunkers". *The Irrawaddy*, 25 November 2009.

May, Reginald le. *The Culture of Southeast Asia: The Heritage of India*. London: George Allen & Unwin Ltd., 1956.

McCargo, Duncan. "Can Thaksin Lead Southeast Asia?". *Time*, 31 January 2005.

_____. "Network Monarchy and Legitimacy Crises in Thailand". *Pacific Review* 18, no. 4 (December 2005).

_____. "Thailand: State of Anxiety". In *Southeast Asian Affairs 2008*. Singapore: Institute of Southeast Asian Studies, 2008.

_____. "The Politics of Buddhist Identity in Thailand's Deep South: The Demise of Civil Religion?". *Journal of Southeast Asian Studies* 40, no. 1 (February 2009).

_____ and Ukrist Pathmanand. *The Thaksinisation of Thailand*. Copenhagen: Nordic Institute of Asian Studies, 2005.

McCarten, Brian. "Hmong Still Hinder Lao-Thai Links". *Asia Times*. <http://www.atimes.com/atimes/Southeast_Asia/KA21Ae02.html>. Accessed 21 April 2009.

McLean, Robert T. "Change is Slow at Turtle Bay". *American Spectator*, 18 April 2006.

Minder, Raphael. "Cambodia's Transforming Tycoon". *Financial Times*, 18 August 2008.

Ministry of Foreign Affairs of Thailand. *Karn Thood Yook Mai Hua Jai Kue Prachachon* [New-Age Diplomacy with the People at its Heart] Bangkok: Cyber Print, 2003.

Miscellaneous Articles Written for the JSS by His Late Highness Prince Damrong. Bangkok: The Siam Society, 1962.

Moe, Wai. "Will Thailand Create a Friendly Burma Policy?". *The Irrawaddy*, 7 February 2008.

Montesano, Michael J. "Contextualising the Pattaya Summit Debacle: Four April Days, Four Thai Pathologies". *Contemporary Southeast Asia*, 31, no. 2 (August 2009): 217–48.

Naing, Saw Yan. "No Freedom, No Independence". *The Irrawaddy*, 4 January 2008 <http://www.irrawaddy.org/article.php?art_id=9816> (accessed 8 February 2009).

Narine, Shaun. *Explaining ASEAN: Regionalism in Southeast Asia*. Boulder and London: Lynne Rienner Publishers, 2002.

Nathan, S. R. *Singapore's Foreign Policy: Beginnings and Future*. Singapore: MFA Diplomatic Academy, 2008.

Nelson, Michael H., ed. *Thai Politics: Global and Local Perspective*. King Prajadhipok's Institute Yearbook no. 2, 2002–2003. Nonthaburi: King Prajadhipok's Institute, 2004.

Nongnuch Singhadecha. *Pon Saehai Rairaeng Khong Karnthood Prachaniyom* [Disastrous Implications of Populist Diplomacy]. *Matichon*, 19 October 2005.

Nopporn Wong-Anan. "Temple Tantrums Stalk Thai-Cambodia Relations". *Reuters*, 20 July 2008.

Oh, Kap-Soo. "Promoting the Asian Bond Market". *Asian Bond Market: Issues and Prospects*. Basel: Bank for International Settlements, No. 30 (November 2006).

Olarn Chaipravat. *Developing the Asian Bond Market*. Singapore: Institute of Southeast Asian Studies, 2005.

Oplas, Nonoy. "Killing in Thailand during the Military Crackdown". 16 April 2009. <http://funwithgovernment.blogspot.com/2009/04/killings-in-thailand-during-military.html>. Accessed 18 May 2009.

Pachara Lochindaratn. *The Evolution of Thailand's Preferential Trading Agreements with Australia, New Zealand, Japan, China and India – The CGE Approach*, The Global Trade Analysis Project, Centre for Global Trade Analysis, Department of Agricultural Economics, Purdue University. 10 April 2008. <https://www.gtap.agecon.purdue.edu/resources/download/3726.pdf>. Accessed 26 April 2009.

Palmer, R. R. and Colton, Joel. *A History of the Modern World*. New York: Alfred A Knopf, 1965.

Pasuk Phongpaichit. "A Country is a Company, a PM is a CEO". Paper presented at the seminar on "Statesman or Manager? Image and Reality of Leadership in Southeast Asia", organized by the Bangkok Office of the Centre of Southeast Asian Studies (CSEAS), Kyoto University, Political Economy Centre, Faculty of Economics and Faculty of Political Science, Chulalongkorn University, Bangkok, Thailand, 2 April 2004.

_____. "Thailand Under Thaksin: A Regional and International Perspective". Core University Project, Centre for Southeast Asian Studies, Kyoto University, Japan, 6–8 September 2004.

_____. "Impact on JTEPA on the Bilateral Relationship between Japan and Thailand". Speech delivered at Symposium on Future of Japan-Thailand Economic Partnership on the occasion of 120th anniversary of Japan-Thailand Diplomatic Relations, 1 November 2007, Hotel New Otani, Tokyo, Japan.

_____ and Chris Baker. *Thaksin: The Business of Politics in Thailand*. Chiang Mai: Silkworm Books, 2004.

_____ and Chris Baker. *The Only Good Populist is a Rich Populist: Thaksin Shinawatra and Thailand's Democracy*. Southeast Asia Research Centre

Working Paper Series no. 36. Hong Kong: Southeast Asia Research Centre, City University of Hong Kong, 2002.

_____ and Chris Baker. "Thaksin's Populism". *Journal of Contemporary Asia* 38, no. 1 (February 2008).

Pavin Chachavalpongpun. *A Plastic Nation: The Curse of Thainess in Thai-Burmese Relations*. Lanham: University Press of America, 2005.

_____. "ASEM Forum to Boost Asian Bond Market". *The Nation*, 23 July 2003.

_____. "Thai Position toward Burma". *Alliances and the Problems of Burma/Myanmar Policy: The United States, Japan, Thailand, Australia and the European Union*. Asian Voices Seminar Series Transcript. Washington D.C.: Sasakawa Peace Foundation, 2006.

_____. "History Matters: Sticky Thai-Lao Ties". *Opinion Asia*, 26 February 2007. <http://www.opinionasia.org/HistorymattersStickyThai Laoties>. Accessed 21 April 2009.

_____. "China's Heavy Handedness in Tibet Could Have Far-Reaching Consequences for the Country". *The Nation*, 16 April 2008.

_____. "Economics Trumps Politics". *Straits Times*, 5 May 2008.

_____. "Improving Thai-Singaporean Relations at the People Level". *The Nation*, 8 July 2008.

_____. "Conflict Leaves Nation's Reputation Abroad in Tatters". *Bangkok Post*, 12 December 2008.

_____. "Thailand: Bending with the (Chinese) Wind?". Paper presented at the International Workshop on "East Asia Facing a Rising China", jointly organized by the East Asia Institute of Singapore and the Konrad Adenauer Stiftung, Singapore, 11–12 August 2008.

_____. "Neither Constructive Nor Engaging: The Debacle of ASEAN's Burma Policy". In *Between Isolation and Internationalisation: The State of Burma*, edited by Johan Lagerkvist, no. 4. Stockholm: The Swedish Institute of International Affairs, 2008.

_____. "A Sad State of Affairs at the Thai Foreign Ministry". *Bangkok Post*, 2 March 2009.

_____. "Thai Power Drama Enters its Most Dangerous Stage". *Straits Times*, 13 April 2009.

_____. "For the Hi-So and Lo-So, the 'Mo-So' is Surely a No-Go". *Bangkok Post*, 17 August 2009.

_____. "Diplomacy Under Siege: Thailand's Political Crisis and the Impact on Foreign Policy", *Contemporary Southeast Asia* 31, no. 3 (December 2009): 447–67.

_____. "Temple of Doom: Hysteria about the Preach Vihear Temple in the Thai Nationalist Discourse". In *Legitimacy Crisis and Conflict in Thailand*, edited by Marc Askew (Chiang Mai: Silkworm Books, 2010).

Petchanet Pratraungkrai. "ACMECS Cooperation: 50% Rise in Mekong Region Trade Expected". *The Nation*, 13 October 2005.

Petty, Martin. "Too Much Diplomacy for Surakiart". *International Herald Tribune*, 16 February 2006.

_____. "Standoff Exposes Discontent in Foreign Ministry". *Thai Day*, 26 March 2006.

Pheaktra, Neth. "Koh Kong to Become Second Hong Kong". *Mekong Times*, 26 May 2008.

Phochana Phichitsiri. "Litany of Woes". *The Nation*, 19 September 2007.

Phon Ngan Daan Karn Tangprathet Khong Rattaban Pol-Ek Surayud Chulanont, Tulakhom 2549–Mokkarakhom 2551 [Foreign Policy Performance of the Surayud Chulanont Government, October 2006–January 2008]. Ministry of Foreign Affairs of Thailand. Bangkok: Aroon Printing, 2008.

Pisanu Sunthraraks. "Luang Wichit Watakan: Hegemony and Literature". Ph.D. dissertation, University of Wisconsin-Madison, 1986.

Piyanart Srivalo. "Newin Shares His Hand as Blue-Shirts' Boss", *The Nation*, 9 April 2009.

Pleaw See Ngern. *Uttaprawat Badsop Thaksin Maethap Daeng* [Disreputable Biography: The Red Army Chief Thaksin]. *Thai Post*, 26 March 2009.

Postlewaite, Susan. "Real Estate Boom in Cambodia's Capital". *Business Week*, 3 June 2008.

Pranee Chantrakul. "Surakiart Peud Chai Kiewkap Karn Ronnarong Tamnaeng Laykhathikarn Sahaprachachart" [Surakiart Opens His Heart on the UNSG Campaign]. *Kaosod*, 1 March 2006.

Prasong Visuth. "Kuen Tamnieb Torrara" [Becoming Tyrant], *Matichon Online*, 10 October 2008. <http://www.matichon.com.th/news_detail. php?newsid=1223646263&catid=01>. Accessed 7 January 2010.

Prizzia, Ross. *Thailand in Transition: The Role of Oppositional Forces*. Hawaii: University of Hawaii Press, 1985.

Pronina, Lyuba. "Thailand Inks Deal for 12 Fighters", *Moscow Times*, 19 December 2005.

Puangthong Rungswasdisub. *Thailand's Response to the Cambodian Genocide*, Genocide. Working Programme Working Paper no. 12. Connecticut: Yale University, 1999.

Raman, B. "My Southeast Asia Diary I: Thai Agitation: Focus on Thaksin's Indian Visits". Paper published by Southeast Asia Analysis Group. <http://www.southasiaanalysis.org/%5Cpapers18%5Cpaper1749. html>. Accessed 27 April 2009.

Rana, Kishan S. *Asian Diplomacy: The Foreign Ministries of China, India, Japan, Singapore and Thailand*. Washington D.C.: The Johns Hopkins University Press, 2007.

Randolph, Sean. *The United States and Thailand: Alliance Dynamics, 1950–*

1985. Berkeley: Institute of Southeast Asian Studies, University of California, 1986.

Rao, P. V., ed. *India and ASEAN: Partners at Summit*. New Delhi: KW Publishers Book, 2008.

Reynolds, E. Bruce. *Thailand and Japan's Southern Advance, 1940–1945*. New York: St. Martin's Press, 1994.

———. *Thailand's Secret War: OSS, SOE and the Free Thai Underground During World War II*. California: San José State University, 2004.

Roberts, John. "Repression in Southern Thailand Fuels Diplomatic Tensions with Malaysia". *Asian Tribune*, 18 October 2005

———. "Thaksin Stokes Further Conflict in Southeast Thailand" <http://www.wsws.org/articles/2004/nov2004/thai-n26.shtml> Accessed 11 December 2008.

Rosenau, James N. *Linkage Politics*. New York: The Free Press, 1969.

Roughol, Isabelle. "1980s Thai-Lao Border Conflict Bears Resemblance to Preah Vihear". *Cambodian Daily*, 24 October 2008.

Sajin Prachason. "Thailand-US FTA: Whatever we have to sacrifice must be sacrificed, if that helps get a better deal". Focus on Global South, 26 April 2005. <http://www.bilaterals.org/article.php3?id_article=1753>. Accessed 12 December 2009.

Sarasin Viraphol. *Tribute and Profit: Sino-Siamese Trade, 1652–1853*. Cambridge: Harvard University Press, 1977.

Schmidt, Johannes Dragsbaek. "From Thaksin's Social Capitalism to Self-Sufficiency Economics in Thailand". Paper presented at the workshop "Autochthoneity or Development? Asian 'Tigers' in the World: Ten Years after the Crisis", organized by the Working Group "Transformations in the World System — Comparative Studies of Development" under EDAI (European Association of Development Research and Training Institutes) Vienna, 19–21 September 2007. <http://docs.google.com/gview?a=v&q=cache:ZFYJoQKNaDMJ:vbn.aau.dk/fbspretrieve/13639418/From_Thaksin_s_Social_Capitalism_to_Self-sufficiency_Economics_in_Thailand+thaksin+globalisation+localisation&hl=en&gl=sg>. Accessed 22 August 2009.

Severino, Rodolfo C. *Southeast Asia in Search of an ASEAN Community: Insights from the Former ASEAN Secretary-General*. Singapore: Institute of Southeast Asian Studies, 2006.

Sirin Phathanothai. *The Dragon's Pearl*. New York: Simon & Schuster, 1994.

Smith, Anthony. "Thailand's Security and the Sino-Thai Relationship". *China Brief* 5, no. 3. Washington D.C.: The Jamestown Foundation, 1 February 2005.

Somkiart Tangkitvanich. "Toon Niyom Thai Bon Naewthang Thaksinomics Lae Pontor Nayobai Karnpattana" [Thai Capitalism à la Thaksinomics and Its Impact on Development Policy]. In *Fah Daew Kan* [Same Sky]

2, no. 1 (January–March 2004). <http://www.thailandelite.com/home.php>. Accessed 11 April 2009.

Sopon Onkgara. "Secret of Thaksin's Burma Trip might be in the Skies". *The Nation*, 6 August 2006.

"Sovereignty Not for Sale", Say Thailand's Civil Society in Opposing the Government's Free Trade Agreements (FTAs). FTA Watch Group. <http://www.ftawatch.org/autopage1/show_page.php?t=21&s_id=5&d_id=5>. Accessed 12 April 2009.

Storey, Ian. "China and Vietnam's Tug of War over Laos". *China Brief* 5, no. 13. Washington D.C.: The Jamestown Foundation, 7 June 2005.

———. "A Hiatus in the Sino-Thai Special Relation". *China Brief* 6, no. 19 Washington D.C.: The Jamestown Foundation, 20 September 2006.

———. "China and Thailand: Enhancing Military-Security Ties in the 21st Century". *China Brief* 8, no. 14 Washington D.C.: The Jamestown Foundation, 3 July 2008.

Suchat Sritama. "Thailand Elite Card Holders Reassured". *The Nation*, 17 January 2009.

Suchit Bunbongkarn. "National Security and the Contemporary Political Role of the Thai Military". Paper presented at the International Conference on Thai Studies at Chulalongkorn University, Bangkok, 22–24 August 1983.

Sukhumbhand Paribatra. "From Enmity to Alignment: Thailand's Evolving Relations with China". ISIS paper no. 1. Bangkok: Institute of Security and International Studies, Chulalongkorn University, 1987.

———. *Beyond Cambodia: Some Thoughts on Southeast Asia in the 1990s*. Bangkok: Institute of Security and International Studies, Chulalongkorn University, 1989.

Sunai Phasuk. *Nayobai Tang Prathet Khong Thai: Suksa Krabuankarnkamnod Nayobai Khong Ratthaban Pon-ek Chatichai Choonhavan Tor Panha Kumphucha, Si Singhakom 1988–23 Kumphaphan 1991* [Thai Foreign Policy: A Study of Foreign Policy-making Process under the Chatichai Choonhavan Government, 4 August 1988–23 February 1991]. Bangkok: Institute of Asian Studies, 1997.

Supalak Ganjanakhundee. "Drug-Related Killing: Verify the Toll, Says Diplomat". *The Nation*, 4 March 2003.

———. "Retired Diplomat Nitya to Retain Foreign Policy". *The Nation*, 10 October 2006.

———. "Sompong Faces Twins Tasks in New York". *The Nation*, 29 September 2008.

———. "Thailand Urges Burma to End Aung San Suu Kyi's Detention". *The Nation*, 18 May 2009.

Surachia Sirikrai. "Thai-American Relations in the Laotian Crisis of 1960–1962". Ph.D. dissertation, Western Michigan University, 1979.

Surapong Jayanama. *Karn Thood Karn Muang Maichai Ruang Suantua* [Diplomacy and Politics are not Personal Issues]. Bangkok: Siam Publishing Company, 2007.

Suwinai Paranawalai. *Kaeroi Thaksinomics Kapkhwamchampen Khong Thangluekthisam* [Tracing Thaksinomics: the Necessity of the Third Option]. Bangkok: Openbooks, 2004.

Tanner John C. "Braced for Change". *Telecom Asia*, October 2004. <http://findarticles.com/p/articles/mi_m0FGI/is_10_15/ai_n 8563863/>. Accessed 21 April 2009.

Tej Bunnag. *The Provincial Administration of Siam, 1892–1995: The Ministry of the Interior under Prince Damrong Rajanubhab*. Kuala Lumpur: Oxford University Press, 1977.

Thailand: Calming the Political Turmoil, Policy Briefing, Asia Briefing no. 82. Bangkok and Brussels: International Crisis Group, 22 September 2008.

"Thailand's Free Trade Agreements and the Human Rights Obligations". Paper prepared by FTA Watch Thailand for submission to the 84th Session of the UN Human Rights Committee, March 2005. <http://www.ftawatch.org/autopage1/ show_page.php?t=22&s_id= 3&d_id=3 >. Accessed 12 April 2009.

Thak Chaloemtiarana. *Thailand: The Politics of Despotic Paternalism*. Cornell Southeast Asia Publications, 2007.

Thamsook Numnonda. *Fyn Adit* [Reconstructing the Past]. Bangkok, 1979.

Thanong Khanthong. "Thaksin and Bush are Like Two Peas in a Pod". *The Nation*, 19 November 2004.

Thiradej Iamsamran and Ram Indaravichit. *Thodsalak Khadi Prasat Phra Viharn: Wiwatha Guru Sudyod Haeng Thosawad* [Decoding the Phra Viharn Temple Case: Opinion of the Guru, The Best of the Decade]. Bangkok: Matichon Publishing House, 2008.

Thitinan Pongsudhirak. World War II and Thailand after Sixty Years". In *Legacies of World War II: South and East Asia*, edited by David Koh Wee Hock. Singapore: Institute of Southeast Asian Studies, 2007.

_____. "Mainland Southeast Asia: ASEAN and the Major Powers in East Asian Regional Order". *Regional Order in East Asia: ASEAN and Japan Perspectives*, edited by Jun Tsunekawa. NIDS Joint Research Series no. 1. Tokyo: National Institute for Defense Studies, 2007.

_____. "Thai Foreign Policy under the Thaksin Government: Out of the Box for Whom", 29 September 2004. <http://www.thaiworld. org/en/thailand_ monitor/answer.php?question_id=70>. Accessed 14 November 2008.

_____. "Thaksin Rising as Regional Leader?". *Korea Herald*, 13 April 2005.

_____. "Thaksin Bends the Wind". *ISEAS Newsletter*, no. 3. Singapore: Institute of Southeast Asian Studies, July 2005.

_____. "A Win-Win-Win Proposition for Thaksin". *The Irrawaddy*, 17 August 2005.

_____. "Singapore's Miscalculation". *Bangkok Post*, 23 January 2007.

_____. "Asia's Age of Thaksin?". *Project Syndicate*, 11 April 2005. <http://www.project-syndicate.org/commentary/pongsudhirak1>. Accessed 17 April 2009.

Thongchai Winichakul. *Siam Mapped: A History of the Geo-Body of a Nation*. Hawaii: University of Hawaii Press, 1994.

_____. "Preah Vihear Can Be Time Bomb". *The Nation*, 30 June 2008.

Udom Deth, Sok. "The Geopolitics of Cambodia during the Cold War Period". *Explorations*, vol. 9 (Spring 2009).

Ukrist Pathmanand. "The Thaksin Shinawatra Group: A Study of the Relationship between Money and Politics in Thailand". *Copenhagen Journal of Asian Studies* 13 (1998).

_____. *Thai Kap Asia: Karnmuang Toon Lae Khwammankong Yuk Lang Wikrit Setthakit* [Thailand and Asia: Politics, Capitals and Security in Post-Crisis Era]. Bangkok: Chulalongkorn University, 2003.

Usa Pichai. "Thaksin Wanted Leniency Towards Burmese Junta", *Mizzima*, 23 December 2009. <http://www.mizzima.com/news/regional/3798 -thaksin-wanted-leniency-towards-burmese-junta.html>. Accessed 2 January 2010.

Veera Prateepchaikul. "Does Hun Sen Want to Play in One Political Sandbox". *Bangkok Post*, 26 October 2009.

_____. "Gen Chavalit: Mediator or Divider?". *Bangkok Post*, 27 October 2009.

Warr, Peter. "The Economy under the Thaksin Government: Stalled Recovery". In *Divided over Thaksin*, edited by John Funston. Singapore: Institute of Southeast Asian Studies, 2009.

Wassana Nanuam. "Thaksin Set to Invest Big Time in Cambodia". *Bangkok Post*, 19 June 2008.

_____, Thanida Tansubhapon and Prasit Tangprasert. "Thailand Shuts Tourist Spots after Fatal Clashes". *Bangkok Post*, 4 April 2009.

Weatherbee, Donald E. and Emmers, Ralf. *International Relations in Southeast Asia: The Struggle for Autonomy*. Lanham: Rowman annd Littlefield Publishers Inc., 2005.

White, George W. *Nationalism and Territory: Constructing Group Identity in Southeastern Europe*. Lanham: Rowman and Littlefield Publishers Inc., 2000.

Withaya Sucharithanarugse. "Concept and the Function of ACMECS". *South Asian Survey* 13, no. 2 (2006).

Wyatt, David K. *A Short History*. New Haven: Yale University Press, 1984.

Yos Santasombat. "Power and Personality: An Anthropological Study of the Thai Political Elite". Ph.D. dissertation, University of California Berkeley, 1985.

Yusuf, Imtiyah. *Faces of Islam in Southern Thailand*. East-West Centre Washington Working Paper no. 7 (March 2007).

Zahariadis, Nikolaos. *Emotion and Manipulation in Comparative Foreign Policy*. New York: Peter Lang, forthcoming.

Zaw, Aung. "Thai, Burmese Troops Clash near Tachilek". *The Irrawaddy*, 2 January 2001.

_____. "Thaksin's Burma Blunder". *The Irrawaddy*, 6 March 2006.

_____. "The Upside-Down World of Thaksin and Hun Sen". *Bangkok Post*, 27 October 2009.

Zola, Anthony M. *Contract Farming for Exports in ACMECS: Lessons and Policy Implications*. Paper presented at the meeting on "Investment, Trade and Transport Facilitation in ACMECS", Bangkok, Thailand, 13 March 2007.

Printed and Electronic Media
Agence France-Presse (AFP)
American Spectator
Asia Sentinel
Asia Times
Asian Tribune
Associated Press (AP)
Bangkok Post
Bernama
Boston Globe
British Broadcasting Corporation (BBC)
Business Week
Cable News Network (CNN)
Cambodian Daily
Daily Digest
Deutsche Presse-Agentur
Economic Times
Financial Times
Hua Hin Today
International Herald Tribune
International Press Report
International Press Service
Japan Times
Kaosod
Korea Herald
Matichon
Mekong Times
Mizzima
Newsweek International

New Light of Myanmar
New York Times
Opinion Asia
People's Daily
Phuchadkan
Prachathai
Press Trust of India
Project Syndicate
Reuters
Straits Times
Telecom Asia
Thai Daily Digest
Thai Day
Thai Post
Thai Rath
The Economist
The Hindu
The Independent
The Irrawaddy
The Moscow Times
The Nation
Time
USA Today
Weekend Standard
Xinhua

INDEX

A

ABAC (Assumption University) Poll, 305, 314
Abhisit Vejjajiva, 128, 174, 233, 276, 280, 285, 295–306
absolute monarchy, 70, 246
ACD Ambassadorial Retreats, 100
ACD (Asia Cooperation Dialogue), 14–15, 25, 34, 39, 53, 97–110, 146, 192–93, 195, 204, 210, 212–13, 215–19, 244–45, 258–59, 267–68, 270–75, 284
  areas of cooperation, 102
  China endorsement of, 200
  in neglect, 107
  member countries, 98
  objectives, 98–99
  ownership of ACD initiative, 97, 107
  project mechanism, 99, 101
  Thaksinization of, 109
  weaknesses of, 108–109
ACD Agricultural Officials' Seminar, 102
ACD Agricultural Policies Forum, 101
ACD Energy Action Plan, 100

ACD Energy Forum, 100
ACD Ministerial Meeting, First, 97–98
ACD Ministerial Meeting, Second, 103
ACD Think-Tanks Network Meeting, 101
ACD Trade and Investment forum, 101
ACMECS (Ayeyawady-Chao Phraya-Mekong Economic Cooperation Strategy), 20, 22, 34, 51, 53, 96–97, 107, 110–24, 140, 152, 166–67, 171–72, 175, 179, 182, 192–93, 204, 213, 218–19, 244–45, 257, 267–68, 270–72, 275, 283–84, 294
  areas of cooperation, 112–13
  challenges, three levels of, 121
  hidden agenda, 122–23
  objectives, 111
  projects, 114–15
  see also ECS
ACMECS Ministerial Meeting, 122, 213
Acquisition and Cross-Servicing Agreement, 201
activism in diplomacy, 11, 50, 52

ADB (Asian Development Bank),
    113, 172
Administration Court, 287
AEC (Assets Examination
    Committee), 40–41, 283
Afghanistan, U.S. invasion of, 202
AFTA (ASEAN Free Trade Area),
    84, 127, 191
    see also EFTA; FTA
Air Asia, 240
Airports of Thailand, 293
Albar, Syed Hamid, 187
Al-Qaeda, 108, 203
Amarin Khoman, 236
ambassador, as CEO, 41, 43, 45,
    47–48, 53, 174, 219, 236, 245,
    249–50, 269, 275, 284
    see also Ministry of Foreign
    Affairs, Thailand
Anand Panyarachun, 2, 84–85,
    118, 187, 191
Angkor empire, 169
Angkor temple, and Thailand,
    175
Anglo-Siamese Treaties, 186
Annan, Kofi, 143
Annual Ambassadorial Meeting,
    117
Anocha Panjoy, 216
Anupong Paojinda, 287
APEC (Asia-Pacific Economic
    Cooperation), 26, 98, 219,
    259, 294
Apiphong Jayanama, 253
ARF (ASEAN Regional Forum),
    84–85, 191, 215
Arroyo, Gloria Macapagal, 34
ASC (Assets Scrutiny
    Committee), 253–54
Asda Jayanama, 54, 150, 214–15,
    243, 252, 254
ASEAN (Association of Southeast
    Asian Nations), 2–3, 11, 18,

    33, 45–46, 53, 57, 83, 93, 108,
    116, 121, 137, 145, 163, 167,
    189, 206–208, 220, 247, 256,
    273, 281–82, 284, 292–93, 298,
    300, 304
    Secretary-General, 165
    tagline, 192
    Thai role in, 25, 69, 82, 291, 294
    Thaksinized diplomacy with,
        190–95
    Vietnam, joins, 160
ASEAN+3, 98, 105–106, 192, 194,
    298, 301–302
ASEAN Business and Investment
    Summit, 110
ASEAN Charter, signing of, 298
ASEAN Community, 256, 279
ASEAN Economic Community,
    25
ASEAN Foreign Ministers
    Meeting, 97
ASEAN Free Trade Area, see
    AFTA
ASEAN Regional Forum, see ARF
ASEAN SARS Summit, 111
ASEAN Standing Committee, 279
ASEAN Vision 2020, 62
"Aseanize" policy, 191
ASEM (Asia-Europe Meeting), 58,
    98, 105
Asia
    Euro Bond Market in, 58, 106
    foreign reserves, 104–105
Asia-Africa Conference, 81
Asia Bond Market Development,
    100
Asia Cooperation Dialogue, see
    ACD
Asia-first policy, 2
"Asia for Asians", 16, 18, 26, 94,
    218, 258
Asia-Pacific Economic
    Cooperation, see APEC

Asian Bond Fund, 26
Asian Bond Fund II, 15
Asian Bond Market, 18, 103–106,
    155, 192, 213
"Asian Community", 97
Asian Development Bank, *see*
    ADB
Asian-Euro Bonds linkage, 58, 106
Asian financial crisis, 8, 20–21, 66,
    103–104, 212
Asian regionalism, 14, 95, 106
Asian Wall Street Journal, 209
"Asian way", 24
Askew, Marc, 188
Assets Examination Committee,
    see AEC
Assets Scrutiny Committee, *see*
    ASC
Association of Southeast Asian
    Nations, *see* ASEAN
Assumption University Poll, *see*
    ABAC
Aung San Suu Kyi, 137–38, 143,
    291, 298, 304
"authoritarian democracy", 206
authoritarianism, 2, 198, 204,
    233–34
Ayeyawady-Chao Phraya-
    Mekong Economic
    Cooperation Strategy, *see*
    ACMECS
Ayutthaya, 164, 169, 210
    dynasty, 68
    Kingdom of, 10
    period, 76
    see also Siam; Thailand

B
"Backward Engagement", 34
Badawi, Abdullah, 187, 282, 288
Bagan Cybertech, 166
Bagan Declaration, 111, 254
baht diplomacy, 119

Baker, Chris, 234, 237
balance-of-power policy, 3, 15, 74,
    76
Ball, Desmond, 166
"bamboo in the wind",
    see "bending with the wind"
Ban Ki-moon, 294
Ban Manangkhasila, policy
    planning unit, 61
Ban Pee Muang Nong, brotherly
    neighbourhood, 177, 182
Ban Phitsanulok, policy planning
    unit, 44, 61
Bandung Conference, 81
Bangkok Bank, 197
Bangkok Post, 252, 296–97
"Bangkok Process", 23, 25, 31, 36,
    53, 96, 137–43, 166, 218, 244,
    246, 273
    first meeting, 140
    personal interest in, 142
    second meeting, failure of, 141
Bangkok University, poll, 303
Banharn Silpa-archa, 8–9, 92
Bank of America, 136
battle of Hill 1428, 177
Bay of Bengal Initiative for Multi-
    Sectoral Technical and
    Economic Cooperation, *see*
    BIMSTEC
"bending with the wind",
    strategy, 5, 15, 53, 64, 72, 74,
    77–79, 82, 86, 218, 270
    change of strategy, 34–36,
        272–74
    end of, 84
Bhokin Balakula, 189
Bhum Jai Thai party, 301
Bhumibol Adulyadej, King, 27
    6th Cycle Birthday
        Anniversary, 62
BIMSTEC (Bay of Bengal
    Initiative for Multi-Sectoral

Technical and Economic
    Cooperation), 23, 85, 98, 128,
    132, 195, 213
biometric passport, 50
bird flu, 121
Black May demonstrations, 8
Blair, Tony, 148, 281
blue-shirt protestors, 301
BOI (Board of Investment),
    Thailand, 128, 211
Bounyang Vorachit, 179
British annexation of Burma, 67
Brunei, Sultan of, 172
"Bt30 Curing all" scheme, 9
Buddhist chauvinism, 185
"Building a Better Future
    Foundation", 38
Bun Rany, 304
Burma, see Myanmar
Bush, George W., 148, 200, 202,
    204–205
Buszynski, Leszek, 74, 191

C
Cambodia
    border demarcation, 170
    conflict, 83, 170, 222, 256
    corruption, 173
    nationalism, 3, 52, 175
    sister cities, 171–72
    Thailand, relations with, 12, 15,
        44, 51–52, 66, 116, 250,
        299–300, 302–306
    Thaksinized diplomacy with,
        169–76
    Vietnam invasion of, 144
Cambodia Air Traffic Services,
    305
Cambodia, Laos, Myanmar,
    Thailand, see CLMT
Cambodia, Laos, Myanmar,
    Vietnam, see CLMV

"Cambodia Shinawatra" (Cam
    Shin), 171, 270
"CamNet", 171
capital outflow, 106
capitalism, 9, 16, 31, 96, 181, 235,
    250, 269
CCP (Cambodian People's Party),
    175
Celestial Empire, 75
Central Intelligence Agency
    (CIA), 203
CEO ambassador, 41, 43, 45,
    47–48, 53, 174, 219, 236, 245,
    249–50, 269, 275, 284
    see also Ministry of Foreign
        Affairs, Thailand
CEO prime minister, 37, 53, 238,
    240
Chaiyasit Shinawatra, 243
Chalerm Yoobamrung, 288
Chamlong Srimuang, 7, 55, 305
Chao Phraya Bhanuwong, 10
Chao Phraya River, 77
Charoen Pokphand (CP), 197, 200
Chatchawed Chartsuwan, 174, 253
Chavalit Yongchaiyuth, 8–9, 11,
    83, 85, 143, 304, 306
Chiang Mai Declaration, 100
"Chiang Mai Declaration on Asia
    Bond Market Development",
    103
Chiang Mai Initiative, 37, 105–106
China
    ACD, endorsement of, 200
    Islamic insurgency, 198, 227
    Laos, relations with, 180–81
    rise of, 14–17, 83, 196, 199, 257
    Thailand, relations with, 2,
        14–17, 22, 35, 51, 57, 81, 85, 90
    Thaksinized diplomacy with,
        195–200
    Tibet, crackdown in, 16, 57

see also Sino-Thai FTA; Sino-
Thai joint military relations
Chirdchu Raktabutr, 297
Chockanand Bussracumpakorn, 45
Chongkittavorn, Kavi, 57, 87, 163,
284
Choonhavan, Chatichai, 2, 11, 27,
28, 45–46, 71–72, 82–84, 95,
97, 117, 120, 124, 163, 165,
170, 178, 243, 250–51, 253,
307
Christianity, spread of, 76–77
Chuan Leekpai, 8, 11, 23, 85,
165–66, 256
Chulacheeb Chinwanno, 57
Chulalongkorn, King, 10, 31, 77,
207
  Great King, as, 73
  reforms under, 68
Chulalongkorn University, 163
CIA (Central Intelligence
Agency), 203
Ciorciari, John, 18
CIS (Commonwealth of
Independent States), 251
  FTA with, 133
Citibank, 136
Civil Service Exchange
Programme (CSEP), 207–209
Clinton, Hillary, 299
CLMT (Cambodia, Laos,
Myanmar, Thailand), 171
CLMV (Cambodia, Laos,
Myanmar, Vietnam), 108,
116–17
CNN, 209
CNS (Council of National
Security), 278
Cobra Gold exercise, 196, 201,
207, 281
Cold War, 12–13, 21–22, 28, 35,
44, 56, 64–65, 69, 71, 73–74,

83–84, 86–87, 121, 124, 163,
181, 190–92, 196, 201, 250,
257, 266, 268, 276
  Thai diplomacy during the,
  80–82
Colombo Declaration, 154
Commonwealth of Independent
States, see CIS
communism, 12, 65, 69, 80–82,
191, 201
Communist Party of Thailand, 71,
81, 178
Communist Pathet Lao, 177
Concept Paper on Asian
(Regional) Bond Market
Development, 104
Connors, Michael K., 104, 202
Constitutional Court, 39, 292–93,
296
"Constructive Engagement
Policy", 84, 165, 220
consumerism, 13
contract farming, 122, 257
Cook, Robin, 281
Council of National Security
(CNS), 208
CP (Charoen Pokphand), 197,
200
cronyism, 249, 252
CSEP (Civil Service Exchange
Programme), 207–209
"Cultural Diplomacy", 23–24,
51–52
  see also diplomacy; foreign policy;
  "megaphone diplomacy";
  Thai diplomacy; Thaksinized
  diplomacy
Cybertech, Myanmar, 271

D
Dalai Lama, 198
dam project, Nam Theun 1, 179

Damaphong, Samoe, 7
decentralization of international
    order, 15
Declaration of the Seoul
    Information Technology (IT),
    101
Declaration on Asia Cooperation,
    100
Democrat Party, 8, 40, 107, 188,
    194, 280, 295–96, 298–99, 304
"Detroit of Asia", 236, 240
Devavongse Varoprakarn, Prince, 10
Dhanin Chearavanont, 200, 271
diplomacy
    activism in, 11, 50, 52
    baht, 119
    Cold War, 80–82
    controlled by monarchs, 70
    economic, 250
    ethical, 281–85
    people-centric, 5, 10, 48–52, 234
    populist, 42, 233–38, 243, 259,
        261
    "second track", 191
    submissive, 76
    trade, 136
    unrealistic, 241–46
    zones of, 162–64
    see also "Cultural Diplomacy";
        foreign policy; "megaphone
        diplomacy"; Ministry of
        Foreign Affairs, Thailand;
        Thai diplomacy; Thaksinized
        diplomacy
diplomats, as salesmen, 125
Doha Declaration, 154
dual-track policy, 20, 125
Dyer, Gwynne, 41

E
e-government system, 50
Early Harvest Programme, 127,
    130–31

"Early Harvest Scheme", 214
East Asia Summit (EAS), 194–95,
    298, 301–302
Economic Cooperation Strategy,
    see ECS
economic diplomacy, 250
economic imperialism, 124
economic nationalism, 30–31,
    124–25
"economy of speed", 245
e-consular system, 50
ECS (Economic Cooperation
    Strategy), 110–11, 140, 156,
    166, 171
    see also ACMECS
EFTA (European Free Trade
    Association), 128, 132
    see also AFTA; FTA
EGAT (Electricity Generating
    Authority of Thailand), 179
EMEAP (Executive's Meeting of
    East Asia Pacific Central
    Banks), 105
English Premier League football
    club, 38
Entre d'Etat des Postes et
    Telecommunications Lao, 181
Entwistle, L. Brooks, 173
Eriksson, Sven-Goren, 238
ETCF (Emerald Triangular
    Cooperative Framework),
    179
ethical diplomacy, under Surayud
    Chulanont, 281–85
Euro Bond Market, in Asia, 58,
    106
European Free Trade Association,
    see EFTA
European Union, 217–18
Executive's Meeting of East Asia
    Pacific Central Banks
    (EMEAP), 105
EXIM Bank, 41, 167

Export-Import Bank of Thailand, 239
extreme mercantilism, 241

F
Fa Ngum, Great King, 184
Falun Gong sect, 198
FBA (Foreign Business Act), 280, 283
FCCT (Foreign Correspondents' Club of Thailand), 253, 284
financial crisis of 1997, *see* Asian financial crisis
"Flexible Engagement Policy", 11, 32, 194, 298
foreign affairs, military in, 70–72
Foreign Business Act (FBA), 280, 283
Foreign Correspondents' Club of Thailand (FCCT), 253, 284
Foreign Ministry, *see* Ministry of Foreign Affairs
foreign policy, 4–6, 10–11, 13, 92–95
  advisory team, 44–46, 53
  business-oriented policy, 27–29, 164–65, 190
  classic Thai, 64–74
  corrupt practices in, 40–42, 60
  five objectives, 93
  Forward Engagement Policy, 32–34, 49, 51, 92, 94, 116, 118, 142, 151, 275
  key goals and themes, 19–36
  legitimization of, 20
  military role, 170, 222
  motivations and incentives, 36–41
  national interests, securing, 38–39
  national interests, and personal profits, 238–41, 270–72, 275
  nationalism, and, 29–32, 202,

    236–37, 266, 276, 280, *see also* nationalism *under* Thailand
  pan-Asia focus, 24–27
  performance, 268–70
  personalization of, 42–43
  post-Thaksin, 278–309
  process of, 41–52
  sustainability, 274–76
  trend, 298–301
  see also diplomacy; "Cultural Diplomacy"; "megaphone diplomacy"; Ministry of Foreign Affairs, Thailand; Shinawatra, Thaksin; Thai diplomacy; Thaksinized diplomacy
"Forward Engagement Policy", *see under* foreign policy
Framework Agreement on ASEAN-China Comprehensive Economic Cooperation, 130
Free Thai ("Seri Thai") movement, 79
Friedman, Thomas, 13
"Friends of Newin", 296
FTA (Free Trade Agreement), 13, 16, 25, 34, 37, 40, 43, 53, 96, 200, 203, 206, 210, 213, 217, 244, 271–72, 284, 294
  anti-FTA campaign, 134–35
  bilateral, 124–37
  CIS (Commonwealth of Independent States), with, 133
  contents of, 129–32
  countries involved, 127–28
  effect of, 134–36
  economic liberalization through, 125
  rationale behind, 126
  Sino-Thai FTA, 2–3, 51, 197, 199

Thai-Australian FTA, 215, 240
Thailand-India FTA, 213–15
U.S.-Thai FTA negotiation, 43
  see also AFTA; EFTA
FTA Watch, 135–36
Fujisaki, Ichiro, 211
Fukuyama, Francis, 12, 56

G
G-20 Summit, 297
GCC (Gulf Cooperation Council),
  98, 127
Generalized System of Preference
  (GSP), 133
geopolitics, 28, 66–67, 69, 122, 148,
  245
Goh Chok Tong, 207
Golden Triangle, 179, 237
Gornpot Asavinvichit, 251
Government House, 3, 5, 44–45,
  53, 235, 292–93
globalization, 9–10, 20, 31, 38, 42,
  52, 71, 85, 125, 180, 184, 235,
  237, 274, 308
  force of, 13–14
Greenberg, Maurice R., 13
Greenfeld, Liah, 124
"Green Star", communist
  organization, 177
GSP (Generalized System of
  Preference), 133
GMC (Greater Mekong
  Cooperation), 84
GMS (Greater Mekong Sub-
  region), 20, 23, 172, 176, 179
GSM (Global System Mobile), 181
Gulf Cooperation Council (GCC),
  98, 127
Gulf of Thailand, oil in, 305

H
H1N1 virus, 121
Hall, D.G.E., 67

Hambali, 203
Hidayat, Greenfield, 200
HIV/Aids, 121
Hmong refugees, 178, 183
Hor Namhong, 120, 303
Hu Jintao, 17, 181
Hua Hin Declaration, 298
Human Rights Watch, 168
Hun Sen, 170–72, 233, 280, 286,
  299–300, 302, 304–306
  Thaksin, relation with, 173–75
Hungary, loss of territories, 88

I
IBM, 7
ICJ (International Court of
  Justice), 286–87
IMF (International Monetary
  Fund), 9, 25, 50, 202, 212
India
  relations with Thailand, 14–17
  rise of, 14–17, 257
  Thaksinized diplomacy with,
    213–16
  see also Thailand-India Free
    Trade Agreement
India-Thailand Trade Negotiating
  Committee, 130
Indochina war, 170
International Conference of Asian
  Political Parties, 97
International Court of Justice
  (ICJ), 286–87
International Institute for Trade
  and Development, 134
international relations, 4
IPStar project, 143, 167, 215, 241,
  254, 271
IPStar Satellite, 307
Iraq
  Thai troops in, 202, 228
  U.S. invasion of, 202
Irrawaddy, media, 143

irredentism, 185, 188
irredentist policy, 82, 88
Islamic banks, 282
Islamic fundamentalism, 188
Isorn Pokmontri, 253

J
Jakrapob Penkair, 8, 248–49
Japan
    Thaksinized diplomacy with,
        210–13
    trade with Thailand, 211–12
Japan imperial army, 78
Japan-Thailand Economic
    Partnership Agreement, *see*
    JTEPA
Japan-Thailand Free Trade
    Agreement, 210
Japan Trade Statistics, 211
Japanese invasion, 79
Jayakumar, S., 208–209
JBC (Joint Border Commission),
    172, 221
JC (Joint Commission for Bilateral
    Cooperation), 172
JCR (Joint Cabinet Retreat), 217
Jemaah Islamiyah, 203
Joint Communiquè, 286–87
Jory, Patrick, 197
JTEPA (Japan-Thailand Economic
    Partnership Agreement), 131,
    206, 210–12
"Juan Peron of Thailand", 41
Julawadee Worasakyothin, 134

K
Kantathi Suphamongkhon, 21, 92,
    143, 149, 183, 215, 243, 251–54
    foreign minister, as, 255
Karen National Union, *see* KNU
Kasit Piromya, 29, 47, 206, 214,
    241, 296, 298–99, 308
Kaysone Phomvihane, 178

"key performance indicators", 250
Khien Theeravit, 108
Khieu Kanharith, 300
Khint Nyunt, General, 123,
    141–42, 166, 168, 232
Khmer civilization, 169
Khmer Rouge, 44
    Thai support for, 170, 173
    Khom Chut Leuk, television show,
        299
Kiat Sithi-amorn, 252
Kingdom of Ayutthaya, 10
Kislenko, Arne, 72, 270
Kittiphong Na Ranong, 295, 297
KMT (Kuomintang), 80
KNU (Karen National Union), 140
    attack on, 299
Koh Kong project, 174
Koizumi, Junichiro, 210
Korbsak Sabhavasu, 40
Korean Peninsula, crisis, 216
Korn Dabarangsi, 214
Kriangsak Chomanan, 178, 243
Krit Garnjana-Goonchorn, 28, 48,
    94
Krit Kraichitti, 297
"Krom Phra Klang" (Treasury
    Department), 10
Krue Sae Mosque incident, 185
Kublai Khan, 75
Kukrit Pramoj, M.R., 81
Kuomintang (KMT), 80
Kusuma Snitwongse, 34, 44, 307

L
Lao People's Revolutionary Party
    (LPRP), 181
Lao Shinawatra Telecom (LST),
    181, 270
Lao Telecom, 181–82
Laos
    China, relations with, 180–81
    clash with Thai culture, 183–84

joint commissions, 179
landlocked, 178, 182
largest investor in, 119, 180
loans to, 182–83
Thailand, relations with, 116
Thaksinized diplomacy with,
    177–84
Vietnam, relations with, 180–81
see also Royal Lao government;
    Thai-Lao Friendship
    Association
Laotian Civil War, 177
LDCs (less developed countries),
    22, 119, 122
Lee Hsien Loong, 207, 208, 281
Lee Kuan Yew, 2, 17, 147
Lee Kuan Yew Exchange
    Fellowship (LKYEF), 207
Lee Kuan Yew School of Public
    Policy, 209
Lert Shinawatra, 7
Levine, David, 275
liberalization policy, see "Perd
    Seri"
Likhit Dhiravegin, 73, 59
"linkage politics", 4, 55
"listening tour", 145
Liverpool, football club, 237–38
"Look East" policy, 213–14
"Look West" policy, 213–15
"lost territories", 65–66, 88
Love Song on Both Sides of the
    Mekong, drama, 184
LPRP (Lao People's
    Revolutionary Party), 181
LST (Lao Shinawatra Telecom),
    181, 270
Lynch, Daniel, 198

M
Mahathir Mohamad, 2, 17, 187,
    189

Mahbubani, Kishore, 209
Major Non-NATO Allies,
    members of, 228
Mak Tae Loke Talueng (Lucky Loser)
    film, 184
Malaysia
    Thaksinized diplomacy with,
        184–90
Manchester City, football club,
    238
Manila Pact, 81, 228
Maris Sa-ngiemphong, 8
marketplace policy, 250
Marwaan Macan Markar, 163
McCargo, Duncan, 8, 188
"megaphone diplomacy", 243
    see also "Cultural Diplomacy";
        diplomacy; foreign policy;
        Thai diplomacy;
        Thaksinized diplomacy
meritocracy, 47
"Merlion" mascot, 208
methamphetamine, 168
MGC (Mekong-Ganga
    Cooperation), 213
    member countries, 230
micro-credit lending, 20
Middle Kingdom, 75, 196
militarism, 201
military
    foreign affairs, in, 70–72
    reinvention of, 281
military coup, 11, 52, 209, 233,
    276, 278–79, 291, 301, 306
Ministry of Commerce, Thailand,
    26, 199, 289
    STF (Special Task Force), 133
Ministry of Defence, Thailand,
    244
Ministry of Education, China, 198
Ministry of Foreign Affairs of
    Laos, 184

Ministry of Foreign Affairs,
Thailand, 3, 5, 8–9, 11, 26, 33,
37, 40, 42, 53, 81–82, 94, 122,
126, 141, 175–76, 187, 218,
233, 235, 237, 243, 266, 269,
279–81, 284–86, 289–90, 292,
295–96, 300, 305, 309
ambassador role, 28
ASEAN department, 193
budget, 244
"dinosaur" organization, 10
founder of, 67–68
"junior ministers" in, 45
old guards in, 46
polarization in, 251
politicization of, 46, 251, 261, 308
radical shifts in, 246–56
recruitment process, 247
regional departments in, 246–47
reshuffle, 297
royal family, and, 70, 248
staff strength, 244–45
"twilight zone", 44, 307
versus the Prime Minister, 43–48
see also CEO ambassador;
diplomacy; foreign policy;
Royal Thai Embassy; Thai
diplomacy; Thaksinized
diplomacy
Ministry of Posts and
Telecommunications of
Cambodia, 171
Miyazawa Fund, 212
Mobile Consular Affair Project, 50
monarchy, abolition of, 78
"money politicians", 88
Mongkut, King, 10, 67, 75, 77
modernization under, 68
Myanmar, 164–69, 235
British annexation, 67
crackdown in, 16, 291
Cybertech, 271

gas exports, 120, 160
interest in, reasons for, 137
loans to, 123, 283, 307
new capital, 168
peace talks, 140
political change, steps toward,
138–39
"roadmap proposal", 138–39
trading partner, top, 166–67
Thailand, relations with, 3, 34,
42, 51, 116, 137–38, 148,
191, 290
Thaksinized diplomacy with,
164–69

N
NACC (National Anti-Corruption
Commission), 296
Najib Razak, 188
Nam Theun 1, dam project, 179
Narai, King, 76
Narongsak Sangkhapong, 293
Nation, The, 149, 254
National Anti-Corruption
Commission (NACC), 296
National Convention, 139–41
National Counter-Corruption
Commission (NCCC), 39
National Economic and Social
Development Plan, 62
National Highway, 287
national identity, 269
national interests, 38–39, 270–72
National League for Democracy,
see NLD
National Reconciliation
Commission, *see* NRC
National Security Council, 44, 50,
286
National United Front for
Democracy against
Dictatorship (UDD), 308

NATO (North Atlantic Treaty
    Organization), 3, 39, 200, 203
NCCC (National Counter-
    Corruption Commission), 39
nepotism, 150, 278
"new generation passport", 50
Newin Chidchob, 296, 301
NGOs (non-governmental
    organizations), 19, 134, 136,
    300
9/11, *see* September 11
Nitya Pibulsonggram, 281, 283
NLD (National League for
    Democracy), 137–38, 140, 143,
    304
Nong Duc Manh, 181
Nongnuch Singhadecha, 234–35
Noppadon Patama, 286–87,
    289–90, 297, 308
North Atlantic Treaty
    Organization, *see* NATO
North Korea, 216, 235
NRC (National Reconciliation
    Commission), 187
    members of, 188

O

OAG (Office of the Auditor-
    General), 50
ODA (Official Development
    Assistance), 119, 182
OECD (Organization of Economic
    Cooperation and
    Development), 119
Office of the Foreign Minister,
    150
Office of the United States
    Representative (USTR), 251
OIC (Organization of Islamic
    Conference), 187, 288
Olarn Chaipravat, 155
Olympic Games, 16, 198, 227

one-party system, 9, 12
One Step Ahead of Thaksin, book,
    259
OTOP (One *Tambon*, One
    Product), 9, 20–21, 51, 117,
    237, 245
Overlapping Maritime Claims to
    the Continental Shelf, 172

P

Pacific Telesis, 7
PAD (People's Alliance for
    Democracy), 7, 11–12, 47,
    208, 258, 276, 280, 285–87,
    289–90, 292–97, 299, 303–306,
    308
Pakistan
    Thailand, relations with, 215–16
Palang Dharma Party, 7, 8, 55
Panitan Wattanayagorn, 163, 210
Pansak Winyarat, 45–46, 128, 253
PAS (Parti Islam se-Malaysia), 52,
    188, 288
Pasuk Phongpaichit, 9, 124, 211,
    215, 234, 237, 239–40, 271
Pattaya saga, 301–302
Pawin Talerngsri, 199
peacekeeping efforts, 219
"people-centric diplomacy", 5, 10,
    48–52, 234
    see also diplomacy
People's Alliance for Democracy,
    see PAD
People's Bank programme, 20
People's Power Party, *see* PPP
"Perd Seri" (liberalization) policy,
    scope of, 127–28
Phibun Songkhram, 6, 30, 63,
    79–81, 90, 117, 210
Phote Sarasin, 82
Phra Ruang dynasty, 75
Pisan Manawapat, 211, 236

Pisanu Suvanajata, 297
Pojaman Shinawatra, 7
populist dictatorship, 199
populist diplomacy, 42, 233–38, 243, 259, 261
post-Thaksin era, 279
PPP (People's Power Party), 285, 292–94, 299
Prachuab Chaiyasarn, 251
Prachyadavi Tavedikul, 29
Prakit Prachonpachanuk, 50
Prapat Thepchatree, 275
Pravich Rattanapian, 251
Preah Vihear temple, 12, 52, 66, 124, 170, 174, 176, 194, 259, 279–80, 285–87, 294, 297, 299, 300, 303, 305, 308
Preecha Laohapongchana, 249
Prem Tinsulanonda, 301
Premier League club, 238
Pridi Banomyong, 79
Prime Minister
  as CEO, 37, 53, 238, 240
  versus the Ministry of Foreign Affairs, 43–48
Prime Ministerial Retreat, 207
Privy Council, 301
"prosper thy neighbour" policy, 116
"protocol states", 82
pro-Thaksin movement, 279, 295
  see also Shinawatra, Thaksin
PSI (Proliferation Security Initiative), 39
PTTEP (PTT Exploration and Production Co Ltd), 159
Puea Thai Party, 299, 303–306
Putin, Vladimir, 217
Pyithu Hluttaws, legislative bodies, 139

Q
Qingdao Initiative, 100

R
Radio Saranrom, 183
Rainsy, Sam, 173
Rama IV, King, *see* Mongkut, King
Ramkhamhaeng, King, 75
Razali Ismail, 140
red-shirt protestors, 285, 296–98, 301–302, 304–306
Rice, Condoleezza, 255
Riduan Isamuddin, 203
"roadmap proposal", 138–39
Roberts, John, 189
Rohingya refugees, 300
Rosenau, James N., 4, 55
"Roving Buakeaw Project", 49, 62
Royal Lao government, 177
  see also Laos
Royal Thai Embassy
  attack on, 120, 124, 171, 174, 194, 237
  see also Ministry of Foreign Affairs, Thailand
Royal Thai Police Department, 7
royalists movement, 12, 279, 295
Ru Than Thaksin, book, 259
Rusk-Thanat Communiquè, 201

S
SAARC (South Asian Association for Regional Cooperation), 98
Saddam Hussein, 203
Sam Houston State University, 7
Samak Sundaravej, 8, 16, 57, 198, 209, 238, 251
  erratic approach of, 285–92
Sarasin Viraphol, 75, 90
Sarit Thanarat, 6
SARS (Severe Acute Respiratory Syndrome), 110
SATTEL (Shinawatra Satellite), 41, 171, 181, 215, 239, 307

Sawanit Kongsiri, 235, 262, 281
SEATO (Southeast Asia Treaty
    Organization), 81–82, 201
    members of, 228
"second track" diplomacy, 191
Seni Pramoj, 79
September 11 (9/11), 16, 72, 200,
    202, 205
"Seri Thai" (Free Thai)
    movement, 79
Severe Acute Respiratory
    Syndrome (SARS), 110
Severino, Rodolfo, 194
Shan State Army, 168, 221
Shaukat Aziz, 216
Shin-Temasek controversy, 40,
    258, 290
Shinawatra Corporation (Shin
    Corp), 166, 206, 208, 239–41,
    271, 280, 283, 306
    Shin-Temasek controversy, 40,
        258, 290
Shinawatra Satellite (Shin
    Satellite), see SATTEL
Siam
    Ayutthaya period, 76–77
    buffer zone, as, 73, 86, 89
    diplomacy controlled by
        monarchs, 70
    lost territories, 65, 170
    modernization, 68
    policy of accommodation,
        67–68, 78, 86
    relations with ancient China,
        67, 75
    sphere of influence, 66, 122
    suzerainty over Laos, 177
    see also Ayutthaya; Thailand
Sihamoni, King, 304, 306
Singapore
    Thaksinized diplomacy with,
        206–10

see also Temasek Holdings;
    Thailand-Singapore Civil
    Service Exchange
    Programme
Singapore Airlines, 208
Singapore Institute of
    International Affairs, 270
Singapore-Thailand Enhanced
    Economic Relationship
    (STEER), 207–208, 290
Sino-Thai FTA, 2–3, 51, 197, 199
    see also China
Sino-Thai joint military relations,
    3, 197, 226
Sivarak Chutiphong, 305–306
Smith, Anthony, 197
Snoh Thienthong, 242
Sok An, 286–87
Somchai Wongsawat, 106, 286,
    292–95
Somkiati Ariyapruchya, 253
Somkid Jatusripitak, 45, 128, 242
Sompong Amornwiwat, 251,
    293–94
Somsavat Lengsavad, 120, 180
Sondhi Limthongkul, 287, 310
Sonthi Boonyaratglin, 149, 281
South Asian Association for
    Regional Cooperation
    (SAARC), 98
Southeast Asia
    colonialism in, 67
    Thailand, and, 22–23
    United States withdrawal from,
        81
Southeast Asia Treaty
    Organization, see SEATO
southern Thailand, conflict,
    188–90, 198, 203–204, 287–89
SPDC (State Peace and
    Development Council), 18,
    141–42, 290

Special Task Force (STF), Ministry
of Commerce, 133
*Spirit of Capitalism: Nationalism
and Economic Growth, The,*
book, 124
STEER (Singapore-Thailand
Enhanced Economic
Relationship), 207–208, 290
student activism, 71
Student Federation of Thailand,
210
submissive diplomacy, 76
Suchinda Kraprayoon, 7
sufficiency economy, 153, 284
Suharto, 17, 256
Sukhothai, kingdom of, 64
Supachai Panitchpakdi, 144, 148,
158, 195
Supreme Court, 306
rulings on Thaksin case,
306–307
Surachai Sirikrai, 80
Surakiart Sathirathai, 9, 14, 18,
20–21, 24, 26–27, 34, 40, 46,
49–50, 87, 92–93, 95–97, 103,
107–108, 120–21, 139, 164,
255, 267
candidate for UNSG, 143–51,
244, 246, 252, 258, 273
deputy prime minister, as,
143–44
personality, 252–54
Suraphan Shinawatra, 7
Surapong Jayanama, 42, 123, 167,
190, 214
Surapong Posayanonda, 253
Surayud Chulanont, 40, 209, 280
ethical diplomacy under,
281–85
Surin Pitsuwan, 11, 37, 148, 165,
194, 241, 291
Suriya Jungrungreangkit, 240

Suthad Setboonsarng, 252
Suthep Thaugsuban, 301
Suvanand Kongying, 175
Suvarnabhumi International
Airport, 38, 41, 118, 293, 296
Suvarnabhumi concept, 83, 117–18,
156, 183
swap agreements, 105

T
Tak Bai, murder of Muslim
protestors in, 25, 52
Taksin, King, 90
Task Force for Closer Economic
Partnership, 106
Teah Banh, General, 173
"Team Thailand", 48, 249–50
Tej Bunnag, 40, 144, 297
Tekhua Pung, 198
Telephone Organisation of
Thailand (TOT), 307
Temasek Holdings, 206, 208, 241,
271, 280, 283
Shin-Temasek controversy, 40,
258, 290
see also Singapore
Thai Airways International
(THAI), 240, 293
Thai-Australian FTA, 215, 240
Thai-Bahrain Framework
Agreement on Closer
Economic partnership, 127
Thai-Cambodia border crisis, 66
Thai-Chinese Chamber of
Commerce, 197
Thai-Chinese FTA, *see* Sino-Thai
FTA
Thai colonialism, 122
Thai currency, wide use of, 183
Thai diplomacy, 258
art of, 63
Cold War, during the, 80–82

history of, 74–85
periodic opportunism, 78–80,
    274
policy of appeasement, 75–78
pre-Thaksin policy, 83–85
see also "Cultural Diplomacy";
    diplomacy; foreign policy;
    "megaphone diplomacy";
    Ministry of Foreign Affairs,
    Thailand; Thaksinized
    diplomacy
Thai-E.U. bilateral trade, 218
Thai Foreign Trade Department,
    172
Thai-Lao Friendship Association,
    179, 183
Thai-Lao Friendship Bridge, 182
Thai monarchs, astuteness of, 73,
    89
Thai Rak Thai Party, *see* TRT
Thai Royal Navy, 300
Thai Trade Representatives, 158
Thai-United States Consultative
    Joint Council, 127
Thai-U.S. Plan of Action, 205
Thai-U.S. Strategic Dialogue, 205
ThaiCom, communications
    satellites, 166
Thailand
    Angkor temple, and, 175
    anti-Chinese policy, 81, 90
    arms purchase from Russia, 217
    Cambodia, relations with, 12, 15,
        44, 51–52, 66, 116, 169–76,
        250, 299–300, 302–306
    China, relations with, 2, 14–17,
        22, 35, 51, 57, 81, 85, 90,
        195–200
    clash with Lao culture, 183–84
    client state, as, 22, 80, 163, 201
    colonialism, and, 63, 65, 67,
        73–74, 78

communism, threat of, 69
credibility, 148
donor country, as, 2, 22, 38, 94,
    118–20, 122, 257
First World nation, as, 38, 242
GDP (Gross Domestic Product),
    51
GNI (Gross National Income),
    119
hegemonization of, 22, 36, 52,
    83–84, 117–18, 124, 152,
    174, 268, 272, 275
India, relations with, 14–17
Iraq, troops in, 202, 228
Japan, trade with, 211–12
joint commissions, 179
Khmer Rouge, support for, 170,
    173
Laos, relations with, 116, 177–84
Major Non-NATO Allies status,
    200, 203
Malaysia, relations with, 184–90
Muslim insurgents, 15, 185–86,
    188
Myanmar, relations with, 3, 34,
    42, 51, 116, 137–38, 148,
    164–69, 191, 290
nationalism, and, 65–66, 124,
    185, 202, 208, 210, 236, 259,
    299, 305, *see also*
    nationalism *under* foreign
    policy
Pakistan, relations with, 215–16
peacekeeping efforts, 219
political cultures, 243
poverty in, 126
separatist movement in, 185,
    188
sister cities, 171–72
Southeast Asia, and, 22–23
southern conflict, 188–90, 198,
    203–204, 287–89

Tak Bai, murder of Muslim
    protestors in, 25, 52, 148,
    185–87, 282, 287
United States, exports to, 203
United States, relations with, 3,
    85
United States, sympathetic to
    coup, 281
United Nations, as member,
    79–80, 93
Vietnam, relations with, 217
wartime period, 78–80
WTO, role in, 158
    see also Ayutthaya; Siam
Thailand and New Zealand
    Closer Economic Partnership
    (TNZCEP), 129
Thailand Elite Card, 128
Thailand-India Free Trade
    Agreement (TIFTA), 213–15
    see also India
Thailand International
    Development Cooperation
    Agency (TICA), 247
Thailand-Laos Cooperation
    Commission Meeting, 180
"Thailand Not for Sale", 208
Thailand-Singapore Civil Service
    Exchange Programme, 290
"Thailand through the Lens", 24
Thailand Trade Representatives
    (TTR), 251–52
Thaksin Shinawatra
    ambition, 37–38
    ASEAN policy, 190–95
    "big brother", 122
    born, 6
    brother-in-law, 286, 293
    childhood, 7
    corrupt practices, 39–42, 60
    deputy prime minister, as, 8
    diplomacy, zones of, 162–64

domestic policy, 19, 20, 232–33,
    236, 261
economic advisor, appointed
    as, 304
economic programmes, 28–29
election, 9, 37, 60
enemy of Muslims, as, 187
foreign minister, as, 8, 232
foreign policy, and, 4–6, 10–11, 13
fugitive, as, 2
guilty verdict, 306–309
Hun Sen, relation with, 173–75
Myanmar apologist, as, 141–43
network of elites, 271
passport revoked, 300
personal life, 37
policy booklet, 96, 153
power, centralization of, 249
private businesses in
    Cambodia, 123
rise to power, 6
Thai-Chinese, model for, 196
Twitter account, 304
    see also foreign policy; pro-
    Thaksin movement
Thaksinized diplomacy, 261,
    268–76, 289–92
    ASEAN, with, 190–95
    Cambodia, with, 169–76
    China, with, 195–200
    India, with, 213–16
    Japan, with, 210–13
    Laos, with, 177–84
    Malaysia, with, 184–90
    Myanmar, with, 164–69
    Singapore, with, 206–10
    United States, with, 200–206
        see also "Cultural Diplomacy";
        diplomacy; foreign policy;
        "megaphone diplomacy";
        Ministry of Foreign Affairs,
        Thailand; Thai diplomacy

"Thaksiplomacy", 2
Thaksinomics, 9, 135
Thammasat University, 252
Than Shwe, General, 18, 141, 290
Thanat Khoman, 11
Thanom Kittikachorn, 6
Theun-Hinboun Expansion
    Project, 179
Thien Sein, 290, 291
"Think new, act new" slogan, 11
Thitinan Pongsudhirak, 48, 123,
    142, 147
Thonburi dynasty, 77
Thongchai Winichakul, 66
Tibet
    China crackdown in, 16, 57
TICA (Thailand International
    Development Cooperation
    Agency), 247
TNZCEP (Thailand and New
    Zealand Closer Economic
    Partnership), 129
top-down decision, 54
TOT (Telephone Organisation of
    Thailand), 307
trade diplomacy, 136
Treasury Department, 10
Treaty of Amity and Commerce
    1833, 201
TRT (Thai Rak Thai) Party, 8, 10,
    24, 45, 96–97, 109, 118, 124,
    126, 144, 163, 167, 200, 239,
    276, 285, 299
    meaning, 1, 29
    one-party system, 9, 12
    populist programme, 9, 17, 124
    region hostile to, 185
TTR (Thailand Trade
    Representatives), 251–52
"2+X principle", 207–208

U
U Thant, 144

UDD (National United Front for
    Democracy against
    Dictatorship), 308
U.K. Sports Investment, 238
Ukrist Pathmanand, 232
UMNO (United Malays National
    Organization), 187–88
UNCTAD (United Nations
    Conference on Trade and
    Development), 144
UNDP (United Nations
    Development Programme),
    119
UNESCO (United Nations
    Educational, Scientific and
    Cultural Organisation), 286,
    302–303
UNHCR (United Nations High
    Commissioner for Refugees),
    187, 234, 300
United Malays National
    Organization (UMNO),
    187–88
United Nations, 18, 36, 282, 293
United Nations Charter, 278
United Nations Conference on
    Trade and Development
    (UNCTAD), 144
United Nations Development
    Programme (UNDP), 119
United Nations Educational,
    Scientific and Cultural
    Organisation, see UNESCO
United Nations General
    Assembly, 100, 145
United Nations High
    Commissioner for Refugees,
    see UNHCR
United Nations Millennium
    Development Goals, 111, 119,
    144
United Nations Secretary-
    General, see UNSG

United Nations Security Council,
see UNSC
United States
Afghanistan, invasion of, 202
combating communism, 69
exports to Thailand, 203
hegemony, 201
Iraq, invasion of, 202
sympathetic to Thailand coup,
281
Thai-United States Consultative
Joint Council, 127
Thai-U.S. Plan of Action, 205
Thai-U.S. Strategic Dialogue,
205
Thailand, aid to, 80, 201
Thailand, relations with, 3, 12,
85
Thaksinized diplomacy with,
200–206
withdrawal from Southeast
Asia, 81
United Wa State Army, *see*
UWSA
UNSC (United Nations Security
Council), 27, 146, 212, 215,
284
UNSG (United Nations Secretary-
General), 18, 26, 27, 96, 140,
244
Sathirathai, Surakiart, as
candidate, 143–51, 244, 246,
252, 258, 273
U.S.-Thai FTA negotiation, 43
USTR (Office of the United States
Representative), 251
UWSA (United Wa State Army),
168, 221

V
Vajpayee, Atal Behari, 214
Vatchara Pannachet, 252
Vatikiotis, Michael, 198

VCP (Vietnamese Communist
Party), 181
Versailles, 76
Vichak Visetnoi, 172
Vietnam
ASEAN, joins, 160
invasion of Cambodia, 144
Laos, relations with, 180–81
Thailand, relations with, 217
Vietnam War, 201
Village Fund programme, 20
Virachai Palasai, 297
Virasakdi Futrakul, 297

W
Wa army, 168, 237
war on terrorism, 3, 12, 36, 200,
203–204
Warr, Peter, 126
weapons of mass destruction, 39
Who Says the Rich Don't Cheat?,
book, 40
Win Aung, 120, 141
Withaya Sucharithanarugse, 123
"World Heritage" site, 286, 297,
302
World War I, 72, 88
World War II, 63–64, 68–70,
78–80, 201, 210
WTO (World Trade
Organization), 126, 144–45
Thailand role, 158
Wyatt, David, 169

X
Xinhua, 227

Y
yaa baa, 168
Yaowapha Shinawatra, 293
Yawd Serk, Colonel, 168
Ye Naing Win, 166

Yeo, George, 209
Yettaw, John, 298
Yong Chantalangsy, 182
"Young Ambassador of Virtue
    Project", 49, 62
"Young Turks", 7

Yongyuth Tiyapairat, 294
Yudhoyono, Susilo Bambang, 288

Z
Zhang Xin-Sheng, 198
Zhou Enlai, 90

ABOUT THE AUTHOR

Pavin Chachavalpongpun is a Fellow in the Regional Strategic and Political Studies Unit (RSPS) and Lead Researcher for Political and Strategic Affairs at the ASEAN Studies Centre, Institute of Southeast Asian Studies, Singapore. A former diplomat, Pavin served with the Ministry of Foreign Affairs of Thailand in many capacities from 1994–2010, including most recently at the Royal Thai Embassy in Singapore. He received his B.A. Honours in International Relations from Chulalongkorn University's Faculty of Political Science, and his Ph.D. from the Department of Political Studies, School of Oriental and African Studies, University of London. He is the author of *A Plastic Nation: The Curse of Thainess in Thai-Burmese Relations* (2005), and contributor to five chapters on "Neither Constructive nor Engaging: The Debacle of ASEAN's Burmese Policy", in *Between Isolation and Internationalisation: The State of Burma* (2008); "Thailand", in *Southeast Asia in a New Era: Ten Countries, One Region in ASEAN* (2010); "Confusing Democracies: Diagnosing Thailand's Democratic Crisis 2001–2008", in *Political Change, Democratic Transitions and Security in Southeast Asia* (2009); "A Fading Wave, Sinking Tide: A Southeast Asian Perspective on the Korean Wave", in *Korea's Changing Roles in Southeast Asia: Expanding Influence and Relations* (2010); and "Dealing with Burma's Gordian Knot: Thailand, China, ASEAN and the Burmese Conundrum", in *Myanmar: Prospect for Change* (2010). Pavin is also editor of *The Road to Ratification and Implementation of the ASEAN Charter* (2009), and co-wrote with Moe Thuzar a book titled *Myanmar: Life After Nargis* (2009);. His forthcoming publications include "Thai-Burmese Relations: Old

353

Animosity in a New Bilateral Setting", in *Bilateralism Versus Multilateralism in Southeast Asia*; "Thailand: Bending with the (Chinese) Wind?", in *East Asia Facing a Rising China*; "Thai Political Parties in the Age of the Great Divide", in *Political Parties, Party System and Democratisation in East Asia*; "The Last Bus to Naypyidaw: The Shift in US's Burma Policy and the Marginalised ASEAN?", in *Myanmar/Burma: Outside Interests and Inside Challenges*; and "Temple of Doom: Hysteria about the Preah Vihear Temple in the Thai Nationalist Discourse", in *Legitimacy Crisis and Conflict in Thailand*. He is a regular contributor to *The Nation, Bangkok Post, Straits Times, South China Morning Post, Japan Times, Korea Herald, OpinionAsia, Asia Sentinel* and *The Irrawaddy*, writing mostly on topic related to Thai and Myanmar politics, nationalism and national identity, Thai foreign policy and international relations in general. His opinion is sought nationally and internationally through interviews with local and international media.

1. Prime Minister Thaksin Shinawatra performs classical dance at a reception in Vientiane, during his visit to Laos, 13–14 June 2001. *Photo courtesy of Thailand's Government House*.

2. Prime Minister Samdech Hun Sen receives his Thai counterpart at Phnom Penh Airport, 18 June 2001. *Photo courtesy of Thailand's Government House*.

3. Thaksin visits the Shwedagon Pagoda, Yangon, during his trip to Myanmar, 19–20 June 2001. On his left is Foreign Minister Surakiart Sathirathai. *Photo courtesy of Thailand's Government House*.

4. Thaksin with a group of Thai workers in Brunei Darussalam. He pays an official visit to the Sultanate state on 16 August 2001. *Photo courtesy of Thailand's Government House*.

5. Senior Minister Lee Kuan Yew and Thaksin, 22 August 2001, in Singapore.
Photo courtesy of Thailand's Government House .

6. Thaksin is received by Chinese President Jiang Zemin, Beijing, during his visit to China, 27–29 August 2001. *Photo courtesy of Thailand's Government House* .

7. Thaksin and his wife, Khunying Pojaman, tour China's Forbidden City, 28 August 2001. *Photo courtesy of Thailand's Government House* .

8. Thaksin meets with Cambodian Prime Minister Hun Sen, again, on 11 October 2001, in Phnom Penh. *Photo courtesy of Thailand's Government House* .

9. His Majesty King Norodom Sihanouk of Cambodia grants an audience to Thaksin and his two daughters, 11 October 2001. *Photo courtesy of Thailand's Government House* .

10. Thaksin and Surakiart, with President Gloria Macapacal-Arroyo of the Philippines, during their visit to Manila, 12–13 October 2001. *Photo courtesy of Thailand's Government House* .

11. At number 10 Downing Street, Thaksin meets with British Prime Minister Tony Blair, during his official visit to the United Kingdom, 13–15 May 2002. *Photo courtesy of Thailand's Government House.*

12. Australian Prime Minister John Howard and Thaksin, during his trip to Canberra, Australia, 29–31 May 2002. *Photo courtesy of Thailand's Government House.*

13. On 10 June 2002, at the International Airport in Manama, Thaksin shakes hands with His Royal Highness Shaikh Salman Bin Hamad Bin Isa Al-Khalifa, Crown Prince and Deputy Supreme Commander of the Kingdom of Bahrain, with Prime Minister His Highness Shaikh Khalifa Bin Salman Al Khalifa in the background.
Photo courtesy of Thailand's Government House .

14. Pakistani President Pervez Musharraf and Thaksin meet in Islamabad, 1 July 2002.
Photo courtesy of Thailand's Government House .

15. During his visit to Dhaka from 8–10 July 2002, Thaksin meets with Prime Minister Begum Khaleda Zia of Bangladesh. *Photo courtesy of Thailand's Government House* .

16. Portraits of the two leaders, central Dhaka, Bangladesh. *Photo courtesy of Thailand's Government House* .

17. At the Signing Ceremony of the Memorandum of Understanding (MOU) on the setting up of the tripartite rubber trade venture at the Tampasiring Ubud Summer Palace, Indonesia, 8 August 2002. From left, Malaysia's Prime Minister Mahathir Mohamad, Thaksin, and Indonesian President Megawati Sukarnoputri. *Photo courtesy of Thailand's Government House* .

18. Thaksin speaks at the East Asia Economic Summit 2002, in Kuala Lumpur, 6–8 October 2002. *Photo courtesy of Thailand's Government House* .

19. In Moscow, Thaksin meets with President Vladimir Putin. Thaksin pays an official visit to Russia on 16–18 October 2002. *Photo courtesy of Thailand's Government House* .

20. Thaksin returns to Yangon for a two-day official visit, on 9–10 February 2003. He meets with Senior General Than Shwe, Chairman of the State Peace and Development Council, Myanmar. *Photo courtesy of Thailand's Government House*.

21. During this trip, 9–10 February 2003, Thaksin also meets with Prime Minister Khint Nyunt before the latter's downfall in October 2004. *Photo courtesy of Thailand's Government House* .

22. Thaksin with Myanmar's Foreign Minister Win Aung, during his visit to Yangon, 9–10 February 2003. *Photo courtesy of Thailand's Government House* .

23. Thaksin attends the 9th International Conference on the Future of Asia, 5 June 2003, Tokyo, Japan. On the right of Thaksin is Sorajak Kasemsuwan, Vice Minister of Foreign Affairs. *Photo courtesy of Thailand's Government House* .

24. While in Tokyo, Prime Minister Thaksin holds talks with Japanese Prime Minister Junichiro Koizumi, 5 June 2003. *Photo courtesy of Thailand's Government House* .

25. Thaksin attended the 9th International Conference on the Future of Asia, Tokyo, Japan, on 6 June 2003. On his right is Kasit Piromya, Thai Ambassador to Tokyo.   *Photo courtesy of Thailand's Government House.*

26. Thaksin, on the sidelines of the US-ASEAN Business Council meeting in the United States, meets with U.S. President George W. Bush at the White House, 10 June 2003.   *Photo courtesy of Thailand's Government House.*

27. Thaksin with Malaysia's Prime Minister Mahathir Mohamad, in Kuala Lumpur. His visit to Malaysia is on 27–28 June 2003. *Photo courtesy of Thailand's Government House*.

28. At a bilateral meeting between Thailand and South Korea, with Thaksin and President Roh Moo-Hyun. Thaksin pays an official visit to South Korea on 24–26 August 2003. *Photo courtesy of Thailand's Government House*.

29. During his visit to Singapore on 5–6 September 2003, Thaksin has lunch with Prime Minister Goh Chok Tong and Deputy Prime Minister Lee Hsien Loong. *Photo courtesy of Thailand's Government House* .

30. Wearing "happi" or traditional Japanese overcoats, Thaksin attends the ASEAN-Japan Summit, Tokyo, on 11 December 2003. *Photo courtesy of Thailand's Government House* .

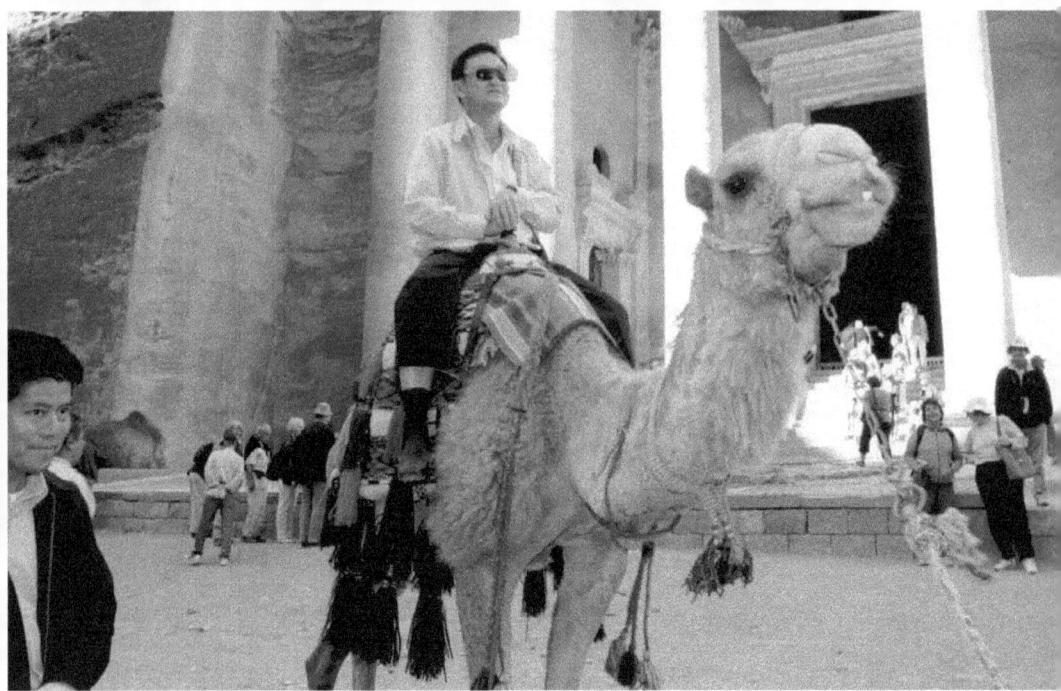

31. Thaksin, on the back of a camel during his visit to Jordan and Oman, 25–27 April 2006, five months before the military coup. In the left-hand corner is Foreign Minister Kantathi Suphamongkhon. *Photo courtesy of Thailand's Government House* .

32. Surakiart, during his "listening tour" in preparation for his United Nations Secretary-General campaign, exchanges views with Minister Mentor Lee Kuan Yew of Singapore, Istana, 10 June 2006. *The author's photo*.

www.ingramcontent.com/pod-product-compliance
Lightning Source LLC
Chambersburg PA
CBHW021846020426
42334CB00013B/202